THE ENNEAGRAM FOR PERSONAL & SPIRITUAL GROWTH (2 IN 1):

ENHANCE YOUR SELF-DISCOVERY JOURNEY. SHINE LIGHT ON YOUR SHADOW & AWAKEN TO YOUR TRUE SELF

ENNEAGRAM UNWRAPPED

BOOK THREE

PERSONALITY HUB

CONTENTS

THE ENNEAGRAM EXPLAINED:

SECTION I

SECTION II

THE ENNEAGRAM GUIDE TO SELF-DISCOVERY, RELATIONSHIP FULFILMENT & AWAKENING:

PART ONE
THE ENNEAGRAM TOOL

PART TWO
YOU AND THE ENNEAGRAM

PART THREE
DEEPENING RELATIONSHIPS

PART FOUR
USING THE ENNEAGRAM FOR GROWTH IN ALL AREAS

THE ENNEAGRAM EXPLAINED:

SUPERCHARGE YOUR SELF-DISCOVERY JOURNEY, UNCOVER YOUR TRUE PERSONALITY & UNDERSTAND ALL 9 ENNEATYPES PLUS UNIQUE TIPS & PRACTICES FOR ALL 9 TYPES

THE PURPOSE OF
THIS BOOK

To help people uncover their Type. This book explains each of the nine types in detail and provides fun examples that are easy to relate to.

Accompanying each Type are practical tips on the lifestyle changes you can make and some daily practices that are more effective for your specific Type.

INTRODUCTION

What if I told you that your quest for material success and the current goals you've set will do nothing more but delight you for a short while, after which you'll plunge right back into that endless pit of restlessness plaguing your life?

Look around you. The world appears to be more chaotic than ever. There's so much doom and gloom everywhere. Countries continue to war against each other; discrimination, instability, disruption, and hate seem to be the trend. And those who aren't busy spreading hate are working themselves to death trying to be the next big sensation on the Internet.

What is happening to humanity? Have we lost our way? Are we becoming worse as technological advancements continue? Shouldn't we be more at peace, in love, fulfilled, and at one with each other as globalization becomes the order of the day?

It turns out that human beings are great at many things. We can solve big problems, such as traveling across the planet, getting to the moon, and even more complex things like how to eliminate fossil fuels. But, unfortunately, we're terrible at solving the simple problem of finding peace and fulfillment. And unless each human can begin to feel peaceful, fulfilled, happy, and secure in their own life, we will continue to witness the horrible state of the world. And this doesn't only apply to global issues. Think about your own life, where you work, your health, your relationships, and your current lifestyle. How satisfied, fulfilled, and happy are you with what you see when you look in the mirror?

The fact is, if you had found your fulfillment and peace in life, this book would have no appeal to you. I may not know your unique situation, but allow me to risk the credibility of this book by boldly stating the following.

It doesn't matter what you think you desire in life; the real thing you're seeking is a sense of connection, security, and unconditional love. You're seeking peace and fulfillment. You want the "thing" that will finally make you feel complete and whole. Unfortunately, you'll never find that by chasing after a "thing."

So, I'm glad you're here because I can promise you this: if you stick with this book and commit to applying everything you learn, you will break the chains of bondage and lift the veil of illusion that had you chasing after the wrong desires. This book will empower you to have the freedom to know, be, and love yourself.

And when you know, love, and live from your true Self, you become unstoppable on the playground of life. Does that sound like something you'd be interested in? Good. Then let's get started.

KNOW THYSELF

"Know thyself" sounds like a cliché, and maybe it is, but I stand by it nonetheless. It is the golden secret to a life beyond your dreams. As far back as ancient Greece, people have been seeking this knowledge of self.

Few can quench an unshakeable thirst to understand who we are, what we want, and what it takes to experience happiness and fulfillment in life. Entire disciplines exist around this topic of understanding more about ourselves as humans. Most of it only amplifies our differences and breeds wild egos that cause more harm than good.

I am not here to offer scientific lectures. Instead, I want to present a simple solution that can enable you to explore and discover the Truth for yourself.

Our behavior directly results from our character and personality, which typically start taking shape during our childhood years. The core beliefs and values that we hold deep in our subconscious minds make us distinct in approaching and reacting to life. One individual's likes, dislikes, fears, strengths, and weaknesses will lead to different responses compared to another's, even if the two people are facing the same obstacle. What creates this difference? How we grow up, the perspectives and worldviews we hold, and our beliefs, whether true or false, affect our actions, health, lifestyle, and well-being. They make us what we are.

Can you imagine a world in which, instead of using gender, skin color, culture, etc., to determine our identity, we focused on understanding our personality type? What kind of a world would that be?

Don't get me wrong, I'm not saying culture and beliefs are bad. But I can confidently say that there would be better relationships, more compassion, and communities that function efficiently in such a world. This book isn't here to point fingers or establish black and white rules over what's good and what's bad. Life isn't binary. As you get to know your true Self, the discovery you'll make is that the spectrum of life is vast enough to accommodate all differences. The self-discovery quest is transformational and priceless because it finally enables you to understand unity and wholeness. And when one attains that knowledge, nothing in their world is ever the same.

Why did you desire to read this book?

Are you among those who feel broken in some way? Is there an inner restlessness or void that you're trying to resolve? Or perhaps you've realized that success can only come from within, and now you're trying to figure out what "within" means.

I find it good practice to always ask myself, "Why am I doing this thing?" Whenever I clarify my reason for doing something, I always seem to get the most out of that activity.

Regardless of your reasons, I'm glad you're here. This is the right time and season in your life to embark on a journey of self-discovery, to get answers about who you are, why you're here, and what life is all about.

Material success, romantic relationships, and career opportunities can flow more naturally into your life as you get to know yourself more. But don't limit yourself to "getting things ."If love is what you're after, don't limit it to finding a soul mate. Even if you manifest that ideal lover, it will not satiate and fill that void that caused you to yearn for love. If abundance is what you seek, don't limit it to making more money because no amount of money will ever satisfy the feeling of lack and insecurity you have. What you need is abundance and a real sense of security, neither of which can be permanently found in acquiring more money. So before we jump into the specifics of this book, let's clarify what this book can do for you and whom it's intended for.

WHAT THIS BOOK IS AND HOW TO USE IT

This book aims to enable you, dear reader, to finally discover who you really are. It's not about superficially identifying common traits or giving gimmicks that will allow you to manifest whatever you seek. Instead, this is about unlocking your potential. Regardless of your past experiences, upbringing, and environment, who you are is mostly untapped potential. To the extent that you've lost touch with your true self, you will experience the restlessness that most humans try to cover up with material possessions and mindless activities.

The rewards of going through this book:

In this book, you'll find practical tips and specific transformational processes tailored to your Enneagram type. You'll also learn how to cultivate present moment awareness, become better at catching old negative thoughts and behaviors, and gently dissolve those limiting behaviors. Last but not least, you'll get tips on the lifestyle changes you can make and some daily practices that are more effective for your specific Type. Before you begin this quest, I encourage you to get a private journal, notebook, or digital diary where you can take personal notes as you discover new exercises. This is also where you'll record the insights that come to you as you learn about your personality type and the other eight types. Throughout the ensuing chapters, you'll find simple yet powerful exercises that I suggest you consistently engage in. Don't shortchange yourself. Remember, the whole purpose of the Enneagram is to discover your true self. Unless you're willing to be honest and clear about your needs and wants and committed to doing the inner work, this tool will not yield much. What you put in is what you'll get out of the Enneagram tool. Okay, time to clear up the mystery behind the Enneagram tool, what it is, and how it works.

SECTION 1

INTRODUCTION TO THE ENNEAGRAM

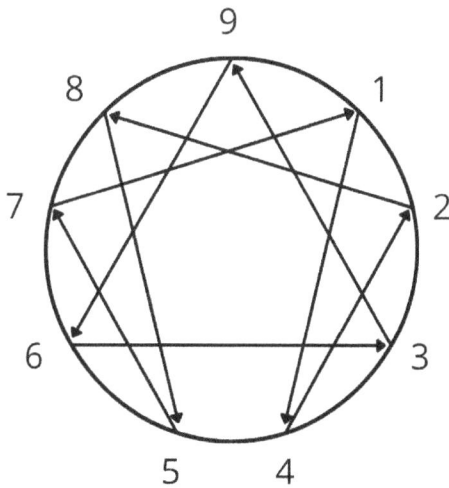

THE ENNEAGRAM SYSTEM

T he Enneagram (*pronounced ANY-a-gram*) is a personality typing system that uses a nine-pointed geometrical diagram to illustrate nine core personality types in the human race and how each Type relates to the other. The term *Ennea* is Greek for "nine," and *Grammos* means "figure." Thus, it is a nine-pointed figure.

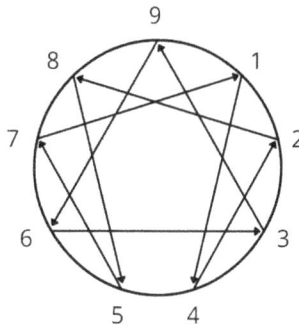

According to the Enneagram system, each of these nine personality types is defined by a particular core belief and frame of mind about how the world works. That core belief drives the Type's deepest fears and highest motivations. When we discover our true Type, we can see how our core beliefs shape our worldview and the lens through which we see others, ourselves, and the world. The Enneagram system aims to teach us that, for the most part, we are working with limited core beliefs. The beliefs may not be harmful per se, just excessively limiting, and may thus become "blinders" that block our minds. Using the Enneagram tool aims to increase our awareness of how our core beliefs color our perceptions so we can ultimately broaden our perspective and approach life more effectively. We look to the Enneagram system to help us discover and understand ourselves better (why do we behave as we do when we're sad, stressed, happy, etc.). And in knowing more about ourselves, we can start to understand why others react and behave as they do. To call it a personality typing system doesn't nearly do it justice. The Enneagram has a long history, and it has evolved over time to become the modern tool that we've adopted here in the West. But we should always remember that, at a fundamental level, the Enneagram's purpose is to awaken and elevate you to greater spiritual heights, not just give you information about personality traits.

Here's an excellent way to think about the Enneagram system:

Imagine yourself running into the ocean for an early morning swim. As the sun rises, everything on the surface is calm; the water is cool, and the sensation of the salty water on your skin feels invigorating. You're swimming on the ocean's surface, and it's impossible to see the world that exists far beneath you from that vantage point. To access that world, you need special gear and a trained professional. But just because you don't see what lies beneath the surface doesn't mean it doesn't exist. You can enjoy the ocean water at the surface with fellow humans, but if you really want to know and experience the true wonders of the ocean, you'll need to swim deep and go where most humans aren't willing to go. If you have the right gear and a good guide, that experience will be transformational. You will never look at the ocean the same way again.

While this is a trivial illustration, it can enable you to gain the proper perspective when it comes to understanding the Enneagram's purpose. Some people only want to stay on the surface, and that's okay. For such people, the Enneagram will tell them their ennea type and what traits correspond to their Type. But the Enneagram tool can also be used to uncover a world you never knew existed. That's what I hope you're here to explore and experience. But I'm getting ahead of myself. Let's first trace the origins and history of this tool before introducing the enneatype.

A BRIEF HISTORY OF THE ENNEAGRAM TOOL

To understand the history of the modern Enneagram tool, we need to clarify a common misunderstanding. The Enneagram symbol and the nine personality types have different origins. The Enneagram symbol is ancient, dating back 2,500 years or more. Indeed, the exact origins of the symbol have been lost to history. The roots of the nine personality types also date far back, perhaps as early as the 4th century A.D. in Alexandria, where a Christian mystic called Evagrius Ponticus identified the eight "deadly thoughts" (or *logismoi*) and an overarching thought that translates to "self-love." Ponticus devoted his life to exploring these thoughts and worked to find a solution to counteract the eight deadly ones. At the time, no one used the term Enneagram, but as you continue to study the tool, you'll make a connection between this modern-day system and the works of Ponticus.

Fast forward to the 19th century, we encounter the man credited with bringing the Enneagram symbol to the modern world. His name was George Ivanovich Gurdjieff. Gurdjieff was a Greek-Armenian born around 1875, and as a young man, he became fascinated with esoteric knowledge. Gurdjieff believed in the existence of a complete science for transforming the human psyche and devoted his entire life to searching for these lost teachings that would enable human beings to find their place in the universe and their purpose.

Through his extensive study and the knowledge he and his colleagues gathered, a synthesized teaching was born that integrated spirituality, psychology, and cosmology. Gurdjieff taught that the Enneagram (which he'd discovered during his travels) was the central and most important symbol in his philosophy. Although Gurdjieff taught using the Enneagram symbol, it wasn't yet a model for psychology, but rather a model of natural processes. Gurdjieff explained that the Enneagram symbol has three parts representing the Divine Laws governing all existence. The first is the circle, which represents unity, wholeness, oneness, and the idea that God is One. The second is the triangle drawn within the circle. The triangle represents trinity, or what Gurdjieff called the Law of Threes, which states everything that exists results from the interaction of three forces (whatever they may be in a given situation or dimension). You'll notice many triads in the Enneagram teachings throughout this book.

The third and last part of the Enneagram symbol is the hexad (the figure that traces the points 1-4-2-8-5-7 in our modern Enneagram symbol. Gurdjieff called this the "Law of Seven," which has to do with process and development over time. He taught that everything constantly changes and moves according to its own nature and the forces acting on them. We get the Enneagram symbol by combining these three parts, i.e., the circle, triangle, and hexad. Gurdjieff taught this philosophy through sacred dances explaining that it should be thought of as a living symbol that was dynamic and ever in motion. It should, however, be noted that Gurdjieff did not teach the Enneagram tool as a personality tool. The combination of the Enneagram symbol and the personality types took place only a few decades ago in the 20th century.

The modern version of the Enneagram symbol and the nine points has been developed according to the teachings of Oscar Ichazo, a Bolivian teacher, healer, and philosopher. Ichazo was just as passionate as Gurdjieff about uncovering lost knowledge. Through extensive study, research, and travel, he synthesized the many elements of the Enneagram symbol and found the connection between the symbol and the personality types.

Ichazo's teachings describe concepts like virtue, holy ideas, passion, and ego. All these are considered traits that represent the basis of the nine personalities of the Enneagram. Ichazo is also credited for coining the term "Enneagram of personality." His young budding student, Claudio Naranjo, developed this method of determining personality into the different branches we see today. Naranjo, a Chilean psychiatrist, had a different view of the Enneagram and wanted to expand it in new ways. That led to other influencers like Jesuit priests also taking the initiative to combine Christian spirituality and the Enneagram of self-discovery and regulation. Others like Don Richard Riso, Helem Palmer, Richard Rohr, and Eli Jaxon Bear were influenced by the works of Naranjo and continue to share their own versions of the Enneagram tool.

For our own point of reference, we can deduce that the Enneagram symbol we know and love here in the West is a synthesis of many different spiritual and religious traditions. Much of what we know about it is a condensation of universal wisdom and philosophies accumulated by Christians, Buddhists, Muslims, and Jews for thousands of years. Though it was passed on from teacher to teacher over the centuries, one thing remains untainted. That is the agreement across all branches of the Enneagram system that we are more than just flesh and bones. We are, in fact, spiritual beings having human experiences. Beneath the surface, regardless of all the differences we seem to have, over and above the veils of illusion, we are pure light and love. Unfortunately, we have given power to obstacles and forces that obscure the light we are and therefore have created a disconnect that each of us experiences as a form of restlessness and void. The Sufi Poet Rumi was accurate and overly wise when he said, "Your task is not to seek our love, but merely to seek and find all the barriers within yourself that you have built against it." This is a call of freedom, your freedom. And the Enneagram system will map out the quest you must embark on to finally attain this absolute freedom. Are you ready?

In the ensuing chapters, you will learn how to interpret the Enneagram symbol and all the nine points so you can apply the teachings to suit the current modern environment we live in.

WHAT YOU NEED TO KNOW ABOUT THE ENNEAGRAM AND HOW IT WORKS

The Enneagram work begins when you learn to identify your Type. This personality typing system describes how you may interpret feelings toward yourself and others. It is a complex framework that consists of nine different personality types, three subtypes, three centers of intelligence, and eighteen distinct wings. Don't be overwhelmed by the complexity of this symbol when you see all the different aspects. Think of these as layers that enable you to go deeper into your quest of self-discovery. As I said before, you are at liberty to decide whether you'll stay at the surface level and use it to determine your personality only or dive deeper to discover who you really are. What makes the Enneagram unique and different from other personality typing systems, e.g., the Myers–Briggs personality typing system, is that you won't just be placed into a rigid category. Instead, you'll see your personality spectrum and the growth opportunities you have to unlock your fullest potential. In other words, the Enneagram affords you the gift of true self-discovery and increased personal awareness.

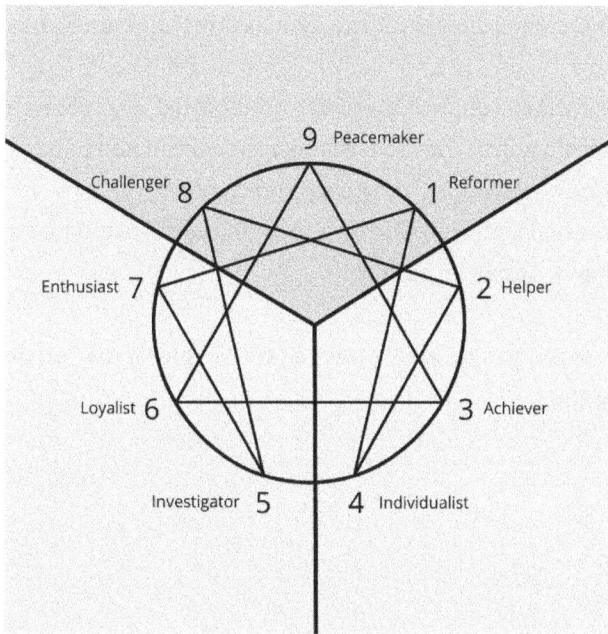

To understand what that diagram means, take note of the outer circle on which the nine personalities are marked. The numbers are evenly spaced around this circle because the circle represents wholeness and the unity and oneness of life. Inside the circle, a triangle connects the numbers 3, 6, and 9. Notice also the hexagonal shape connecting the other numbers, with each Type being joined by two lines to two other personalities. There's another layer to become aware of here. Notice the numbers on each side of any particular type (e.g., Type 3 will have adjacent to it 2 and 4). These adjacent personality types become Wings for that particular Enneatype. They represent the personalities that can influence that Type in different circumstances. We'll unpack all these different layers as the book unfolds, but for now, I invite you to sit in quiet observation for a moment or two before moving to the next chapter. See if you can find some resonance with the symbol above.

Ask yourself questions like:

- Do I feel resonance with the idea of unity and wholeness of life?
- Does it make sense to me that I am not just a single rigid personality, and that specific influences can shift my behavior depending on the circumstance?
- Does it feel right to approach myself as a spiritual being having a human experience?

If you answered yes to all or most of these questions, let the inward journey begin.

THE FIRST STEP IS TAKING A JOURNEY INWARD

T he quest for self-discovery is an inward journey that begins the moment one makes a solid commitment that they will stop living from the inside out. Until you decide to stop approaching life as others have, you will not get the most out of this book or the Enneagram tool. I believe you're here because you want transformation. If so, make the decision that, from this moment on, you will no longer play as a victim in life and instead approach it as a co-creative experience. The fact is, you are co-creating the story of your life, and the more connected you are to your higher self, the less random life becomes. The Enneagram tool facilitates this shift from living outside-in to living inside-out. The first step is to identify your Enneagram Type.

INTRODUCING THE NINE TYPES

The Enneagram tool will begin to serve its purpose in your life as you identify your Type and understand your Type's most dominant issues. If you recognize a bit of yourself in more than one Type, that's perfectly normal. There's a little bit of us in every Type because we are all connected, but our most defining characteristics are rooted in one of the nine Types. That's what you want to hone in. At the end of this chapter, you'll find a questionnaire developed by Riso and Hudson called the Riso-Hudson Quest that will help you narrow down your primary Type. Then as you go through each of the Enneagram Type chapters, you'll have the chance to dig deeper and learn a little more about each Type. By the time you're done reading all the descriptions and doing the exercises provided, you should have a firm grasp of your personality type. However, if you want to be extra certain, you can go online and take a final Enneagram test to see how you score and whether your self-assessment matches the professional assessment. Some tests are free, but the best ones tend to be paid. I will leave some links in the resource section of this book for both free and paid online tests.

For now, read the brief descriptions for each Type to see if you can spot two or three that strike you as most typical of yourself. Creating a shortlist of two or three as you go through this book is an excellent first step toward narrowing down this process. That way, you can give these as much attention as possible when going through self-discovery exercises. Keep in mind the characteristics listed in this chapter are merely an introduction and do not represent the full spectrum of each personality.

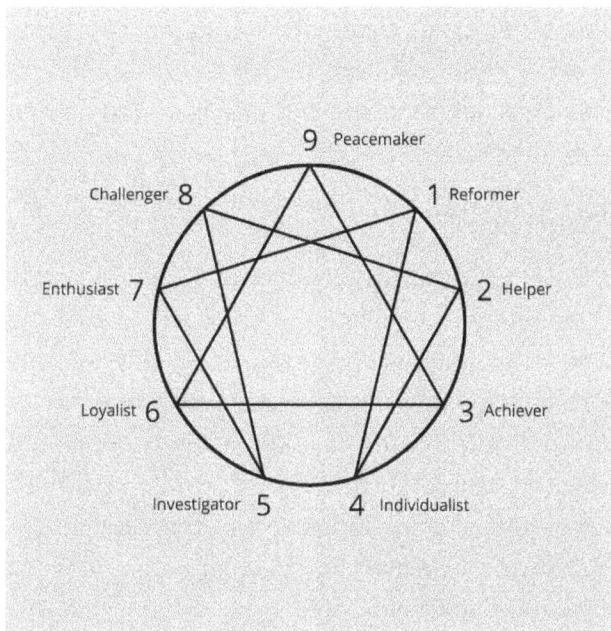

Type One: The Reformer

They are the highly moral, principled, and idealistic Type. Ones are ethical and conscientious, with a strong sense of right and wrong. They tend to be the teachers, crusaders, and activists who strive to improve things and are super afraid of error. Ones are organized, orderly, and fastidious. They have extremely high standards, which can lead to perfectionism. Ones have problems with repressed anger and impatience. At their best, healthy Ones are wise, noble, realistic, discerning, and morally heroic.

Type Two: The Helper

They are the caring, nurturing Type. Twos are empathetic, warm-hearted, sincere, friendly, and generous. Think of that self-sacrificing person who is always putting themselves first and is naturally great at developing solid relationships. Twos are driven to be close to others and often do things for others to be needed. As serious people-pleasers, Twos struggle with setting healthy bounders and often over-extend themselves to the point of self-neglect. At their best, healthy Twos are altruistic and unselfish. They ooze unconditional love for themselves and others.

Type Three: The Achiever

Threes are the adaptable, success-oriented Type. They are attractive, charming, ambitious, competent, self-assured, and energetic, and most are very status conscious. Threes are usually concerned about their personal advancement, some even more concerned about their image and what others think of them. A fundamental struggle for Type Threes is knowing when to slow down and relax. That's why many have trouble with workaholism and competitiveness. At their best, healthy Threes are authentic, self-accepting, and tend to be role models that others look up to.

Type Four: The Individualist

They are the introspective, romantic Type. Fours are highly sensitive, emotionally attuned to themselves and others, self-aware, and reserved. Some can come across as highly moody depending on their level of development, but, in all cases, they tend to be emotionally honest and self-revealing. Fours typically have trouble with the victim mindset and often engage in self-pity. At their best, healthy Fours are highly creative, inspired, and able to renew themselves and transform experiences from mundane to magical.

Type Five: The Investigator

They are the intense, logical, cerebral Type, with an insatiable curiosity and a thirst for knowledge. Thinking is a Type Five's comfort zone. Fives are typically highly alert, insightful, and focused. They can concentrate on things for a long time and tackle extremely complex ideas that the rest of us wouldn't dare. And the best part is they do it with such grace and poise that we can't help but admire them. Perhaps you've encountered such a person, or you are that person.

Fives are independent and innovative, but they can easily become too detached from the world and relationships with others. They typically have problems with eccentricity, isolation, and nihilism. At their best, healthy Fives are visionary pioneers and often ahead of their time. They see the world in an entirely new way.

Type Six: The Loyalist

Loyalists are committed, reliable, hardworking, responsible, and security-oriented. They are often cautious and indecisive, though some can also be rebellious, defiant, and reactive, especially under high stress. Sixes have trouble trusting others and themselves, so they often grapple with suspicion and self-doubt. At their best, healthy Sixes are confident, emotionally stable, courageous, self-reliant, and most enjoy championing the weak and powerless.

Type Seven: The Enthusiast

They are the busy, productive Type, always playful and high-spirited. Sevens are optimistic, spontaneous, versatile, and crave adventure. Seeking out new and exciting experiences that amplify pleasure is a Seven's comfort zone. Although Sevens tend to be multitalented and passionate about their various activities, they can easily overextend themselves and become scattered and undisciplined. Sevens typically struggle with impulsiveness and a fear of commitment. At their best, healthy Sevens are joyous, focused, purposeful, highly accomplished, and full of gratitude. They know how to see things through to completion without losing their sense of freedom and adventure.

Type Eight: The Challenger

Eights are powerful, dominating, confident, strong, assertive, and resourceful. They believe that they must be in control of their environment at all times and aren't afraid to be confrontational and intimidating if that's what it takes to win respect. They can also be prideful and domineering. Many Eights have to grapple with vulnerability and let in those they love because, for the most part, they associate intimacy and emotions with weakness. At their best, healthy Eights are heroic, magnanimous, and strong. They have the strong urge and potential to become historically significant in society.

Type Nine: The Peacemaker

Nines are easy-going, calm, trusting, accepting, and stable. They are kind-hearted, gentle, good-natured, and very supportive, and people just love being around them. Some Nines can easily go too far and lose their identity in the name of "fitting in" and keeping the peace. Their strong desire for stability and peace often causes them to avoid confrontation at all costs. They typically struggle with passive-aggressiveness, loss of identity, and hidden anger issues. At their best, healthy Nines have the powerful gift of bringing healing and understanding wherever they are. They can bring people together, heal conflicts, and create a sense of stability that allows others to let their guard down.

Now that you've had a brief introduction to the Nine Enneagram Types, you may have been drawn to certain qualities that felt very real for you. If not, that's pretty normal too. Various indicators will enable you to determine your primary personality type. These include the Wings, Sub-types, and Centers of Intelligence. Let's elaborate on what each of these is.

WHAT ARE WINGS?

Enneagram Wings are the numbers located on each side of your Enneagram Type. So if you discover you're a Type Two, your Wings would naturally be One and Three; if you're a Type Six, then your Wings are Five and Seven. Why are Wings important? Our Wings enable us to "borrow" and become influenced by the energy and qualities of said Wings. Having Wings adds a lot of depth to our overall Enneagram Type. The borrowing of energy shows in real action as similar traits and qualities. The jury is still out whether we're influenced by both Wings equally or whether we only rely on a single Wing. Some teachers emphasize the two-Wing theory, which makes sense because it offers a sense of equilibrium. Others teach the one-Wing theory, which states that only one Wing is dominant and influences a personality. According to one-Wing theory, a person's full Enneagram Type is expressed with both the main Type and an associated wing, e.g., an Enneagram Type Two could be 2w1 (a Type Two with a One Wing) or a 2w3 (a Type Two with a Three Wing).

WHICH THEORY IS CORRECT?

The American Journal of Psychiatry signals validity for both theories: "Individuals are generally more influenced by one Wing than the other, although traits from both wings may emerge in response to different environments. Although an individual's Wing may determine many aspects of his or her personality, the core type describes the primary motivation driving behavior"[1].

The point here isn't which theory is right or wrong, but what most resonates with you. Wings can be seen as personality flavors that you can toggle between depending on your context and level of development.

A great analogy I've heard for understanding the function and importance of the Wings is that of salt and pepper to flavor a dish. The main dish doesn't change, but adding a bit of salt and pepper elevates the taste to new heights. However, even the best meal becomes inedible if poorly done (underseasoned or overseasoned). Similarly, our Wings can flavor our personality as long as we're doing it in the right balance and at healthy levels of development.

It's essential to discover your dominant Wing, as that will give you granular details of your personality. For example, a Type Two is always empathetic, nurturing, and focused on helping others, but if their dominant Wing is One, then this individual will integrate a strong moral compass and principled integrity into their personality. As a result, the 2w1 will come across as someone with a stronger sense of duty. Their helping and nurturing nature may be directed toward community building and advocating for social justice issues instead of just focusing on their immediate loved ones. In comparison, a type Two with a dominant Three Wing will come across as more ambitious than usual. The 2w3 is less concerned about morality and instead emphasizes traits like confidence and competency. This individual may not be as oriented around service and community as the other 2w1 individual. Rather, the 2w3 will be more concerned about their image. Don't get me wrong, their goals and nurturing qualities are still the same. They will still work on fulfilling other people's desires to get what they want. But in behavioral observation, you'll see a difference in how they react to various situations and what they focus on most.

BRIEF DESCRIPTION OF THE 18 ENNEAGRAM TYPES WITH WINGS

All Enneagram Types have Wings; as in the example above, each Type will display additional flavors and focus on certain things depending on which Wing is most dominant. Here's an overview of how each Type would show up under the influence of their Wings.

1w9: Calm, practical, and meticulous perfectionist with a knack for catching inconsistencies in other people's reasoning and judgment. This individual is a deep listener and tends to easily get people to open up and trust them.

1w2: Socially aware activists and advocates who work tirelessly behind the scenes to uphold safety standards for others.

2w1: Deeply empathetic and caring with strong moral principles and integrity. This person finds fulfillment in other people's happiness and well-being.

2w3: Socially outgoing; loves to look good and be around people. This person is a great organizer and connecter of people.

3w2: Socially savvy, charming, and popular go-getter who enjoys meeting new people and networking at events.

3w4: Charismatic, attractive, driven, and organized; the boss who is always on the go with new business ideas and projects. This individual finds great joy in rewards and being efficient.

4w3: Charming, individualistic, and artistic, with a sense of wonder about the underlying beauty in nature, as well as the spectrum of human emotions.

4w5: Intense, curious, and artistic. Constantly creating and seeking to use their self-expression to highlight the universality of the human condition.

5w4: Deep, intense, and idiosyncratic. This individual values autonomy, self-reliance, and mastery of a subject. They mostly enjoy being on their own and are highly creative and a little romantic deep down.

5w6: Deep, intense, detached, and voracious researcher who gains energy from digging into fascinating topics under the radar.

6w5: Resourceful and dutiful team worker who values security and knowledge. This person tends to have a great sense of humor as well.

6w7: Optimistic and fun-loving, this individual loves exploring life but still seeks safety and comfort, which often creates contradiction and confusion.

7w6: The experience junkie who is ever-optimistic, energetic, and always searching for new projects to undertake.

7w8: Bold, creative, and often entrepreneurial, who enjoys experimenting, taking new risks, and creating with new mediums and ideas.

8w7: Headstrong, confident self-starter who loves to work hard and play hard; typically has a fearless attitude.

8w9: Confident servant leader who keeps other people's best interests (especially of those under their care) in mind to preserve harmony. This individual is more gentle and encouraging toward others.

9w8: Calm, independent vagabond on a quiet mission to discover what makes society a kinder, more accepting place.

9w1: Calm, collected, and pragmatic. This individual values cooperation and justice and the feeling of being connected to others in their community.

WHAT ARE SUB-TYPES?

Instinctual sub-types, or instinctual variants as they are also known, combine your core Enneagram Type and your instinct. What do we mean when we say instinct? Simply put, it is your survival mechanism. We are all wired in a particular way, and although there are three fundamental instincts or life forces within each of us, they are stacked differently. The order in which they are stacked, i.e., from the most dominant to the least dominant, influences our actions, thoughts, and feelings. How we navigate the demands of life is based on our sub-type.

What are the three instincts?

Claudio Naranjo teaches that we all have these three instincts. As you read through the following descriptions, try to become aware of which one shows up most in your personality and which one feels the most active in your personality. The dominant instinct is usually the one a person will feel most resonance with. They might feel neutral about their second instinct, and the third will be totally repressed or underdeveloped.

Self-preservation:

Self-preservation (SP) is one of the three basic sub-types. This variant is mainly concerned with safety, security, comfort, and, yes, self-preservation. People with a dominant self-preservation instinct prioritize the basics of life, e.g., food, shelter, family relationships, and tending to their physical and mental well-being. Energy and resource management is essential to such people, and they typically seek to avoid stressors in life or anything that could jeopardize their well-being.

Social:

Social (SO) Instinct is concerned with relationships and a sense of belonging to a group or community. People with a dominant Social Instinct tend to be socially aware and care more about the greater good above personal needs and desires. They know their place in a group, how they're perceived, and who they need to befriend. Such people find their most joy in teams or group settings where people work toward a shared purpose or common goal for the greater good. This instinct values connection and feeling involved with others.

One-to-One:

One-to-One, also referred to as Sexual (SX) instinct, is driven mainly by relationships (whether romantic or platonic) and experiencing life to the fullest. People with a dominant one-to-one instinctual variant value passion, excitement, and intimacy. They possess strong energy and actively seek out experiences where they can build bonds. With the One-to-One instinct, relationship building involves individuals, not groups or communities as with Social Instinct.

In total, adding the layers of the instinctual variants produces 27 subtypes which you'll learn about for each Enneagram type in subsequent chapters. If this all seems too overwhelming to grasp, think about the three instincts through the lens of the Centers of Intelligence. The Self-Preservation Instinct can be associated with the Head center; the One-to-One with the Body center; the Social Instinct with the Heart center. And now you must be wondering what that even means, so let's uncover that mystery next.

THE THREE CENTERS OF INTELLIGENCE

As you do the inner work and identify your true self, you'll notice that even if you type the same as another person, you'll never be identical. In fact, you may come across an individual who is the same Enneagram Type as you, yet is drastically different in their outlook and behavior. Aside from the fact that they might be leaning on a different wing than yourself, we need to consider how their instinctual variant influences their core type. But, to fully grasp the power and implications of that last statement, we'll need to discuss what the centers of intelligence are.

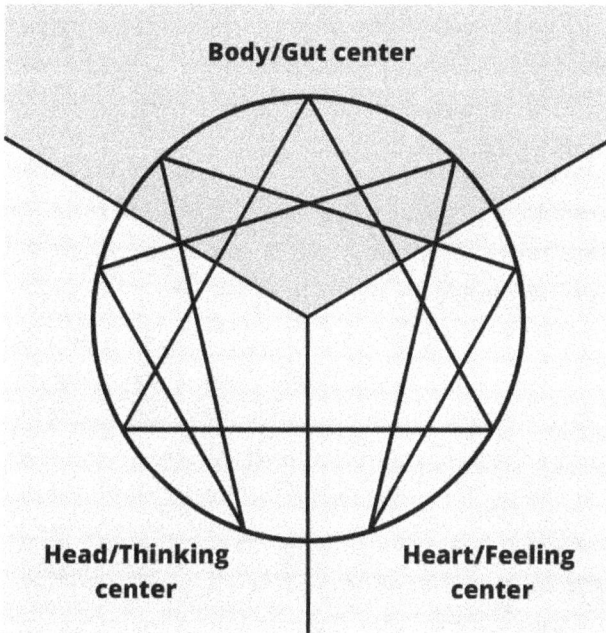

Some teachers like to call these centers of intelligence "the Triad" because they split the nine points into three equal portions, as shown in the illustration. They are the head, body, and heart, each of which provides us with basic skills that we need to navigate life and solve problems. They also indicate the underlying emotional issues that might cause us to behave in specific ways.

The head, also known as the thinking center, is more driven by logic, analysis of information, and deep thinking. Types 5, 6, and 7 make up the head center. Head types tend to be perceptive, creative, and thoughtful when operating at healthy expression levels. They are naturally good at performing cognitive tasks like visualization and imagination. However, if operating at unhealthy levels, fear is the primary underlying emotion that cripples their mind. This fear can wreak havoc if left unchecked. Unhealthy Fives react to anxiety by isolating themselves and retreating into their own minds. Sixes cope by imagining all the worst-case scenarios for everything. Sevens tend to turn their fear outward by actively running toward uncomfortable scenarios and reframing them as something exciting or adventurous —this is their way to escape their anxiety.

The body is also known as the gut center, and is mainly driven by physical sensations. The body center comprises Types 8, 9, and 1. These types are strong, stable, grounded, and connected with life, especially when they operate at healthy levels. Body types like to exert control over their environment and be independent. If operating at unhealthy levels, however, these Types can get consumed by their unchecked anger and may unconsciously act on it negatively. Eights tend to project their anger by lashing out at others when anger is building. Nines are more likely to suppress or reject their anger and hide it under the rug, pretending it doesn't exist. Types Ones deal with their unresolved anger issues by internalizing them, which often makes them overly self-critical. Unlike the other types, Ones will become aware of their anger and attempt to channel it in ways that are often unhealthy for themselves and others.

The heart is the emotional center and is mainly driven by feelings and a strong desire to connect. The feeling center is made of Types 2, 3, and 4. These types are caring, authentic, sensitive to emotional reactions, and connected with others. They love being appreciated and affirmed by others, whether they are aware of this tendency or not. The unresolved emotional issue that this group needs to resolve is shame, and it tends to subconsciously impact each Type in different ways. Type Twos are likely to express shame externally by overextending themselves in acts of service for other people so they can receive praise and affection. Threes may throw themselves into their work to be successful and receive admiration from others, and are more likely to be in denial of their shame. Type Fours attempt to control their shame by emphasizing their uniqueness to receive validation from others.

We all have one dominant Center of Intelligence; however, as with everything else you have learned so far, that doesn't mean the others are not active. We all have the head, body, and heart centers, but we often default to a favorite one that's dominant to our specific Enneagram Type. By identifying your Enneagram type, you will see which group you fall into and what dominant unresolved emotion you will need to consciously work on.

Don't be alarmed by the complexity of the various layers we've uncovered in this chapter. Your intention should be to increase your awareness and notice where you experience most resonance as more details are expressed for each Enneagram type. Trust in this process, and know that as we diver deeper into each Type in upcoming chapters, you'll gain more clarity, and things will start clicking into place.

THE DEEPER PURPOSE OF THE ENNEAGRAM

The real gift of the Enneagram tool is its ability to invite us to ponder and observe the mystery of our true identity. It initiates a process of inquiry that can lead us to a more profound truth about ourselves and our place in the world. If you discover your Type and use it as a scapegoat, as I've observed with a few people who say, "Of course I am critical of everything! After all, I'm a One," or "You know how we Sevens are! Commitment is really not my thing," then we're simply justifying our behavior instead of recognizing our blind spots and areas of growth and expansion. Any time you use your Enneagram tool to rigidly lock yourself into a limiting behavior, you're missing the purpose of this tool. Knowing your Type is important, but it's only valuable if you're using it as the kick-off point of your quest for self-discovery. Your true self can only be found beyond the traits of your Enneagram type. Your aim, and mine, is to do the inner work so we can stop automatic reactions of our personality. We want to approach life and relationships from a higher place than mere personality. The more awareness, insight, and clarity we bring to the mechanisms of our personality, the easier it will be to discover our true Selves. And that is the real purpose of the Enneagram. Head over to the resource section for the online Enneagram test I recommend.

---

1. https://psychiatryonline.org/doi/full/10.1176/appi.ajp-rj.2020.150301

CHAPTER 3

CULTIVATING AWARENESS AND UNDERSTANDING THE 9 PASSIONS

During the introduction and brief history of the Enneagram symbol and personality types, we mentioned the seven deadly sins or passions that Ichazo referenced to develop the modern-day Enneagram. In this chapter and the next, we'll investigate what these terms mean and why they matter to your quest for self-discovery. Before that, let's discuss one of the most critical qualities you must cultivate - self-awareness.

CULTIVATING AWARENESS

It is true that understanding the Enneagram personality types profoundly and with great clarity is a pre-requisite for transformation. But information alone doesn't bring about change. As William Shakespear once wrote in The Merchant of Venice, "If to do were as easy as to know what we're good to do, chapels had been churches, and poor men's cottaged princes' palaces. It is a good divine that follows his own instructions: I can easier teach twenty what were good to be done, than be one of the twenty to follow mine own teaching." In other words, it takes more than just learning about the

Enneagram to transform your life. Most students of personal development struggle to experience new results because they cannot transfer the learned material into everyday living. It's easy to be calm, positive, and think abundance in a workshop or a weekend retreat by the lakeside. But that doesn't guarantee that you'll finally change your life. None of us can will or think or technique our way into transformation. The kind of progress and success we dream of doesn't happen automatically, just because you pick up a book such as this or sign up for a masterclass. Active participation on a consistent daily basis is necessary. Without it, no lasting transformation can occur. So how do you ensure that everything you learn about the Enneagram positively transforms your life forever? How can you shift from intellectual recognition of Truth to living it as a way of life now and always? By cultivating more awareness in your life. The Enneagram will empower you to let go of the limiting mechanisms of your personality so that you can experience more deeply who and what you really are. And you need a tremendous amount of self-awareness to catch yourself moment by moment. As you consciously and intentionally participate in the living of your Truth, that practice will lead to permanent transformation.

Why is self-awareness critical in this quest for self-discovery?

A simple agreed-upon definition of self-awareness is "the ability to observe oneself clearly and objectively through reflection and introspection." In other words, it's about monitoring our inner worlds, thoughts, emotions, and beliefs. According to most sacred traditions around the world, observing ourselves and being vigilant as we interact with the world is one of the most powerful things we can do to gain mastery in life. It is the path to our full awakening to who we really are and realizing that we are more than just physical beings living in a three-dimensional world. As we awaken, we become more aware and learn to "catch ourselves in the act" as we behave according to our personality and conditioning. When we are able to notice what we are doing in the moment, and we are willing to experience our current state completely, without judgment, that's when the magic happens.

On the quest for self-discovery, awareness is vitally important because it enables us to see our habits and conditions more clearly as they occur. And when we can see them in action, those old patterns move from the subconscious, where we have no control over them, to the conscious mind, where we can dissolve and alter them. Analyzing past behavior is helpful, but can never be as powerful as present moment observation. Let me share a story to illustrate this point. I once caught myself in a moment when I was about to enter a heated argument with my girlfriend. At the time, this inner work was still pretty new to me, and we'd only been dating a few months. She said something that triggered some disturbing emotions, and I felt my entire body shift into a different state. Ordinarily, I would have fallen into the trap of arguing, but this was the first time I observed myself and witnessed the sensations in my body, the brewing negativity, and that urge to lash out. It was such an incredible experience because, in that moment of awareness, I realized that I didn't really want to get into an argument and mess up our weekend getaway. I saw that my reaction was just a way to justify something deeper. So, instead, I began to question what was really behind that behavior. What was this important point that I wanted to make, or what was it I was trying to defend and hide? Becoming more curious about myself completely dissipated the situation and resulted in me taking a step back and heading out for a long meditative stroll that revealed a lot more about my approach to romantic relationships. The trick, though, is that I was able to observe without judgment; I was able to stay in that discomfort long enough to question and meet my feelings with curiosity rather than shrink into embarrassment. Then I applied some mindfulness practices that work for my Type—we'll talk more about all these practices for each of the Enneagram types.

The more self-awareness you cultivate, the easier it will be to observe and catch yourself in the moment, enabling you to make different choices. It will also increase your ability to regulate emotions. At first, it might feel embarrassing and uncomfortable; you might have a strong urge to shut down or distract yourself from facing those unwanted sensations, but if you can just stay present and embrace that discomfort, you'll notice something new emerging. With patience and a lot of self-acceptance, you'll start to experience self-compassion and understanding that transcends your personality. That's when you begin to tap into the real you. That's when you begin to awaken.

A Course in Miracles writes, "The Bible says that a deep sleep fell upon Adam, and nowhere is there a reference to his waking up." Gurdjieff and many other spiritual teachers have often asserted that our current normal state is akin to being asleep, at least from the soul's perspective. That sounds strange for someone new to inner work because it's hard to convince your ego as you read this that you're asleep. But what if I told you that there are many levels of awareness? Consider how "real" a dream feels when you're being chased by an animal. Your physiology responds as though you were awake, yet your body in this reality is wholly immobilized on your bed as you dream. Would it be too ridiculous to open up to the possibility that, even at this moment, you could be asleep in relation to other levels of awareness or higher realities? In this current level of awareness, your personality and ego tend to have the most control. They dominate your day and determine your behavior. However, through practice and cultivating more awareness, you could bridge a gap between your personality and a higher version of yourself that remains unseen and unknown. Waking up from the trance of personality and being able to detach yourself from that version of yourself that's driven by impulse, desire, and emotions reveals a you that you might have been seeking since childhood. So this isn't about villainizing your personality; instead, it's about giving you the power to choose how you'll show up in any given moment. Most of us, especially our political leaders, run around in life being led by a mischievous six-year-old. Is it any wonder we are continually recreating drama and chaos? Once we understand, however, the mechanisms of personality, and begin to identify who we really are independent of personality, the game of life takes on new meaning. As we recognize that we are a Type Five or a Type Eight, we're not enslaved by that Fiveness or Eightness. Instead, we can choose at any given moment how to direct our Type, and when we see that it doesn't serve us, we have the choice to override it altogether. Once you begin practicing more self-awareness, you're ready to face your greatest teacher: your Type's passion.

THE 9 PASSIONS

In the context of the modern Enneagram system for personality typing, Ichazo traced early ideas about the ancient "Nine Divine Attributes" from Greece to the desert fathers of the fourth century who first developed the concept of the Seven Deadly Sins (basically the opposite or distortions of the Divine Attributes) and incorporated them into our modern system. Although Christian tradition talked about the Seven Deadly Sins at first, two others were later added: fear and deceit. Ichazo's teaching of the Passions in the context of the Enneagram model that we use tells us we all have each of these "Passions" within us. However, depending on our Enneagram Type, a particular passion will be more pronounced. That's the passion that shows up repeatedly throughout our lives and is the root of our imbalance in life. It distorts and traps our ego in unconstructive ways as it tries to resolve that deep-seated issue.

The idea of the Deadly Sins, aka the Passions, will make more sense if you think of the sin in the following way. Sin means to "miss the mark," but not as most religions teach (something bad or evil). So the 9 Passions represent the nine main ways that we lose our center and become distorted in our thoughts, feelings, and actions.

Passion for type 1: *Anger*
Passion for type 2: *Pride*
Passion for type 3: *Deceit*
Passion for type 4: *Envy*
Passion for type 5: *Avarice*
Passion for type 6: *Fear*
Passion for type 7: *Gluttony*
Passion for type 8: *Lust*
Passion for type 9: *Sloth*

Each of these Passions is discussed in detail under their corresponding Enneagram Type in subsequent chapters. As mentioned before, your passion is your greatest teacher. When you recognize this underlying emotional reaction and how it plays out in your life, you will finally start moving toward your genuine desire in life and your essential nature. What is your essential nature? Great question. Let's unpack that next.

ESSENCE PERSONALITY EGO

A t this point in your quest, you ought to be realizing that while your personality matters, it's not who you are. If you've already landed on that Truth, congratulations. Life is about to get way more intriguing and wonderful. The fundamental Truth of Life is that we are far more than the familiar conditioned concepts we call personality. Our true potential is grand and remains mostly dormant and untapped until we begin this quest of self-discovery. Beyond the accepted limitations of our ego-personality, each of us is a magnificent being. Deepak Chopra likes to refer to this being as our Higher Self. I like that term, so from now on, whenever I desire to make a distinction between your ego personality and True Self, I shall refer to them as the ego self and the Higher Self. The Higher Self cannot be seen, tasted, touched, or analyzed by the logical mind, but there is a simple way to "experience" your Higher Self.

How can you begin to discern the difference between the Higher Self and the ego-self?

- The Higher Self is always certain and clear about things. Your ego-self is influenced by countless outside influences, which creates confusion.
- The Higher Self is always at peace. Your ego-self is restless, agitated, and easily disturbed.
- The Higher Self is stable. Your ego self shifts constantly.
- The Higher Self is love. Your ego self, lacking love, seeks it from external sources, including people and things.

At this moment, while reading the words in this book, become aware that you're reading. Notice yourself and your thoughts as you reflect on my words. Now, ask yourself, "Who is noticing that I am reading?"

If you can sit in self-contemplation with that thought, you'll come to experience the quality of Being or Presence of the observer, aka your Higher Self. Your Higher Self is ever-present in the moment, and is what Enneagram experts call your "Essence." In spiritual language, this Essence is often referred to as the spark of the Divine that rests within. As mentioned before in *A Course in Miracles*, the human race fell into a deep sleep since the time of Adam, and in that sleep, we forgot our true nature. Here's how I've come to understand this teaching. My Higher Self is the Divine spark, the real and powerful me. My ego-self is the everyday little me formed due to my beliefs, culture, childhood, societal norms, and environment. It's the human conditioning aspect of myself that I've grown to believe is who I am. The more I go through life living only from the perspective of my ego-personality self, the more distant and disconnected I am from my Higher Self, and that's where all the problems stem from. That disconnect breeds the restlessness, void, loneliness, fear, and lack that I try to grapple with in my physical world by chasing after things and people, hoping that will finally solve my internal issues. In this "darkness," I do not experience my own Divine nature and certainly cannot perceive divinity in anything or anyone else.

Instead, I get trapped in whatever perspective my ego-personality holds true.

Notice what thoughts, emotions, and beliefs came up for you as you read that last paragraph. Hearing these things for the first time is entirely foreign for many of us, so it's easy for your ego to reject these ideas. I only ask that you suspend unbelief and keep an open mind until you've gone through the entire book. Then you can choose what you want to believe and live by. In normal everyday living, we don't experience our Essence and its many aspects because our awareness is dominated by ego-personality. As we learn to cultivate the awareness discussed in chapter 4 and become aware of ourselves moment-by-moment, it becomes more apparent that there's more to us than our personality and impulses. And in those moments, we can catch glimpses of our Essence. To be clear, reconnecting with your Essence doesn't kill your personality or destroy your ego; you will still function as a human being in the world, but you will do so above ordinary levels of human awareness because you'll have direct contact with Divinity.

This quest is, therefore, one of remembering. It's remembering who you really are and the magnificence within you. It's about returning to your True Self. The Enneagram's purpose is to guide you on this journey of awakening. It's here to give you insights into your specific psychological and spiritual makeup, not so that you can comfortably fit into a particular category, but so you can become aware of the many ways you're limiting your Higher Self through the expressions of your limited personality. Many people think the Enneagram is meant to justify their behaviors or provide them with consolation for being of a particular nature. This is far from the truth. The Enneagram tool wasn't created to place us in a box, but instead to show us the box we are already in and provide a way out. So, if you want out of your old way of living and into something profoundly different and more aligned with your true Essence, rest easy because you have to take that first step today.

SHOULD WE GET RID OF OUR PERSONALITIES?

Most people assume that returning to one's Essence means abandoning or rejecting the personality and ego. This is misinformation and certainly not what the Enneagram teaches. We don't want to villainize or even eliminate the ego-personality because we need it to enjoy and function in human living. So if you've been fearful about losing your identity or becoming less functional in society, don't be. The Enneagram teaches us to get in touch with our Essence and reconnect with our True Self so we can become whole. Wholeness includes and integrates all aspects, including personality. Think about the restlessness, fear, instability, and lack of lack that plagues our ego-personality. The quest for self-discovery and reconnecting finally heals all those issues because our ego can finally receive permanent, unconditional love, strength, stability, and a sense of power that it could not access anywhere else. That transforms our ego-personality from unhealthy levels to the healthiest and most productive version because it's nourished directly from the Divinity within us. Moments of "flow" and peak performance are typically the result of an individual who has become present and aware, aligned with their True Self. In such states, the activity at hand becomes more enjoyable and yields better results.

The solution, therefore, is not to reject our personality but rather to see it for what it really is: a tiny part of who we are in totality. The personality still exists, but there is a more active intelligence, a higher, more powerful presence underlying that personality that is in charge and on the driver's seat of our lives. We shift from a personality identity to an Essence identity. That makes all the difference in our human experience.

How quickly can we make this shift?

It would be inaccurate to claim that you will switch from ego-personality identity to Higher Self identity at the snap of a finger, or that it's a one-time thing that lasts forever. The Truth is, this is an ongoing process that you work on moment-by-moment. With practice, you move further away from the lower levels of awareness to the higher levels. Each moment of self-realization will transform you to some degree, and the more you pile on these moments, the higher you rise until, soon enough, your default expression will be an expanded awareness. As you progress and practice, your identity gradually opens up to include more of your Higher Self. In other words, your inner light and essential nature will shine brighter day by day as you keep doing the work. As long as you never stop working to improve, you will continue to experience deeper, higher, and more profound divine self-expression beyond anything you can imagine.

BASIC DRIVES OF THE PERSONALITY

Before we dive deep into each personality type, let's bring a little more clarity to the fundamental mechanisms that drive the personality. These are basic fear and basic desire.

The basic fear is rooted in a sense of loss that each personality feels consciously or unconsciously. It comes from the loss of contact with our Essential nature in early childhood. Even children born under the best circumstances will not have all their developmental needs perfectly met, no matter how well-intentioned their parents are. For various reasons, parents will at times have difficulty coping with all the needs of their babies (especially in areas they also lacked as children). For example, if an infant expresses joyfulness and delight in being alive, but her mother is depressed, it's unlikely the mother will be comfortable with or even encourage the baby's joy. As a result, the baby learns to suppress her happiness to keep her mother from getting more upset. There are many learned behaviors that, as children, we adopted to enable us to either fit in or protect our caregivers based on observed behavior. Some children contract and suppress their emotions entirely; others go to the other extreme to get a reaction from their caregiver. But in all cases, our conditioned environment always hampers our true and fullest expression in one way or another. We react in ways that correspond to our forming personality depending on our temperament. As we continue to grow in our formative years, our unmet needs and subsequent blockages pile on, and we become keenly aware of a disconnect. Something feels off, and that creates deep-seated anxiety and fear regardless of personality type. Each Type has its own characteristic basic fear. Even if we cannot express it in words, we feel the tug of powerful, unconscious fear and anxiety, especially when under the pressures of life. Keep in mind that part of what drives our basic fear is our ego-personality's fear of nothingness, which is pretty much a universal paradigm. As you go through each of the nine types, you'll recognize that all these fears are present in you to some extent, but your own Type's basic fear will stand out much more than the others. Here's an example to show you what I mean.

EXERCISE 1:

Read the following sentences and notice which one stands out most (maybe even stirs up painful flashbacks or makes you cringe).

#1: It's not okay to make mistakes.
#2: It's not okay to you have your own needs. Don't be selfish.
#3: It's not okay to have your own feelings and identity.
#4: It's not okay to be too happy or too functional.
#5: It's not okay to be comfortable in the world.
#6: It's not okay to trust yourself.
#7: It's not okay to depend on anyone for anything.
#8: It's not okay to be vulnerable or trust anyone.
#9: It's not okay to assert yourself.

Which of these statements really pressed hard on your psyche?

Take note of whatever insights come to you. For now, let's keep exploring.

We talked about Basic Fear and the fact that it arises from a deep sense of disconnect from our Essence nature. Now let's talk about Basic Desire because it's equally important to understand where that's rooted as well.

Basic desire arises as the defense mechanism to counteract that sense of loss and disconnect that our basic fear generates within. It is the ego's way of "handling the situation and making things okay." I like to imagine the ego-self regularly thinks to himself, "If I can just get X, that feeling/void/restlessness/emptiness/loss that we're experiencing will be gone, and I can finally feel whole again." X represents whatever your specific personality type struggles with the most. It could be love, security, peace, and so forth. Many Enneagram teachers refer to the Basic Desire as the "ego agenda" because it's basically what the ego is always striving after. But here's the thing. No one says your ego desires are wrong. In fact, when you dig deeper, they are pointing you to something wonderful and right. The ego just mainly focuses on surface-level humanistic needs. Unfortunately, the ego tends to fixate too much on its specific basic desire to the point of neglect of other human and spiritual needs. Things tend to go wrong when we attempt to fulfill our basic desire in misguided ways. Suppose you are the personality type that is ever-seeking and obsessing over security. Perhaps, you always want to feel safe and secure in everything in your life. In an uncertain world where change is constant, attaining that aim is challenging from an ego perspective. Maybe it has caused you to push too hard to the point where you start self-sabotaging and ruining even the same security your ego needs. As you will see in upcoming chapters when we talk about the Enneagram Type Six, this is a common experience for Sixes operating at lower levels of development. Similarly, each personality type is capable of such self-sabotaging behavior, which, ironically, robs them of the very thing they are chasing after.

Look around the world today. Thanks to technology, the Internet, and social media, we are more connected than ever. And yet, more people claim loneliness and the inability to find their soul mate. There are more divorce cases than ever, and people even take their own lives due to lacking love in their lives. That is the sad outcome when individuals chase after their basic desires in misguided ways. And when that happens, our basic desire turns into a fixation that unwittingly blocks our Essential nature creating a wider gap between our everyday self and our Higher Self. The irony here is that when we are fixated on our basic desire, our personality craves control. It will not relinquish that control until it believes the desire has been fully and permanently attained. Unfortunately, as you might have already experienced, any goal achievement doesn't guarantee the feeling of wholeness or completion. How often have you chased after a money goal thinking it will make you feel rich, only to achieve it and still feel poor and unhappy? Or perhaps it was a romantic partner that you chased after, thinking they would fill a void, yet a few months or years in, that same void persisted?

Going back to our example of the Type Six who relentlessly seeks security in all the wrong ways. That individual would want to control everything in their world, and they wouldn't allow themselves to relax and become present until they feel their world is completely secure. As we know, without Presence, there is no return to the Essential nature. So, of course, that person will feel trapped in a cycle of anxiety and insecurity, trying hard to control the external world and force things to feel stable and secure. Understanding this, can you see the interrelation between the basic fear and basic desire? Are you seeing why most teachers say that human nature is driven by fear and desire? In this construct, we can summarize that our personality operates on a model of fleeing from our basic fear and pursuing our basic desire. The entire feeling-tone of our character emerges out of this dynamic, and it becomes the underlying drive for our ego and sense of self.

Time for another exercise to move you deeper into this quest. In the previous exercise, we focused on statements that would enable you to notice your most prominent basic fear. This time, we're focused on statements that can help you identify your basic desire.

EXERCISE 2:

> #1: I need to live in integrity and do what's right. I operate with a strong moral code, and so should everyone else.
> #2: I need to be loved and needed by others.
> #3: I must become and show that I am valuable and prove to others that I deserve admiration.
> #4: I must find my true identity and express my uniqueness to the world.
> #5: I need to be competent and the most knowledgeable so I can know Truth.
> #6: I need to be secure.
> #7: I must be happy all the time.
> #8: I need to protect myself from the world and show that I am strong at all times.
> #9: I need to find peace in my mind and life at all costs.

After going through this second exercise, can you find a statement of desire, and does it correspond with or match the basic fear that most stood out for you?

The answer you give is already enlightening you on your Enneagram type and also the area of your life where growth seeks to happen. As Andrew Harvey once said, "The very things we wish to avoid, neglect and flee from turn out to be the 'prima materia' from which all real growth comes."

Ready for real growth? It's time to learn about your Enneagram type.

SECTION II

THE 9 TYPES

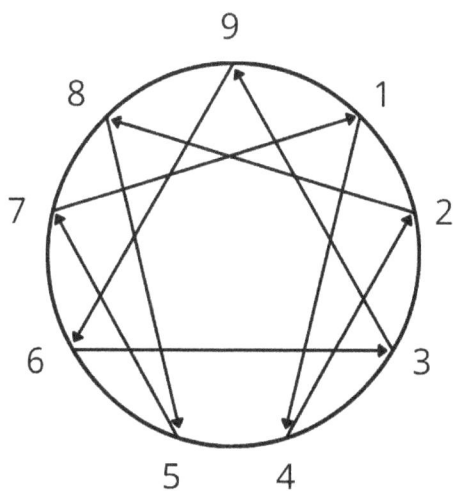

CHAPTER 5

ENNEAGRAM TYPE 1

THE REFORMER OR PERFECTIONIST

This chapter and the next will go in-depth on the Enneagram Type One, commonly referred to as the reformer or perfectionist. The title - reformer is a perfect fit for this enneatype because these individuals thrive when they're changing the world around them for the better. Type Ones are idealistic, purposeful, self-controlled, and highly conscientious. They adhere to strict moral and ethical codes and operate with extremely high standards. Because they desire to make everything around them "right" by their standards, they can easily create friction and resistance when interacting with others. Enneagram Type Ones fall into the Gut or Body Center, making anger one of the main emotions that hinder personal growth and evolution, especially if unresolved.

Many Ones who aren't yet operating at the higher and healthier levels of development often fall into habits of criticism, judgment, and perfectionism. But here's the thing. These great expectations of perfection (as unrealistic as they might be) aren't just placed on others. Ones tend to set exceptionally high standards for themselves, causing them to live in constant self-criticism. Their strong inner critic takes the driver's seat, which dictates how they behave and treat others. From an outside observer, Type Ones might be great at execution, planning, organization, and promoting positive change, but they're also difficult to work with, impossible to please, and in some cases, total jerks.

STRENGTHS OF A ONE:

Ones are great at getting things done, and they don't allow anyone to stand in their way or hold them back. They often make incredible change-makers, crusaders, teachers, and activists.

Ones are also capable of self-leading and efficiently solving setbacks and problems that arise as they pursue their goals.

A defining strength for type One is their ability to go the extra mile to ensure a project or situation is handled exceptionally well. They will stop at nothing to attain perfection.

Due to their idealistic worldview and the need to get everything done right, they pay close attention to details, fuss over the little things and never take shortcuts. That makes this type extremely diligent, hardworking, and reliable.

Key personality traits of Type One

- Focused and purposeful.
- A compulsive need to be right all the time.
- Meritocracy and organization.
- Hard working.
- Being good or perfect.
- Politeness.

Common hobbies for a Type One

- Organizing
- Fundraising
- Tutoring
- Planning

FEARS AND WEAKNESSES

By now, it's evident that one of the distinguishing expressions of a Type One is the need to live by very high moral standards and do things the right way. That comes from the need to be good and to be perceived as good and worthy.

What's the Basic Fear driving this behavior? The fear of being bad, corrupt, evil, or defective.

As a type One, you may fear being misinterpreted, accused, blamed, or considered fraud for not living up to the high standards you've set. The idea that others may not see you as perfect is unbearable because that will mean you're imperfect and therefore defective. In a more practical sense, you are fussy about your physical space and how messy others make it. You fuss over unclear projects or when a loved one acts recklessly. If expectations are unclear and there's a lack of quality in any area, you will lose your mind. For example, a businessman who once attended our virtual meetups shared that whenever he walks into the office if even a single light bulb is off, he loses his mind because it's unacceptable that his office manager would call themselves a professional when they can barely tend to office duties. This is a great example of how detail-oriented and perfectionistic Ones can be. Deep down, it's all about the need to be good and perfect. Instead of criticizing yourself over this habit of perfectionism in a world that's anything but perfect all the time, it's better to get curious about why that fear is prevailing.

Perhaps somewhere during your upbringing, you may have picked up the message that you need to be perfect all the time? You're an idealist at heart, so it makes sense that anything flawed should be fixed immediately, including you.

How does this Basic Fear often manifest itself?

You will often see and catch even the tiniest mistakes in others as you interact with them. If it's in your social life, you may stop dating someone or decline an invitation simply because they didn't live up to the details of your ideal. At work, it might show up as constantly getting into conflict with work colleagues over how something should be done and why your idea is the right way to solve certain challenges. But it doesn't stop there. By far, the biggest issue for a One is the ongoing negative chatter in their mind. It feels almost impossible to tame that inner critic who seems impossible to please. You might become resentful and angry with yourself, others, or a less than ideal situation that throws you off your game. And because you're a body-based type, dealing with feelings (especially anger) isn't a strong suit, so you're likely to suppress emotions that typically leak out in the most unhealthy ways. We'll study different levels of development so you can start identifying where you are on your journey and how to move toward the most connected and healthy version of yourself. But first, let's take a look at your Basic desire and motivations.

DESIRES AND MOTIVATIONS

The Basic Desire for a Type One is to be good and honorable. If you identify as a Type One, there are a few key things to recognize about your personality. First off, leading a purposeful life is extremely important to you, which is praiseworthy. The best way to rise into higher levels of development is to align your goals and work choices with your purpose. People call you a perfectionist or bossy mainly because they don't fully understand how important it is to you that things get done the proper way. Attaining the best in every outcome isn't just a slogan for you. It's part of your personality's DNA, and it's okay to honor that as long as it doesn't enslave you. As a type One, you're extremely responsible and pragmatic and strive to make the world a better place. You rely on your judgment to come up with solutions and do a great job separating emotions from facts so you don't get overwhelmed by emotions like other types. Ethics is also a big issue for you. In fact, as we break down your core values, you'll notice how connected they are and why all are necessary for enabling you to live an honorable life. Let's name the top values your personality identifies with most.

Core values

As a type One, these are some of the core values you may hold dear.

- Integrity
- Honesty
- Ethics
- Duty
- Humility
- Organization, structure
- Cleanliness, tidiness, order
- Service above self

Type One celebrities and famous people you might know include Apple co-founder Steve Jobs, Canadian Singer Celine Dion, Actress Julie Andrews, Actress Natalie Portman, Anti-colonial nationalist and political ethicist Mahatma Gandhi, and the former first lady of the United States, Michelle Obama.

Wondering if you could be a type One? Here are some personality indicators:

1. You hold yourself to very high standards. Some might even say unrealistically high standards.

2. You are a stickler for rules. You always need clarity about what others expect of you and what the boundaries are so you can act accordingly.

3. You exercise high levels of self-restraint and work hard to civilize your natural instincts. That makes you more rational and less impulsive.

4. You care a lot about making a difference in the world and doing your part to make things better for yourself and others.

5. As a child, you may have taken on a lot of responsibility, turning you into the "dependable one" that everyone relies on. People know they can count on you no matter what because you always keep your word and take your duties very seriously. However, this comes with a dark side as well because it means you carry a heavy burden all your life.

6. You have a strong inner critic that judges every action you take. That voice is behind your constant need for perfection in your world. Left unchecked, this voice can be the cause of great anxiety, self-criticism, and self-doubt.

7. You're utterly frustrated at how sloppy and subpar most people are. Because you strive so hard for perfection and work hard to live with integrity, you can't stand it when others act recklessly or neglect their duties.

8. You have a hard time relaxing and just allowing yourself to be a little spontaneous.

9. Being corrupted, evil, or betraying your moral code is simply unacceptable.

10. You worry that expressing the anger that sometimes brews inside you or allowing yourself to just explode emotionally will cause you to fall from the ideals and standards you've set for yourself. So rather than express your negative

emotions, you prefer to hold in your anger and repress it under clenched fists, a tight jawbone, and gritted teeth.

11. Friends and family members may call you overly critical, a bit of a pushover, and too strict if they were asked to describe you. But you don't mind because you know that's what it takes to create the kind of success you desire.

YOUR WINGS

Wings are the numbers that reside directly on the two sides of your Enneagram Type. As an enneatype One, you have -

- The Enneagram One with Nine-Wing: "The idealist."
- The Enneagram One with Two-Wing: "The Advocate"

While you may have tendencies that lean into both wings, you'll likely be more dominant in one than the other, and this will be your dominant Wing.

Meaning of your Wing

If you're a 1w9 (One with Nine-Wing), then you will tend to be more introverted than a 1w2. You're more of that principled idealist and always think before you speak so you can avoid going against your moral code in any way. Sometimes, this leads to delays and procrastination because you just need to be sure and think everything through before acting. A strong aspect of having this Wing as the dominant of the two is that your decisions and actions are almost always failproof.

If you're a 1w2 (One with Two-Wing), then you're more extraverted and outgoing in nature. You're more empathetic and understanding of others compared to a 1w9. You feel deeply inclined to help the people around you. While you are still an excellent problem solver, you struggle a lot with striking that balance between controlling things and people and supporting them.

The Arrows and what they mean

When you look closely at the Enneagram symbol, you'll notice that there are lines within the circle connecting the personality points in the circle's perimeter. These lines aren't arbitrary. They are, in fact, arrows that map how each personality will react in certain situations. Your personality type is linked to two other points (4 and 7). One arrow indicates how you will react in stressful, pressure-filed situations or when you're feeling like your back is up against the wall. It explains the actions or reactions of an unhealthy personality. In Enneagram terminology, this is called the Direction of Stress or the Direction of Disintegration. The other arrow indicates how a healthy version of your personality reacts to situations and how your personality grows in different environments. The term for this is the Direction of Growth or the Direction of Integration. In brief, moving in the direction of stress (4), you would be moody, irrational, and temperamental. However, moving in the direction of growth (7), you become more joyful, spontaneous, and relaxed like a healthy Seven.

To understand the relationship of these arrows and how we came about with healthy and unhealthy levels, let's talk about the various levels of development for type One.

LEVELS OF DEVELOPMENT

Levels of Development arise from Riso and Hudson's teachings and the founders of the Enneagram Institute, which is a great place to take your Enneagram Test. Their theory posits that all individuals fall into one of nine levels of functioning. The lowest level is nine, and the highest is level one. The levels are divided into a triad that subcategorizes these levels as healthy (1,2,3), average levels (4,5,6), and unhealthy levels (7,8,9).

Unhealthy Levels

Level 9: This level of development is the most destructive and unhealthy. Although we all go through this level during infancy when we're purely interested in our needs and nothing else, this level should be outgrown as soon as possible. As babies and infants, operating at a level 9 where you care about nothing else other than getting your way and having your needs met is perfectly normal, but this is extremely unhealthy for adults. Thus an adult One operating at this level is cruel, punitive, and condemnatory toward others. Such a Type One is likely to experience serve depression, nervous breakdowns, and even struggle with obsessive-compulsive disorders.

Level 8: This level is where a type One becomes obsessive about imperfection and the wrongdoing around them. At this level, the One is quite delusional and compulsive. They also tend to be quite contradictory by saying one thing and then doing the opposite.

Level 7: This type One is rigid, intolerant, self-righteous, and highly dogmatic. When dealing with others who are wrong, they tend to be very severe in their judgments and unrespectful of other people's feelings or personal boundaries. At this level of development, the individual only deals in absolutes, and they alone know "The Truth ."

Average Levels

Level 6: This level of development is moving toward the path of healthy expressions but is still highly critical both of themselves and others. Such a type One will be picky, judgmental, and a classic perfectionist. They are opinionated about everything and have a knack for correcting people and tormenting them to do "the right thing" by their standards. This type One is impatient, abrasive, and constantly scolds everyone around them. At this level, type One is overcompensating and still driven by the desire to advance their ego agendas, even if it's at the cost of others.

Level 5: This level of development brings with it the expression of a lot of defensive behavior. Type One at this level is extremely afraid of making mistakes and failing to reach their ideals. Everything has to go according to their plans or lose it. This individual is more organized, orderly, and extremely hardworking. They are rigid, emotionally constricted, and highly impersonal even with people they like. Their main focus is to compulsively tend to each detail so they can achieve their goals.

Level 4: At this average level of development, there's a strong expression of imbalance for type One. The individual is becoming high-minded and quite dissatisfied with reality. They feel it's up to them to improve everything and everyone in their world, often moving them into advocates, critics, and crusaders as they attempt to tame that inner critic so they can reach their highest ideals.

Healthy Levels

Level 3: This level of development gets us into the more healthy expressions of a type One personality where they care about social values. At this point, they have outgrown purely ego-driven goals and now see their role as individuals in society and the world as a whole. This is where the ego begins to heal and operate more constructively. This type One is extremely principled and always wants to be fair, ethical, objective, and embody justice. They have a strong sense of responsibility and personal integrity.

Level 2: This level of development is attained through the commitment to doing the inner work and learning more about oneself. At this level, the Type One's ego reaches the individual's Ideal Self. This Type One is conscientious, reasonable, self-disciplined, mature, and moderate in all things. They have an intense sense of right and wrong and a purpose that drives their life.

Level 1: At this level of development, Type One reaches the holy grail of self-mastery and wholeness. This is indeed a Type One at their best and the level of true freedom. It involves facing your deepest fears and genuinely understanding yourself as both a human and spiritual being. Although you reach your ideal Self at Level Two, transcendence and enlightenment occur at this level. You become extraordinarily wise and discerning, accepting things just as they are. Your ability to discern truth and know what action to take at any given point is awe-inspiring, and you become more hopeful, calm, accepting, humane, and liberated from the inside out. This is the dream for all of us on this quest, and it is within your grasp as you continue to walk this path.

TYPE ONE'S PASSION

The Passions (also called the Deadly Sins) are our teachers. Each type has a dominant passion that can enable the individual to uncover their underlying emotional reaction and unresolved issues when recognized. By following that thread, the person becomes aware of how they've lost sight of their true desire and their essential nature.

For a type One, your Passion is Anger, although many teachers agree that a more accurate description is resentment. Anger in and of itself isn't an issue, so don't villainize the experience of this emotion. The problem is that as a type One, you tend to repress the emotion of anger which leads to continual frustration, dissatisfaction, and resentment. That breeds an inner resentment that influences how you relate to yourself and others.

Pause for a moment. Think about how often you think, feel or even speak the words, "This just isn't right. Nothing is as it should be!" If you can become aware of your Passion of Anger, you'll likely see that it results from a need to change or fix everything around you. So you end up angry with someone (or yourself) for not being good enough.

Increasing awareness of this Passion opens up a new choice. It enables you to transform and start moving toward your Essence, which returns you back to your virtue of Serenity.

CHILDHOOD AND EMOTIONAL PATTERNS OF TYPE ONE

We can now see that Anger is one of the leading emotions for type Ones and really all the types that form the Gut or Body Center. But most Ones have a hard time recognizing that they have anger and resentment issues. So to bring even more clarity so you can take appropriate action, let's talk about how you internalize this emotion and how others experience it. Because you tend to reflect your anger inwardly, it tends to leak out in the form of criticism, judgment, and scolding. And you don't just do it to others, you also do it to yourself. So unlike a type Eight who also has the Passion of Anger and tends to project it externally, you do everything possible to contain and conceal the suffering you experience. Depending on your dominant Wing Type, specific qualities will be more pronounced than others.

Type One Wing 9 - The Idealist

A type One with Wing Nine means the individual has all the qualities of a One and a few qualities of type Nine. Although you can be influenced by both Wings, the more dominant Wing will resonate deeply with you. Some of the traits of that particular Wing will be easy to identify in yourself. As you study and understand more about yourself, it is imperative to identify which Wing is more dominant and, if possible, the proportion of the Wing score if both as active. Studying your main personality and wing types can also give you a better understanding of your childhood wounds and how that's affecting your adult life. Type 1w9 is typically rational, calm, and balanced with a sense of right and wrong. There's a strong emphasis on justice and fairness, especially when dealing with people. Does that sound like you? Here are some more details of this personality:

- Loyal friend
- Extremely detail-oriented
- Improvement oriented
- Stand up for the powerless and underprivileged
- Striving to make a difference in society
- A strong code of ethics

1w9 also prefer to keep to themselves and hardly allow their emotions to show. They may have had a disconnected relationship with their caregiver during their childhood years. They likely grew up in an extreme environment - either too strict or too lenient. If the household was also a religious one, then this child probably developed a need to please an angry, capricious God. Having a dysfunctional relationship with parents and the authority figures in their environment, this child needed to create a personality that didn't express themselves emotionally to avoid evoking anger in others. They also had to learn to create a strict set of boundaries for themselves and a particular of carrying themselves in the world to preserve a spotless, flawless reputation as a child. Control had to be mastered early in life. As adults, we see it playing out in relationships, work life, and social interactions. The need to strive for perfection, maintain control, and remain vigilant and rational comes from childhood experiences.

Type 1w9 personality is extremely cautious and overly protective of their reputation in the workplace. As a 1w9, some of the best careers you can excel at include:

- Judge
- Social Worker
- Journalist
- Consultant
- Guidance Counselor
- Environmentalist
- Public Relations Specialist
- Ambassador

Being averse to criticism, type Ones are advised to avoid career choices that may involve a lot of criticism. It's also not a good idea to go for a job that you don't feel makes a difference. When in the wrong work environment, people will consider you non-adaptable, too demanding, and unrealistic. Be mindful of what your personality requires and the fact that you care about doing work that matters and being recognized for your dedication and commitment as an idealist. While I cannot tell you what your ideal job is, I can encourage you to avoid roles like Customer Service, Auditor, and Management assistant. Such career roles will not align with your strengths and only expose the aspects of you that need healing.

Type One Wing 2 - The Activist

The second Wing influences type One in subtle but significant ways. In this Wing, the emphasis is on service and developing deep relationships. Does that sound like you? Here are some more qualities:

- Sensitive to the needs of the people around you.
- Genuine love for humanity.
- Interested in mentoring opportunities and building one-to-one relationships.

- Always standing for what's right.

The main underlying qualities remain the same, but there will be some changes in the expression of a 1w2. Let's observe the differences between the two.

Healthy 1w9 personalities tend to view the world both imaginatively (as ideal as they wish it to be) and they also consider all the facts to keep themselves grounded. They try their best to maintain peace wherever they are. As a healthy 1w9, these individuals do a better job overcoming some of their shortcomings, e.g., when they make a mistake because they value maintaining that sense of peace. But at the end of the day, they still repress their emotions. This quality stems from the influence of their Nine Wing.

On the other hand, healthy 1w2 are more in tune with their emotions and allow themselves to feel anger, sadness, etc. The 1w2 personality is also more compassionate and helpful, more so with those they have close relationships. For a 1w2, it's not just about doing what's right for the greater good and making a difference in the world; it's also about developing real and deep connections.

Unhealthy 1w9 personalities tend to struggle with severe self-criticism and detachment, especially from their surroundings. Disassociating themselves is one of their coping mechanisms. On the other hand, unhealthy 1w2 personalities tend to become highly bossy. Instead of detaching and closing themselves off, they feel the need to take charge of every situation because they believe they know what's right. They might drown in self-pity in their low periods and whine about how mistreated they are. Unlike unhealthy 1w9, these individuals are incredibly vocal about their disappointment and disapproval of others, including their loved ones, which can make them quite unbearing. Unhealthy 1w2 personalities likely grow into these types of adults because, during their childhood, they received unfair treatment from their parents. As children, the 1w2 felt alone and isolated, especially if they got abused by the same person who was meant to protect them. However, any type One can unlearn their unhealthy emotional patterns and way of thinking. When a 1w2 moves in the direction of growth and heals those old wounds, they transform into compassionate, logical, and caring individuals that people love to be around.

In the workplace, type 1w2 personality loves to be in a leadership position where they can organize and manage people. As a 1w2, some of the best careers you can get into include:

- Nursing
- Law
- Real Estate
- Religious Worker
- Social Worker
- Medicine
- Politics

Again, be mindful of the career or job role you choose because some roles may cause you to feel unappreciated, or it may cut you off from direct day-to-day contact with people you can serve. Accounting, Retail representatives are just a few examples of roles that might not be a good fit for your overall personality and your wing type.

The path from anger to serenity begins when you become aware of your anger and how it drives you and causes suffering. As a classic Type One, you may not necessarily be aware of the underlying anger that manifests are irritation and frustration, but it's time to become aware. You've learned that it's not okay to express your anger directly. So, much of it is hiding in your body. What's needed is for you to move into the healing zone and find your Serenity. In the Enneagram language, serenity is the Virtue of type 1.

If you're a One, then when at your best, you exhibit these strengths:

You're diligent, responsible, reliable, conscientious, and have a high degree of self-discipline. You're very sincere and have a strong sense of idealism.

When your strengths get out of balance or are used in unhealthy ways, they lead to:

Rigidity. Becoming too critical of yourself and others for not living up to your high standards. You also become controlling and moralistic. You might push yourself too hard, becoming obsessed with details and getting things done to perfection. Unfortunately, that also causes you to neglect yourself and cut out rest and relaxation.

SUBTYPES FOR TYPE ONE

An Enneagram subtype (also known as an instinctual subtype or instinctual variant) combines your main Enneagram type One and your survival instinct. There are three survival instincts that we can default to, and although all three are present in each of us, we tend to activate one at any given time. The other two remain neutral and under-developed, respectively. That is, you'll be overly aware of the first subtype (dominant), the second will be neutral (secondary), and the third won't even feel like it's part of you because it's totally underdeveloped, making it your blind spot(tertiary).

So when you read all three types, notice which one feels strongly connected to how you show up and which one you feel zero connection to. That will give you an idea of how your variants are stacked up in order of priority and influence.

Self-Preservation One (SP)

The Pioneer is the self-preservation instinct for a type One and is driven mainly by the need to tend to physical needs and anxiety. An SP 1 needs to conquer their environment and achieve order. We would term this subtype the more stereotypical perfectionist because they care a lot about being right and correct all the time. The main focus is also on being orderly and organized with their health, finances, home, and family matters. SP 1s engage in material achievements to overcome those feelings of worry and anxiety over security and survival. Despite the incessant worry, SP 1 knows how to "keep it together" and often comes across as warmer and friendlier than the other subtypes.

It's easy for an SP 1 to mistype as a type Six. SP 1s tend to suppress their anger even more than their other two subtypes. A common theme here would be the thought, "I need to be good and honorable with my family and meet my physical needs."

Does this sound more like you? Don't worry if it doesn't. Keep reading to identify your most dominant variant.

Social One (SO)

The Social Reformer is the Social One subtype and is driven mainly by the need to belong and be accepted in their community or group. All Type Ones are social and pro-change and reformation, but this particular subtype is more invested in social justice and fairness. They work extra hard to be role models and show others the right way to live. Although the SO 1s also repress anger, they are more okay with showing it.

It's easy to mistype an SO 1 as a type Three or type Five. Unfortunately, they can also be non-adaptable in their quest to uphold society's highest morals and standards. A common theme here would be the thought, "I need to be good and honorable with my community who depend on me."

Does this sound more like you? Don't worry if it doesn't. Just keep reading to identify your most dominant variant.

One-to-One/ Sexual One (SX)

The Evangelist is the one-to-one instinct for a type One, and they are mainly driven by the need to be right and perfect with their intimate connections. Please note that SX instinct refers to both platonic and romantic relationships. SX 1s are the countertype of Type One, which means they don't react to their dark side as a typical One would. Instead of repressing their anger and working hard to achieve self-perfection, they project it outward and focus on perfecting others. SX 1s struggle with zealousness and jealousy if you dig deeper. On the surface, they may still show a lot of self-control but hang around them long enough, and they will leak judgment and envy. Unlike the other subtypes, SX 1s will show their anger and resentment. It's easy to mistype an SX 1 for a type Eight. A common theme here would be the thought, "I need to be good and honorable with my intimate relationships."

Does that sound more like you? If not, that's okay. Keep exploring the rest of the book and become aware of which descriptions resonate most with you. Sometimes it takes a little more digging to uncover your type. If you've already identified as a Type One, you'll love the next chapter on tips for growth and improvement.

CHAPTER 6
WORK AND LIFESTYLE TIPS FOR TYPE 1S

Before we can talk about the positive changes you can make in your life, it's essential to address some of the ways you've been unconsciously holding yourself back and the struggles you're likely to face on this quest for self-improvement. Don't worry, most of this chapter is dedicated to what you can do to make things better in your world, but as I like to say, before shooting an arrow in any direction, be clear on the target.

Every Type One has a few blind spots, and by now, it shouldn't come as a surprise that most of them tend to be impulsive and natural. Anger is the first, and I'm sure, as a Type One, you know this all too well. You may not realize that despite your best attempts to hide your unresolved emotions, they still leak out in the form of body posture, facial expressions, tone, and other body language cues. For a present and observant person, they will feel and read your energy no matter calm you try to be. The anger you tend to experience usually comes from the high standards and expectations you have in your mind, which, unfortunately, few people in the world can live up to. Another way people can tell you have unresolved issues is through your over-criticism. While you do it with good intentions, very few people like to be criticized or judged. I think even you don't enjoy criticizing yourself, right? That's why many consider over criticism to be a negative trait. Let's find a better approach where you can still reform and improve your environment without going overboard in criticism and judgment. The last blindspot I want to make you aware of is the tendency to be too rigid. That tends to come from repressed feelings. If you tend to view emotions as a waste of time and productivity, you're likely repressing yourself and other people's emotions in your interactions. It's a wonderful trait to approach situations rationally and separate emotions from facts, especially when solving a problem, so let's aim to create a balance here. Repressed emotions never end well, and your life and relationships will improve when you learn to process emotions at the appropriate time, of course. What are some other struggles you may encounter on this quest of self-discovery? Let's identify the top ones.

STRUGGLES OF ENNEAGRAM ONE

Setting unrealistic expectations

The urgent need to always be honest, responsible, ethical, and hardworking can lead to unrealistic expectations of yourself. You set such high standards, which is excellent, but that can sometimes become your Achilles heel. Most people appreciate your integrity and would be okay with you even if you only hit 99% of your intended goals. Still, I know with you, nothing is good unless it's 100% right. So you might be in the habit of berating and being too hard on yourself. The lower you are on the development scale, this need to be perfect turns into a dark, twisted personality that's totally unhealthy for you and those around you.

What to do: If you recognize the tendency to push, punish or criticize yourself too much, it's time to learn some self-acceptance practices.

The more you grow towards self-acceptance, the less demanding that inner critic will be and the easier it will be to accept others.

Never good enough

The classic "I'm never good enough" pain on your side is actually a common experience for all Type Ones. Flaws, mistakes, and defects seem more overwhelming for a Type One than any other Enneagram. Unfortunately, living in this energy of not being good enough is extremely draining and terrible for your health.

What to do: The feeling of not being good enough is mainly between the unhealthy and average levels of development. It comes from a lack of self-forgiveness. Take a moment now and observe how you've been extra strict and unforgiving to yourself. Choose to change that for the better.

Corruption and bad people overwhelm you

Our world can be a bit much for an idealistic and goal-oriented individual who lives with integrity. There's so much corruption going on, and a lot of bad goes unpunished. I know it's a lot to take in and impossible to accept. Your desire for ethical integrity for yourself and others is truly noble. As long as you serve to make the world a better place in healthy ways that bring out the highest version of yourself, then, by all means, fight on. However, if you're at average or unhealthy levels of development where you strive to overcome moral adversity at the cost of sacrificing your own needs, we need to take a step back. The desire to promote higher values is a good one to pursue, but you can't do it from a place of remorse, pain, anger, and resentment where you think others are beneath you. That kind of superficial righteousness only turns you into a hypocrite. It makes you cynical, pessimistic, and negative. Nothing good ever comes from those emotional states.

What to do: If you find yourself being sarcastic, cynical, or condescending about the world and the people around you who aren't living up to your standards, it's time to switch gears. Develop a more open mindset and a positive attitude. Find the good that exists instead of only feeding yourself the bad you hate. And yes, that might include cutting out all your news, gossip, and social media consumption or at least minimizing it to a point. At the same time, increase time spent on positive and joyful activities and experiences. Find stories of empathy and great human accomplishments.

Taking things too seriously

One more struggle you'll need to tackle is that of taking yourself a bit too seriously. Are you rigid with your routine, emotions, relationships, and how others should behave around you to the point that it's off-putting? Perhaps for you, it's normal, but I bet those in your life might have a different experience. Let me be clear here, no one is attacking that relentless hardworking, no B.S quality that you have because it does serve a great purpose. We are simply encouraging you to find a healthy balance so you can also relax and enjoy some spontaneity and the "unknown" once in a while. By doing so, you can avoid becoming too rigid in life and creating mountains of tension mentally and physically. Have you ever felt like you were a bubbling pot of boiling water simmering with passion and rage yet too afraid to allow those emotions to come up so you could deal with them once and for all?

For most ones, letting the lid off their emotions is unacceptable. They believe in concealing their feelings and never allowing themselves to reveal anything but total composure. That makes having an intimate and open relationship with a Type One really challenging.

What to do: If you realize you're too rigid with your life, relationships, emotions, and any other area of yourself give yourself permission to just open up to someone you trust and share your plight. Allow yourself to break some eggs and let out that anger or just scream at the top of your voice. I know this will be hard to do, especially at those average and unhealthy levels of development. But awareness is the first step to transformation. Just recognizing some of your inner struggles and allowing yourself to face them instead of denying them is already progress. Now keep going.

OPPORTUNITIES FOR GROWTH PROFESSIONALLY

Let's uncover some of how you can start growing personally and professionally now that you're doing the inner work of moving up in your development.

- Embrace your inner child once again and find your playful side. We all have a curious childlike quality in us. Find yours. Start small with something as simple as playing with a dog at the park, joining Zumba class, or painting again. Did you enjoy baking as a child? Why not join a beginner's cooking class. When was the last time you laughed so hard until a bit of pee came out? Fill your Netflix and Hulu playlist with classics that make you laugh until your ribs hurt.
- Embrace and process all your emotions, especially your anger. Anger or any other emotion isn't inherently wrong to feel. It's when we dwell and make that our dominant state that things go awry. You are not a bad person because you get emotional or feel negative emotions. Pretending emotions aren't really only increases your tension and internal stress. The body will break down when negative emotions are suppressed. That creates room for passive-aggressive behavior, leaky negative emotions, and diseases. It's time to learn healthy ways to process all feelings. We'll discuss some healthy habits that can enable you to process emotions at the end of this chapter.
- Learn to ask for help. I know this will sound crazy at first but asking for help from others makes you a stronger, better, and at times a more responsible person. It's what

leaders know. Being open about what you need help with doesn't make you weak. It enriches your relationships and ensures you don't burn out in the process of achieving greatness. And when you do receive help, allow the person to help and approach the situation in their own way. Let go of the need to micro-control others to do things your way all the time. This is especially important in your professional life while dealing with colleagues.

- Silence that inner critic and retrain your self-talk. Retrain your mind to dwell on positive self-talk and become the cheerleader in your life. Your invitation now is to start speaking to yourself as you would a lover or your child. Be the parent or coach you never had growing up. Approach yourself with the greatest sensitivity and compassion, knowing that no one else can be good to you unless you are good to yourself. That inner critic only replays an old record set by your caregivers during childhood. It's been playing for so long that your brain thinks that's the norm. It's time to teach yourself some new tricks. Things like how to love yourself more, forgive yourself when things go wrong, and effectively communicate with yourself for the best outcome. The relationship with Self is sacred; it is the most important relationship you will ever have in this lifetime. You and your inner voice have been in this game called life since birth, and you'll be together till your last breath. Doesn't it make sense to make the experience one of love instead of criticism?

ENNEAGRAM TYPE ONE UNDER STRESS

When Type One experiences stress, the first fallback is their unhealthy traits, including becoming critical, judgmental, and berating. If the stress and pressure persist, the One falls into the path of disintegration, as we discussed in arrows and their meaning, leading to the expression of some unhealthy traits of Type 4. That turns an average and unhealthy One into a moody, envious, withdrawn, melancholic and irritable person. But it doesn't have to be that way. Perfectionism is dialed up, and they struggle to accept any kind of flaw or mistake in themselves or others.

With this new awareness of how stress might lead you down a path of disintegration and further away from your true and highest version, here are a few healthier ways to deal with stress and pressure.

Schedule a day or chunks of hours to simply relax.

- While at work, take numerous planned breaks between activities to beat burnout and avoid getting too worked up about the problem.
- Invest time nurturing your inner child and being around fun-loving people (e.g., friends, siblings, etc.)
- Resist the urge to binge-watch or listen to sappy or angsty films and songs. That's just the unhealthy individualists (4) trying to take over the situation. Instead, find something upbeat and humorous to watch and laugh at as much as possible.

RELATIONSHIPS

Both romantic and professional relationships must be honored when you're an Enneagram One. So it shouldn't be surprising that people consider you a loyal, reliable, and trustworthy person. They might feel like you can be too rigid or pushy, especially when things aren't getting done to the standards you set, but most people embrace the challenges of dating or working with your personality. Below are some tips to help you make things even better.

Be easy on yourself.

- Whenever you disagree with another, try to remember that neither of you is 100% right or wrong.
- Allow the other person (especially in a romantic relationship) to take the lead and do things their way without imposing your standards. It doesn't have to be all the time, but just periodically give them a chance.
- Sharing your feelings and expressing pleasant and unpleasant emotions is healthy when you're in an intimate relationship. Vulnerability can be a good thing.
- Allow yourself (sometimes) to just let go and be silly. This is especially important when you're dating. Relax and just enjoy the moment.
- While at work, let your co-workers understand you by clearly communicating your expectations, how you like to work, what you value, and how much you care about growth and improvement. The more your colleagues can understand your point of view, the easier it will be for them to support you.

RELATIONSHIP TIPS WITH OTHER TYPES

Here's what you can expect and improve upon when you have a relationship with other Enneagram Types.

Type 1 & Type 1: With a fellow Type One, you're in that perfectly mirrored relationship where you get each other. You have high standards and strong convictions, and you want things done well. You both value integrity, honesty, and goodness. You're responsible, conscientious people who always act appropriately, and you enjoy the mutual respect and trust you've built. It's great to know you're with someone who has the same work ethic, thoughtfulness, and moral code you have.

A challenge you might face in this relationship is that you can become overly critical of each other because you're so similar. When your strong convictions land on different sides, you can become indignant. And when you do have a firm agreement, you may become too judgmental of those that don't see things your way because you believe it's the only "right" way. Another issue is that you both repress anger, especially when operating at average or lower levels of development, and typically those emotions leak out as resentment toward the other. Grow together by developing as a couple to higher levels of expression. Realize that you don't need to fuss over the little details of how the other isn't measuring up. Also, create time for fun and something that enables you to be silly together. A weekend getaway, summer vacation, or a night out can help you keep that fun aspect alive. And when you disagree on opinions, remember to soften your perspectives and allow the other the safety and freedom to have their different point of view even if you don't agree with it.

Type 1 & Type 2: With Type Two, you're in a warm, nurturing relationship. You're both doers who care about serving others and making the world better. Your partner brings grace and softness that's beneficial to your more rigid personality. You're good at taking care of the practical things in life and paying detailed attention to things which makes the Two feel valued. You're both present with each other, enjoy completing tasks, and working together toward a shared purpose.

A challenge you might face is during the conflict. You believe staying rational is the best way to move forward, and your partner tends to be more emotional. Another issue might arise due to the Two's desire for a more profound emotional connection, which might feel overwhelming to you, creating some distance. Grow together by openly communicating what you both need in the relationship. Be more intentional and descriptive to avoid misunderstanding. Carve out time to nurture and discuss your relationship without discussing other projects.

Type 1 & Type 3: With Type Three, the relationship is dynamic and task-oriented, and you enjoy accomplishing things together. You admire the Three's can-do attitude and ability to get things done, while your partner appreciates your sense of responsibility and unwavering commitment. You support each other's endeavors, and when conflict arises, you both believe that staying rational is the best way to figure things out.

A challenge you might face with this relationship is getting so consumed by your projects and talks that date nights can feel like a business meeting. In other words, you may not really be nurturing the relationship itself even when you're spending time together. Another issue is that Threes are shapeshifters, which might make you feel like your partner is manipulative or shallow. On the other hand, your partner might feel like you're too rigid or stifling, and your perfectionism may not be well received, especially if you're giving critical feedback. Grow together by prioritizing rest time. Make time for your relationship outside of projects and tasks. Keep an open communication at all times and avoid letting disagreements get out of hand.

Type 1 & Type 4: With a Four, you can cultivate a deep, meaningful relationship. You're both idealists with a vision of how the world could be. You help the Four create boundaries in their life and get a bit more structured, and they help you loosen up a bit and think outside the box. While you are opposites in many ways, your energies complement each other well, especially when operating under healthy levels of development.

A challenge you might face in this relationship is the negative impact of internalizing criticism. You can easily get overwhelmed by the Four's emotions and become resentful. On the other hand, the Four can lash out at your critique and constant correction even though you might just be trying to help them become better. Grow together by embracing your different approaches to life. Emphasize the things you have in common and find value in the things that make you different.

Type 1 & Type 5: With a Five, you're in a stable, dependable relationship with someone who pays attention to details almost as much as you. You and your partner are quick to observe things that others typically miss. You're thoughtful, hard-working, and understand each other well. The Five brings thoughtfulness, curiosity, competence, and depth to the relationship. Your high standards and steadiness are desirable to the Five. You enjoy being independent and structured boundaries in your relationship because it means you never overwhelm each other.

A challenge you might encounter in your relationship is when you have a difference in opinion. You believe in objectivity, so there's no changing your mind once you find the truth. On the other hand, Fives are open to evolving all their ideas as they learn more information. This difference can create frustration as your partner perceives you as too rigid while you might feel like they are not predictable. Another issue that might arise is that your advice may feel more like criticism for a Five who is very sensitive to criticism, which may cause them to withdraw and turn silent. This silence may cause you to feel insecure about your relationship. Grow together by openly communicating and learning to hold each other's ideas as valid even when you're not in agreement. Affirm each other and remind one another that you are there for each other.

Type 1 & Type 6: With a Six, you're in a committed, responsible, secure relationship. You both value duty and loyalty. The community matters to you, and you both want to make the world a better place. The Six is witty and help you lighten up, and you help your partner feel more grounded and safe. The relationship thrives because you feel like you can count on each other and make an effort to show each other love.

A challenge you might face in this relationship is during conflicts because you tend to become critical and resentful, making the already anxious Six insecure and fearful about the relationship. It turns the Six into a doubtful, skeptical person, which can frustrate you because they seem inconsistent and irrational when insecurity levels rise. Grow together by maintaining calm during conflicts. Try to keep a level head and encourage the Six to express how they feel without overreacting. You should regularly find little ways to be spontaneous together and add more fun into your life.

Type 1 & Type 7: With a Seven, the relationship is dynamic and adventurous, and there's a lot of spontaneity that takes you out of your comfort zone. In many ways, you're opposites, but when operating at healthy levels of development, the relationship thrives because you complement each other well. The Seven helps you celebrate life every day and find fun in all you do. You help ground the Seven and create a sense of stability and conscientiousness that they need.

A challenge you might experience is when the relationship hits a slump. Sevens get bored super fast and tend to feel trapped when they have to be in a predictable routine which is your thing. You might feel like you're in a relationship with a child who doesn't want to grow up, and your partner may feel like you're being a bully. At average and unhealthy levels, Sevens don't know how to handle slumps or obstacles, so they tend to run away from any kind of conflict or unpleasantness. While you're trying to be rational and work things out, they might be completely unwilling to work through problems. Invest time learning how to process unpleasant emotions together. Have those tough talks, and then reward yourselves for doing it. Appreciate the balance the other brings. Grow together by working on rising to higher levels of development.

Type 1 & Type 8: With an Eight, your relationship is truthful, dependable, and profound. You stand firm in your convictions, and both take responsibility for right the wrongs in the world around us. The Eight is intensely loyal and protective of you and the relationship, and you love that. You're trustworthy, detailed, systematic, fair, and truthful, and that's very attractive to an Eight. This can be a very intentional and deeply fulfilling relationship when cultivated correctly.

A challenge you might face is your differing energies and how you deal with tension or conflict. You prioritize self-control and choose your words carefully, but the Eight is more expressive and, at times, explosive with anger. Their directness may come across the wrong way, which can be highly frustrating for you. You both need to be in control, which often leads to a battle of wills during conflicts. Grow together by reminding each other that you're on the same team. Find activities like mindfulness practices that you enjoy doing together to help you be more present and calm.

Type 1 & Type 9: With a Nine, you're in a comfortable, stable, harmonious easy going relationship. Both of you are ethical, considerate, and self-sacrificing, and you're propelled by a deep sense of purpose. The Nine enables you to be more self-accepting and self-forgiving because they are always comforting and accepting. You help bring a sense of duty and work ethic to the Nine so they can create more of what they desire.

A challenge you might face in this relationship is how you deal with anger and conflict. Although you're both in the body triad, where is the emotional wound, you process it very differently. The Nine avoids it and tries to repress anger to keep the peace while you suppress it and do everything to be appropriate at all times. All this pent-up anger leaks from time to time, especially during tension. Stubbornness, resentment, and passive-aggressiveness are issues you'll need to overcome to keep your relationship healthy. Grow together by finding healthy ways to deal with conflict and clear the air. Affirm one another and the relationship whenever you're working through a conflict. Encourage your partner to voice their issue and let it go once resolved.

AFFIRMATIONS FOR ENNEAGRAM TYPE 1

Read through the following affirmations and find a handful that resonates to help you shift into a healthier version of yourself.

- I embrace and accept myself completely.
- I forgive myself easily and move on.
- I forgive others easily and move on.
- I accept who I am.
- I choose to focus on finding good in others and giving my attention to what's working.
- I choose to be kind and compassionate to those I work with.
- I accept that everyone is doing the best they can with their level of awareness.
- I choose to see mistakes as learning opportunities.
- I love and approve of myself.

Remember, affirmations only work when what you say and feel are in synch.

DAILY ROUTINES FOR GROWTH AND HAPPINESS

- Practice self-care daily. By making self-care a priority, you allow yourself to dissolve the critical aspects of your personality. You could list different self-care activities that you could do for each day of the week, including taking a bubble bath and treating yourself to a spa session or a massage. Get creative and really show yourself some love.

- To make sure the tendency for perfection isn't stressing you out, follow the path of integration and pick up healthy, fun habits that you enjoy. Do you love board games? Great. Why not play games over the weekend with a friend. What about dancing? Consider signing up for some dance classes or try cooking a new recipe.
- Practice mindfulness. Some people prefer to meditate or do some yoga as part of their mindfulness practice. Try both and see which aligns with your lifestyle. If neither brings you to that present state of mindfulness, experiment with taking mindfulness walks or mindfulness showers. There is no right or wrong way to center yourself and become fully present. The only thing that matters is that you do it consistently.
- Keep investing in your personal and professional growth. Don't be afraid to stretch beyond your comfort zone and join educational activities that aren't necessarily related to your work. The more range you can give yourself, the more you'll expand your awareness and perspective. An ever-expanding perspective is a key to development for a Type One.
- Make time to process your emotions. Nothing will change your life experiences more than choosing to face and process all your feelings boldly. You can schedule weekly emotions time where you step back and meet with all the emotions you had to check during the week. That enables you to have more control over your feelings rather than being controlled by them. It also eliminates the danger of falling into stress and disintegration.

ENNEAGRAM TYPE 2

THE HELPER OR GIVER

This chapter and the next will go in-depth on the Enneagram type Two, commonly referred to as the helper or giver. The title - helper is a perfect fit for this enneatype because these individuals thrive when taking care of and nurturing others. Type Twos are empathetic, warm-hearted, gentle, generous, caring, and naturally friendly. Their need to feel and be loved is predicated on how much others need and appreciate them. Helpers tend to be self-sacrificing to the point of self-neglect because they have such a strong belief that their value comes from helping others first. Enneagram Type Twos fall into the heart or Feeling Center making shame one of the main emotions that hinder personal growth and evolution, especially if unresolved. One of the great gifts of an Enneagram Type Two is their interpersonal skills. You'll find them at the center of action either at work or in a family set-up doing everything they can to ensure all parties have what they need. That can be everything from lending a hand on a project, offering a shoulder to cry on, or babysitting your child so you can have an hour to rest. There's no task too big for a Two to say yes to, and sometimes, this can backfire on them, creating a lot of inner turmoil.

Although Twos are always gentle, positive, and caring towards others, they have a dark side that sometimes leaks out in temperamental outbursts, especially when they feel underappreciated. Most people get surprised that Twos can get angry, and indeed this doesn't happen very often. Still, it's good to realize that even the gentle Two can be pushed to their point of emotional eruption. Do you recognize any of these signs in yourself? If you've already done an Enneagram Test that typed you as a Two, continue reading to learn more about some unconscious patterns you may not have recognized. I like to combine self-study and the Enneagram Test because it enables me to concentrate more on my enneatype and uncover more of myself without wasting time. But even if you didn't take the test, you might still type yourself accurately if you read each chapter in the book and reflect honestly. With the information you learn here, begin to notice your patterns and incorporate the suggestions and recommendations given in the next chapter so that you can stop self-neglecting.

As a Type Two, your greatest desire is to see others happy, and that's a great intention. We just need to make sure achieving that goal doesn't come at the cost of your well-being and personal evolution.

Many Twos who aren't yet operating at higher and healthier levels of development often fall into self-neglect and people-pleasing habits. It's a slippery slope when sacrificing one's need to help others. The end result is typically emotions of resentment, anger, frustration, and disappointment. That's especially the case when Twos don't receive the rewards or the credit they feel they deserve for all their efforts.

STRENGTHS OF A TWO

Twos have a natural ability to recognize the needs of others. They play a strong supporting and encouraging role for those around them.

Twos have tremendous empathy, especially for the lonely, marginalized, and undervalued people around them. They always act from a place of generosity and love. Nothing is too much of an ask for a Two, which is why people love being around them.

Type Twos know how to build welcoming homes for themselves and others.

Key personality traits of Type Two

- Warm, approachable, and kind.
- Excellent team player.
- Gentle and caring.

Common hobbies for a Type Two

- Cooking
- Gardening
- Volunteering
- Socializing

FEARS AND WEAKNESSES

By now, you have enough clarity about a Type Two's need to be and feel loved and how that's tied into their self-worth. Love is one of the highest and most important human needs that we all have. For Type Two, having that sense of being loved by others is core to their identity and happiness.

At times this push to receive love because they give it to others first is actually rooted in fear.

What's the Basic Fear driving this behavior? The fear of being unworthy of receiving unconditional love.

As a Type Two, you want to be needed by other people because that reassures you of your place in their lives and affections. Much of this thinking comes from childhood experiences that we'll touch upon shortly. Still, we realize now that people pleasing and caring for others so you can receive love isn't a sustainable way of experiencing unconditional love. A fundamental weakness you must overcome is the continuous need to seek approval from others. That only perpetuates your self-doubt and causes further damage to your self-image.

Your sensitivity to other people's emotions and needs is a strength, but only if it doesn't override your own needs. I know that saying "No" is one of the hardest things you could ever do because nothing matters more than maintaining great relationships. Still, it's time you learned that sometimes being a good caregiver and nurturer requires one to say NO. And just so you know, that doesn't make you any less loveable or worthy of love.

Our goal is to move you higher in your development, into the healthy levels of expression where you can finally find the balance between helping others and fulfilling your needs and purpose.

Growing up in an environment where your basic emotional needs (especially unconditional love) were lacking means you had to adapt to other people's expectations and repress your own desires to survive. Perhaps somewhere during your upbringing, you may have picked up the message that you can only receive affection when you do something good for those who care for you. Now that you're past that stage in your life, it's time to heal some of these wounds and step into your true power.

How does this Basic Fear often manifest itself?

The conditioned belief that stating your needs is wrong has caused you to fear saying "NO" to anyone because you're afraid of rejection or losing love. So you keep saying yes even when it hurts. That dissolves all personal boundaries and likely leads to self-neglect.

You may also have difficulty dealing with tension, relationship conflicts, and disagreements. Many Twos share that whenever they get into an argument with a loved one, they can't focus on work or anything else until that situation is resolved. We also know that this topic of addressing needs is a bit tricky for a Type Two to face. If you're feeling all kinds of discomfort as you read this, that's okay. You're not alone. You might have been raised with the belief that your needs don't matter, and maybe you even feel ashamed that you have needs (I have a friend who once shared that she felt ashamed to ask her husband for anything). Some fears manifest in extreme ways where the individual becomes resentful because they recognize they have unmet needs. Still, they're too ashamed to boldly ask for what they need, and so they just hate on others. Some unconsciously become manipulative. They offer help and serve others purely because they want to get something in return. These are the people in the lower levels of development. As a Type Two, it's essential, to be honest with yourself, get clear on where you stand when it comes to meeting your needs, and then begin the work of moving through and out of that fear state. That's when you will finally stop living at the mercy of others and their approval and instead discover your true value and unconditional love.

DESIRES AND MOTIVATIONS

The Basic Desire for a Type Two is to be loved. With that desire comes the core motivation or the energy that pushes an individual forward in life. By understanding the motivations behind your Enneagram Type Two, you can better identify where you are meant to be in life or what purpose you would best serve. For Type Two, the desire to achieve a sense of belonging and be loved and needed by others is inherent in their thoughts and actions. As a Two, you've seen how easy it is for you to step into any situation and immediately identify what other is feeling and what they need. You're the person that's always there to cheer others on and support them on their journey. It takes keen attentiveness and care to respond to other people's needs. True to your personality, your purpose is closely tied to nurturing and building relationships. Being the friend everyone would love to have, you have a lot to give. So as you begin your journey of self-healing and growth, don't discard these qualities that make you exceptional. Instead, find healthy ways to integrate them into your life in healthy ways that promote unconditional love. Notice how important love is in your life. In fact, as we break down your core values, you'll realize that becoming more of yourself doesn't cancel out your relationships. It only enables you to serve and care for others from a place of overfill rather than dependency and lack. Let's name some of the top values your personality identifies with most.

Core values

- Love
- Family and friendship
- Kindness and empathy
- Altruism, selflessness
- Compassion
- Serving others
- Thoughtfulness
- Appreciation
- Generosity

Type Two celebrities and famous people you might know include Singer Dolly Parton, Mathematician and Writer Lewis Carrol, Singer and music producer Stevie Wonder, Actress and First lady of the United States Nancy Reagan, Catholic nun and missionary leader Mother Teresa, Television host Mr. Rogers and Actress Debbie Reynolds.

Wondering if you could be a Type Two? Here are some personality indicators:

1. You value relationships above all else. Nothing is more important to you than family, friends, and even acquaintances.
2. Offering support, helping, and serving others is something you genuinely enjoy.
3. You're drawn to careers that are service-oriented and people-facing.
4. You feel deeply hurt when people don't reciprocate your generosity and helpfulness.
5. You're sensitive to criticism
6. You have an innate ability to know what people are seeking in a friend and always seem to know exactly what to say and do
7. One of the things you struggle with is the concept of selfishness. You do not want to ever come across as selfish, but you also don't like it in others.
8. You tend to overcommit and struggle with setting clear boundaries.
9. Having a warm, inviting home is extremely important to you.
10. You sometimes worry that you're worthless unless you give to others or help them somehow.
11. At your best, you feel creative, authentic, comfortable with who you are, and very much enjoy creative expression.

YOUR WINGS

Wings are the numbers that you find directly adjacent to your Enneagram Type. As a Type Two, you have -

- The Enneagram Two with One-Wing
- The Enneagram Two with Three-Wing

While many believe both wings are active in each of us, one Wing tends to be more dominant and influential in our lives. Studying the arrows and their meaning can enable you to figure out which Wing is influencing your behavior and thought patterns at any given stage of life.

Meaning of your Wing

If you're a *2w1 (Two with One-Wing)*, then you're more concerned about supporting others and being seen as a responsible figure. With this Wing, your morals play an important role in behaving and relating to others. You're willing to do anything for a friend or loved one as long as it matches your morals. Unfortunately, you also tend to be too critical of yourself, as is common to an enneatype One. You have lots of trouble openly expressing your needs.

If you're a *2w3 (Two with Three-Wing)*, you're more ambitious than the 2w1 and way more extraverted. You also make an excellent leader because you have a bit of that competitive and winner's mindset that's influenced by the enneatype Three.

The Arrows and what they mean

Looking closely at the Enneagram symbol, we can see the connecting lines and arrows for your type, giving us further insight into how you react to stress and challenges and what opportunities for growth you have at any given point. Thus, moving toward disintegration or unhealthy stress (8), you would be overly needy, aggressive, and even a little dominating at Eight. However, moving toward growth and integration (4), you transform that prideful quality and become more self-nurturing and emotionally aware like a healthy Four. Although you can move in the direction of disintegration or integration at any point in your life, the primary influencer of your behavior and what you express is determined by your current level of development. Let's see if you can spot where you are so you can start moving upward to the highest version of yourself.

LEVELS OF DEVELOPMENT

Levels of Development arise from Riso and Hudson's teachings and the founders of the Enneagram Institute, which is a great place to take your Enneagram Test. Their theory posits that all individuals fall into one of nine levels of functioning. The lowest level is nine, and the highest is level one. The levels are divided into a triad that subcategorizes these levels as healthy (1,2,3), average levels (4,5,6), and unhealthy levels (7,8,9).

Unhealthy Levels

Level 9: This is the lowest and most destructive state for a Type Two to be at unless they are still in infancy. As adults, if a person is still trapped here, they feel victimized, abused, and powerless. They can excuse and rationalize their actions no matter how horrible because they are resentful and angry at the world and others. Twos at this stage struggle with a lot of health problems as they vindicate themselves by "falling apart" and burdening others.

Level 8: At this level, an unhealthy Type Two is very prideful and entitled. They are domineering, aggressive, and coercive. This individual chooses to use manipulation to get what they want from others. Nothing they give comes from a place of generosity because they always expect something back.

Level 7: This is the least dangerous unhealthy level for a Two. A Type Two at this level is highly deceptive and selfish in their behavior. Although they can be manipulative and self-serving, they're not extreme or overly aggressive. Instead, they will use guilt to get what they want, belittle and undermine others, and abuse things like food and medication to get sympathy.

Average Levels

Level 6: A Type Two at this level is overbearing, condescending, presumptuous, and walks with an air of self-righteousness for all the good they do. This Two tends to overrate just how much good they are doing and feel indispensable (as though people owe them). Although their efforts are directed toward others, it is done to garner praise, love, and affection.

Level 5: At this level of development, Type Two expresses their neediness by becoming too possessive, co-dependent, and intrusive. This Type Two wants others to depend on them, but at the same time, they expect something in return. They simply overdo their acts of kindness to the point of meddling and control, all in the name of love.

Level 4: This average Type Two craves a connection with others and struggles the most with people pleasing. They are overly friendly, emotionally demonstrative, and full of "good intentions" about everything. Showing and receiving love is of supreme importance for this Two. They will wear themselves out trying to get approval and do things for others that demonstrate how loving they can be.

Healthy Levels

Level 3: At this level, we begin to see real growth and transformation as this Type Two expresses a more nurturing, generous, and genuinely loving aspect of their nature. This individual is awakening, encouraging and appreciative. They can see good in others, and although serving others is still super important, they also tend to their own needs. That makes them pretty stable and genuinely kind in their acts.

Level 2: At this level of development, the total transformation has occurred for a Type Two, and we see the rise of a more empathetic, compassionate individual. This Two knows how to set clear boundaries and tend to their own needs and wants. They do not depend on the affection or approval of anyone but instead give from a place of fullness. This Type Two is warm-hearted, forgiving, sincere, thoughtful, and wonderful to be around.

Level 1: This is the holy grail for a Type Two. It's where the individual transcends and becomes their highest and most spiritually mature version. This Two knows how to love themselves and others. They are altruistic, humble, unselfish, and filled with unconditional love that radiates wherever they go.

TYPE TWO'S PASSIONS

Your dominant Passion as a Type Two is Pride. Pride in this context refers to the inability or unwillingness to acknowledge one's own suffering (something all Twos are very guilty of). The Passions (also known as the Deadly Sins) are our teachers. Most of us were taught to hide, avoid, and run away from the aspects that aren't pleasant. But here, we are encouraged to boldly face the parts of us that need healing so we can dissolve and transform a negative into a positive. You can also think of this Passion as vainglory because it's essentially pride in one's virtue. As a Two, helping others even at the cost of your own well-being and to the point of self-neglect is something you take great pride in. Yet, there is a deep lack in all that "giving" because it violates your wholeness. By following the thread presented by your Passion, you become aware of where you are relative to your highest Self and essential nature.

Pause for a moment and think about how often you feel the injustice or "unfairness" of others when you feel like the other didn't appreciate you or reciprocate enough. Wasn't it coming from a sense of entitlement and pride? As though they "owed" you for what you did for them? If you can become more aware of your Passion of Pride, you'll likely see that it's rooted in this sense of feeling unloveable or unworthy of receiving love. So you end up giving and ensuring others need you to guarantee that they will approve of and love you. Increasing your awareness of this opens up a new choice. It enables you to transform and start moving toward your Essence, which returns you back to your virtue of Humility.

CHILDHOOD AND EMOTIONAL PATTERNS OF TYPE TWO

Enneagram Type Twos are part of the Feeling or Heart Center of Intelligence, where shame is a dominant emotion that needs healing. The deadly sin for a Two is pride, but pride comes in various flavors. It's not just a matter of entitlement. It can also be an air of self-righteousness and need to be praised and outwardly appreciated for your strong support and good work. The worldview that to gain love and approval, you need to give to others and be needed by them causes you to attach your sense of value to this external validation. And while being a generous, supportive and attentive partner, friend, colleague, boss, or parent is an excellent thing, if you're doing it from a place of lack and disconnect, its expression may not be healthy. You might end up neglecting yourself and becoming too needy and co-dependent. What's needed for growth is humility so you can free yourself from the need to give to others to feel loved and valued. It's about realizing that you are whole, worthy of love, and complete just as you are. The path from pride to humility is the path of healthy integration and growth.

Type Two Wing 1- The Companion

A type Two with Wing One means the individual has all the qualities of a Two and a few of Enneagram One. Although you can be influenced by both Wings, the more dominant one will resonate deeply with you as your read these descriptions and learn how that shows up in behavior. Studying your primary personality and identifying your wing type will give you more insight into your behavior, childhood trauma, and how that's affecting your adult life. Type 2w1 comes across as optimistic and warm with high standards and expectations. Does that sound like you? Here are some more details of this personality:

- Caring
- Responsible

- Hardworking
- Empathetic
- Excellent listener
- Extremely likable and approachable
- Friendships and relationships are a bigger priority than anything else, even your own needs

Unfortunately, they struggle to live up to their own expectations. That perfectionism tends to be a constant source of anguish. They try hard to ensure they don't disappoint anyone because they fear rejection and failure as that would prove their hidden belief of not being good enough. The Companion puts everyone else's needs ahead of their own to cope with their fears and mitigate the constant worry of being alone. This constant need to do things for others turns a 2w1 into a total pushover at extreme levels.

The behavior may be rooted in a very strict childhood where parents or caregivers demanded a lot from this type. Often we find the 2w1 was given loads of responsibility at a really young age which made them learn to take on other people's problems and to feel guilty when things go wrong. It also made them associate receiving love and approval with giving to others first.

Type Two Wing 3- The Host

The Host is the charming and eloquent variation of the Enneagram Two. That might be one of the reasons they tend to be super popular in their social group and at work. Unlike the more worrisome and fearful 2w1, this type Two is bold, ambitious, and fearless. Despite this boldness, 2w3 still has a strong need to be loved and needed by others. Hence, they tend to be more extravagant and outgoing than the 2w1 variation of their type. They are also more driven to take up leadership roles and might go as far as being a little rebellious to stand out from the crowd and prove themselves. 2w3 can be less emotionally sensitive. Despite the many similarities these two Wing types will have, the 2w3 experiences less personal distress than the 2w1. On the one hand, that increases traits like:

- Confidence
- Boldness
- Decisiveness

The natural ability in type Two to build deep relationships is expressed in healthy ways when a 2w3 is on the Path of Integration which causes others to trust and follow them naturally. On the other hand, it makes them more arrogant, pretentious, insensitive, and obsessive, especially at the lower levels of development. At their best, however, 2w3s are more self-aware and self-assured. They know how to support others even as they pursue their own ambitions. They develop a greater sense of balance between work and play.

If you're a Type Two, then at your best, you express these strengths:

You're generous, helpful, and love to provide support, guidance, and advice to others. You're a romantic at heart and easily maintain lasting relational connections. Tuning in to people's needs and feelings comes naturally to you. You always know what others need. You're energetic, engaging, enthusiastic, and great at getting things done.

When you move toward the unhealthy aspects of your personality, you exhibit these characteristics:

- You feel unlovable and unworthy if you're not giving to others. When you don't feel needed, you experience deep worry and fear that you're no longer valuable or loved. You're prone to a lot of self-shaming, self-judgment, and comparing yourself to others. Sometimes it oscillates between self-loathing and feeling superior to others. You get resentful and angry when you feel like your giving isn't reciprocated. You're prone to chronic self-neglect. You exhaust yourself by giving too much and investing too much in relationships.

- You're caring, energetic, loved by all, and quite popular in the workplace because people enjoy working with you. Your ability to uplift anyone and everyone is admirable. When operating from a healthy level of development, you easily convert negative energy into positive. Classic Type Twos have high emotional intelligence and always work productively and efficiently.

Best and worst careers for Type Twos

For any Type Two, a career that involves teamwork and supporting others is highly recommended. Choose a career that fulfills your social needs and allows you to influence others directly because that's one of your strengths. Your desire for approval and reassurance will be satiated if you work with superiors and co-workers who aren't afraid to express their appreciation of you. An environment where high energy, collaboration, and joy are promoted. Some careers that may offer this experience include teaching, counseling, therapy, psychology, becoming a religious leader, social worker, non-profit worker, or even a doctor.

Careers to avoid include salesperson, stockbroker, acting, modeling, or any industries that are likely full of rejection, criticism, and high competition. Such jobs may not be as fulfilling for a classic Two.

SUBTYPES FOR TYPE TWO

Your primary Enneagram Type Two further combines with your natural instincts to create subtypes generally stacked in order of dominance.

There are three survival instincts that we can default to, and although all three are present in each of us, we tend to activate one at any given time. The other two remain neutral and under-developed, respectively. Hence you'll be overly aware of the first subtype (dominant), the second will be neutral (secondary), and the third won't even feel like it's part of you because it's totally underdeveloped, making it your blind spot(tertiary).

So when you read all three types, notice which one feels strongly connected to how you show up and which one you feel zero connection to. That will give you an idea of how your variants are stacked up in order of priority and influence.

The Self-Preservation Two (SP)

The main quality is Privilege. SO Twos express themselves as the "cute" and charming individuals with very childlike energy. This Two is the countertype of the group and tends to display behavior that causes them to be mistyped for a different Enneagram Type like a 6 or 7. This individual is shy, charming, and wants to be loved and cared for. However, they resist being dependent on others and tend to be a little more withdrawn in an attempt to self-protect. Self-preservation Twos are more self-indulgent and hedonistic, always searching for pleasurable experiences to distract themselves from feelings of self-abandonment and inner deprivation.

The Social Two (SO)

Ambition is the main quality for this subtype. The SO Two is more interested in utilizing their seductive power intellectually to influence and attract groups, communities, and broader systems. They like to stand out from the crowd and often seek leadership roles. Such individuals enjoy being in the know and building their connections and competence. Less childlike than the other subtypes, it's easy to mistype this SO Two for an Eight or Three.

The One-to-One/ Sexual Two (SX)

Seduction is the main quality of this variant. This Type Two is more focused on their talent, seductive abilities, and using their energy to attract and build strong relationships. They care more about close connections on a 1-1 basis, whether that's a romantic or platonic setting. This Two can express personal needs a little better in an intimate setting. SX Twos are passionate, flexible, strong-willed, and even a little wild at heart, sometimes leading to a mistype with a 4.

WORK AND LIFESTYLE TIPS FOR TYPE 2S

B efore we discuss how you can improve yourself on this quest of self-discovery, we must explore some of the struggles you may experience on your journey. For some of you, the struggles already dominate your life, and if that's the case, you'll find the suggestions offered pretty helpful.

STRUGGLES OF AN ENNEAGRAM TWO

Learning to say "NO."

Type Two's biggest struggle is learning to add NO into their vocabulary. By not learning to say no, you also create opportunities for unkind people to take advantage of your goodness. The core desire to be loved and feel worthy is so attached to helping and serving others. So when someone asks for something, it feels like a battle to just say you can't or won't help out. Unfortunately, when you don't learn to set clear and healthy boundaries for yourself, you wear yourself thin and overgiving at the cost of your personal well-being. As a Two, your self-esteem revolves around giving and being selfless, but you need to know the difference between generosity, where you give from an overflow, and selfish giving, where you give because you believe it will get you the love, affection, and assurance you need.

What to do: Learn to give generously from a place of overflow and unconditional love, not neediness. Those who genuinely love you will not change their attitude or your relationship simply because you said no to a request. And when a favor or demand is placed on you that goes against your values or jeopardizes your well-being, have the courage to say no.

Feeling unloved

If you grew up in an environment where you were taught that love comes at a price, you only felt loved when you did something for someone. This unresolved emotion will likely influence your adulthood. Average and unhealthy Type Twos will struggle with this feeling the most, and it often leads to all kinds of diseases. Pause for a moment and honestly think about how you feel. Do you constantly worry that people only love you for what you do and not for who you are as a human being?

What to do: Work on increasing your understanding of love. It's time to learn that people love you for who you are, not what you do.

Feeling misunderstood

Type Twos are naturally empathetic, highly attuned to other people's emotions, and perceptive. Being this sensitive and tactful, you tend to know what others need even before they admit or recognize it. And while it's great for those around you, it can also lead to a lot of neglect because most of the time, you pay more attention and even prioritize the needs you recognize in others. Over time, that causes you to communicate your needs even less.

I have a friend who was stuck in an unhappy relationship for five years because she couldn't find the right time to break up with her boyfriend. It sounds silly for the rest of us, but as a Type Two, you probably understand what it's like to live an empty and unseen life. If you've spent your life feeling like a dumping ground for other people's emotional baggage, it's time to put an end to that.

What to do: If you feel misunderstood or being taken advantage of, cultivate the courage to express your needs and emotions. Don't let resentment fester.

Grappling with the topic of selfishness

What qualifies as selfish in your world? That is a question you need to answer for yourself if you want real growth. It's okay to recognize that you have trouble taking care of yourself or giving yourself a break because you don't want to come across as selfish. Many Twos say they feel guilty when they get sick or can't help out a friend. That stirs up more feelings of unworthiness, and some even worry that people they love will abandon them if they ever act in selfish ways. No one can tell you what you should believe, but I do encourage you to rewrite your rules on what selfishness looks like for your own sake.

What to do: Assess your understanding of selfishness and make sure it allows you to take care of yourself and prioritize your needs.

OPPORTUNITIES FOR GROWTH

Let's uncover some of the ways you can start growing personally and professionally now that you're doing the inner work of moving to higher levels of development.

Prioritize your needs

The biggest growth area for you and the opportunity at hand is learning to tend to your needs first. If you don't, no one else will. Giving someone else the responsibility of keeping you happy and fulfilled gives away too much power and always results in disappointment and misunderstanding. The key to successful relation-ships, a sense of fulfillment, and increased self-worth is taking complete charge of your needs. So learn to take care of your mind, body, and spirit. Figure out what you need to lead a happy, balanced and healthy life. If you need assistance with resources or certain activities, ask for help but never hand over responsibility.

Assuming you did the inner work of determining what selfish is and isn't, start applying that in your daily engagements. For example, if while at work this week a colleague asks for you to help them complete a task over lunch hour, what should you do? Well, old, you would immediately say yes without giving it a thought. But now that you're growing and learning to become the best version of yourself, recall that your body needs nourishment. What impact will that have on your energy, focus, mood, and overall health by skipping lunch? Unless it's an emergency, the proper answer would be, "No, I'm sorry I can't help you during lunch, but I can try to find a different option if that works for you?"

This isn't an act of selfishness. It's common sense behavior from someone who has their priorities right.

Analyze your motives

Type Twos can be so selfless and giving for all the wrong reasons. I'm not here to judge but instead to expand your awareness so you can judge for yourself what your motives are at any given point. Do you frequently help someone because you expect them to reciprocate somehow? If so, that's a motive rooted in lack and selfishness that will not serve your sense of worthiness. It's easy for average and unhealthy Twos to become manipulative in their good deeds, so you always want to check in to ensure you are doing good because it feels good, not because you want something in return.

Tune into your real value

Most of the inner turmoil and struggles you experience with people will evaporate as you rise higher in your personal development. That's because the more you discover your true Self, the more you learn your true value. Soon enough, you stop being dependent on others to love you. If you do something good for someone, you don't do it for validation, affection, or to feel worthwhile. In fact, you only do it because you're overflowing with unconditional love. And whether the person acknowledges your efforts or not, it won't matter to you because your value and sense of worth are no longer attached to what others think of you but who you think you are. Can you feel the difference? This is such a powerful shift for a Two, and it will transform your life, so keep working at this. Keep walking this path of self-discovery until you know your value and who you really are.

ENNEAGRAM TYPE TWO UNDER STRESS

Type Twos dip into unhealthier versions of their traits, including pride, manipulation, and martyrdom, when under stress, either personal or professional. If the stress persists, they'll often move into the full-blown path of Disintegration we talked about earlier and pick up the average and unhealthy traits of Type 8. That includes becoming aggressive, pushy, controlling, demanding, argumentative, and tyrannical. As a Two, you may have noticed that you don't even feel or behave like yourself under certain stressful conditions. For instance, your usual caring, generous nature and deep desire to help others around you may get hijacked by some unknown dark force. You find yourself more harsh and blunt than usual. You probably become edgy and more aggressive, careless less about other people's feelings, and even lashing out when you feel invalidated. That often causes you pain and grief as you push away the people you care about or even avoid certain people in your life who need you just because you're trying to prove a point. This isn't true to your nature. So how can you beat stressful situations that trigger this dark side?

Things that typically stress a Two include:

- Being taken for granted
- Too much time alone
- Feeling left out
- Not getting affirmation or gratitude for their kind deeds
- Saying "yes" to too many things to the point of burnout.
- Not feeling needed

One of the most important things you can do for yourself when feeling stressed or irritated is to pause, step out of that stressful environment and just be with yourself for a little while.

Often the stress is triggered by taking on too many things all at once or focusing too much on others and neglecting yourself. When you can step away for an hour or a day and just tend to your own needs first, it usually brings back the sense of balance and harmony disrupted by stress.

Some of the activities you could indulge in to get you off that stress frequency include music therapy, painting, or some kind of artistic expression. You can even treat yourself by going for a massage, shopping, or booking a table for 1 at your favorite restaurant. Whatever uplifts you and centers your energy is a must if you want to process stress quickly and in a healthy way.

As you take time off to replenish your needs, remember to communicate with others. Let them know you're taking some alone time to heal, grow and nourish yourself and that you'll be back in communication at a specific time. That enables people to give you some space.

RELATIONSHIPS

Type Twos are naturally intuitive, empathetic, and caring in nature. So when it comes to friendships, professional team relationships, and companionships, Twos always excel.

You naturally make a wonderful parent, boss, team leader, and friend as a Two because of your supporting and compassionate nature. You're the person people come to when they feel hurt or troubled by something. People naturally open up, and your warmth is very soothing. At work, you'll always put others. First, your emotional intelligence is off the charts, so you know how to handle different personalities and facilitate healthy teamwork and collaboration. That enables you to be efficient, productive, and uplifting even in less-than-ideal situations. But you can only be this soothing warm light when you've grown to healthier levels of your own development.

RELATIONSHIP TIPS WITH OTHER TYPES

As a Two, you give yourself freely in any and all relationships because you desire to cultivate a fun, passionate, and happy partnership. Here are some ways to improve your relationships with other Enneagram Types.

Type 2 & Type 1: With a One, you're both doers who want to improve the world. You see the needs of others and act on them quickly. Type One is good at taking care of the practical things, and you as a Two offer softness and grace, which Ones typically struggle with. Since you have different approaches to emotional conflict, it can be overwhelming for Type One to understand your deep desire for connection. So grow together by finding time to be intentional about your relationship. Have an open dialogue that is strictly about your relationship and the balance between both your emotional needs.

Type 2 & Type 2: This is a match made in heaven with a fellow Two because you intuitively know what the other needs. You're generous and thoughtful toward each other, kind-hearted and affectionate. You constantly affirm each other, making you feel loved, valued, and seen. Be mindful about exhausting yourself and using up all your energy helping others, especially if it's starting to impact your relationship. Don't be afraid to admit that you both need help learning to tend to your individual needs. Never let pride or resentment get in the way of cultivating unconditional love in your relationship. Grow by learning to identify your own feelings and prioritize self-care.

Type 2 & Type 3: With a Three, you're a charming, passionate, engaging, and impactful power couple. You bring warmth, affirmation, and acceptance to the Three and that kind of love reminds the Type Three that they don't have to perform to be valuable. The Threes bring ambition, energy, and liveliness to your relationship, which inspires you to follow your dreams. Your confidence, attractiveness, and radiant energy make you a dynamic couple. The challenge comes in acknowledging and understanding your own feelings. Your helpfulness and desire for deeper emotional connection can get overwhelming for a Three. If you start feeling overlooked, taken for granted, or forgotten by your ambitious, task-oriented three, speak up. Grow together by learning how to have an open, intimate dialogue. Ask high-quality questions and engage with each other through reflective conversations to help you get in touch with your own feelings.

Type 2 & Type 4: With a Four, you're an intimate, deeply connected, and emotionally fulfilling couple. You see the Four's needs and offer friendly, supportive, understanding energy, while the Type Four brings creativity, humor, and honesty that you deeply enjoy. There are high expectations in this relationship, but you're not always good at communicating these expectations with each other. Because a Type Four is naturally reflective, they may not realize your needs. So grow together by affirming one another, being attentive to each other's emotional needs but don't be too absorbed in them.

Type 2 & Type 5: The old saying of "opposites attract" holds true with a Five. You're all warmth, comfort, communication, and caring, while Type Five is pretty much the opposite. Yet even with these differences, the Five's wisdom, commitment, and trustworthiness are very attractive to you. Fives pay great attention to detail, and once they "let in" a partner, they go all in. That makes you feel pretty special and important. The deep mystery and loyalty between the two sets you off on a lifelong journey to know more about each other and life. The greatest challenge is how you respond to stress and conflict. You're emotionally expressive, while the Five is calm and always rational. That can often leave you feeling like they are not as engaged in a conversation. You can be pretty overwhelming for a Type Five, causing them to walk away and isolate themselves for a while, often leaving you feeling abandoned and rejected. Grow together by realizing that you have some similarities in that you're both sensitive in your own way, and your needs aren't at odds with each other. Learn to work through your differences and find ways to communicate that don't overwhelm the Five while at the same time engaging enough for you to also feel understood.

Type 2 & Type 6: A relationship with a Six is deep, steadfast, loyal, and based on serving each other. Your empathetic and affectionate nature is very comforting to the Six because they feel like someone has their back at all times. They work hard at the relationship to create a sense of stability for you, which makes you feel prioritized and valued. Perhaps the best part about this relationship is the strong friendship that exists, which creates a kind of supportive, attentive, and responsible relationship that can be extremely fulfilling for you.

One of the challenges you may face with a Six is their subconscious tendency to test their partner. Sometimes they might just push you away and go cold for no reason. Their constant need to be reassured that you love and trust them might become overwhelming for you, especially if you feel like you've done everything possible to prove your love. On the other hand, the Six can easily misunderstand your constant prodding and overbearing help as being pushy and controlling. You like to "fix" things when you see a problem, but a Six tends to work through concerns by verbalizing them. So, grow together by continually working on your friendship & connection. Have an open dialogue regarding your needs and how you'd like those needs to be met.

Type 2 & Type 7: With a Type Seven, life is a never-ending adventure, and spontaneity is the norm. The energy, fun, enthusiasm, and pleasant nature that Type Seven radiates inspires you to become more in tune with your own desires. You bring generosity, empathy, and a concern for the welfare of others that grounds the Seven in healthy ways. It reminds them to slow down and pay attention to their loved ones. Your giving nature inspires the Seven to think about others more instead of always focusing on their own needs. You get to see how bold they are at chasing after their own dreams and thinking outside the box. That rubs off on you in positive ways.

One of the challenges you face in the relationship is the tension created by your emotional connection or lack thereof. From your point of view, Sevens isn't as present as you'd like them to be, especially when feelings come up and that can make you feel unseen. You might react to this by demanding that the Seven pay more attention to your needs or by trying to "fix" the Seven because you feel like they just need help to get better. In either case, the result is often more tension because the Seven often feel too caged or cornered and may run, fearing that they'll get trapped and lose their freedom. Grow together by prioritizing open dialogue. Don't repress or skim through conflict and unpleasant thoughts. Encourage your partner to face these unpleasant emotions courageously because it's part of a healthy human experience. Reassure one another of your commitment before wadding into difficult topics, then reward yourselves for having hard conversations.

Type 2 & Type 8: With an Eight, the attraction is strong because you see something in the other that's needed. The Eight needs the gentle, warm nature that it can protect, and you are deeply attracted to the power and tenacity you admire in the Eight. You soften some of the rough edges of the Eight. The Eight helps you set healthy boundaries and learn to boldly say NO! Together, you bring out the best in each other and become caring and passionate people.

A big challenge in this relationship is the difference in perspectives regarding defining independence. A Type Eight is guarded, self-reliant, and enjoys autonomy a lot, but as a Two, you're constantly seeking affection and affirmation. The Eight's independent streak can sometimes feel unloving because you'd rarely go off and do your own thing without considering your partner, yet that often happens to you. Suppose the relationship is between two average or unhealthy Enneagram types. In that case, things can get pretty ugly as both of you become overbearing and demanding. Grow together by embracing the safety, consistency, and security you provide for one another.

Type 2 & Type 9: With a Type Nine, the relationship is loving, warm, and serene. Things are comfortable and always easy going. The Nine is accepting and understanding and allows you the freedom to just be yourself. That helps you feel secure in the relationship because you feel loved without working for it. Your helpful, empathetic nature and the attention you give the Nine can help them tune in to their own desires and find their voice in the relationship.

A challenge you might experience in this relationship would be finding that balance between your active, action-oriented, and emotionally expressive nature and the Nine's relaxed way of moving through life. At times, your vibrant and helpful energy may become too much for the Nine. Because they don't like conflict, it can lead to avoidance and passive aggressive behavior. That can create distance between your relationship and cause you to become resentful and indignant.

AFFIRMATIONS FOR ENNEAGRAM TYPE 2

Affirmations can be a great tool when you begin replacing your negative thoughts and habits. Learn to become your own cheerlead and direct some of that tender loving care inward by speaking words that uplift and encourage you. Here is a list for you to try out.

- I am my best self when helping others.
- I love and approve of myself.
- I am worthy of all the love in the universe simply because I exist.
- I give and receive unconditional love.
- Loving others is easier when I love myself first.
- I know my true worth.
- I take time to tend to my own needs.

Remember, these affirmations only work if you feel and believe in what you're saying. Pick a few that resonate with you emotionally and use them as often as needed.

DAILY LIFESTYLE TIPS FOR GROWTH AND HAPPINESS

Invest time daily focusing on yourself

It's time to start investing time in your growth and development. The more you rise to healthier levels of development, the greater your impact will be on others. Ask yourself, "when was the last time I tended to my own needs and desires?" If you can't answer this question quickly, you need to self-reflect and take some new action. Make some adjustments and ask for help where needed so you can nurture yourself into a balanced life. Your giving should come from a place of overflow and unconditional love.

Open your mind to receive

It might seem easy to other people, but I know how hard this must be for you. Twos struggle with receiving because it appears selfish to ask another to do something for you. However, asking for help and opening your heart toward the kindness coming from others isn't selfish. It's an act of love. The more you cultivate your essential value of humility, the easier it will be to receive. To help your mind shift into openness, ask yourself the following questions. Will receiving this assistance or thing make the person providing it genuinely happy? Will loving myself help me interact with others on a more emotional level? Is it possible for me to experience the same joy while receiving that I do while giving?

Create a daily routine for self-care

Dear Two, it's essential to realize that your ability to help, support, and love others must come from a place of overflow, not co-dependency. The more you work on rising to higher and healthier levels of development, the more you'll see that you can't pour from an empty cup. Your cup must be filled to the brim first, so practicing self-care is imperative.

Some self-care rituals to integrate into your life include morning walks, yoga, personal development studies, and embodied meditations. You also want to pay more attention to your self-talk and the tone you use yourself. Ensure that inner dialogue carries the same compassion, love, and gentleness you extend to others. One last suggestion I can offer for self-care is to give yourself a treat regularly. If you enjoy massages or pedicures, give yourself a treat as often as possible. Remember, your friends and family love you for who you are, not because of your availability and hospitality.

Engage in some solo activities that you enjoy

Do you enjoy baking, cooking, painting, dancing, or poetry? Sign up for an in-person or virtual class and learn something new for yourself. Curl up with a new novel on a Saturday night or watch your favorite comedy in bed. Make a list of activities you can enjoy doing alone and use that time to just be in your own company. You'll be amazed at what transformation that can give you.

Practice mindfulness

Mindfulness is part of self-care practices and can include various activities, including mindfulness walks, meditation, gratitude practices, mindfulness eating, etc. Think of it like this - anytime you're practicing present moment awareness and fully engrossed in the activity at hand, you're tapping into mindfulness. Done each day consistently, you can experience new levels of self-love and self-acceptance, which are critical to the health of your mental, emotional and spiritual well-being.

Journal

Using a private journal to record your thoughts, express your emotions and practice gratitude is a powerful way to connect with your inner world. When journaling down your feelings, you create an outlet and a more objective way of recognizing what's really going on. It can enable you to see how you react to situations and the underlying thoughts so you can know what's driving your behavior. Another added benefit of journaling is practicing daily gratitude. The benefits of gratitude are widely known and scientifically proven, including lowering blood pressure, improving mood, and improving overall mental health. Practice gratitude daily, and you'll naturally feel more loved and loving.

ENNEAGRAM TYPE 3

THE ACHIEVER OR PERFORMER

Over the following two chapters, we'll go in-depth on my favorite Type. The Enneagram Type Three is commonly referred to as the Achiever or performer. The title is quite fitting because, as Threes (yes, I am a Three), we are success-oriented, driven, and strive to be the best. Threes want to be significant and distinguished through their personal achievements. We must continue advancing and achieving in life because that adds to our sense of worth. It's easy to spot a Three because they are usually the confident, ambitious, image-conscious, and goal-oriented individual in the group who isn't afraid to speak up. Threes tend to be quite charming, attractive, eloquent, energetic, diplomatic, and poised. When operating at higher levels of development, a Type Three is authentic, self-accepting, inspirational, and makes a great role model for others.

An essential defining quality of a Three is this innate desire to achieve great things in life. Threes dream big, make a plan, and then take massive actions toward said goals. If you're a three, your word and reputation matter, and you consider these priceless assets. It's essential to leave a mark on any project you work on, and you want to be remembered for being unique. People look up to you, and you like that, so you keep pushing people forward, motivating them to succeed. You've got a natural knack for identifying people's strengths and weaknesses. That enables you to place people in positions that are more likely to succeed.

In the Enneagram system, Threes are one of the most successful and popular personalities because they naturally have high self-assuredness and work extra hard to build on their skills and talents.

Many Threes who aren't yet operating at higher and healthier levels of development struggle with workaholism and competitiveness, which can become detrimental to their well-being and relationships. They might get trapped into being to image consciousness and trying to keep up a status that others admire even when things aren't going right, which can take a toll on them. This need to look good and save face creates a lot of pressure for average and unhealthy Threes, leading to a downward spiral and inner disconnect. When that natural energy is out of control and negative, Threes can be highly destructive. The average and unhealthy Three may appear malicious, self-absorbed, self-aggrandizing, narcissistic, and even untrustworthy from an outside observer. That's why we need to work on rising higher in our development.

STRENGTHS OF A THREE

Threes are self-starters and very intelligent. They constantly search for ways to improve and get better at their game. While each individual will have their definition of success, for most Threes, success is about having the finer things in life, being surrounded by the right kind of people, and being around power. To have all these, Threes go the extra mile each day and leverage their strengths which include some of the following:

- Adaptability and quickly pivoting in situations so they can keep moving in the direction of the target.
- A charisma and enthusiasm that's contagious and attractive.
- Commitment and dedication to goal achievement.
- Being open to new opportunities and unafraid of responsibility and accountability.
- Strong will, ability to think critically, and act pragmatically.

Key personality traits of Type Three

- Charisma
- Focus
- Productive and efficient
- Intense work ethic

Common hobbies for a Type Three

- Dancing
- Modeling
- Singing
- Competitive sports
- Developing talents

FEARS AND WEAKNESSES

By now, it's evident that one of the distinguishing expressions of Type Three is the need to accomplish great things and be greatly admired and loved for all their achievements. A Threes biggest fear is to be worthless, insignificant, and a failure.

What's the Basic Fear driving this behavior? The fear of being worthless or without inherent value. For many Type Threes, there's a subconscious belief that to be loved and worthy in the eyes of others, they must succeed or at least appear successful. Deep down, all they want is to ve valuable, and so Threes do anything and everything to demonstrate that. Many times, this basic fear is expressed in one of two ways. The first is through constant activity. Always doing anything and everything to move the needle. The second is through emotional neglect. I can attest to both things because I struggled with hyperactivity for a long time. I adapted my life to meeting certain expectations that I perceived would enable me to maintain a particular image of success. I would engage in projects I didn't even enjoy or care about just because I thought it would bring more achievement and recognition. And when projects weren't that good, I dropped them quickly because I didn't want those failures to hurt my image. The other issue I had was dealing with my emotions. I always tried to put them on hold or stuff them on the back burner as much as possible because "I didn't have time" to deal with them. But the truth is that I just didn't want to deal with my feelings. If these are struggles you've had, keep reading because I'll show you how to move past this level of development.

DESIRES AND MOTIVATIONS

The Basic Desire for a Type Three is to feel valuable and worthwhile. Threes want to be accepted, loved, and desirable. Now, I know what you're thinking. Isn't that a selfish desire? If you're a Three, you understand that it's anything but selfish. This overwhelming care to be valuable and desired translates into the desire to help others. I can confidently say that I am eager and driven to help others as much as I want to help myself. After all, helping others means I get to fulfill my own goals. Many Threes are doing this unconsciously because they innately know that the more they lift others up, the higher they will rise. The respect and admiration we crave are earned. We're not afraid to work for it. Of course, when dealing with unhealthy levels of development, that craving to be successful does turn dark. It may involve deceit, manipulation, and other means that may not be for the highest good of anyone. But when dealing with healthy Threes, success means success for everyone around them.

Core values

- Productivity
- Goal-oriented, results-oriented
- Personal growth
- Competency
- Respect
- Adaptability, Flexibility
- Prestige, Reputation

Type Three celebrities and famous people you might know to include American talk show host, author, actress, and entrepreneur Oprah Winfrey, Actor, rapper Will Smith, Former Pro NBA superstar, and Entrepreneur Michael Jordan, and Actor Tom Cruise.

Wondering if you could be a Type Three? Here are some personality indicators

1. Winning is everything. You need to win and be the best at whatever you've set your mind on.
2. You're internally driven and motivated to be productive.
3. You hate and possibly even fear failure as it goes against your primary desire.
4. You care deeply about your image. Even at healthy levels, Threes still care about how they present themselves to the world.
5. Your vision of what you want is clear, and you're consistently thinking about the future and how it could be better.
6. You're a natural leader and find it easy to motivate, inspire and lead others into their greatness.

7. You love setting big goals, accomplishing them, and doing it all over again.
8. It's a struggle for you to have downtime and just unwind, especially when you've got an exciting goal on your mind.
9. You have a hard time celebrating your successes. You're already chasing the next big project as soon as you hit a target.
10. You have the natural ability to read a room and adapt to fit the audience you want to win over. That gives you the edge over others and makes it easy to build connections with almost anyone.

YOUR WINGS

Wings are the numbers adjacent to your primary Enneagram number. As a Three, you have

- The Enneagram Three with a Two-Wing: "The Charmer"
- The Enneagram Three with a Four-Wing: "The Professional"

While you may have tendencies that lean into both wings, you'll likely be more dominant in one than the other. That will become your Dominant Wing. The Charmer, aka enchanter, is highly personable, extroverted, caring, and compassionate. They will be more community-oriented and passionate about community development. Although goal-oriented like any other Three, the charmer is more invested in making relationships succeed and motivating others into greatness.

The Professional (sometimes referred to as the expert) is highly success-driven and more focused on personal goals rather than communal ones. They tend to have strict and clearly defined boundaries between the various parts of their lives, such as work, friendship, etc., and they generally like to be admired from afar. This particular Three is more in tune with their emotions. Unlike the charmer, they have a closer-knit friend and family group.

Meaning of your Wing

If you're a 3w2(Three with Two-Wing), you're naturally people-oriented and genuinely care about building relationships. Sure, you're still highly image-conscious, success-driven ambitious, but you have the added benefit of not needing to over-extend yourself or "fake it" when it comes to relationships. Your efforts and desire to accomplish greatness are intensely focused on family, friends, and the community you care about. In other words, you're likely pouring more of your energy into relationship success rather than worldly success.

Type 3w2 are drawn to careers that offer authority and the opportunity for advancement. Their competitiveness often means they'll thrive in fields where this aspect of their personality is an asset rather than a hindrance. That includes:

- Lawyer
- Journalist
- Politician
- Event planner
- Television anchor
- Advertising consultant
- Entrepnreneur

Welcome to my world. If you're a 3w4 (Three with Four-Wing), then your personality type is one of the more complex ones. As a Three with a Four Wing, our personality is a bit contradictory because, on the one hand, we can be chameleons, changing color to blend in whenever we feel the need to. But with a dominant Four Wing, authenticity is a massive influence. Finding that alignment between being a Three and the strong urge to be authentically myself has been one of the most challenging aspects of my self-discovery journey. So if it gets scary and hard as you go through this, rest easy. You're not alone. The intention is to grow in your development to the point where your focus shifts from superficial to meaningful things where you can leverage all your natural abilities, including that perceptive shape-shifting gift.

As a type 3w4, certain roles will be better suited for your personality, including:

- Lawyer
- Financial analyst
- Architect
- Publicist
- Venture capitalist
- Marketer
- Investment banker
- Politician

The Arrows and what they mean

Your Enneagram personality type is linked to two other points worth discussing. These lines are called arrows, and each indicates how you show up at your best and worst. That simply means you get to learn the full spectrum of your personality and the best path towards growth, alerting you to the red flags you need to become aware of so you can pause, step back and avoid crashing and burning again. One arrow is called the Arrow of Disintegration, which shows our stress number. The other is called the Arrow of Integration.

For us as Threes, we have 9 as the arrow of Disintegration and 6 as the arrow of Integration. When we move toward the unhealthy path of Disintegration, we take on traits from an unhealthy Nine because our dominant need for attention and significance has been challenged. That might express itself as withdrawal, anxiety, fear, and uncertainty. If you've ever faced too much pressure at work and fell into overwhelm, guilt for not meeting your goals, or anger towards everyone, that was you on the path of Disintegration. Many unhealthy Threes on this path will drink excessively, become overly aggressive and engage in all kinds of substance abuse to cope.

On the other hand, when we move toward Integration, we cultivate and activate the healthier qualities of a Six. That causes us to move through situations and life feeling more secure and accepting of ourselves and others. We no longer feel the need to be validated by others because we are content with who we are and the life choices we've made. By developing more traits of a healthy Six, we become more focused and forgiving. We set clear boundaries that enable us to take care of our emotional needs. To understand the relationship of these arrows and how we came about with healthy and unhealthy levels, let's talk about Type Three's various levels of development.

THE 9 LEVELS OF DEVELOPMENT, FROM LOWEST TO HIGHEST

Levels of Development arise from Riso and Hudson's teachings and the founders of the Enneagram Institute, which is a great place to take your Enneagram Test. Their theory posits that all individuals fall into one of nine levels of functioning. The lowest level is nine, and the highest is level one. The levels are divided into a triad that subcategorizes these levels as healthy (1,2,3), average levels (4,5,6), and unhealthy levels (7,8,9).

Unhealthy

Level 9: This is the darkest, lowest, and most dangerous level an adult could live from for any Enneagram number. It's okay at infancy to be here—in fact, this is where we all start when we are infants. However, many adults have never developed past this stage or, even worse, keep falling back to this level. For Type Threes who are ambitious and image- and status-conscious, being at this level is highly destructive for them and those around them. At this stage of a Three's development, they are vindictive, relentless, and obsessive about destroying whatever reminds them of their own shortcomings and failures. The person will likely exhibit psychopathic behavior, generally displaying Narcissistic Personality Disorder.

Level 8: At this unhealthy level, the Three has developed a little, but is still stuck in harmful levels of expression, so they are highly devious and deceptive. The individual at this level will do anything to cover up their mistakes and failures because they want to keep that front that they are winning in life. This Three is also delusionally jealous of others, untrustworthy, malicious, and tends to sabotage and betray people if that's what it takes to win.

Level 7: This Three struggles mostly with fear of failure and is driven by that innate urge to avoid failure. Usually, that means doing whatever it takes to win and preserve their illusion of superiority. The individual at this level isn't really successful, but they "fake" things in their world to appear more successful than they really are. That makes them highly opportunistic and exploitative, seeking to covet the success of others at any chance they get.

Average

Level 6: At this level, the Enneagram Three has developed enough to rise to average levels of expression. This Three is self-focused, arrogant, grandiose, narcissistic, and has inflated notions about their success and talents. The struggle with jealousy is still prevalent, and they do anything to impress others with their superiority. It's easy to spot this Three because they are always the loudest in the room, trying to show others that they are the best even though they don't believe it.

Level 5: At this average level, Type Three is more concerned about accomplishing as much as possible and winning the admiration of others. On a more positive note, this Three is pragmatic and efficient. They are solely focused on crushing their goal and getting what they want. Being intimate with another or "letting anyone in" is a challenge. The smooth facade used to win over people keeps them out of tune with their authentic self, and they avoid dealing with their feelings.

Level 4: This Type Three is career and performance-focused. They want to be the best and constantly strive to achieve bigger and bigger goals. Fear of failure is still a considerable challenge. At times, they may compare themselves to others who are more successful.

Healthy

Level 3: The rise in development for Type Three to this healthy phase is liberating. While the Three is still ambitious, striving to become outstanding and the best they can be, they are more geared toward becoming an exceptional human and not just winning in their career. This three works hard to embody widely admired qualities and invests a lot in personal growth. They are also highly effective, and others naturally follow and get motivated by being around this individual.

Level 2: At this level, Type Three is self-assured, desirable, charming, gracious, adaptable, and possesses high levels of self-esteem. They are competent and believe in themselves and the value they bring to the table.

Level 1: This is the highest and most advanced level that a Three can hope to attain. At this level, transcendence has occurred, and the Three truly is operating at their best (in complete alignment with their divine Self). They are authentic, self-accepting, gentle, benevolent, modest, and full of heart in all they do. People love and follow this individual.

TYPE THREE'S PASSION

The Enneagram identifies the Passion or vice of a Three as deceit or, better said - vanity and false self-image. I view the Passion as our ego's primary coping tool to reconnect with essence. Although it's not the best path and often leads to Disintegration and unhealthy habits, the underlying intention is to find our way back home. Usually, this Passion is born out of childhood experiences or some wound that caused us to wear a mask and protect ourselves from the world. The more we wore this mask, the harder it became to recognize our true self. As members of the Heart Triad, losing our essence and true self meant we also lost touch with our emotions and the innate joy and love we know we deserve. So in an attempt to have some of that feeling of wholeness, we tend to deceive ourselves and others. For a Three, the passion of deceit is expressed in the attitudes and behavior of becoming what others admire and desire. It can be in the form of mimicking another person, promoting personal success over all else while ignoring failures, disguising perceived flaws, and being overly obsessed with image and status. Take a moment now to candidly reflect on the following questions:

- Do I believe that I have to earn love by being worthy?
- Do I tend to shape-shift and become what others want me to be just to get what I want?
- Am I overly identified with my personality and outer image?
- Do I often take on the ideas of others, especially role models, and wear them as my personal identity?

The honest response you get from this simple exercise will move you toward your virtue and a step closer to your true essence. What is virtue? Your virtue represents your most accurate, most authentic expression of yourself. It's typically the exact opposite of your Passion or ego fixation. For a Three, that virtue is Truth and Integrity. And it expresses itself in behavior as:

- becoming authentically yourself without regarding what others think
- slowing down frequently to acknowledge and process your emotions
- becoming more self-accepting and content to just be yourself
- feeling whole and confident in your Truth

CHILDHOOD AND EMOTIONAL PATTERNS OF TYPE THREE

Emotional patterns for an adult are often shaped by early childhood experiences and how one interprets their upbringing. Each of us has a filter through which we understand the world around us. For Enneagram Threes, that filter is associated with external success. As children, Threes were deeply connected to the nurturing figure in their life and learned to intuit that person's needs before they were expressly stated. In my case, it was my mother, and I did everything possible to meet those needs because there was no "man of the house," and I needed to step in to fill the gap left by that protective presence. Some Threes were part of a big family and didn't receive the attention they needed, so they used performance to stand out and get attention. I also have Type Threes friends who grew up with amazing parents who praised them for their accomplishments. So as kids, they learned to associate love with "doing" instead of "being."

All Threes strive to win or accomplish something because we get that look of approval we've loved receiving since childhood. It doesn't matter what kind of a family set-up you had. If the messaging your brain received is that winning gets you love and attention, you do whatever it takes to keep that reality going. That could have been in sports, academics, and even a career now that you're an adult.

There's nothing wrong with wanting to win and succeed in life but where things get tricky is when it's founded on a false sense of self.

Suppose you're only going after success in life because you've attached that to your self-worth and love. In that case, you're dealing with the fear of rejection and abandonment. That's what the Enneagram is attempting to help you uncover so that you can heal those emotional wounds and live your ambitious life from a place of wholeness. Instead of using external accomplishments and successes as distractions and masks to cover up the disconnect from your true Self, make the shift and heal from the inside out. Let's get a little granular on your particular personality type by discussing the subtypes to enable this transformation. Then we'll cover lifestyle tips and changes you can integrate.

SUBTYPES FOR TYPE THREE

The Enneagram profiling system allows for 3 subtypes in each Type. These are Self-Preservation, Social, and One-to-One (Sexual) variants. Remember, all three instinctual variants exist in all of us. Still, the order in which they stack up determines their influence on our lives. One will be most dominant and the easiest for you to resonate with and observe as behavior and thought patterns in your life. The second will feel a little neutral and less influential, and the third will be the least significant. The third instinct becomes a blind spot for many because it's totally underdeveloped and out of their conscious recognition. Depending on which instinct is most dominant will shape your unique personality and how you approach life as a Three.

Self-Preservation Three (SP)

Security is the main focus for this Enneagram Three, which is also the countertype of the group. As the countertype, this Three will act in ways that make it easy to mistype the SP Three. SP Threes have boundless energy and high drive, which they use to accomplish personal goals like buying lovely homes and establishing financial security. Unlike classic Threes, this individual dislikes being a show-off. They prefer not to advertise their accomplishments and strengths.

While they still value winning and looking good, they don't want to be seen as image-oriented. Don't get me wrong, this Three wishes to be recognized for their hard work and excellence but not in the vain and often materialistic way other Threes enjoy.

This subtype is reliable, efficient, and productive and aspires to do the right thing for themselves and others. Their pursuit of security and self-sufficiency through hard work may lead to struggles with workaholism.

Social Three (SO)

Prestige is the main focus for this individual. Driven by the vain need to look good, impress others, and get the job done, Social Threes enjoy being on stage in the spotlight. Social Threes know how to climb the social ladder and achieve success. Of all the subtypes, Social Threes are the most aggressive and competitive. Success and gaining influence are critical to these Threes and may even cut corners or cover up failure as long as they get the desired outcome.

Sexual/ One-to-One Three (SX)

Charisma is the main focus for this Threes, and it's expressed in how much time, energy, and attention they place on their physical appearance. While this Three isn't as obvious and overt about their vanity as in the case of a Social Three, they are also not in denial in conflict with it as is the case with the Self-preservation Three. Their vanity and personal attractiveness are employed to make others feel good. Sexual Threes have a harder time talking about themselves and often put the focus on the people they want to promote. There are some people-pleasing tendencies in a Sexual Three, especially around family, friends, or team members that they care about. It can be easy to mistype this subtype Three as a Two because they tend to think and act along the lines of "If those around me achieve success, then I am more successful."

CHAPTER 10

WORK AND LIFESTYLE TIPS FOR TYPE 3S

There's a lot to cover about the growth opportunities for all Enneagram Threes. Before that, let's address some of the struggles you'll face at some point in your journey. The battles are already a present-day reality for some of my readers. They might be avoiding this topic altogether. If that's you, it's time to face the demons and put them to rest.

STRUGGLES OF AN ENNEAGRAM TYPE 3

The feeling that success is always out of reach

That is a feeling every Three can relate to somehow, mainly when operating at average or unhealthy levels of development. The person works hard to climb the ladder and hit the target, but it's an ever-moving target. And if you look around, there's always someone more skilled, successful, famous, better looking, etc. For average and unhealthy Threes, this ever-moving target causes them to feel unsuccessful and worthless, so they need to keep upgrading and reaching for the next best thing. When handled poorly, this feeling becomes a breeding ground for a lot of pain and lack of gratitude.

What to do: Let's spend a few moments writing down your goals over the next year, five years, and ten years respectively. Are those goals really yours? Did you pick them because you're trying to compete with someone or prove something to someone? Do you have any goals you chose because you feel achieving them will enable you to become the highest and best version of yourself? What would you have as goals over the next year if there were no rewards and people loved you for yourself?

Comparisons

Another unhelpful behavior for average and unhealthy Threes is the habit of comparing their success to the successes of others. No matter how good they get, if they feel someone else has it better, they immediately feel insecure. When around people less successful, they feel proud and competent but perhaps bored because there's no challenge. It takes a lot of personal growth to shed this habit of comparison and stop feeling insecure when around more successful people.

What to do: Consider doing activities that take you out of that competitive mindset and enable you to see that you're on a unique path, and so is everyone else. You could even collaborate on a charitable activity like cooking for kids with special needs or building an educational facility for a local school (with the people you tend to compare yourself with). It's important to realize that your success is yours, and no one can take it away from you. And the same is true for the people around you. The scarcity mindset of comparison is more hurtful than helpful to your success on this abundant planet.

Always being "on."

This is super common across the board for Threes because we just don't know how to "unwind." In fact, many Threes hate that word. The lower the level of development (average and unhealthy levels), the more problematic this becomes because this tendency leads to vanity, false images, and exaggerations. When a Three starts to "fake it," whether emotionally, physically, or through their status, just to appear like they're "on," that's a big issue. Because it only amplifies their hidden insecurities and forces them to overextend themselves trying to save face.

What to do: It's okay to be enthusiastic, energetic, and always on as long as it comes from an authentic place. Make sure you're in control of that "on" switch.

Burnout

Another significant struggle for average and unhealthy Threes is overworking to the point of a breakdown. Because the person tends to get too obsessed with success and goal achievement, they can quickly fall out of touch with their physical and emotional needs. That leads to sleep debt, poor diet, lack of exercise, and overall health issues from self-neglect. Threes can easily over-extend themselves in the name of making dreams come true. The other area they often neglect is their relationships. When focused on a goal, they'll ignore everything and everyone, including loved ones, if they don't see how the relationship is helping them achieve their goal.

What to do: Prioritize your self-care routine. Do a daily check-in with yourself to ensure everything is okay internally. Stop and take deep breaths every so often. Give yourself permission to nap, eat lunch and dinner in peace, take long walks, etc. Plan your busy schedule accordingly so you can have ample sleep each night and include some family and social life every so often to give the people in your life a little attention and affection.

Feeling unloved and struggling with self-acceptance and self-love

This is the holy grail for a Three. The journey to self-discovery isn't to make your ambitions and desires a bad thing but rather to enable you to experience true and unconditional love. That love comes from within by learning to accept and love yourself first. Then allow others to love you. I know this is hard and definitely requires some serious self-development. Still, once you get it, you'll no longer fixate on perfecting your outer image or impressing people.

The awards, fancy cars, homes, and social status will be nice to have, but they won't define you. The struggle for love started at a young age. Most Threes felt unloved for who they were and, in turn, grew into people who cage their emotions and strive for achievement. It's a survival mechanism that served its purpose. If you want to express and experience the highest and best version of your life, it's time to shed this belief and find your true self.

What to do: Invest time getting to know who you really are. Partake in some self-love activities, read a book or attend a seminar that introduces you to the aspects of you that are beyond what you know. Once you know who you really are, beyond your ego-personality, you will learn to love and accept yourself. This may take time, but the more you move in this direction, the sooner you'll find your "lost self."

OPPORTUNITIES FOR GROWTH

Let's uncover some of the ways you can start growing personally and professionally now that you're doing the inner work of moving to higher levels of development.

Develop the intention to accept and love yourself

You can shift into more positive traits by challenging your current value system. Choose to stop relying on achievement and recognition. According to Enneagram teachings, the integrated path of growth is influenced by the Enneagram Six. So as a Three moving into higher levels of development, these lines of growth Influenced by Six will enable you to realize that your value isn't determined by other people. Their approval or lack thereof has nothing to do with your self-worth. You still possess tremendous value whether you're winning accolades or not. This growth path helps you embrace who you really are, and you become more honest, authentic, and loyal to your true self.

Practice active listening

As a Three, I can attest that listening to other people's advice isn't easy. I've trained myself to develop this quality because it is essential. Our stubborn nature tends to be at odds with other people's suggestions of how things should be done. When working in a team environment or even with a spouse, allowing two-way communication is healthy and critical to thriving relationships. This is an area of growth for all Type Three, so be gentle with yourself and notice each time you shut down someone's ideas because your mind is already made up. Learning to listen to other people's ideas and their side of the story gives you a broader perspective and makes you seem less self-centered.

Shedding the urge to lie

The core Passion or sin for a Type Three is deceit. The higher up your development you rise, the easier it will be to resist the temptation to deceive, lie or twist things around to your advantage. As you find your authentic self and reconnect with that higher version of you, vanity and deceit will naturally fade away. You won't feel the constant need to maintain a false image or wear a deceptive mask.

Let's get something straight. Achieving success and following your ambitions and dreams is right, and it's wonderful to desire a better lifestyle, that eight-figure income, and global travel for yourself. Just don't "chase" after these things to impress others or as a coping mechanism to hide your shame. If the success you seek is only a shell to cover feelings of emptiness, then no growth occurs. Heal the inside first, find who you really are, and then make manifest whatever feels right to your Higher Self.

Give back to your community

Find a cause within your community that resonates with you. Making contributions to society can be a great way to train yourself to share the spotlight and see abundance at different levels of life. Your perspective of success will expand as you interact with others totally different from you and yet successful in their own right.

We associate success with power, material accomplishments, and status as Threes. Success in this new discovery expands to other areas as well. You'll learn to embrace teamwork and altruism, and it's a great way to inspire and take care of the people in your community. Consider volunteering for a project or activities that resonate with you.

ENNEAGRAM TYPE 3 UNDER STRESS

When Type Threes get stressed, we become disconnected and fall into average and unhealthy levels. We express behavior that's typically influenced by the arrow Nine. When that happens, things take a downward spiral because, as you can imagine, being influenced by the poor qualities of an Enneagram Nine like procrastination, slothfulness, and indifference spell doom for our typically high-energy personality. So you'll sense a disconnect within yourself and realize that you're getting caught up in busy work that means nothing to you and doesn't really move the needle in your life. You'll also start putting things on hold, and feelings of apathy will increase exponentially.

As Threes, we get really stressed out by some of the following:

- Feeling incompetent about something we care about.
- Being around incompetent people.
- Losing
- Not seeing progress toward a set objective or goal.
- Being around people who lack vision.
- Not being recognized for our hard work and accomplishments.
- Feeling undesirable or worthless.
- Not being challenged enough.

How to ease your back into a healthy state:

The best way to shift from that paralyzing, unhealthy state of stress and Disintegration is to recognize that you're behaving like an unhealthy Nine. And just pause and take some time to decompress and let out the stuff weighing you down. Find someone you can trust and tell them what's going on and why you're so stressed. If you don't trust anyone, consider journaling everything in a private journal. What matters is that you recognize that it's happening and immediately release it from your system.

Take deep breaths and tune into your body. What's going on there? Are you tired? Hungry? In pain? What could you do for your body now to bring it into a state of ease and good health? Once you've let out the stress either verbally or through journaling and taken care of your bodily needs, shift your attention to something creative that you can do to start a new momentum. For most Threes, creative expression comes easy. There's always something we enjoy doing, such as writing, drawing, painting, playing an instrument, pottery, listening to music, etc. You already know your thing, so block out time immediately and engage in this activity until it consumes you and shifts your energy. Now that you've got a new momentum started keep adding activities to build on it until you get back on track.

RELATIONSHIPS

Type Threes are naturally energetic, devoted, and value genuine care. When it comes to personal and professional relationships, a Three typically assumes a competitive, ally, or mentoring role with the other person. Where they position you determines how your relationship plays out.

In romantic relationships, Threes usually seek partners capable of bringing something unique and beneficial to the relationship. Depending on the level of development, the Three will be drawn to different qualities in the other, whether that is intelligence, mutual interests, or support of some kind. In the workplace, Threes are attracted to the people who can grant them access to attain their chosen objective. Depending on the situation, that could be the manager, an executive, or the company owner. When less healthy, Threes become too preoccupied with achievement and success, sometimes at the expense of the people around them. That's why it's essential to become self-aware and keep creating that balance as a Three so that your loved ones don't feel neglected or lose interest in being part of your journey.

RELATIONSHIP TIPS WITH OTHER TYPES

As a Three, you desire someone who will love and appreciate you, compliment or match your intensity and keep you challenged in all the right ways. Here are some ways to improve your relationships with other Enneagram Types.

Type 3 & Type 1: You have a partner that genuinely supports your endeavors with a Type One. Someone who also believes just as you do that staying rational is the best way to deal with conflict and figure things out. The One admires your can-do attitude and the fact that you always get things done. You appreciate Type One's commitment, sense of responsibility, and high standards. When both of you operate at higher levels of development, this can be a beautiful relationship.

Some of the challenges you might face together is stepping out of that serious, strict, task-oriented mindset and into friendship and romance. The One might also see your shape-shifting as manipulative and shallow, while you might see the One's principled approach to everything, including date night, as too rigid, dull, and stifling.

You can grow together by softening each other's edginess and learning what it truly means to rest, relax and reset. Practice this in your relationship.

Type 3 & Type 2: You're a charming, passionate couple with a Type Two. The Two brings a lot of warmth, acceptance, and affirmation to your world, which you love. You bring the ambition, energy, and liveliness that inspires the Two to follow their dreams. There's plenty of attention, affection, and interpersonal connection when operating at healthy levels between you and your partner. It's easy to maintain healthy, positive social engagements. Your combined attractiveness and confidence radiate dynamic energy that people can't help but admire.

Some of the challenges you might face include a lack of understanding of your own feelings. Sure, you can pick up on the other person's energy and feelings but are you investing enough time to do the same with your inner feelings? When there's inner self-neglect, the relationship faces many issues. You might feel overwhelmed by the Two's helpfulness and desire for emotional connection, especially when under stress. The Two can feel neglected as you drown in your ambition and tasks.

You can grow together by learning to have an open dialogue with high-quality questions that enable you to reflect on what's really going on inside. Get in touch with your own feelings first. It will enrich your relationships far more than any therapy.

Type 3 & Type 3: With another Three as your partner, it's like being with a perfect mirror that enables you to do extraordinary things together. You bring out the best in each other. You're charming, successful, and pleasant, and you just get each other. A pair of Threes in a relationship means both parties understand the importance of being outstanding and admired. Yet beneath all that, you still get to see behind the mask and realize there's a caring, genuine and loving person underneath all that hard work and great ambition.

While I think Threes in a relationship is a match made in heaven, the best time to be in a relationship with another Three is at higher levels of development. Otherwise, the challenge you'll face is hitting a wall with your partner when they get worn out from the busy demanding schedule you both run. With such hectic days and big ambitions driving both of you, it's easy to neglect feelings or down-time together. That tends to create gaps in your relationship, and you'll often find yourselves caught up in opposite cycles of achievement and exhaustion. The fact that you don't like to admit failure or even apologize when something is your fault can also become a huge issue.

Grow together by prioritizing the "feelings" part of your relationship as much as everything else. Train yourself to sit with the discomfort of dealing with emotions until it stops being too uncomfortable. When you feel like withdrawing, make an effort to do the opposite and communicate with your partner. Realize that apologizing isn't a sign of failure or weakness.

Type 3 & Type 4: With a Type Four, the relationship is earnest and intense and facilitates plenty of open communication. The Four brings introspection, depth, and meaning to the relationship, which is excellent for you because it helps you slow down and do your inner work. Your ambition, energy, and structure are desirable to the Four. It helps them become more present in the world and increase their self-confidence. The relationship is very balanced, and you become more sensitive and comfortable expressing yourself.

The main challenge you might face with a Four is how different their emotional temperaments are to you. You might find too much "emotion" to be overwhelming or irrational. They might see you as "fake" or apathetic because you just don't get as emotional about things as they do. In other words, sometimes you just don't understand them, and they feel the same about you.

Grow together by setting realistic expectations in your relationship. When tension arises, meet it head on as soon as you notice its ugly head. Be open and clear about how far you're willing to go to prioritize your partner's emotional needs and allow them to speak their heart. Listen with your head and heart if you truly want to maintain that long-lasting connection.

Type 3 & Type 5: With a Five, your relationship is efficient and stable. You both shine as you become more inventive and competent together. The Five bring creativity, depth, and objectivity to the relationship. They admire the work you put in to be the best at what you do because that's something they value. Your energy, confidence, and sociability is also very attractive to the Five and helps the Five out of their shell. When your assertiveness is combined with your partner's thoughtfulness and penchant for thorough research, the relationship brims with a dynamic steadiness that keeps you wanting more.

A common challenge you'll face is how you operate things and move through life. Fives tend to move at a thoughtful pace. Their measured approach helps them conserve energy, remaining steady and poised. As a Three, you're always thinking on your feet, so the speed is the name of your game. That can often create frustration, primarily if you're operating at average and unhealthy levels. You may feel like you're in a tug-of-war pulling in opposite directions.

Grow together by being open-minded enough to learn from the other. Get in touch with your feelings in a meaningful way and talk about them together. Work on rising to higher levels of development as partners.

Type 3 & Type 6: With a Six, you have a transparent, stable relationship that's resilient. The Six is encouraging, faithful, dutiful, and knows how to keep you grounded and encouraged. You know how to bring out the best in people, so as you highlight the good in your partner, they feel more encouraged to pursue their passions. The relationship is comfortable and makes it easy for you to find an emotional connection with your partner. With high levels of responsibility and hard work, you become unstoppable once you trust each other.

The main challenge you may encounter is the difference in fundamental values. A Six values loyalty above all else, and your shape-shifting tendencies can cause them to doubt your trustworthiness. They are also pretty cautious, which may conflict with your hard driving, less careful personality. And sometimes, you may feel like they're holding you back.

Work through your feelings as a couple. You can grow together by validating one another's focus of attention and staying present in the relationship. Keep an open dialogue and let your partner know that you respect their values even though how you express trustworthiness may not be what they're used to.

Type 3 & Type 7: There's never a dull moment in the relationship with a seven. Sevens are adventurous, courageous, and vibrant, which is excellent because that fun, spontaneous energy keeps things interesting for a Three. You are able to help the Seven become more focused, sensitive, and poised. It's a fun-filled, high-energy relationship.

The challenge you might face is the emotional neglect and avoidance that may build up over time. You tend to be busy, and Sevens don't like confrontation or negativity, so they might let things slide, creating gaps in your relationship. Your partner might also get frustrated with your constant desire for productivity. Because you're both sensitive to feelings of loss or rejection, it's likely that you'll quit avoiding abandonment.

Grow together by sharing your feelings and making time for open dialogue, even the uncomfortable stuff. Learn to slow down every once in a while.

Type 3 & Type 8: You're in for an intense, lively relationship with a Type Eight. The Eight brings just as much, if not more, assertiveness and passion, which is great because it allows you to be the fullest version of yourself without judgment. You help your partner let go of the need to control everything because they feel you're competent, responsible, and powerful enough to be trusted. It moves them out of that "lone wolf" energy, trying to do everything alone. It's a powerful, influential relationship, and you can build a solid unbreachable fort together.

The challenge, of course, is how extreme both your personalities are. Just as you match each other in positive ways, you also match each other in tension and conflict. Eights fear being vulnerable or betrayed, and given how easily you can shape-shift, that can cause alarm for a Type Eight. You may also struggle to deal with your partner's anger issues.

Grow together by letting go and working on your trust level. Have fun and allow yourself to be in situations where you're not in total control.

Type 3 & Type 9: With a Nine, you're in a serene, purposeful, easy-going relationship. Nines offer love, acceptance, and a sense of calm which makes you feel that they love you just for being. You give them the encouragement they need to find their voice and follow their dreams because you can see untapped potential. The relationship is very reciprocal, balanced, steady, and peaceful. You are each other's cheerleaders.

The main challenge you might face is conflicting energies. You might feel like the Nine is holding you back and your partner may feel neglected because you're always busy chasing after the next big goal. There's also the issue of procrastination and inaction that Nines often fall into, which can be utterly frustrating for you. However, pushing your partner to take action leads to withdrawal and suppressed resentment.

You can grow together by listening to each other more with an open mind. If your partner says you need to slow down a little, remember it's well-intended. There may be some truth in their concern.

AFFIRMATIONS FOR ENNEAGRAM TYPE 3

Affirmations can be a great tool when you begin replacing your negative thoughts and habits. Learn to become your own cheerlead and direct some of that tender loving care inward by speaking words that uplift and encourage you. Here is a list to help you out.

- I am more patient and find my own flow in life.
- I accept and love myself.
- I am full of energy and life.
- I allow myself to breathe and relax.

- I embrace myself despite my mistakes and imperfections.
- I am grateful for all my successes.
- I embrace leadership centered on truth, integrity, and compassion.
- I am authentic.

Remember, these affirmations only work if you feel and believe in what you're saying. Pick a few that resonate with you emotionally and use them as often as needed.

DAILY LIFESTYLE TIPS FOR GROWTH AND HAPPINESS

Schedule some regular time to unplug and reset

Our work is vital to us, and no one is asking you to give up on what you believe in. However, it's good for your mental, emotional, physical, and spiritual well-being to have some periods of rest and relaxation. That doesn't mean spending weeks lying on a hammock doing nothing (that would drive me crazy). It means figuring out what helps you feel relaxed and rested and adding that to your schedule as part of your downtime. Creating space to "unplug" from the world and daily demands is good. Find ways you enjoy unplugging. For me, it's going for a swim. I take laps each day before heading home for the evening. No phone, no people, just me and the water for 30min. That resets me.

Practice mindfulness

You can practice mindfulness eating, take mindful showers, or even take a yoga/meditation class if that resonates with you. Learning to be more mindful will also improve your ability to be present in each moment.

Focus on a relationship you care about

Your schedule is hectic, and there's barely enough time to get everything done. I get that. But if you have a few people in your life who matter to you, figure out a way to give them the attention and love they deserve. You can choose to focus on improving one relationship at a time. Prioritize some time this week to interact with someone you love. Be present during the interaction and show them how much you love and appreciate them. Communicate your feelings and let them know you're working hard to be more involved in the relationship. Then next week or next month, add one more person to your list. Relationships are critical to our success, so we need to figure out a way to prioritize them in our pursuit of success.

Keep a gratitude journal

I take five minutes daily to write down 3 things I feel grateful for. This simple practice has transformed my life. So many Threes get caught up in competing and accomplishing the next big thing. That constant strain and stress can quickly turn into bad habits and diseases for the body. I find that gratitude enables me to maintain that delicate balance between feeling content with who I am (what I have) and embracing the desire for more. Scientific evidence shows that gratitude helps the mind and body in various ways, including lowering blood pressure, stress management, and maintaining homeostasis. As a Three, I want to keep a healthy mind and body so I can keep growing and moving toward my dreams.

Explore spirituality

The topic of spirituality isn't easy, and not everyone is ready for it. But you should know that you don't need to be religious to have a strong spiritual connection. All Threes would benefit significantly from exploring spiritual enlightenment because most of us fall into average and unhealthy levels of expression due to a disconnect with our Higher Self. To find your true self, you'll need to walk that mysterious path of spiritual enlightenment because anything less is just your ego-talk. We struggle with false image, ego fixation, vanity, or wearing too many masks because we're not in touch with our true selves. So we have to perform and make stuff up because that's the only way we know to garner the love we crave deep down.

But once you find your true self and experience unconditional love, your personality morphs into one that doesn't need to fake anything. You learn to be yourself no matter what, and in so doing, you cease to attach your worthiness to accomplishments or external possessions. Dealing with your emotions also becomes easy. The self-image you wear is even more attractive than anything you'd created before the spiritual transformation. It's a lot to take in, so start slowly and consider following spiritual teachers like Deepak Chopra or Neale Donald Walsch, depending on your personal preference.

CHAPTER 11

ENNEAGRAM TYPE 4

THE INDIVIDUALIST OR ROMANTIC

I n the following two chapters, we'll cover everything you need to know about the Enneagram Type 4, often referred to as the Romantic or the Individualist. Aptly named, this Enneagram type is most concerned about expressing their individuality and finding their true identity. Similar to the Enneagram Types Two and Three, The Fours are also part of the heart triad. Their core emotion is shame, but unlike the other Types, Fours really embrace and almost drown in this emotion, expressing it more as a sense of deep sadness or melancholy.

Fours believe they are innately different and uniquely talented; therefore, no one can truly understand them or their unique gifts. They are also highly sensitive and acutely aware of their deficiencies. Creativity comes naturally and abundantly to all Fours. When operating at high levels of development, they are plain-spoken, truthful with themselves and others, and possess great emotional depth. These Fours are comfortable being vulnerable and showing who they are unapologetic. This authenticity and intensity is often very attractive. At unhealthy and lower levels of development, however, Fours can be tough to bear, too moody, erratic, full of self-doubt, and inclined to play the victim card as a coping mechanism.

STRENGTHS OF A FOUR

Four are highly sensitive to other people's feelings. They value emotions, and connecting with others emotionally is one of the ways they bond with people. That makes a Four a great listener. People often find comfort and genuine understanding when interacting with this Type.

Fours are also creative and rely heavily on their imagination. Their minds delve into places others are too afraid of or incapable of exploring. That's why some of the greatest artists in human history are type Fours. When a Four finds their artistic expression, they can create endlessly. Each creation is a magnificent performance that enables them to continually find and express who they believe they are.

Another strength you'll find in a Four is how authentic and self-aware they are about their own emotions, strengths, and weaknesses. It gives them the benefit of constant growth and continued learning, which is common among healthy Fours. Unhealthy Fours tend to be hindered by this quality of introspection, causing them to be too self-conscious to the point of paralysis. They may get easily frustrated by their lack or weaknesses, and when they fail, it's harder for them to bounce back.

Key personality traits of Type Four

- Creative
- Authentic
- Compassion
- Passionate

Common hobbies for a Type Four

- Designing
- Photography
- Reading
- Acting
- Listening to music and/or watching movies

FEARS AND WEAKNESSES

Fours have a most complex relationship with their emotions. On the one hand, they aren't afraid to deal with their feelings. Still, they get completely overwhelmed and lost in the melancholy of their unresolved issues. Although they long to be loved and accepted for who they really are, they also believe it's impossible. Talk about emotional chaos. Fours are afraid that they are too flawed and that something is wrong with them or missing, so unconditional love and lasting happiness are impossible. To cope with this fear, they amplify what is different and unique about them, what they can do that others can't. By standing out and pointing out how special they are, they avoid dealing with the real underlying issue, just as we all do.

Another issue Fours experience is this gnawing feeling that no one gets them. They feel misunderstood by others, and in some dark, twisted way, some even assume that they are too "unique" and extraordinary for others to get them. When this thought is entertained by an individual operating at lower levels of development, it can get really destructive to the person's wellbeing and relationships. Unhealthy Fours can become withdrawn, erratic and unbearable because they can't stop feeling sorry for themselves and creating pity parties wherever they go.

It's common to hear statements like, "What I do is so hard and so special, you would never understand me!"

What's the Basic Fear driving this behavior? The fear of being without a unique identity or personal significance.

Fours are idealistic, deeply feeling and sincere people. They are intense and whatever they focus on tends to amplify. Indulging in feelings of inadequacy or that something's missing causes them to become self-absorbed, cynical, passive-aggressive, and at times even manipulative.

How does this basic fear often manifest itself?

Depending on the Four's level of development, there are many forms of expression one might observe in the behavior. For example, it might be overwhelming emotions that manifest as crazy mood swings. It could also be constant jealousy and envy, especially when they see others happy, prosperous, and getting the things they dream about. Another negative expression is manipulating people so they can keep a relationship going in fear of abandonment or comparing themselves to others too much and showing how deficient they are in a particular area. But as I said, it all depends on how developed the Type Four is, so we'll study more about the different levels of development shortly. But first, let's shift focus to the driving desires of a Four.

DESIRES AND MOTIVATIONS

The basic desire for a Type Four is to express their unique individuality and find their true identity. To most Fours, identity is the most important aspect of their entire being. Without a unique identity, life has no meaning for this Enneagram type. So they work tirelessly to find and express this truth about who they really are. Fours are driven to stand out and be spectacular in what they do because they're different. Everyone around them is there "mundane" and unoriginal. They hate people they consider fake and cringe at people who just seem to follow trends. Due to this exaggerated need for authenticity, sticking to their individuality and continuing that personal quest for truth and uniqueness is always at the heart of everything they do.

Core values

As a Type Four, these are some of the core values you may hold dear.

- Originality and creativity
- Authenticity
- Romance
- Beauty, aesthetics
- Imagination
- Self-awareness
- Depth and intensity

Type Four celebrities and famous people you might know include Actress Kate Winslet, Singer Taylor Swift, Writer Edgar Allen Poe, Actress Dakota Fanning, Poet Rumi, Composer, and Pianist Frédéric Chopin, Writer Virginia Wolf, Singer, and Actress Cher, Composer Pytor I. Tchaikovsky, Actor Jonny Depp, Actress Angelina Jolie, Actor Nicholas Cage, Singer Alanis Morrisette, and Singer Song-writer Prince.

Wondering if you could be a Type Four? Here are some personality indicators:

1. As far back as you can remember, you always felt like you were different, even as a little child.
2. You frequently have days where your emotions and thoughts are so loud you can barely focus on the outside world.
3. At your core, you feel that your ability to navigate the deep end of the human experience is a unique gift that you alone

have to offer the world - and for that reason, you wouldn't trade it in even if you could.

4. You consider yourself a compassionate and in-tune person.

5. You're incredibly in tune with the thoughts, emotions, and motivations of yourself and those close to you, and it's easy to detect even subtle shifts in other people's moods.

6. The worst thing that can happen to you is feeling nothing or lacking emotion. In fact, you'd rather feel anything than neutral.

7. You hate mundane things, experiences, or people that lack originality.

8. You're always seeking the magical side of everything. More than anything else, you enjoy getting lost in the world of your own vivid imagination.

9. You struggle with envy and feeling that you're always missing out while others have what you want.

10. You're motivated by the pursuit of beauty, originality, and truth.

11. Letting go of the past, especially childhood or painful trauma, is extremely hard for you.

12. You secretly fantasize about meeting someone who understands and loves you so completely that they can, at last, save you from the loneliness and emptiness you've been feeling for so long.

YOUR WINGS

Wings are the numbers adjacent to your Enneagram Type. As a Four, you have-

- The Enneagram Four with Three Wing: "The Aristocrat"
- The Enneagram Four with Five Wing: "The Bohemian"

While you may have tendencies that lean into both wings at various stages of your life, you'll likely be more dominant in one than the other. This will be your most influential and dominant Wing.

Meaning of your Wing

If you're a 4w3 (Four with Three-Wing), you're more enthusiastic, hardworking, and care more about the external world than a classic Four. Your intelligence and creativity are applied in all things, including business and other accomplishments. Operating at healthy levels, the influence of this Wing enables you to become more practical, and it balances out the dreamy, melancholy state with confidence, goal setting, and execution. Unfortunately, average and unhealthy levels could elevate negative traits like envy, competition, and an obsession for validation and appreciation from others.

As a 4w3, you probably want to be in a work environment where your thirst for knowledge and curiosity is quenched. You also want to work with bosses and managers who appreciate and acknowledge all your hard work because that matters to you. Careers best suited to you include but aren't limited to:

- Motivational speaker
- Personal trainer
- Journalist
- Artist (Dancer, Poet, Actor, Painter)
- Graphic Designer
- Interior Designer
- Novelist
- Psychologist
- Career advisor
- Photographer

If you're a 4w5(Four with Five-Wing), you're more self-analyzing, free-spirited, and value your space. Relationships with others and showcasing your skills or motivating others isn't your thing, unlike the 4w3 type. When operating at healthy levels, you're emotionally secure, insightful, intelligent, observant, and fond of understanding people and the world around you. The influence of this Wing at healthy levels is almost like a perfect combination of the heart and head, which makes you very wise and profound. You see beyond what ordinary mortals could. That's why social sciences and arts call to you naturally. That doesn't mean you care about other people's opinions. In fact, you prefer to create things for yourself to fulfill your authentic desires. You enjoy Solitude, and some might even call you a bit eccentric. At average and unhealthy levels, however, the influence of this Wing can cause you to become detached and filled with self-doubt.

As a 4w5, you probably want to be in a work environment where you don't need to have too much people interaction because small talk bores you. You do, however, need an environment where you're free to express your creativity, reflect and seek knowledge and Truth. Careers best suited to you include but aren't limited to:

- Architect
- Actor
- Videographer
- Graphic designer
- Musician
- Librarian

The Arrows and what they mean

Your Enneagram personality type is linked to lines or arrows that show the path of growth or disintegration depending on where you are in life. When moving on a path of disintegration, a Four will fall into the negative trappings of the arrow Two (2), and they'll become more insecure and clingy. This is known as the Direction of Stress or the Direction of Disintegration and typically occurs in the face of pressure or surmounting stress. The other arrow indicates how a healthy version of your personality reacts and grows in more healthy environments. In this case, a Four develops more of the healthier qualities of the arrow One (1), becoming more objective and principled. To understand the concept behind healthy and unhealthy levels, let's go over the various levels of development for a Four.

THE 9 LEVELS OF DEVELOPMENT, FROM LOWEST TO HIGHEST

Levels of Development arise from Riso and Hudson's teachings and the founders of the Enneagram Institute, which is a great place to take your Enneagram Test. Their theory posits that all individuals fall into one of nine levels of functioning. The lowest level is nine, and the highest is level one. The levels are divided into a triad that subcategorizes these levels as healthy (1, 2, 3), average levels (4, 5, 6), and unhealthy levels (7, 8, 9).

Unhealthy Levels

Level 9: This is the lowest and most dangerous level for an adult Four. Typically we are all at this level during infancy. If we fail to rise to higher levels, we experience unhealthy qualities and conditions. For a Type Four, this is where the person feels hopeless, depressed, and highly self-destructive. Some abuse drugs or alcohol to escape, and others have major emotional breakdowns and become suicidal.

Level 8: Although this level is slightly higher than the previous, this Type Four is still stuck in the dark dungeons of their own mind. They are delusional, blameful, highly self-loathing, self-hating, and morbid in their thinking. Everything is tormenting them, and life has no color or beauty. Helping such an individual is challenging, mainly because they try to do everything to drive you away.

Level 7: The Four is a little more productive at this level, but they have difficulty dealing with failure or setbacks. When something goes wrong, they can't handle that sense of shame. It causes them to fall into depression, become alienated from others, and get emotionally paralyzed.

Average Levels

Level 6: At this level, we see a somewhat functional Four, although filled with melancholy, disdain, self-pity, and envy. This Four feels different from others, and they hate seeing others leading a life they presume to be better. While they may wallow in self-pity, they're not really moved to take action to improve what they can't stand about their deficiencies.

Level 5: This Four is moody, hypersensitive, shy, overly self-conscious, and tends to be withdrawn. They are the kind of person that takes every comment, remark, and feedback personally. Emotional outbursts are a common occurrence, and they're not quite in control of their mood swings.

Level 4: At this level, we see a functional individual more capable of being healthy and productive in their world. This Four is artistic, romantic, and obsessed with beauty. They're focused on cultivating an environment around them that's aesthetically beautiful and in tune with their inner fantasies and imagination.

Healthy Levels

Level 3: At this level, the Four is emotionally honest, humane, and true to themselves. They are highly personal and individualistic with a somewhat ironic view of life and themselves.

Level 2: This Type Four is self-aware, introspective, intuitive, gentle, compassionate, and keenly aware of their and other people's emotions. The search for "self" is prominent at this stage of their development, but they do it in healthy, life-giving ways.

Level 1: At this level, the Type Four is at their best. This individual is inspiring to observe, abundantly creative, and they can transform every experience they've ever had into something valuable. They have transcended into their highest expression, and they know their true identity.

ENNEAGRAM FOUR'S PASSION

Type Four's Passion or deadly sin is envy. It typically expresses itself as a sense of lack. Fours have this gnawing feeling that something is missing in them and that others have it, but they were somehow left out. That causes them to look at others we happier, better in some way, and to some extent, even more deserving. Unfortunately, this only creates a sense of inner deficiency, superiority, and inferiority complex.

What the Four needs is equanimity. This is the virtue that will bring much-needed balance, inner peace, wholeness, and healing for the Four. With equanimity, the Four will learn to detach from emotions and stop being controlled by them. They will be grounded in their bodies and recognize that they already have everything they will ever need for a delicious human experience. If you're reading this and realize that you're a Four, this is the work you must do. Bring yourself back to wholeness, back to equanimity.

CHILDHOOD AND EMOTIONAL PATTERNS OF TYPE FOUR

One might wonder, how did the Four develop this belief of lack? Most of the time, it begins in childhood. As children, Fours felt disconnected from both the parental figures in their lives. For some, it was due to extreme reasons like abuse, and for others, it was milder. Regardless of the reasons, Fours felt like their caregivers didn't see them for who they really were.

In many cases, they felt like the advice or comfort offered was too generic and meant for a child totally different from them. This feeling of being unseen and misunderstood within the family unit created a coping mechanism for the Four. They learned to deal with feelings of rejection, isolation, and loneliness by learning to embrace what they felt made them different. More than anything else, a Four just wants to find their identity. As adults, many Fours confess they had fantasies of meeting someone who will really see them for who they are and love them unconditionally– something they've longed for all their lives.

However, to experience that kind of connection requires a certain maturity on the part of the Four, which is why this Enneagram work is vital. The Four must realize that idealizing unconditional love and focusing more on what makes them different isn't beneficial. Instead, they must learn to see where bonds with others can form, which requires conscious effort. The intense, almost uncontrollable emotions that average and unhealthy Fours experience can be trans- formed through self-awareness and self-acceptance. That's also the path to discovering that nothing is missing. You're not flawed, and you can experience the wholeness you've desired your whole life.

To heal the childhood wound, a Four must reconnect with their Higher Self and recognize that they are worthy. They need to embrace positive feedback and learn to disregard the unhelpful negative emotions that often drown them.

SUBTYPES FOR TYPE FOUR

The Enneagram profiling system allows for 3 subtypes in each type. These are Self-Preservation, Social, and One-to-One (Sexual) vari- ants. Remember, all three instinctual variants exist in all of us. Still, the order in which they stack up determines their influence on our lives. One will be most dominant and the easiest for you to resonate with and observe as behavior and thought patterns in your life. The second will feel a little neutral and less influential, and the third will be the least significant. The third instinct becomes a blind spot for many because it's totally underdeveloped and out of their conscious recognition. Depending on which instinct is most dominant, it will shape your unique personality and how you approach life as a Four.

Self Preservation Four (SP)

Tenacity is the distinct quality of this subtype. It's also the counter-type of the Four, so rather than wallow in self-pity, this Four wants to be recognized for being "tough." Even though they are pretty sensitive, they prefer not to complain or share their pain and suffering with others. Instead, they are empathetic and look out for and try to support others. It's easy to mistype this Four as a Type One or Type Seven.

Social Four (SO)

Social Fours are emotionally sensitive and most connected to their suffering. For SO Fours, there's a sense of comfort and familiarity in agony. They enjoy basking in the sweetness of sad poetry and the painful beauty of melancholic music. SO Fours feel everything profoundly and somehow think that their suffering is also what makes them unique and special. Shame is a distinctive quality, and they find comfort in expressing their pain and suffering to others, often attracting support and admiration. The strong emotion of shame triggers plenty of envy and comparison. SO Fours blame themselves for being inadequate and inferior, which only plunges them deeper into shame.

One-to-One/ Sexual Four (SX)

The Sexual Four is intense and has a distinctive quality of competition. They are easy to mistype as an Enneagram Three or an Enneagram Eight because of how demanding, and competitive they tend to be. One-to-One Fours seek to escape their suffering by being the best at what they do and demanding recognition for their work. Surprisingly, these individuals are more shameless than shameful about their personality traits and have no problem getting extremely vocal about their unmet needs. More often than not, the anger or demanding nature of the SX Four is a mask to cover up how sad or confused they really feel.

CHAPTER 12
WORK AND LIFESTYLE TIPS FOR TYPE 4S

A s part of your discovery and transformation, it's essential to recognize your triggers, the areas that you struggle with most, and where your opportunities for growth lie.

STRUGGLES OF AN ENNEAGRAM FOUR

Envy

All Fours struggle with feelings of envy in various shades. It stems from that feeling of being deficient or lacking in some way. The average or unhealthy Four feels wholeness, friendship and ease are forever out of reach.

What to do: Take time to notice what you have and the things you've excelled at. Instead of criticizing yourself or comparing yourself with others, acknowledge and focus on the abundance you've got going and let that expand. Practice gratitude and yes, count your blessings. Where your attention goes, energy will flow.

Feeding creativity with pain

Creativity and originality can only come through great suffering for many average and unhealthy Fours. Many believe that they must experience emotional intensity to produce their best work, so they might seek out anguish and grief to channel their creative works. This can be a tormenting experience, not to mention quite destructive.

What to do: Train yourself to realize that creativity is possible even with positive energy. You don't need to dwell on the negative to be the energy. You don't need to stay on the negative to be the creative genius you were born to be.

Finding people who "see you."

When you spend your whole life feeling misunderstood and different, it translates into a life where you just feel invisible and possess a strong desire to connect with someone who can get on your level when it comes to feelings, struggles, and values. That longing creates a terrible existence, and you deserve and can have better.

What to do: Make an effort to connect with people you trust and form genuine bonds. Believe in your ability to attract love into your life. The more you learn to love yourself, the easier it will be for others to appreciate all the long-ignored parts of you. Still, you need to stop idealizing what such a relationship should look like in your imagination.

ENNEAGRAM TYPE FOUR UNDER STRESS

Enneagram Fours are typically stressed when there's too much external pressure. They hate being micro-managed or being forced to follow many rules and guidelines. When their feelings are ignored or if they can't express their true feelings, Fours tend to isolate and brood over their negative emotions and misfortune.

Fours also can't stand being in an environment where they have to put on a happy face when struggling emotionally. Suppose they're working on something and get a creativity block, or there's a lack of progress on their goals. In that case, they'll quickly fall into stress and land on the path of disintegration.

If you're a Four and stress is mounting, don't wait for things to get out of hand. Instead, find someone you trust and just speak it all out. If there's no one to talk to, journal it. Once you've emptied your mind and heart, remember that while emotions are important, they are not always accurate in life. Bring yourself back to the point of recalling your strengths, talents, and what's working. Be in the present moment and engage in some mindfulness practices. Have a set of sticky notes or reminders on your phone for encouragement during this time.

RELATIONSHIPS

Type Fours are deep, novel, and passionate. When it comes to personal and professional relationships, a Four longs to be mirrored, deeply understood, and affirmed by their partner. They spend a great deal of time thinking about their own identity and who they are in the partnership.

In romantic relationships, Fours usually seek partners who will give them the affirmation, love, and understanding that's been missing in their life.

Fours work hard to make the workplace meaningful and special. A leader who is a Four is often authentic, empathetic, creative, expressive, and aesthetically driven. All Fours long to receive appreciation and recognition for the great works they produce at every level of the organization.

RELATIONSHIP TIPS WITH OTHER TYPES

Here are some ways to improve your relationships with other Enneagram Types.

Type 4 & Type 1: The relationship is deep and meaningful with a Type One. You both have a vision of how the world could be. Even though you are opposite in many ways, your energies complement each other well when operating from healthy levels. Type One helps you create some boundaries and get more focused, and you help your partner relax and loosen up a bit. You encourage them to think outside the box and embrace a little creativity.

The main challenge you might face is the internalized criticism and negative self-talk that plagues you, especially if you're at average or unhealthy levels. Your partner can easily get overwhelmed by your emotions, stirring up resentment because they believe you're being improper. On the other hand, you might start to feel like you're constantly critiqued for being different and expressive, and you might lash out when all the One is doing is trying to help you.Grow together by openly communicating your expectations and prioritizing growing to higher levels of development together.

Type 4 & Type 2: You enjoy a deep, emotionally fulfilling relationship with a Type Two. The Two brings a caring, friendly, and warm energy to the relationship. You care about understanding the depth of your partner's heart which helps them become more in tune with their own feelings. The attention you give your partner is also well received. They can pull you out of your inner world and out into the physical world, where you can make real connections with others.

A significant challenge you might face is a communication breakdown, especially since you expect so much from each other but aren't always good at stating it. There are a lot of assumptions, and sometimes those can create blindspots.

Grow together by affirming each other, being more attentive to each other's actual needs, and explicitly stating what you need in the relationship, so there's no room for misunderstandings.

Type 4 & Type 3: With a Three, you'll have a strong, dynamic, high-energy, sensitive relationship. Communication is often transparent and earnest with a Three. They bring a lot of ambition, practicality, and structure to the relationship, and that's good for you. Your self-doubts and negativity tend to take a back seat when with a Three because they are great at bringing out the best of you and cheering you on. Your creativity and emotional depth are great for the Three because it helps them reflect more, slow down, and find deeper meaning in the world.

A significant challenge you might encounter is your different temperaments and how you individually move through life. Sometimes you don't understand each other. Often, the Three finds you emotionally overwhelming and irrational, and you might consider your partner fake or apathetic. They're always moving fast and chasing after something which, at times, you might consider a distraction and something futile that gets in the way of enjoying the beauty of life.

Grow together by setting realistic expectations for one another and notice when tension arises. If you're feeling emotionally neglected, don't allow it to brew into something terrible. Have an open dialogue and find a way to have the experiences you want.

Type 4 & Type 4: With a Type Four, you're essentially in a mirrored relationship that's romantic, thoughtful, passionate, and profound. It's like sharing your life with someone who has the same longing for meaning, beauty, and understanding. You can talk for hours about your deepest thoughts and get lost in your fantasy worlds. You see how things could be perfect and mourn for what's missing.

The main challenge with this relationship is that you both struggle with the same weaknesses. That means you both get moody, you're highly sensitive to rejection, and you experience criticism as a confirmation that you're fatally flawed.

You can grow together by making lifestyle changes and rising to higher levels of development. Incorporate mindfulness practices, journal daily, and practice gratitude. Find enjoyable and healthy ways to stay active together. Become accountability partners and help each other avoid spiraling into negativity when something goes wrong.

Type 4 & Type 5: With a Five, you're in a stable, complex, and comfortable relationship. The Five is well-reasoned and emotionally present, bringing a lot of objective wisdom, rationality, and thoughtfulness. You enjoy long conversations and love to explore obscure topics of interest. You empower your partner to become more comfortable with their emotional side and self-expression.

The main challenge you face with a Five is that you both live in your own little worlds, so you need to make an effort to stay grounded in reality. You might also struggle with your partner's constant objectivity and detachment, and the Five might find your emotions overwhelming.

Grow together by appreciating the balance you bring each other. Respect each other's needs and find a way to be together while still giving each other the necessary space.

Type 4 & Type 6: With a Six, the relationship is affectionate, sensitive, and comforting. A Six is loyal and practical, and they can persevere a lot where there is trust. You bring a lot of compassion, emotionality, and self-awareness to the relationship. Your longing to go deeper and discover more helps the Six find more of who they are.

The Six's desire for predictability and steadiness can be difficult for you. You might face a challenge when the Six feels like you're going too far or you're too impractical and unrealistic. That can be deeply wounding for you and may cause you to resent or reject your partner.

Grow together by learning to express your truths in ways that don't wound the other. Ask yourself, "Do I need to express this now? Will it be helpful to us?"

Type 4 & Type 7: With a Seven, you're pretty much the opposite, yet it somehow works because you both enjoy thinking outside the box. The Seven sees all the positive and beautiful things you have, boosting your confidence. And you help the Seven stay a little more grounded and get more comfortable with experiencing all kinds of emotions. There's never a dull or stagnant season in this relationship.

One of the main challenges you might face is when conflicts arise. Your partner likes to avoid any negative emotions, and they might even feel stifled by your need for emotional connection all the time. They might even consider you a killjoy who just wants to keep them down.

Grow together by learning to stay present with each other even when you don't agree rather than escaping or internalizing your emotions. You can also benefit from letting go of the past, especially the things that didn't work out.

Type 4 & Type 8: With an Eight, it's a highly intuitive, intense, and passionate relationship. The Eight offers a sense of protection, strength, and practicality that you crave. There's a magnetic pull between you because you're both on a quest to understand or conquer the mystery in the other. Your sensitivity and emotional vulnerability are something the Eight knows they need. They appreciate how intense you can be in your own way.

A challenge you'll face in this relationship is how reactive, intense and explosive your conflicts and disagreements can be. While it might seem okay, this isn't the healthy version of yourself. Neither of you likes to be controlled. You can't stand feeling misunderstood, so there are likely constant fighting and making up cycles.

Grow together by rising to higher levels of development so you can enjoy your magnetic connection without constantly creating a battlefield. Always start every conflict or disagreement with compassion.

Type 4 & Type 9: You have a sensitive, easy-going deep relationship with a nine. The Nine is non-judgmental and offers you a sense of acceptance that enables you to move toward self-love. Your partner keeps your feet on the ground so-to-speak and allows you to dream. Your energy and creativity are inspiring for your partner. It helps them get more in tune with their emotions and reconnect with the world.

A challenge you might face is during conflicts due to your opposite stress responses. Nines disengage during conflicts because keeping the peace is the only thing that matters to them. You might view this as neglect or not being present, making you more emotionally reactive. That can be overwhelming and unsettling for a Nine.

Grow together by learning to be more thoughtful during conflicts and disagreements. Remember how brutal confrontation is for their personality. Think about your words before using them and allow your partner the space to express their words, too but be kind in this approach.

AFFIRMATIONS FOR ENNEAGRAM TYPE 4

Affirmations can be a great tool when you begin replacing your negative thoughts and habits. Learn to become your own cheerlead and direct some of that tender loving care inward by speaking words that uplift and encourage you. Here is a list to help you out.

- I heal from my past.

- I appreciate the present moment
- I see beauty and abundance all around me.
- My life is good, and I am grateful.
- I use my experiences to grow.
- I love and accept myself.
- I am whole and abundant.
- I deserve unconditional love.
- I am willing to see others as equals.
- I release myself from overthinking.
- I am willing to make feeling good a priority.
- I am enough.

Remember affirmations only work when what you say and feel are in synch.

DAILY LIFESTYLE TIPS FOR GROWTH AND HAPPINESS

Practice mindfulness

Incorporate mindfulness into your daily routine by finding activities and techniques that help you connect with the present moment. Mindfulness practices enable you to be more non-judgmental, tolerant, and honest with yourself. Consider experimenting with mindfulness meditation or yoga.

Do some volunteer work

Volunteer work is one of the best ways to give back to your community and help people who need and appreciate your help. By pouring your energy into charity, you're putting your energy into the right places. It will be received with deep gratitude. You'll also experience a strong sense of peace knowing that you're doing something meaningful and purposeful.

Cultivate a positive attitude

Adopting a positive mindset doesn't mean faking it. It means keeping an optimistic outlook on life. Notice your inner dialogue and the lens through which you view life. Is it optimistic or pessimistic most of the time? A positive attitude enables you to attract better people and opportunities into your life. It actually allows you to be more gentle and forgiving of yourself when you make mistakes.

Practice self-discipline

Falling into unhealthy habits is super easy for a Four, but as you've learned in this book, spiraling into negativity is not the best way to uncover your true identity and reconnect with your higher self. So I want to encourage you to practice more self-discipline. Refrain from indulging in unhealthy behavior and thought patterns for your growth. You don't need to stop having fun, but you need to eliminate self-destructive behavior. Make this commitment to yourself, and you'll start to see significant shifts internally.

CHAPTER 13

ENNEAGRAM TYPE 5

THE INVESTIGATOR OR OBSERVER

I t's time to uncover the deep mysteries of the Enneagram Type 5, commonly referred to as the Investigator or Observer. Some also like to use the term "quite specialist," and as you read along, you'll soon discover why all these names fit this personality. Fives belong to the thinking center of intelligence or the "head-based" triad. They are the cerebral type, always going with their head and logic. Type Fives are intense, mentally alert, curious, perceptive, secretive, innovative, and prefer to keep to themselves. They are exceptional at focusing on and developing complex skills and ideas. When operating at healthy levels of development, Fives are visionary pioneers, often ahead of their time. They can see the world and universe in ways the rest of humanity can't. That makes them truly extraordinary.

An essential defining quality of a Five is the deep insatiable desire to understand more of the world or the universe. They thirst for knowledge and truth. Many Fives who aren't yet operating at higher and healthier levels of development tend to struggle with detachment and dealing with human interactions or even the daily societal obligations. This can be highly destructive and unhealthy for them and for those engaged with them because they'll come across as absent-minded, aloof, difficult stingy, and eccentric. That's why it's imperative to keep working on personal growth as a Five.

STRENGTHS OF A FIVE

Fives are independent thinkers with a natural knack for thinking through and problem-solving. While other personality types may struggle to understand a complex problem, fives tend to get excited by it. They love challenges and prefer environments where they are free to do whatever it takes to find solutions to a problem.

In fact, fives get bored and easily fall into destructive habits when things aren't challenging enough. Their innovative and inventive nature typically leads them to follow new unchartered grounds and explore concepts yet unknown to society. Type Fives can continually learn and pick up new skills at incredible speeds. That's why many will often become masters at more than a single subject. Another strong quality of a Five is how cool and composed they are, regardless of external conditions. That's mainly due to their natural inclination to focus on problem-solving rather than the emotional charge of any given situation. Other strengths that Fives leverage to their advantage include some of the following:

- The ability to easily cut through complex intellectual ideas and problems
- Creating excellent boundaries for themselves to protect their time and resources
- Maintaining confidentiality and trustworthiness
- Respecting other people's boundaries and space

Key personality traits for a Five

- Curiosity
- Perceptive
- Calm
- Objective and emotionally composed in a crisis
- Insightfulness
- Autonomous and fully independent
- Thoughtful
- Trustworthy
- Often introverted
- Extremely knowledgeable on specific subjects of interests

Common hobbies for a Five

- Working with computers
- Playing board games
- Learning new trivia
- Reading non-fiction
- Participating in solo sports

FEARS AND WEAKNESSES

By now, it's evident that one of the distinguishing expressions of Type Five is the quest for knowledge, truth, and understanding of their world. Fives value time as their most precious resource because it's the one thing they need (that's limited) to achieve their goals. That means they care about doing everything possible to materialize this desire, which indicates that one of their biggest fears is their lack of attainment. For many Fives, anyone or anything that threatens this resource is something they avoid altogether. They easily get overwhelmed when others demand too much from them. Even their own needs can become overwhelming if they feel it's draining too much of their precious resource. Fives tend to withdraw from relationships and maintain a minimalistic lifestyle to focus solely on their intellect and escape worldly demands as a way to cope with this fear.

What's the Basic Fear driving this behavior? The fear of being incompetent, incapable, ignorant, and useless.

Fives get their strength and earn respect for their knowledge and the objective perspectives they offer. In the absence of this, Fives believe they wouldn't get the respect due to them. The fear of being ignorant, helpless, and having their privacy invaded is poignant for a Five. It often expresses itself as withdrawal from people, environments, or situations that conflict with their desires. When some worldly issue demands their attention, they'll try to put them off and deflect those needs and desires as long as possible. In other cases, a Five will get really angry if they are interrupted or pulled from their inner thinking or work. When a demand is made, the first impulse for a Five is to analyze and dissect it as much as possible, aka overthinking. It works when dealing with big problems, but it creates analysis paralysis for everyday stuff.

Depending on their level of development, some of the weaknesses a Type Five might experience include being disconnected from their own feelings, struggling to relate to other people's emotions, and coming off as condescending when interacting with others.

DESIRES AND MOTIVATIONS

The basic desire for a Type Five is to be competent, knowledgeable, and capable. Fives are motivated by the need to possess understanding and knowledge, figure things out and find objective truth. That's why Fives will feel energized and invigorated when learning something new. It can be a new skill, concept, or anything else they haven't learned before. The more challenging it is, the better. They are also happiest when they're discovering something new and when they are by themselves, thinking and reconnecting with their own minds. Of all the Enneagram Types, Fives are the most introverted and analytical. They find great joy in focusing all their energy inward and pursuing knowledge instead of relationships like most other personality types. Because they allocate such little energy toward external demands, Fives take great care to conserve their energy for the things that matter. While that makes relationships with others challenging, the few people they do let in get to experience the richness, stability, and companionship this personality type brings. The Fives also appreciate receiving praise and validation from the few they bring into their world.

CORE VALUES

- Freedom and self-sufficiency
- Knowledge and understanding
- Competency and productivity
- Reputation
- Respect
- Prestige
- Success, achievement, and accomplishment
- Acknowledgment and recognition

Type Five celebrities and famous people you might know to include Billionaire and Microsoft founder Bill Gates, Celebrated scientist and Nobel Prize Winner Albert Einstein, Poet Emily Dickenson, Theoretical Physicist Stephen Hawking, Retired German Politician, and Scientist Angela Merkel, Arthur Stephen King, Geologist, and Biologist Charles Darwin and Dutch Painter Vincent van Gogh.

Wondering if you could be a Type 5? Here are some personality indicators

1. You hate small talk.

2. You see the world and people as things to be gradually understood and won't stop learning until you do.

3. People often underestimate how intense your feelings are since you always seem so calm.

4. You don't open up to people often, but you're fiercely loyal and supportive when you do.

5. You love observing and taking note of every detail in your surroundings.

6. Being self-sufficient and autonomous are non-negotiables in life.

7. Emotions are seldom felt in public and will only be adequately explored in the privacy of your own home. And if it happens in front of someone, you really trust them.

8. You come up with theories about basically everything.

9. You enjoy imagining yourself in the fortress of your own mind, watching your 'avatar' interact with humans.

10. Although life can seem too infinite to truly understand, you know that ultimately, the unexamined life is one not worth loving. And people love you for it.

YOUR WINGS

Wings are the numbers adjacent to your Enneagram Type. As a Five, you have-

- The Enneagram Five with Four Wing: "The Iconoclast"
- The Enneagram Five with Six Wing: "The Problem Solver"

While you may have tendencies that lean into both wings at various stages of your life, you'll likely be more dominant in one than the other. This will be your most influential and Dominant Wing.

Meaning of your Wing

If you're a 5w4 (Five with Four-Wing), you're more of a philosopher who possesses unique beliefs. Your beliefs help you break down your surrounding and societal views. You like to defy the norms, and through the knowledge, you're on a quest to confront the conventional ways. A true innovator at heart, darkness is alluring to you. The unknown is where you enjoy exploring the most, and societal taboos and boundaries mean nothing to you. In fact, half the time, you don't even get why people limit themselves to what's known. Along with your love for dark, hidden, and the unknown sciences, you tend to be more artistic than a classic Five with a Six Wing.

As Five with a Four Wing, you're more in touch with your emotions, giving you more depth than a classic Five, enabling you to be sensitive, reflective, and highly creative. You have the perfect combination of intuition and knowledge when operating at healthy levels. At unhealthy levels, however, the combination of the overly sensitive aspects of the Four Wing and the analytical, detached mind of the Five can lead to a lot of isolation, self-hatred, and contempt for others.

Common career types that best suit a 5w4 include:

- Inventor
- Professor
- Writer
- Artist
- Composer
- Entrepreneur
- Engineering

If you're a 5w6 (Five with a Six-Wing), you're more a troubleshooter than a philosopher. You tend to be more practical disciplined, and organized. Your greatest gift is your ability to use your mind, and you are a little more social than the 5w4. Still, you struggle tremendously with tuning into your feelings or handling stress. You are very observant of the world around you but not particularly introspective. Having the influence of the Six Wing means you can use your analytical mind on practical things that ensure the world will be easier to navigate, more predictable, and maybe even a little safer.

Common career types that best suit a 5w6 include:

- Computer programming
- Accounting
- Law enforcement
- Mathematics
- Engineering

Arrows and what they mean

Your Enneagram personality type is linked to two other "lines" or points worth noting. These lines are called arrows, and each indicates how you show up at your best and worst. One arrow called the Arrow of Disintegration shows the lines of stress (your path of destruction), and for you, that path lies in number 7. As you disintegrate, you pick up the unhealthy habits of an Enneagram Seven and become more scattered, detached, and hyperactive. We'll talk more about stress and how to avoid falling into disintegration in the next chapter.

The other line connected to your Enneagram type is 8, the Arrow of integration. That means that moving on the path of growth and integration, you take on healthy traits from an Eight that make you decisive and more self-confident like a healthy Eight. To understand the relationship between these arrows and how we fall into unhealthy patterns or rise into healthy ones, let's discuss the nine levels of development. The goal is to identify where you might be and move toward the highest level, i.e., healthy level 1.

THE 9 LEVELS OF DEVELOPMENT, FROM LOWEST TO HIGHEST

Levels of Development arise from Riso and Hudson's teachings and the founders of the Enneagram Institute, which is a great place to take your Enneagram Test. Their theory posits that all individuals fall into one of nine levels of functioning. The lowest level is nine, and the highest is level one. The levels are divided into a triad that subcategorizes these levels as healthy (1, 2, 3), average levels (4, 5, 6), and unhealthy levels (7, 8, 9).

Unhealthy

Level 9: As the lowest and darkest level for a Five, we see a deranged, self-destructive adult if they are still stuck at this level. The person is suicidal with psychotic breakdowns, and all they see is oblivion. That's because level Nine is where we begin as infants. For a Five, growing into an adult while stuck at this level of inner growth proves absolutely detrimental for themselves and those around them.

Level 8: At this level, the unhealthy Five is obsessed yet frightened by their own ideas. They are extremely phobic about everything and prey to gross distortions. Everything scares them, and they are pretty hysterical.

Level 7: At this level, the Five is still highly unstable and fearful of aggression. They are nihilistic and eccentric and feel repulsed by others and all social attachments. This person does everything possible to avoid reality.

Average

Level 6: The rise to average levels means that now we're dealing with a person who is cynical, argumentative, radical in their views, and abrasive. They prioritize their inner world and personal vision above all else and can turn pretty antagonistic toward anything that interferes.

Level 5: At this level, we encounter a detached Five who is more preoccupied with their visions and interpretations rather than reality. They are high-strung-intense and still pretty disconnected from the world. Their fascination is more with off-beat esoteric subjects.

Level 4: At this level, the Five is more intellectual and studious and invests a lot of time in model building, preparing, practicing, and gathering more resources. This type of Five loves conceptualizing and fine-tuning things before taking action.

Healthy

Level 3: The rise to this level sees the Five attain skillful mastery of whatever interests them. This individual is excited by knowledge and the quest for truth and understanding. They tend to become an expert in some fields. The Five is inventive, innovative, highly productive, independent, idiosyncratic, and even a little whimsical.

Level 2: At this level, the Five is extraordinarily perceptive and possesses excellent insight. They spend much of their time observing everything and noticing even the tiniest details. Their ability to focus and the insatiable curiosity that engulfs their personality are remarkable.

Level 1: This is the holy grail for a Five, and at this level, we reach the highest and best version of this individual's expression. This Type Five is a visionary. They are open-minded and pioneer discoveries finding entirely new ways of doing and perceiving things.

TYPE FIVE'S PASSION

Fives feel they lack enough inner resources to invest in others, especially for social interaction. They think too much interaction will lead to catastrophic depletion, leading them to withhold themselves from contact with the world. In the Enneagram teaching, this Passion or ego impoverishment is called avarice, although some prefer greed. It simply means that Fives have an insatiable desire for gain or wealth. For a Five, their internal resources and time are the most precious resources they possess if they want to accomplish all their big goals. Unfortunately, too much hoarding of resources and energy out of fear shuts down the heart. It makes it impossible for the Five to receive or give.

What is needed is for the Five to grow and activate the virtue of non-attachment. When this occurs, the Five will become more in sync with the flow of life. They will realize there's no need to hoard anything because life is abundant. There is always enough time, knowledge, energy, and everything they need to complete their mission. The Five will finally be free from the fear that hardens their heart, making them more open-hearted and generous.

CHILDHOOD AND EMOTIONAL PATTERNS OF TYPE FIVE

Fives grew up in an environment that made them feel ambivalent toward their parents. They felt that there was little they did that was wanted or needed by the family. For one reason or another, the Five always felt like an "outsider" looking in rather than nurtured and accepted as one of the group. Sometimes that was because they had abusive or alcoholic parents. Other times, they were the unfavored child, so they felt like the odd duck. In other situations, it could just be that they didn't feel understood or picked up on clues that made them feel a particular way, even if their parents didn't intend it. For instance, certain Fives wanted to feel equal to their parents, so they turned to learning and using their problem-solving skills to master their environments.

Whatever the case, Fives felt they were "odd," so they retreated from the outside world and their families to cope with this loneliness. They spent most of their time hiding in their rooms, looking for a subject they could master or an area of expertise that would allow them to find their place in their family or society. But they always looked for something unique to themselves. So if their siblings were learning to play piano, they would learn to play the cello. They also learned there's a lot of safety, stability, and comfort in being lost in their own mind.

Growing up, Fives become good at expressing either verbally or non-verbally how much they value independence. "Don't ask too much of me, and I won't ask too much of you." Even as adults, Fives hate intrusion, and close physical affection can feel overwhelming and bothersome. They also don't like getting overwhelmed by the thoughts and emotions they experience while spending too much time around people. Thus, even those interested in the people around them prefer to watch and observe from a distance to process their behaviors and understand more about them.

Whether at school or work, Fives need as much time as possible to themselves to devote to mastering their subjects of interest. They are more in their head and identify mainly with their thoughts than emotions.

Average to unhealthy levels, Fives believe that shutting others out and having little to no interaction with the world will lead to happiness.

To heal the childhood wound, the Five must reconnect with their Higher Self and recognize that abundance is the only truth. They need to engage in activities that encourage the mind-body-spirit connection.

SUBTYPES FOR TYPE FIVE

Self-Preservation Five (SP)

SP Five is called "Castle Defender" because this individual is highly protective of their home, personal space, and privacy. This Five has clear and strong boundaries and enjoys living a relatively solitary life with just a few close friends. This Five prefers to observe social life than participate in it. SP Fives are the classic introverts, preferring to reveal very little about their inner world.

Social Five (SO)

SO Five is called "the Professor" and is characterized by a deep insatiable thirst for knowledge and wisdom. This Five loves focusing on big questions, mastering languages and secret symbols of a society or group. A social Five does enjoy connecting with small groups and experts who share their brilliance and high ideal. Still, they are often disconnected from everyday issues and emotions. This Five is more than happy and enthusiastic about sharing values, ideas, and ideals, but they're not too keen on sharing space, time, or inner resources. They also run the risk of being driven by over analysis and over-thinking.

Sexual One-to-One Five (SX)

SX Five is called the "Secret Agent" or "Confidant." This one's also the countertype of the group—some of their expressed behavior might come across as counterintuitive for a Five. This individual is cool, analytical, and passionate. Their passion, however, is limited to their life goals and one or two people in an otherwise reserved life. Once they experience "chemistry" with another person, they enjoy the connection, trust, and openness that the relationship fosters. SX Fives risk becoming dependent on the other for that feeling of aliveness and vibrancy, which can lead them to resist sharing that person with others.

WORK AND LIFESTYLE TIPS FOR TYPE 5S

I n this chapter, we'll go over the struggles and stresses that a Type Five may encounter. We'll also cover some strategies to reduce or eliminate stress, and tips for relationship and personal success.

STRUGGLES OF AN ENNEAGRAM FIVE

Emotional unavailability

As a Type Five, you prioritize privacy over everything else. You also know how to disconnect from emotions in real-time. These qualities make it extra challenging to form bonds or experience intimacy in any kind of relationship.

What to do: While you don't need to open up and let in everyone, make an effort to "let in" the few you choose to be in a relationship with. Explore your emotions more openly and at the moment as you feel them, especially when you're with the person you love.

Distractions

All Fives at any level can relate to this because all hate to be interrupted by the outside world. Dealing with the noise of the outside world is often overwhelming and unpleasant. You'd rather pursue ideas and theories in a quiet, safe space void of interruptions, obligations, and people. You need time to tinker with ideas, inventions, art, or other explorations.

What to do: It's okay to protect your space, but I also encourage you to make room for the people you trust. Instead of seeing all people and activities as distractions, see them as investments. Choose the people you will invest in and some activities that you both enjoy, then include that into your strategy as you plan out your life.

Grappling with meaningless purposeless activities

One of the biggest struggles an average and unhealthy Five will experience is a sense of purposelessness and meaninglessness in life. That is especially the case if they allow themselves to turn pessimistic and cynical about the world, people, and the universe. It's hard to see good in the universe when everything around you feels random and absurd.

A Five will have this experience if they don't find an area of mastery and consuming interest, turning them into agitated, stressed-out individuals.

What to do: Find your purpose and bring meaning to everything you do. Pick an area of mastery and keep exploring.

Not having their alone time-respected

As a Five, you're more likely introverted, which means you prefer to be alone more than most people. You also hate small talk and people who barge into your life unannounced. Most people overwhelm you, and it's easy to get overstimulated and irritated when people hijack your time with chatter and socialization.

What to do: Detach healthily. That means you need to carve out time for socialization while still leaving yourself solid unstructured time to just be with yourself daily. Communicate this to your friends and loved ones so they can refrain from barging in and crossing over your boundaries.

Feeling misunderstood

It's common for most Fives to feel misunderstood by family and people in general. Your deep insatiable desire for mastery and competency isn't something many will get. At average and unhealthy levels, this feeling can take a downswing and cause you to feel like what you want to attain is always out of reach.

What to do: If you find yourself feeling that way, work on your inner game so that it doesn't become a weakness that leads you down the path of disintegration.

Facing their darkness and being haunted by it

As a Five, you might notice a peculiar attraction to the darker aspects of life. At healthy levels, this isn't much of a struggle; at average and unhealthy levels, it can turn into an uncontrollable obsession. Some Fives spend a lot of time thinking about the stuff they find most frightening. They might even make a career out of it by studying or creating works of art out of things that scare them.

What to do: While learning how to control and override your fear is a good thing, there is a better and healthier way to deal with the dark side. The higher up your development you go, the easier it will be to face your fears and the dark side healthily.

STRESS AND OPPORTUNITIES FOR GROWTH

Fives often spiral down into unhealthy thinking and behavior patterns when stress mounts. If they're unable to connect with their inner world, a lack of clarity kicks in, causing them to be hazy. When this is left unchecked, the Five will develop traits of an unhealthy Seven. They might behave recklessly, become impulsive and find unhealthy ways to distract them from their stress as a way to shut down "thinking."

What stresses out a Five?

- Feeling like life is meaningless and without purpose
- Physical malnutrition and neglect
- Not finding an area of expertise to master
- Feeling incompetent or incapable
- Becoming dependent on others
- Having their time or privacy invaded
- Extreme isolation and lack of connection
- Not getting enough alone time

Opportunities for growth and ways to avoid disintegration

- Engage in activities that enable you to reconnect with your body and your emotions. Experiment with yoga, playing an instrument, creative writing, or whatever idea excites you as long as it engages your emotions and brings you close to understanding your physical and emotional side.
- Prioritize time outside connecting with nature or make some time for socializing with others.
- Read books and watch videos on emotional intelligence, then find a few people to practice these skills with.
- Prioritize your health by developing a healthy eating lifestyle and regularly working out.

RELATIONSHIPS

As a Five, you take a more intellectual and objective approach to everything. In relationships, that curious, investigative and independent nature is attractive, but it can also create problems if you're not making an effort to express intimacy and open up with loved ones.

RELATIONSHIP TIPS WITH OTHER TYPES

Type 5 & Type 1: With a One, you're in a stable, dependable relationship where each partner respects boundaries and structure. The One brings curiosity, independence, hard work, high standards, ethics, and mutual interests. You bring that sense of self-sufficiency, independence, steadiness, and a judgment-free environment that gives your partner great comfort.

A challenge you might encounter in this relationship comes down to values. Ones believe in objectivity, but they hold fast to their convictions once they find the truth. On the other hand, you are very open-minded and flexible, so your truths can evolve as you learn more. This "rigidity" with your partner is often frustrating, and you tend to appear "unpredictable." Your partner's constant advice and help can also feel more like criticism because you're sensitive to feedback, which might cause you to withdraw. However, that only makes the Type One feel insecure about the relationship. Grow together by appreciating differing perspectives and validating each other's viewpoints. You should also remind each other frequently that you're there for each other, especially when you don't see eye to eye.

Type 5 & Type 2: With a Two, you're in a loyal, nurturing, warm and comfortable relationship. The Two brings your feelings to the foreground and enables you to be more grounded in the present moment. Your commitment, trustworthiness, wisdom, and competence are highly desirable for a Two. Remembering even the tiniest details about your partner makes them feel special and loved.

A challenge you might find with your partner is your emotional temperament and how you respond to stress and conflict. Twos are naturally passionate and expressive, while you are always calm and rational. This might leave your partner feeling like you're disengaged and detached. On the other hand, you might feel overwhelmed by all that emotion or as though your partner is too intrusive. It's essential to work through these differences and find healthy ways to deal with stress and misunderstandings. Grow together by recognizing that your needs are not at odds despite your differences. Remind your partner that you're not abandoning or rejecting them when you seem detached.

Type 5 & Type 3: With a Three, the relationship is dynamic, full of energy, stable, and filled with creativity. Your partner brings confidence, high energy, and sociability, and you admire their expertise and accomplishments. The Three admires your creativity, depth, objectivity, and thoughtfulness. You stabilize your partner, and they help take you out of your shell.

A challenge you might encounter is how you both move through life. Threes are fast and tend to think on their feet. You're more steady and prefer to conserve your energy. That can sometimes brew frustration, creating a tug-of-war as you pull in opposite directions. Grow together by getting in touch with your feelings and openly communicating expectations. Choose to learn from each other and leverage each other's strengths.

Type 5 & Type 4: With a Four, the relationship is deep, meaningful, and full of new explorations. You both enjoy indulging in lengthy conversations on topics of interest. The Four is emotionally present and imaginative and enables you to become more comfortable with your emotions and self-expression. You help the Four become more rational and thoughtful about their ideas and actions. It helps to keep your partner grounded and stable.

A common challenge occurs when the Four become frustrated with your detachment and objectivity. They might feel that you're not present or understanding of their emotions. You might become overwhelmed by the emotions of a Four, especially when they fall into average or unhealthy levels. Grow together by respecting and openly communicating each other's needs.

Type 5 & Type 5: With a fellow Type Five, the relationship is stable, founded on a deep respect for each other's privacy, and enriched by the thirst you both have for knowledge. Having a partner who truly gets you and values the same things you value can be extremely comforting.

A challenge you will face in this relationship is how you both withdraw when things get challenging. Because you both love space and privacy, you can easily get complacent, and things may just naturally fall apart due to mutual neglect. Although you deal with conflict calmly, objectively, and rationally, it might be tough to have an emotional connection and, in turn, real intimacy. Grow together by reaching out and connecting emotionally at a human level. It's okay to exert some social and emotional energy, so put a little more effort into this.

Type 5 & Type 6: With a Six, you have a balanced, secure relationship that allows both of you to be yourselves without the fear of getting overwhelmed. The Six brings thoughtfulness, loyalty, and attentiveness. They enjoy how careful and thoughtful you are with your words, actions, and approach to life. Your partner enables you to stay more connected and become less isolated.

A challenge you might face with this relationship might be how you approach problems and situations. The Six trusts in rules and procedures more than their own thoughts, and you are an out-of-the-box thinker who only trusts in your own intellect. That can create a lot of frustration for both of you. So, grow together by embracing each other's differences and dedicate time each week to do something you both enjoy and like to learn about. Practice working through little differences often so that, when big issues show up, you can move through those without picking each other apart.

Type 5 & Type 7: With a Seven as your partner, life is an exciting adventure with more to discover daily. Your relationship is whimsical, and there's never a dull moment. The Seven brings spontaneity, freshness, and even a little bit of a rebellious streak. You enjoy having someone bursting with curiosity to explore the world together. You also help your partner become a little more grounded and serious in their pursuits.

You may encounter a challenge with this relationship when you're both stressed. When stress hits, you withdraw and choose to conserve your energy by becoming undemanding and focusing on things that matter. Your partner goes in the opposite direction and becomes more demanding, expending more energy and chasing yet another new thing. That can lead to significant misunderstandings. Grow together by having an open dialogue about how you'll manage stressful situations together and incorporate both your strengths.

Type 5 & Type 8: With an Eight as a partner, you find something you need in them and vice versa. Your partner helps you become more in tune with your intuition and power. They get you focused on being more practical and tending to your needs. You help the Eight become more aware of their impact on others and the importance of slowing down every now and then. The relationship is deep, self-assured, loyal, and rich with thought-provoking conversation.

A challenge you might encounter regularly is what happens when that good debate becomes too intense or what happens when conflict arises. You both hate being anything but self-reliant. Vulnerability doesn't come easy, so there's a natural tendency for communication and connection to break down. Grow together by making an effort to ensure you don't drive a wedge between you. Work on finding a deep emotional connection and admit your own needs. Be vulnerable together and protect that safe space.

Type 5 & Type 9: With a Nine as your partner, the relationship is comforting and stable, and they just accept you as you are for all that you are. Your partner brings ease, kindness, and patience into the relationship, and you enable the Nine to reconnect with their inner childlike curiosity. The relationship allows for self-awareness, peace, and autonomy.

A challenge you might encounter is that your partner may become passive-aggressive and stubborn when conflicts arise. Your rational and objective approach tends to make your partner feel distanced. Still, because they prefer to avoid conflicts at all costs, they might not say anything, which may create resentment. Grow together by keeping an open dialogue at all times, especially during disagreements. Give each other time and space to process your thoughts and feelings but always have the conversation to air things out. You should also find ways to stay grounded and present by doing something you enjoy.

AFFIRMATIONS FOR ENNEAGRAM TYPE 5

- I am present and mindful
- I make peace with uncertainty
- My life has great meaning and purpose, and I am living it
- I support others lovingly
- I feel secure knowing what is needed, and I trust that I will receive what I need
- I practice being in flow and tapping into the generosity of the universe because life is abundant

Remember affirmations only work is what you say, and feel are in alignment.

DAILY LIFESTYLE TIPS FOR GROWTH AND HAPPINESS

Find your purpose. This won't happen instantly, but with a bit of self-discovery, you can uncover the purpose that lights up your life.

Practice mindfulness daily

Find a practice that resonates with you. Think of this as an exploration or an experiment and test yoga, meditation, pilates, journaling, gratitude, or simply taking long walks daily. Whatever enables you to come into the present moment and reconnect mind-body-spirit is what you need for growth and happiness.

Make time to tune into your emotions

This one will feel like a challenge at first because it's easy to shelf emotions or not deal with them, so here are two ways you can work on this. The first is to journal how you feel at the end of each day. The second is to pause when you experience that emotion and then do the STOP method. STOP means: **S**top; **T**ake three deep breaths; **O**bserve your breath and your body; **P**roceed from this new calm state. As you observe your body, notice the emotion and how you're experiencing it, then just release it. Allow it to flow like water flowing downstream.

Make time for the relationships that matter to you. And if you don't have any relationship, it's time to allow one into your life. I'm not saying you meet the world, but I am encouraging you to reach out to someone you feel you can trust and allow that bond to form over time.

ENNEAGRAM TYPE 6

THE LOYALIST OR SKEPTIC

T he loyalist, sometimes referred to as the skeptic, is one of the more interesting paradigms in the Enneagram teachings. They tend to be complex and intriguing. It's often easy to mistype them for other personality types because of their character complexities. Loyalists are witty, practical, and always think about everything that could go wrong in any given situation. The title skeptic is quite apt because this personality type has serious trust issues and constantly doubts everything, including their own thoughts. They have difficulty trusting anyone, so they always need reassurance from the few they deem authoritative. Inherent in their personality is a tendency to be anxious and nervous about everything. But I suppose that makes sense given their need to consider worst-case scenarios at every new turn.

Loyalists belong to the head triad of thinking center alongside Fives and Sevens. They need to feel safe and attempt to do so through meaningful relationships. Safety and security are of primary importance to Sixes, so most of their decisions are rooted in the need to be in a safe space with people they can trust.

STRENGTHS OF A SIX

Loyalists are inquisitive and always curious to learn new things. They're great problem solvers and highly perceptive. Sixes tend to be great strategic thinkers. They are organized and well-liked because they have a certain warmth to them.

Another strength of a Six is their trustworthiness and the warmth they bring to their relationships.

Key personality traits for a Six

- Committed
- Problem solver
- Trustworthy
- Responsible
- Detail-oriented and precise
- Excellent team player

Common hobbies for a Type Six

- Volunteering
- Writing fiction
- Reading
- List-making
- Listening to music

FEARS AND WEAKNESSES

Sixes fear that things will go wrong in their life. No matter where they are or what's happening, Sixes want security so bad and fear not having the support and guidance they need to the point where they trust no one. On the one hand, they crave safety, support, and reassurance, but on the other, they don't trust anyone, including themselves, to provide it when it matters. So they're constantly seeking to close this gap by looking for some external authoritative power.

What's the Basic Fear driving this behavior? The fear of being unsupported and lacking proper guidance.

This fear shows in behavior as constant anxiety and overplanning to prepare for the worst. The brain of a Six is on constant overdrive, ever thinking and rethinking plans to find all possible solutions.

DESIRES AND MOTIVATIONS

The primary desire of a Six is to be supported and feel secure. That's why loyalists surround themselves with people they feel will support them unconditionally. In turn, the Six is also extremely loyal and trustworthy. While it may seem a little needy because they need constant reassurance and support, the Sixes make wonderful friends and companions.

Core values

- Commitment
- Trust
- Security
- Reliability

Type Six celebrities and famous people you might know include author Mark Twain, Actress and model Marylin Monroe, Director and producer Woody Allen, Actress Jennifer Aniston, Actress Julia Roberts, Comedian Ellen Degeneres, Actor Tom Hanks, and former U.S. Presidents George H.W. Bush and Richard Nixon.

Wondering if you could be a Type Six? Here are some personality indicators:

1. You need a lot of reassurance with almost everything you do.
2. You're critical of yourself because you constantly worry you've let others down.
3. You hang on to relationships/friendships for much longer than you should.
4. Decision making is a daunting task because you see an infinite number of options.
5. You fear being abandoned by others and left alone.
6. You thrive on stability and predictability.
7. You're good at deciphering between logic and emotion.

YOUR WINGS

Wings are the number adjacent to your Enneagram Type. As a Six, you have -

- The Enneagram Six with Five-Wing: "The Defender"
- The Enneagram Six with Seven Wing: "The Buddy"

While you may have tendencies that lean into both wings at various stages of your life, you'll likely be more dominant in one than the other. This will be your most influential and dominant Wing.

Meaning of your Wing

If you're a 6w5 (Six with a Five-Wing), you're more independent, analytical, and more interested in pursuing solitary hobbies than communal ones. Sixes with this Wing find they have a greater need for time alone whether they can concentrate on the things they need to solve, whether personal or professional. They like to work in fixed systems like academics or analytical jobs where the rules are well established, and a predictable path is clearly outlined.

As a 6w5, you're also great at taking care of your family and serving others, doing things the right way, and ensuring those loyal to you are happy.

You're incredibly reliable, responsible, intellectual, and excellent at problem-solving. Careers best suited to you include but aren't limited to:

- Banker
- Web developer
- Paralegal
- Professor
- Business consultant
- Financial analyst

If you're a 6w7 (Six with a Seven-Wing), you're much more extroverted and playful than the Six with a Five-Wing. The influence of the Seven Wing enables you to be more easy-going and adventurous. You're willing to take on a bit more risk, and you're not afraid to fail and make mistakes as you grow. Although you're still cautious, you tend to approach the world more light-heartedly. Sixes with this Wing are more empathetic and connected to others. There's a strong desire to create bonds and relationships they can depend on, making their relationships enriching and dynamic. Unfortunately, this makes them less independent than the 6w5; however, this social need only increases their self-confidence and fuels their energy at healthy levels.

You're energetic, a great team player, and quite social at work. Careers best suited to you include but aren't limited to:

- New anchor
- Real estate agent
- Professor
- Nurse

- Actor
- Author
- Sales representative

The Arrows and what they mean

Your Enneagram personality type is linked to lines or arrows that show the path of growth or disintegration depending on where you are in life. When moving on a path of disintegration, a Six will fall into the negative trappings of the arrow Three (3), and they'll become competitive and arrogant. This is known as the Direction of Stress or the Direction of Disintegration and typically occurs in the face of pressure or surmounting stress. The other arrow indicates how a healthy version of your personality reacts and grows in more healthy environments. In this case, a Six develops more of the healthier qualities of the arrow Nine(9), becoming more relaxed and optimistic. To understand the concept behind healthy and unhealthy levels, let's go over the various levels of development for a Six.

THE 9 LEVELS OF DEVELOPMENT, FROM LOWEST TO HIGHEST

Levels of Development arise from Riso and Hudson's teachings and the founders of the Enneagram Institute, which is a great place to take your Enneagram Test. Their theory posits that all individuals fall into one of nine levels of functioning. The lowest level is nine, and the highest is level one. The levels are divided into a triad that subcategorizes these levels as healthy (1,2,3), average levels (4,5,6), and unhealthy levels (7,8,9).

Unhealthy

Level 9: This is the most dangerous level for any human being. It's rock bottom for a Six, especially if they are adults going through life at this level. The adult Six at this level is hysterical, self-destructive, and seeks any means (even suicide) to escape punishment. They tend to cope by turning to alcoholism and drug abuse.

Level 8: Still pretty unhealthy, this Six is violent, fearful, and completely irrational. They feel persecuted and that others are out to get them. Unfortunately, they're stuck in a self-manufactured torture cycle where what they fear becomes their experience.

Level 7: The Six are fearful about their safety and security at this level. They are panicky, volatile, and feel powerless. Such a person typically seeks out a stronger authority or belief to act as their safety net. They also criticize everyone who isn't part of their safe zone.

Average

Level 6: As the Six rises to average levels of operations, we see the person compensating for the internal turmoil and insecurities. They blame everyone for their problems and mistrust everything and everyone except those they look up to for security. This person may come across as authoritarian while being fearful of authority, and they often use fear to silence others.

Level 5: At this level, the person is indecisive, cautious, ambivalent, anxious, and tends to give mixed signals. The internal confusion makes them react unpredictably.

Level 4: This Six invests all their time and energy into whatever they believe will keep them safe and create stability in their life. At this level, the Six is constantly overthinking and overanalyzing every-thing. They are more organized and structured. They anticipate problems at every turn and find comfort in their alliances.

Healthy

Level 3: This is the beginning of the journey to the highest and best version of an Enneagram Six. This individual is a community builder. They are responsible, reliable, trustworthy, and hardworking and invest their energy doing work that helps others.

Level 2: At this level, the Six can inspire others and makes a great leader. They are affectionate, lovable, and form strong bonds with others.

Level 1: This is the highest and best level for a Six. The individual is self-affirming, independent yet symbiotically interdependent, and cooperative at this level. They have great courage, optimism, and love for serving others—a true inspiration for everyone in their world.

ENNEAGRAM SIX'S PASSION

The Six's Passion of deadly sin is Angst or anxiety. It typically expresses itself as the subconscious need to protect yourself from everything happening around you. Sixes tend to spin out of control mentally as they worry about everything that could go wrong.

What the Six needs is courage. This is the virtue that will bring back your power and reassurance that you can handle life and whatever challenges lie ahead. It will enable you to see that the only absolute security you can have is the one you create for yourself and that power exists within you.

If you're reading this and recognize that you're a Six, this is the work you must do. Bring yourself back to wholeness, back to courage.

CHILDHOOD AND EMOTIONAL PATTERNS FOR ENNEAGRAM SIX

You might be wondering how the Six developed this anxiety and where the ego fixation came from. As children, Sixes felt their environment was too unpredictable and dangerous. Even though they had a protective figure, the protection they received also experienced constant threats for whatever reason. That could be because the protector was abusive at times, or maybe they struggled with addiction or mental health issues, making them highly volatile. It could also be that the protector was too strict with illogical and over-the-top punishment whenever the child made a mistake. Regardless of the root cause, the child learned to depend on protection from the caregiver, who at times betrayed the very essence of security that the child believed in. That caused the child to develop the habit of constant analysis to prepare for any unpleasant situations. It also conditioned the child to view themselves as powerless.

In adulthood, this conditioning leads to an adult who constantly seeks that exact protective and authoritative figure because they aren't used to being their own source of security. At the same time, they tend to be skeptical of everything and everyone - always hoping for the best but expecting the worst.

Sixes feel separated from their internal guidance. They are plagued by the need to find the right course of action and be around their "people," making them very divisive. The constant doubt and anxiety are detrimental to their success in life and can only be eliminated through growth and inner work.

To heal the childhood wound, a Six must walk the path of self-empowerment and self-love. They need to learn to depend on the safety and security of their Higher Self instead of relying on others.

SUBTYPES FOR ENNEAGRAM TYPE SIX

The Enneagram profiling system allows for three subtypes in each type. These are Self-Preservation, Social, and One-to-One (Sexual) variants. Remember, all three instinctual variants exist in all of us, but the order in which they stack up determines their influence on our lives. One will be most dominant and the easiest for you to resonate with and observe as behavior and thought patterns in your life. The second will feel a little neutral and less influential, and the third will be the least significant. The third instinct becomes a blind spot for many because it's underdeveloped and out of their conscious recognition. Depending on which instinct is most dominant, it will shape your unique personality and how you approach life as a Six.

Self Preservation Six (SP)

For this subtype, warmth is the essential quality that stands out. Although they are the most fearful and insecure of the subtypes, SP Sixes are also warm-hearted in their interactions with others. They repress their anger and tend to be overly cautious with everything because they never want to make mistakes or disappoint others. They focus on building strong familial alliances as a coping mechanism to create a strong fort for themselves and those they love.

Social Six (SO)

SO Sixes are dutiful. It's easy to mistype them for Enneagram One because of their strong moral compass and tendency to see things are black and white. These individuals are rational and prefer to follow the rules and do things the right way.

One-to-One/Sexual Six (SX)

As the countertype of the subtype Sixes, SX Sixes are intimidating. They come across as bold, assertive, and a little rebellious. It's easy to mistype them for Enneagram Eight because they always run in the direction of their fears as a way to counteract their anxiety. Because the Sixes naturally mistrust people, SX Sixes will seek out concrete and pragmatic ideologies because they feel more truthful and grounded.

WORK AND LIFESTYLE TIPS FOR TYPE 6S

Before we discuss how you can improve yourself on this quest of self-discovery, we must explore some of the struggles you may experience on your journey. For some of you, the struggles already dominate your life, and if that's the case, you'll find the suggestions offered pretty helpful.

STRUGGLES OF AN ENNEAGRAM SIX

The love-hate relationship with authority

By this, I mean you love the security that comes with looking to others for authority, but at the same time, you're skeptical about people who call themselves authority. People who seem self-assured and confident that their way is the only right way seem "too good to be true ."That's probably why you start playing the devil's advocate as soon as you find someone you like.

What to do: The only real solution to the issue of security and authority comes down to trusting your inner guidance. I know that's a tall order, but that's why you're reading this book, isn't it?

The battle with uncertainty

Is there anything you don't doubt? The lower you are in your development, the higher and more overwhelming your doubts become. On the outside, people see a charming, good-humored, or even self-assured person, but you know the truth. Deep down, you live in a constantly shaky world. You're scared of abandonment, rejection, deception, betrayal, death, and everything that lies in between. You worry that you'll screw up your relationships, job, or assigned project. It's a hard battle, and you face it daily. While other Enneagram types might succeed in distracting themselves from their fears, your fear seems to live face-to-face with you.

What to do: The only way to overcome fear is to find your Higher Self and live from that strength and fundamental Truth. Work on developing to higher levels in your spiritual connection. The more you work on your mind and spirit, the more grounded you'll become, and fear will no longer stand in your way.

Perfectionism and rigidity

Often as a Six, you might feel like you can only relax and feel secure once all your problems are solved. In other words, you'll be happy and at ease when X happens (X is the thing you're working on or worried about). You might also struggle with perfectionism, especially in your relationships. That could be because you tend to be overly critical to avoid making mistakes or disappointing the people you care about. Both these issues are rooted in the same false belief, and it's because of that unceasing anxiety that you become so rigid in your behavior.

What to do: Recognize and quantify how much time goes into worrying and catastrophizing everything. Notice how much time this takes away from being happy, present, and effective in your daily life. Incorporate some mindfulness practices, so you can learn to accept yourself and silence the mental chatter that robs you.

You don't trust yourself

As a child, you may have deliberately or unintentionally received the conditioning that you shouldn't trust your instincts. As a result, you spend most of your time looking to teachers, mentors, coaches, and institutions to tell you what's right. Unfortunately, giving away that much power erodes your ability to become all you were born to be. It creates a breeding ground for mistrust. If you can't trust yourself first, you can never truly trust anyone else because Truth is always unknown to you.

What to do: Invest in anything and everything that enables you to cultivate a healthy and unshakeable self-belief. This should not be an ego-based belief but rather a Higher Self belief. You will know absolute freedom when you learn to trust in that voice above and beyond what others say, no matter how authoritative they might be.

ENNEAGRAM TYPE 6 UNDER STRESS

Sixes are typically stressed when they feel unsafe or there's a disorder in their environment. They also cannot stand disorder in their environment, corruption, lack of structure or clarity, and wishy-washy behavior from others.

When stress is more than they can handle, Sixes naturally disintegrate into the arrow 3, meaning they pick up unhealthy behaviors from Enneagram Three. That causes them to ignore their values and focus on covering up their insecurities, fear of rejection, failure, and abandonment. They might even become super boastful about their accomplishments, especially around the people they want to impress. Suppose they are stressed because they're not feeling the reassurance and support needed from their group or an authoritative figure. In that case, they might become overly self-absorbed and arrogant, playing the devil's advocate. All of which are rooted in the internal stress and mounting fears they're attempting to conceal.

If you're a Six and you're wondering how to deal with burnout or the fear of chaos and uncertainty, here are a few things you can do:

When the idea of the worst-case scenario hijacks your mind, instead of succumbing to that fear, play it out like a movie in your head. Ask yourself, "if that bad thing happens, then what?" Keep asking yourself that question until you either prove that you're not going to die out of this situation, and your brain will naturally give in to a more calm and optimistic state. You'll find calm and solid ground by realistically assessing the situation.

You can also consider playing the simple game "what if I'm wrong and the opposite thing happens?" By asking this question, you give your brain permission to consider the opposite (the positive) aspects of things. This is a simple yet powerful game for Sixes because often, the brain leaps into the worst-case scenarios for everything.

RELATIONSHIPS

Sixes are thoughtful and protective of those they love. They make great partners, especially when operating at healthy levels of development. If, however, the Six isn't well developed in their self-mastery, they do struggle with trust. That makes the relationship challenging because they can be considered controlling and too skeptical.

As a Six, you know all too well how hard it can be to trust someone, especially a romantic partner. Consistency, commitment, responsibility, and devotion matter to you, so your right partner needs to bring a certain level of compassion, kindness, and trustworthiness to your relationship. They need to be transparent for things to work well.

Below are tips on cultivating a healthy, loving relationship with other types and what you might expect. If none of the suggestions resonate, that's okay. This is to raise your curiosity and awareness of your strengths and weaknesses in relationships.

RELATIONSHIP TIPS WITH OTHER TYPES

Type 6 & Type 1: With a One, you have a relationship you can count on because you're both committed, responsible, and value loyalty. You and your partner are dutiful and want to make the world better. The One grounds you and creates a safety net that soothes your skepticism. Your wittiness helps the One lighten up, and you're able to see various possible outcomes to any scenario, which can be helpful for the Enneagram One, who tends to be rigid in their choices.

Although the Enneagram One's self-assuredness and decisiveness can inspire you to cultivate the same qualities leading to an enriching relationship, you may encounter a challenge when your partner becomes resentful or overly critical of you. That could make you reactive and anxious, making you appear hypocritical to your partner. Sixes and Ones are very uncomfortable with conflict, leading to the blame game. Grow together by keeping open communication and leaning into your fun side. Find ways to be spontaneous together and not take each other's missteps too seriously.

Type 6 & Type 2: With a Two, you're in a supportive, warm, attentive relationship. Your connection is built on friendship and responsibility. The Two brings empathy, affection, and comfort, making you feel that your partner always has your back. Your desire for steadiness offers the Two a sense of feeling prioritized and valued.

A challenge you might face in this relationship is your ambivalence. The tendency to test your partner by pulling them close and then pushing them away only amplifies insecurity for your partner. The Two might go into "fix it" mode, trying to help you win back your love. Unfortunately, that might make you feel like they are too controlling.

Grow together by finding time to continue growing your friendship and connection. Both of you need to verbalize your needs and how you can meet those needs. Don't play the assumption game in your relationship.

Type 6 & Type 3: With a Three, the relationship is dynamic, dutiful, responsible, and resilient. You trust each other and make a great team. The Three brings ambition, a great work ethic, encouragement, and optimism that inspires you to pursue your passions. You keep your partner grounded and help them slow down a little more.

A challenge you might face in this relationship comes down to your values. As a Six, you might struggle with the shape-shifting nature of a Three, causing you to have trust issues. The Threes hard-driving "always on" energy can also conflict with your cautious and more conservative nature. That can cause the Three to feel like you're holding them back.

Grow together by validating each other's focus of attention and staying present in the relationship. Have an open dialogue about your emotions, and make sure you work through the minor issues that could create cracks in the relationship.

Type 6 & Type 4: With a Four, you've got a deep relationship. The Four always wants to go emotionally deeper, and your commitment to the relationship facilitates that level of expressiveness and exploration. The Four brings compassion and self-awareness, and you're practical, loyal, and sensitive. You have plenty of similarities, and that can be pretty comforting.

A challenge you might face here is that you're extremely practical while your partner tends to be driven by their passions. That can create conflict, especially when you don't see eye to eye on something. The Four might also struggle with the fact that you want everything to be predictable with strict boundaries, and they don't like being boxed in or limited in life. Grow together by handling your conflicts better. Recognize that sometimes, your partner's pursuit of authenticity may not align with your need for consistency. And that's okay. Work through these experiences and be thoughtful in your responses. Ask yourself, "do I need to express this right now? Will it be helpful to our relationship?"

Type 6 & Type 5: With a Five, you have a deep relationship that allows you to be yourself without fear of judgment or overwhelm. Your thoughtfulness, loyalty, attentiveness, and balance enable the Five to stay more connected and less isolated from the world. The Five's steadiness, stability, cautious approach, and trustworthiness appeal to you.

A challenge you might face in this relationship is when it comes to decision-making. Your tendency to trust existing rules and proce- dures can be frustrating for your partner because Fives trust their intellect more than other people's opinions. While you're both analytical in your approaches, when you don't see eye to eye, things can become pretty messy because you may start picking apart the relationship instead of focusing on the issue at hand.

Grow together by learning to step back from a heated situation and giving each other some space to realign internally, then come back and work through the differences compassionately. Find something your both enjoy and like to learn about and dedicate time to that activity each week.

Type 6 & Type 6: Being in a mirrored relationship is easy and comfortable, and it's like having a best friend who just gets you. Establishing the deep trust necessary for a lasting partnership can take time because you're both Sixes, but nothing can separate you once you find it. You can relax, have fun together, and know that you've got each other's backs. There's no guesswork about where you stand in the relationship.

A challenge you'll face is how you deal with conflict. You may say things in the heat of the moment that you don't mean, which may crack the trust you've worked so hard to build. Grow together by expressing compassion regularly and step back from the heat of the moment to avoid saying things you'll regret later.

Type 6 & Type 7: You're in a fun-loving relationship with a seven. You're kindred souls who play off one another's strengths. The Seven brings adventure, light-heartedness, and fun to the relationship, and you offer stability, balance, and light caution, which enables the Seven to get grounded.

A challenge you might face in this relationship is that you both struggle deeply with anxiety, fear, and insecurities. But the way you cope with them differs significantly. You create structure, stability, and systems to deal with your anxiety and fears, whereas Seven copes by constantly looking for external distractions and things that spark their energy. Your partner can quickly get tired of your pessimism and desire to be free of the rules and "silly" considerations that you hold dear. Be respectful of each other's ways and find that middle ground where you can agree. Grow together by recognizing that both your perspectives in life carry significant value.

Type 6 & Type 8: With an Eight, you're in a protective, dependable relationship. You compliment each other well. The Eight brings clarity, decisiveness, and transparency, enabling you to trust them. Your warmth and kindness make the Eight feel embraced and cared for.

A challenge you might face here is that you're both reactive in conflicts, and when things go wrong, you don't feel like you can trust each other. You might find the Eight's bullish approach a little off-putting, and your partner sees your concerns and questioning as a lack of trust. If you're counterphobic, conflicts may become explosive as neither party will back down easily. Grow together by developing your self-control and recognizing that you're both work in progress. Being vulnerable is a tough call for both of you, and that's okay.

Support each other and offer reassurance because you're both looking for safety, not control. Remind each other that you're in this together.

Type 6 & Type 9: With a Nine, you're in a supportive, affectionate, and loyal relationship with many shared values. You share a mutual devotion and comfort. The Nine brings kindness, acceptance, and stability to the relationship. Your action-oriented nature can help the Nine become more active in their own life.

A challenge you might face is during stressful periods because the Nine tends to withdraw, which can feel like abandonment. Your emotional reactivity can also be detrimental because the Nine likes to avoid all conflict and prefers to tip-toe around things which may also feel like they are not being transparent. Grow together by supporting each other in voicing your needs and wants. Figure out what you really want in a relationship and encourage your partner to do the same, then openly share this vision so you can move toward it together.

AFFIRMATIONS

- I am safe in this present moment
- I am willing to trust more
- I know my worth
- I am compassionate with others and myself
- I choose to see the best in others

Remember affirmations only work when what you say and feel are in synch. Only use affirmations you deeply resonate with.

DAILY LIFESTYLE TIPS FOR GROWTH AND HAPPINESS

- Work on your self-talk. Mental chatter is one of the leading causes of the high stress and health issues you might experience. The more you work on your mindset and train your brain to maintain healthy, loving self-talk, the easier it will be to keep calm. Consider learning how to meditate. It's one of the best ways to calm a worrying mind and elevate your physiological state.
- Invest some time daily to decompress and tune into your body. Use deep breathing techniques to bring a sense of calm throughout your body.
- Learn to let go of non-essential responsibilities that overwhelm you. There's nothing wrong with letting others take over a project. Recognize when you're simply taking on too much and just say no.
- Move your body daily. Exercising is a great way to increase stress-reducing endorphins in the brain. Find exercises you enjoy and work up a sweat daily or at least three times a week.

ENNEAGRAM TYPE 7

THE ENTHUSIAST OR ADVENTURER

The Enthusiast or Adventurer is the Enneagram Type Seven. This personality is best known for their carefree, adventurous behavior. They are bubbly and bursting with energy. In this chapter and the next, we'll dig deeper into the personality, fears, desires, strengths, struggles, and ways to reconnect with your higher self while increasing happiness in your life.

The Enneagram Seven is an idealist and visionary. They are energetic, charismatic, creative, and love taking risks. A Seven is a big picture thinker and prefers to live outside the box of conventional advice. Most Sevens are multi-talented and passionate about various things. They have a genuine concern for human growth and progress while at the same time having little regard for social status or etiquette.

Sevens have a strong desire to learn more about themselves and discover new things. They can be pretty impulsive and abstract in their communication, but they are great storytellers. Sevens love to animate everything they say and constantly seek the good in life and others. In fact, they tend to struggle to deal with anything in themselves or others that aren't positive. But more on that later.

Enneagram Seven is part of the head triad or thinking center, making them witty and intellectual. Like Fives and Sixes, they are very observant of their environment and use their creative imagination to make decisions. However, the main difference is that, unlike the Fives and Sixes, who are very grounded and careful with their choices, Sevens tend to be more impulsive with their decisions and actions.

STRENGTHS OF A SEVEN

One of the greatest strengths of an enthusiast is their belief in the positive aspects of life and people. They are good finders in the truest strengths of the word, always encouraging, uplifting, and cheering others to pursue their dreams.

Sevens are great at seeing the big picture in almost everything. They have an agile mind that can switch between multiple things quickly. If you're with a Seven, things are always dynamic and fun because they know how to brighten the mood and uplift everyone around them.

Another strength is that Sevens never take themselves too seriously. That enables them to bounce back quickly in the face of a setback or failure.

Key personality traits of a Seven

- Versatile
- Curious
- Bold
- Playful
- Energetic

- Cheerful
- Resilient

Common hobbies for type Seven

- Podcasting
- Stand-up comedy
- Adrenaline inducing activities
- Trying new foods

FEARS AND WEAKNESSES

Sevens fear missing out on the good life or getting trapped and stuck in a rut. That's because of the core fear of being deprived or experiencing pain. They constantly seek exciting, novel, and fun experiences to cope with this fear.

The idea of limitations and restrictions is very unappealing to a Seven. Unfortunately, this can lead to behaviors like escapism, impatience, avoidance, and overindulgence, especially when the individual isn't operating at healthy levels.

What's the Basic Fear driving this behavior? The fear of being trapped in pain or lacking something.

This fear can manifest itself in constant busyness, which brings with it fatigue. It also shows up as a lack of follow-through and withdrawing from commitments without notice. But the Seven would rather put up with exhaustion than deal with mundane experiences or pain.

Some Sevens go on the opposite extreme and excessively plan their fun adventures. This over-enthusiasm and constant need for movement and entertainment is also an unhealthy manifestation of the same core fear.

DESIRES AND MOTIVATION

As pleasure-seeking personalities, all Sevens have a fundamental desire to be stress-free, happy, and satisfied. Sevens are motivated by the desire to have their needs fulfilled. If faced with dull, boring, or scary experiences, Sevens do everything possible to retreat from that environment. They typically go to great lengths to find happiness and excitement. When operating at average or unhealthy levels, the Seven will jump from one exciting thing to another, chasing after the next big high.

Core values

- Fun
- Pleasure
- Optimism
- Flexibility

Type Seven celebrities and famous people you might know include singer and songwriter Elton John, entrepreneur Richard Branson, Singer Katy Perry, actress Elizabeth Taylor, Comedian Eddie Murphy, President John F. Kennedy, Actor Jack Black, and Robin Williams.

Wondering if you could be a Type Seven? Here are some personality indicators:

1. It's easy for you to pick up new skills, but you don't put much into mastering any of them.
2. You quickly feel depressed if you're resources are limited in any way. You're happiest when you can experience and achieve whatever you want.
3. Most of the time, you find the present pretty dull.
4. Despite your seemingly carefree attitude, you know exactly what you want out of life and won't stop till you get it.

5. Your enthusiasm level mirrors that of a five-year-old regardless of your actual age.
6. Patience isn't something you handle well because you want everything you've planned to happen a.s.a.p
7. FOMO is real and alive!
8. You can't stand people who say, "Be realistic."
9. You're passionate and obsessed with the future and its possibilities. In fact, you spend most of your time thinking about and planning the future.

YOUR WINGS

Wings are the number adjacent to your Enneagram Type. As a Seven, you have -

- The Enneagram Seven with Six-Wing: "The Entertainer"
- The Enneagram Seven with Eight-Wing: "The Realist"

While you may have tendencies that lean into both wings at various stages of your life, you'll likely be more dominant in one than the other. This will be your most influential and dominant Wing.

Meaning of your Wing

If you're a 7w6 (Seven with a Six-Wing), the influence of this Wing makes you more focused and responsible. Your spontaneity and the need to be steady, secure, and focused make you the most sociable personality type across the Enneagram system. You also become more disciplined, productive, and organized with greater foresight.

At work, you'll get along with practically everyone. You're charming, funny, adult, and childlike at the same time and, at times, a little cheeky. People love working and being around you. They also feel they can rely on you. Some of the best careers you can go for include but aren't limited to:

- Photographer
- Journalist
- Media planner
- Travel agent
- Tour Guide
- Publicist
- Travel writer

If you're a 7w8 (Seven with an Eight-Wing), the influence of this Wing makes you more assertive and driven. You're not as concerned with relationships as the 7w6 because your focus is on creating your own experiences and winning in life. If you fancy material success and power, your willpower is strong enough to get you there. However, you'll need to be mindful not to fall into unhealthy habits like workaholism, power games, and overstimulation that tend to be the downfall of an Enneagram 8. Living on the edge of life is excellent but make sure you're operating at high levels of development which we'll discuss shortly.

Careers best suited to you include:

- TV anchor
- Sales manager
- Promoter
- Travel agent
- Motivational speaker
- Firefighter
- Paramedic
- Travel writer

The Arrows and what they mean

Your Enneagram personality type is linked to lines or arrows that show the path of growth or disintegration depending on where you are in life. When moving on a path of disintegration, a Seven will fall into the negative trappings of the arrow One (1), and they'll become more self-critical and perfectionistic. This is known as the Direction of Stress or the Direction of Disintegration and typically occurs in the face of pressure or surmounting stress. The other arrow indicates how a healthy version of your personality reacts and grows in more healthy environments. In this case, a Seven develops more of the healthier qualities of the arrow Five (5), becoming more focused and curious about life. To understand the concept behind healthy and unhealthy levels, let's go over the various levels of development for a Seven.

THE 9 LEVELS OF DEVELOPMENT, FROM LOWEST TO HIGHEST

Levels of Development arise from Riso and Hudson's teachings and the founders of the Enneagram Institute, which is a great place to take your Enneagram Test. Their theory posits that all individuals fall into one of nine levels of functioning. The lowest level is nine, and the highest is level one. The levels are divided into a triad that subcategorizes these levels as healthy (1,2,3), average levels (4,5,6), and unhealthy levels (7,8,9).

Unhealthy

Level 9: At this level, the Seven is at their lowest and most destructive state as an adult. This is where the person is completely burned out, panic-stricken, depressed, and in deep despair. They lose their health and energy, and some become suicidal or addicted to drugs. It's pretty common to overdose at this stage of their life because they are entirely out of control.

Level 8: At this level, the person is still out of control, erratic and compulsive in their behavior. They have massive mood swings and feel like they'll never fully understand life or get what they want. This person can't get grounded or stabilize their emotions.

Level 7: This Enneagram Seven is narcissistic, flashy, and exuberant. They jump from place to place and person to person, desperate to quell their insurmountable anxiety. Many tend to cope through drugs and other addictive behaviors.

Average

Level 6: The rise to this level does bring some relief, but the Seven is still struggling with addiction. They engage in a slew of constant activities, trying to seek the next "high" through adventure and new projects. As an adrenaline junkie, this Seven doesn't know when to stop and lacks follow-through in whatever task they start. They come across as pushy, demanding, jaded and insensitive.

Level 5: This Seven is constantly busy because they fear being bored. They are great storytellers, flamboyant, and always have tons of ideas. Unfortunately, they're still not grounded or focused enough to complete what they start making them unreliable. Unable to discriminate what they need, this person tends to exaggerate and overindulge in almost everything.

Level 4: At this level, the person is future-oriented and almost always excited about some new plan. They always want to have more options and choices available to them, and they enjoy keeping up with the latest trends in society. This person is adventurous and worldly-wise.

Healthy

Level 3: At this level, the Seven is stepping into the path of integration, becoming a more practical, productive, and reliable individual. They can channel their multi-talents in prolific ways and quickly become accomplished achievers who generally do many things well.

Level 2: At this level, we encounter a Seven who is inspiring and contagious because of their high positive energy and enthusiasm. This individual is reliable and eager to learn, and they've finally learned to be grounded while still enjoying their adventurous spirit.

Level 1: The holy grail for an Enneagram Seven is where the individual rises to their best version becoming spiritually reunited. That, in turn, raises their curiosity, thirst for knowledge, and new experiences while simultaneously being grounded and grateful in the present. They develop more depth in life and become joyfully awed by the simple wonders of life. Better still, they find their perfect work-life balance while still making time for new adventures.

ENNEAGRAM SEVEN'S PASSION

The Seven's Passion or deadly sin is gluttony. It typically expresses itself as overindulgence in life and the pursuit of more. Sevens tend to jump from one experience to another, always seeking to taste a little bit of everything.

What the Seven needs is sobriety. That's the virtue that will get you in touch with your true Self and the present moment. By coming to the deeper part of the Self, you become more grounded in the moment, less distracted, and fearful of boredom or unpleasant emotions. You realize that you can enjoy life fully and have it all without overindulging.

If you're reading this and recognize that you're a Seven, that's the work you must do. Bring yourself back to wholeness, back to sobriety.

CHILDHOOD AND EMOTIONAL PATTERNS FOR ENNEAGRAM SEVEN

One might wonder how the Seven developed this reckless, carefree, gluttonous quality. The ego fixation can be traced back to childhood when the disconnect took place thanks to what's referred to as "nurturing deficiency." As children, Sevens experienced neglect resulting in a lack of bond with the supposed caregiver. Whether that was because the primary caregiver was abusive, struggling with addiction, or having mental health issues, the child developed a deep sense of emptiness. Sevens filled that loneliness with distractions, activities, objects, and possibilities that would excite their senses and keep them busy. They chased after anything and everything they thought would make them happy because they felt that would compensate for the nurture they always felt was out of reach.

As adults, the same emotional patterns play out as excessive optimism, constant adventure, and chasing after whatever they believe will keep them stimulated and happy. Unfortunately, they don't know how to deal with long-standing issues or even face uncomfortable situations. Sevens fear being alone or being hurt and sometimes walk away from projects or a relationship purely because they're afraid of being disappointed.

To heal the childhood wound, a Seven must reconnect with their Higher Self and learn to receive love, care, and affection from others. They need to enjoy the present moment and prioritize creating meaningful relationships.

SUBTYPES FOR ENNEAGRAM TYPE SEVEN

The Enneagram profiling system allows for 3 subtypes in each type. These are Self-Preservation, Social, and One-to-One (Sexual) variants. Remember, all three instinctual variants exist in all of us, but the order in which they stack up determines their influence on our lives. One will be most dominant and the easiest for you to resonate with and observe as behavior and thought patterns in your life. The second will feel a little neutral and less influential, and the third will be the least significant. The third instinct becomes a blind spot for many because it's underdeveloped and out of their conscious recognition. Depending on which instinct is most dominant, it will shape your unique personality and how you approach life as a Seven.

Self Preservation Seven (SP)

The SP Seven is a masterful networker and connector, always looking to build a strong "family" of people they can leverage to fuel their adventure-seeking prowess. These individuals love the good things in life, and everyone in their world plays a vital role in meeting their needs. These are the kinds of people who brag about how they have friends all over that they can call on at any time. They're good at getting what they want and are perhaps the most practical and rational of the three subtypes.

Social Seven (SO)

As the countertype for the subtype, Sacrifice is the key quality for the Social Seven. They act against their gluttony by being of service to create a better world. It's easy to mistype this SO Seven with an Enneagram 2 because they are warm and often put the needs of others (or a group they support) ahead of their own. The fun-loving, adventurous spirit is still alive, but they tend to direct their energy toward a mission of helping everyone enjoy life more.

One-to-One/Sexual Seven (SX)

With the SX Seven, the key quality is fascination. This Seven experiences life through rose-colored lenses. They have a contagious enthusiasm and optimism and only see good in all people and all things. SX Sevens believe that life is a fantasy novel, and they are very good at helping those they're interested in "fit into the magical costume" the Seven creates for them. In other words, SX Sevens know how to make others feel special, and that attracts a lot of interest. Unfortunately, getting swept away into the charm, intensity, and sparkles of a Seven can lead to heartache because their attention is typically temporary. As soon as they find a new object of attention, they immediately disappear, which can be deeply shocking to the person interacting with a Seven. One more thing to note is that SX Sevens cannot stand anything they consider dull and dreary and often walk away from overly predictable relationships.

CHAPTER 18
WORK AND LIFESTYLE TIPS FOR TYPE 7S

As part of your discovery and transformation, it's essential to recognize your triggers, the areas that you struggle with most, and where your opportunities for growth lie.

STRUGGLES OF AN ENNEAGRAM 7

Getting bored

You get bored most of the time because you're mismanaging your energy and focus. However, this boredom is rooted in deficiency at average and unhealthy levels and typically leads to very unhealthy actions. Almost all Sevens will struggle with this because the truth is, even the healthy ones need that sense of adventure and challenge in their life.

What to do: Study your boredom. How soon after you get bored do you seek out distractions? What emotions lie in your boredom? What does that feel like in your body? What memories does your boredom bring up? Is there pain associated with it that you're trying to avoid? Journal whatever revelations you get. Writing down what you really feel can help you become more self-aware and heal some of those hidden wounds. Again, it won't be easy, but it will change your life.

Feeling trapped

Freedom is one of the core values and the basic desire for a Seven. The world is an endless treasure trove of activities and experiences, so commitments can make you feel like a bird trapped in a cage. Even if you crave marriage, long work contracts, and family commitments, these things also give you tremendous anxiety.

What to do: Open your mind to the possibility that commitment, discipline, and freedom can go hand in hand. Relationships and work opportunities can last a long time but still facilitate the sense of novelty and adventure you crave. Seek out these types of engagements.

Feeling distracted and unfocused

It's easy for average and unhealthy Sevens to be invaded by too many ideas and possibilities. Many complain of feeling out of control and even overwhelmed. Then focusing does become an arduous task.

What to do: Meditation is a great way to help your mind calm down. It also enables you to practice being in the present moment, strengthening your focus. Find meditation practices that excite you and turn them into a daily ritual.

No follow-through

This behavior is often rooted in a lack of focus and discipline. When a Seven gets distracted or bored, they tend to abandon what they were doing and find something new to excite them.

What to do: Cultivate discipline in your life. It won't be easy, but you must do it. If you can train your brain to stick with something to completion, it will change your life and improve your professional perception.

ENNEAGRAM TYPE SEVEN UNDER STRESS

Sevens tend to get really stressed when they're micro-managed, bored, or when they feel like they don't have enough personal freedom. They also don't like being cooped up for too long or stuck in the same place. Other things that stress Sevens significantly include financial problems because they can't do and have everything they want. They also don't like being stuck in detail work or doing nitty-gritty stuff because they're big picture thinkers. Suppose you give a Seven too much responsibility or rigid deadlines. In that case, they can easily fall into high-stress levels, which may, over time, cause them to disintegrate into the unhealthy habits of an Enneagram One. That's quite alarming for everyone around this individual because they go from a carefree, fun-loving, and optimistic person to a rigid control freak. They can become overly critical and bury themselves in work or projects to take their mind off their struggles.

If you're a Seven and wondering how to deal with high-stress levels, consider meditation and other mindfulness practices. These will bring you into the present moment and calm you down. You can also use music to help you mirror your emotions. Once you determine which emotions are creating this unpleasant feeling, don't run and hide. Instead, find healthy ways to process those emotions. Journaling your feelings is a great way to release them. Realize that both positive and negative emotions are essential for the full human experience.

RELATIONSHIPS

Type Sevens are fun, enthusiastic, energetic, and spontaneous. When it comes to personal and professional relationships, a Seven never wants to feel caged or restricted.

In romantic relationships, Fours usually seek partners who will enable them to feel connected and grounded without being stifled.

Sevens work hard to make the workplace fun and exciting. They enjoy new events, sharing their creative ideas, and boosting morale, but they need support to remain accountable and follow through on their assignments.

RELATIONSHIP TIPS WITH OTHER TYPES

Here are some ways to improve your relationships with other Enneagram Types.

Type 7 & Type 1: With a One, you're in a case of "opposites attract," which can be profoundly fulfilling if both operate at healthy levels. In many ways, you complement each other because you bring curiosity, reliability, and hard work into the relationship dynamic. The One helps you become more steady and conscientious, and you help them see the little ways that everyday life can be worth celebrating.

A challenge you might face in this relationship is the feeling of being trapped in the boredom of routine, strict rules, and predictability that your partner adores. Meanwhile, your partner might feel like the "adult" in the relationship.

Grow together by developing higher levels of awareness so you can appreciate the balance the other brings.

Type 7 & Type 2: With a Two, the relationship is warm, nurturing, spontaneous, and fun. The Two bring generosity, concern for the welfare of others, and loving attention and dedication to your needs. You inspire them to dream bigger and think outside the box. In this relationship, the Two show you that it's okay to think beyond your personal needs.

A challenge you might face is the difference in perspectives regarding emotional connection. The Two might feel that you're not present enough, especially when feelings arise. That will cause your partner to respond by either demanding that you understand their needs or trying to "fix" you. Regardless, this doesn't end well because it causes you to feel trapped in the relationship. Grow together by learning to talk through conflicts rather than staying positive and avoiding tough talks. Reassure each other of your commitment and when you have these unpleasant talks, reward yourselves with something fun.

Type 7 & Type 3: With a Three, the relationship is adventurous and gregarious, and you play off each other's strengths. There's never a dull moment here. The Three is ambitious, focused, poised, and sensitive to the relationship. You're relaxed, courageous, and resilient, and you know how to keep things interesting, which makes you super attractive.

A challenge you might face since you're both constantly doing things and keeping busy is that you may avoid dealing with feelings and conflicts. Your partner may also feel embarrassed by your naturally boisterous nature and the tendency to say whatever comes to your mind. Meanwhile, you might get frustrated by the Three's constant desire for productivity and work. Grow together by sharing feelings. Be open and yes, it will be uncomfortable but do it anyway. Learn to slow down every once in a while and just enjoy being in each other's company.

Type 7 & Type 4: With a Four, you're in a colorful, emotionally expressive relationship. The Four helps you stay grounded and creates a safe space to explore your emotions. You help your partner see all the wonderful positive things in life, which helps boost their confidence. Although you're opposite in many ways, you both tend to think outside the box, and you're constantly intrigued and fascinated by each other's way of life.

A challenge you might face in this relationship is how you handle conflict. Given your varying reactions to emotions and conflict, your partner may feel like you don't care about them or respect their feelings. Meanwhile, the constant need for emotional exploration and connection could feel a bit stifling to you, and at times your partner might feel like a killjoy who just wants to keep you down. Grow together by practicing a lot more present moment mindfulness. Instead of escaping or internalizing disappointment or unpleasant moments, talk it out and let things go. When things don't go as planned, learn to be okay with that.

Type 7 & Type 5: With a Five, you're in a thoughtful relationship with constant learning, investigation, and deep diving into hobbies and things of interest. The Five brings knowledge and curiosity that you find highly appealing. Your spontaneity is quite refreshing for your partner and gets them out of their head so they can enjoy life a little more.

A challenge you might face is how opposite you are when stress hits. You like to run into the future without care. The Five is more conservative and self-reliant. While you both want to meet your own needs, the way you approach them is very different and often leads to misunderstandings. Grow together by openly communicating your needs and leveraging each other's strengths. The combination of knowledge and intrigue can work in your favor as long as you take the time to integrate this into the relationship.

Type 7 and Type 6: With a Six, you're stable, predictable relationship, and you enjoy playing off one another's strengths. The Six brings stability, caution, and pragmatism that you appreciate, and your fun, adventurous spirit lightens their careful disposition. Your partner appreciates the fact that you've got their back.

A challenge you might face in this relationship is that you both struggle deeply with anxiety, fear, and insecurities. But the way you cope with them differs greatly. You get bored quickly, and your partner's structure and pessimistic outlook might become frustrating. Meanwhile, the Six might see your carefree attitude as too unstable and untrustworthy, creating cracks in your relationship. Grow together by recognizing that both your perspectives in life carry significant value. Be respectful of each other's ways and find that middle ground where you can both agree.

Type 7 & Type 7: With a Seven, you're in a mirrored relationship where you understand each other's need for independence. You ride the waves of fun and possibility, the relationship is light-hearted and full of energy, and you're constantly bouncing ideas off one another. You can enjoy a resilient, deeply loving, thriving, and joyous connection.

You might face a challenge in this relationship when conflict or adverse events arise. Your natural impulse is to avoid all unpleasant experiences. You might also have difficulty finding common ground on what you want out of the relationship and life. Grow together by being more intentional about the relationship. You should also prioritize downtime together and connect emotionally at a deeper level, especially when conflicts arise.

Type 7 & Type 8: With an Eight, the relationship is captivating, dynamic, and intense. The Eight keeps you grounded in reality, attentive to practical matters, and focused. You help your partner lighten up a little and have more fun in life.

A challenge you might face is that you quickly get frustrated when you don't get what you want. Eights need to feel in control and have things their way, so when you go off on your own, that might get a little intense. Your cheerful disposition may also come across as inauthentic, and when an Eight is around people they consider inauthentic, they tend to be more self-protective. Because you're both strong-willed, your relationship can quickly tune into a battle for autonomy. Grow together by slowing down long enough to notice your emotional reactions and ask yourself if these reactions are constructive. Be present with your emotions and learn to process them in healthier ways.

Type 7 & Type 9: With a Nine, the relationship is calm, steady, and flexible. The Nine offers a very reassuring calmness as it makes you feel accepted and loved just as you are. You bring a sense of fun and aliveness that helps the Nine break out of their shell and try new things.

A common challenge you might face is due to your stubbornness, especially when things aren't going well. You're more likely to be the first to surface conflict since you hate feeling trapped by negative emotions. Unfortunately, your tendency to move past conflicts too quickly may cause your partner to feel trampled. Nines take time to process things, and when they're not encouraged to speak their Truth, they tend to withdraw and become passive aggressive. Grow together by learning to work through conflict together. Have those tough conversations with compassion. After a successful unpleasant conversation, reward yourself with something fun. It's also a great idea to remind each other that conflict will not jeopardize the relationship.

AFFIRMATIONS

- I am satisfied and grateful for every experience
- Every obstacle is just a learning opportunity
- I choose to be happy and content
- I am willing to trust the timing of my life
- I can slow down and still have fun

DAILY LIFESTYLE TIPS FOR GROWTH AND HAPPINESS

Avoid stimulants

Addiction is a common issue with Sevens, so I want to encourage you to avoid using any stimulants as much as possible. Besides, you already have boundless energy. Do you really need 5 cups of coffee?

Instead of more coffee or other addictive substances, find ways to raise your feel-good hormones even more, either through daily exercise or giving yourself healthy treats like a spa day each week.

Learn some deep breathing techniques.

Deep breathing techniques are a great way to process emotions. You can find YouTube videos from various teachers with numerous techniques to apply. Just stick with the teacher you best resonate with.

Confide in a friend you trust

When boredom, distractions, and negative emotions kick in, instead of avoiding them, talk to a trusted friend or a coach so they can support you and keep you accountable, especially if you're working on an important project.

Spend time practicing stillness and just being in the present moment

Find daily practices of solitude, whether through sitting alone with some soothing music, journaling, or walking in nature. Learn to fall in love with yourself and enjoy being in your company. Your path to healing starts with solitude.

ENNEAGRAM TYPE 8

THE CHALLENGER OR PROTECTOR

The following two chapters cover everything you need to know about the Enneagram Type 8, often referred to as the challenger or the protector. Similar to Nines and Ones, Eights make up the Body triad of the gut center of intelligence. Aptly named, this Enneagram type is self-assured, assertive, and loves to be in charge. Eights are most concerned with protecting themselves and those under their care. They don't like authorities that impose ideologies or regulations on them, so they're constantly looking to lead the group/family/company. That means they have trouble processing and dealing with feelings of anger. But unlike the Nines and Ones, Enneagram Eights don't repress or hide their anger. If anything, they use it to their advantage as an intimidation technique.

Eights believe they must always be in control of everything. Their primary focus is to control the situation internally and externally in personal or professional settings. That makes vulnerability one of the peeves for an Eight. Letting their guard down and allowing themselves to be influenced by someone they trust is tough, but it can happen with maturity and a lot of inner work. Eights are unapologetic in their demeanor and communication. They are straight shooters who sometimes come across as arrogant and insensitive. One thing you can depend on is that an Eight will always be honest, direct, and straight to the point, and they expect the same from others.

STRENGTHS OF TYPE EIGHT

One of the strengths an Eight possesses is finding that balance between indulging in the things they love and nurturing the people they care about. Eights can relax and unwind when it's time to do so.

Resourcefulness is also a strength you find with the Eight because they know how to leverage what they have to get what they want. If there's something they need but lack, Eights are excellent at forming allies to leverage other people's resources.

Another great thing about Eights is how bold and courageous they are. They love to stand up for the underdogs and the little guys in their world and aren't afraid to use their power to protect the weak. That behavior is rooted in the mindset that the world is unjust and weak people are at a disadvantage. So the strong must defend the defenseless.

Key personality traits of an Eight

- Self-confident
- Resourceful
- Assertive
- Decisive
- Strong
- Domineering

Common hobbies for an Eight

- Public speaking
- Debating
- Exercising
- Extreme sports

FEARS AND WEAKNESSES

The primary fear of Type Eight is being controlled or harmed by others. This individual sees vulnerability as a weakness that could lead to powerlessness, loss of control, and getting hurt. Type Eight will attempt to remedy this fear by avoiding all situations that may cause them to feel vulnerable or powerless.

For most Eights, the issue becomes complex because they deny their fears and weaknesses. Because they don't want to admit that they're afraid to lower their guard, their relationships tend to be pretty rocky, especially with those they love the most. At average and unhealthy levels, their intensity and passion for life and goals can be overwhelming and intimidating to others. Control and domination may turn dark, and they might mix their need for justice with revenge. Because power is a focal point for an Eight, they must be mindful of how they acquire and utilize the power they crave. Used well, an Eight's power can do a lot of good but used poorly, it can bring a lot of heartache and devastation to others. Many people interacting with average or unhealthy Eights also describe a lack of respect and too much confrontation from the Eight.

What's the Basic Fear driving this behavior? The fear of being controlled and harmed by others.

Type Eights believe that you are what you do. Somewhere along their life journey, they were conditioned to believe that the world is a tough place where only the strong survive. So they decided to be among the survivors by taking the lead and always striving to be in charge so they could keep their power.

How does this basic fear often manifest itself?

This fear is expressed in behavior as being too pushy, domineering, and even ego-centric. The person may come across as aggressive, confrontational, rude, impolite, and intense. In some cases, especially the very unhealthy Eights, they are notorious for creating drama around them, making it difficult to have real connections with anyone.

DESIRES AND MOTIVATIONS

The basic desire for a Type Eight is independence. They want to protect themselves and remain in control of their own lives. Being self-governed and in charge is their primary aim for a Type Eight, and nothing should jeopardize that. That typically makes an Eight incredibly courageous, strong, and dependable.

Enneagram Eights march to the beat of their own drum, unfettered by external sources' demands and perceived obligations. Once they feel secure about their actions and plans, they attack head-on with force and willpower until they get the job done.

They also love nurturing the people they care about, although they do it authoritatively. As challengers, they aren't afraid to impose their ideas and wills on others. While it tends to work out well for everyone under their care, things can get heated pretty quickly if you're on the opposing side of type Eight.

Core values

- Power
- Influence
- Achievement

- Perseverance
- Strength

Type Eight celebrities and famous people you might know to include minister Martin Luther King, Jr., Billionaire and former President Donald Trump, author Ernest Hemmingway, Comedian, and actor Jack Black, Singer Franck Sinatra, actor Sean Penn, Actress Susan Sarandon, actor Alec Baldwin, singer Aretha Franklin, Former U.K Prime Minister Winston Churchill, and President Franklin D. Roosevelt.

Wondering if you could be a Type Eight? Here are some personality indicators

1. When you're up against a problem, your first instinct is to tackle it single-handedly and head-on. Asking for help doesn't even cross your mind.
2. You refuse to enable self-pity or self-sabotage in the people you love. You want to see your loved ones thrive, even if that means you have to be the one who doles out some tough love.
3. You're not one to bend over backward trying to please people. You are fair and just in your decision-making, but you also know you can't make everyone happy all the time.
4. It's essential to have firm boundaries within your relationships. That way, you still feel as though you'd be in control of every other aspect of your life should the relationship end.
5. Often, your attitude comes off as intimidation or abrasive to others. But you know the world absolutely needs people like you, and in that crisis, you're the first person everyone would want by their side.

YOUR WINGS

Wings are the numbers adjacent to your Enneagram Type. As a Type Eight, you have-

- Enneagram Eight with a Seven-Wing: "The Maverick"
- Enneagram Eight with a Nine-Wing: "The Bear"

While you may have tendencies that lean into both wings at various stages of your life, you'll likely be more dominant in one than the other. This will be your most influential and dominant Wing.

Meaning of your Wing

If you're an 8w7 (Eight with Seven-Wing), you're more extroverted than the Eight with a Nine-Wing. The combination of Seven's fun, outgoing and impulsive personality combined with your natural assertiveness and energy makes you quite the supernova of every. It also means you're less guarded and more eager to enjoy life. Of course, the downside to this powerful combination is that 8W7 can quickly turn into an oppressive, uncaring, cruel maniac who thinks themselves omnipotent when operating at unhealthy levels. But on the other hand, a mature and highly developed individual will be the opposite, with great strength, vitality, and compassion. Basically unstoppable. Such individuals can have a lasting, sometimes legendary impact.

As an 8W7, you likely want to be in an entrepreneurial environment. Whether you work for yourself or the board of directors, it's essential that you are in charge and leading the rest of the people. You're most fulfilled when you can create optimistic and innovative plans, share your thoughts and opinions openly, and go after big things. Careers best suited to you include but aren't limited to:

- Politician

- Lawyer
- Entrepreneur
- Financial advisor
- Sales director
- Pilot
- Performer

If you're an 8W9 (Eight with Wing-Nine), you're more cooperative, less intense, and more family-oriented, thanks to the influence of the Nine Wing. While the Enneagram Nine is pretty much the opposite of an Enneagram Eight, the effect of having this peace-loving conflict avoiding Wing soothes the aggressive nature of the Eight. The term "Bear" comes from that visual of having a powerful figure fully equipped with claws that will destroy you but snuggly in their own way and less prone to use their power unnecessarily. Of course, this may vary from person to person. Some people with this wing may be more influenced, so the peaceful quality may vary. As a general rule, 8W9 will be more open to other people's opinions, calm, reassuring, and tend to use less of an iron fist in their leadership style. The combination of aggression and indifference can be tricky at average and unhealthy levels. At unhealthy levels, the influence of this Nine Wing leads to an unpredictable individual - calm and friendly one minute, then explosive and temperamental the next. For a healthy 8W9, the opposite is true, and in fact, we see this individual being extremely wise, generous, and protective of the people they love. They turn into great and benevolent patriarchs and matriarchs, at ease with themselves, strong-willed yet mild-mannered. People enjoy being led by such an individual.

As an 8w9, you probably want to be in a work environment where you have the space and freedom to be autonomous and still around others that you can help.

Careers best suited to you include but aren't limited to:

- Business owner
- Judge
- Activist
- Counselor
- Director
- Professor

The Arrows and what they mean

Your Enneagram personality type is linked to lines or arrows that show the path of growth or disintegration depending on where you are in life. When moving on a path of disintegration, a Type Eight will fall into the negative tappings of the arrow Five (5), where they suddenly become secretive and fearful. This is known as the Direction of Stress or Direction of Disintegration and typically occurs in the face of prolonged high stress. The other arrow indicates how a healthy version of your personality reacts and grows in more healthy environments. In this case, Type Eight integrates into the arrow Two (2), adopting the healthy aspects of the Two. That turns the lustful, controlling Eight into a more open-hearted, caring, and approachable individual. To understand the concept behind healthy and unhealthy levels, let's discuss the nine levels of development for a Type Eight.

THE 9 LEVELS OF DEVELOPMENT, FROM LOWEST TO HIGHEST

Levels of Development arise from Riso and Hudson's teachings and the founders of the Enneagram Institute, which is a great place to take your Enneagram Test. Their theory posits that all individuals fall into one of nine levels of functioning. The lowest level is nine, and the highest is level one. The levels are divided into a triad that subcategorizes these levels as healthy (1,2,3), average levels (4,5,6), and unhealthy levels (7,8,9).

Unhealthy Levels

Level 9: This is the lowest and most dangerous level for an adult Eight. Typically, we are all at this level during infancy. If we fail to rise to higher levels, we experience very unhealthy expressions and behavior with devastating consequences. For an Eight, this is where the person feels vengeful and murderous. They are barbaric with sociopathic tendencies. All this person cares about is getting what they want. When something or someone stands in their way, they may brutally destroy everything that doesn't conform to their will. Surrender is never an option.

Level 8: At this level, the Eight is delusional about their power, invincibility, and what they can achieve. They feel omnipotent and invulnerable and may recklessly over-extend themselves to get what they want.

Level 7: This unhealthy level for a Type Eight exhibits a hard-hearted, immoral, and potentially violent person. They hate any attempt to be controlled by anything or anyone and believe that might makes right. This Eight is completely ruthless and dictatorial in their approach.

Average Levels

Level 6: At this average level, we see an unhealthy Eight making progress toward maturity, but they are still combative, intimidating, aggressive, and use threats and reprisals to get obedience from others. Everything is a test of will for a Type Eight at this level of expression, and they're not very good at having healthy relationships because they use fear to control others.

Level 5: Type Eight is boastful, forceful, and ego-centric at this level. Being "the boss" and having everyone follow orders matters to this individual, and they want to impose their will and vision on everything. They don't see others as equal, so treating people with respect is challenging. What they want most is total domination of their environment.

Level 4: A Type Eight at this level of development is more enterprising, pragmatic, self-sufficient, and desires to have enough resources. They are risk takers who aren't afraid to bend the rules to get what they want. While they are hardworking and a little better with people, they struggle with emotions, often denying and neglecting their emotional needs.

Healthy Levels

Level 3: The individual at this level has grown into a healthy version of themselves, exhibiting more of their leadership and good people skills. This Eight is more decisive, authoritative, and commanding but in a more healthy way, championing people and protecting those under their wing. They are more honorable and courageously carry others with their strength.

Level 2: At this healthy level, we witness a mature individual who is self-assertive, confident, and strong, and people love to look up to this Eight. A Type Eight at this level has learned to stand up for what they need and want without stifling others, and they have respect for the people around them. They are extremely resourceful with a "can do" attitude that's contagious.

Level 1: Type Eight is at their best and healthiest version. Healing and transcendence bring about an individual who is self-restrained and magnanimous, merciful and forbearing. They are courageous, passionate, driven, and willing to put themselves in serious jeopardy to achieve their vision. A lasting influence is what they care about. In many cases, these individuals achieve historical greatness and true heroism.

ENNEAGRAM EIGHT'S PASSION

The Eight's Passion or deadly sin is lust. It typically expresses itself as intensity and excessiveness. Eights tend to think that anything worth doing is worth overdoing.

What the Eight needs is innocence. This is the virtue that will bring much-needed openness and calmness. It will enable the Eight to be more vulnerable and to respond (rather than react) in a fresh way to each moment without judgment or force. If you're reading this and recognize that you're an Eight, this is the work you must do. Bring yourself back to wholeness by embracing your innocence.

CHILDHOOD AND EMOTIONAL PATTERNS FOR A TYPE EIGHT

The Eight's belief that vulnerability is a sign of weakness likely started in childhood. For most Eights, their childhood environment had plenty of turmoil, and conflict or combat was necessary to survive. Perhaps due to violence, neglect, or simply being the youngest or smallest in a big family, the Eight child saw the need to adopt a tough persona. They decided to grow up quickly and portray a "strong" personality because vulnerability or "softness" would lead to rejection, hurt, or betrayal. If they had a relatively nurturing childhood, they'd probably take on a strong protective role (especially when raised with a single mother). And if they came from an abusive childhood, they'll live in constant anticipation of rejection and betrayal. The more rejected they feel, the more they harden their hearts and become aggressive.

As adults, Eights carry the same worldview and do everything in their power to maintain an upper hand in all circumstances. They are the ones people turn to and rely on when in need of guidance and strength. While this does make them quite formidable, it also makes it hard to develop an intimate connection because they never want to let their guard down. The childhood would is experienced in behavior even as an adult through anger, avoidance of affection, imposing their control and will on others, etc.

To heal the childhood wound, an Eight must reconnect with their Higher Self and recognize that vulnerability is strength. They must learn to practice self-compassion and recognize that it's okay to trust and lower their guard with a small trusted group of people. As an Enneagram Eight, your path to healing begins the moment you become aware that you have a need to be seen as a strong unstoppable, impenetrable force at all times.

SUBTYPES FOR TYPE EIGHT

The Enneagram profiling system allows for 3 subtypes in each type. These are Self-Preservation, Social, and One-to-One (Sexual) variants. Remember, all three instinctual variants exist in all of us, but the order in which they stack up determines their influence on our lives. One will be most dominant and the easiest for you to resonate with and observe as behavior and thought patterns in your life. The second will feel a little neutral and less influential, and the third will be the least significant. The third instinct becomes a blind spot for many because it's underdeveloped and out of their conscious recognition. Depending on which instinct is most dominant, it will shape your unique personality and how you approach life as an Eight.

Self Preservation Eight (SP)

SP Eight possesses the quality of seeking satisfaction at all costs. SP Eights are strong, direct, aggressive, and highly productive. They are great at getting results and often the pillars of strength for many as they take on the role of guardian, father, or mother figure. They are protective of their family and loved ones and are most concerned with survival and meeting their needs. If their conditions aren't met satisfactorily, SP Eights forcefully push things forward without guilt until they get what they want.

Social Eight (SO)

The SO Eight is the most rebellious of the subtypes and enjoys being a rebel and trailblazer. They enjoy being the group leader because they are intense in their desire to create change and authentically stand out. SO Eights are pretty impulsive, and their key quality is possession. They are driven by the need to accumulate power and influence so they can serve a worthy cause.

One-to-One/Sexual Eight (SX)

The SX Eight is the countertype of the Eights, and their key quality is solidarity. It's easy to mistype this Eight for a Type Two because, unlike the SP Eights and the SO Eights, these individuals use their power and influence more in the service of others rather than asserting their own needs. They are extremely sensitive to injustice and unfair social norms. SX Eights are loyal and protective and believe it's their duty to protect and shield their people from harm, unjust authority, and other abusive powers. While they aren't big on emotions and vulnerability, they tend to be more open, receptive to feedback, and have close allies they trust.

WORK AND LIFESTYLE TIPS FOR TYPE 8S

As part of your discovery and transformation, it's essential to recognize your triggers, the areas that you struggle with most, and where your opportunities for growth lie. Let's start with some of the struggles associated with your Enneagram Type.

STRUGGLES OF AN ENNEAGRAM EIGHT

Impatience

All Eights hate being around people who procrastinate or easily get distracted. They also can't stand waiting too long for results because they want results immediately. This quality of impatience can become a struggle if you don't find a better perspective when approaching big goals. Most of the time, it takes teamwork to achieve grand visions.

What to do: Be mindful of the goals and milestones you set for yourself and your team. Realize that people move at different paces, and some accomplishments do take time. Focus on progress instead of getting angry and impatient at the missing results.

Intimidating to others

Many people find you highly intimidating and perhaps too aggressive. That's probably because you hate sugarcoating things or beating around the bush. Some call it "intense," others call it "aggressive," and you don't get it. But it is something that's going to impact all your relationships.

What to do: Recognize that you are intense by nature and perhaps overly direct. With that awareness, approach your interactions mindfully and see if you can recognize instances where it's better to be calmer and let go a little. What would happen if you worked on bringing in a little more zen and harmony? Would you be less stressed? or healthier? Grateful?

Vulnerability and letting your guard down

Having a heart-to-heart and letting your guard down is tough. Ever since you can remember, you always needed to keep your defenses up to survive. Emotions and being vulnerable are signs of weakness, right? Turns out that's not entirely true. This struggle is real for all Eights until they learn how to rise to the higher levels of development and heal.

What to do: I know a part of you craves intimacy and tenderness. There is a way for you to be strong and still allow a few trusted people into your softer, gentler side. So let me encourage you to explore more about this topic.

Putting too much pressure on yourself

With big ambitious goals and the need to be the leader and protector of your universe, it's easy to put a lot of pressure on yourself. Asking for help is something all Enneagram Eights struggle with because it could lead to feelings of inadequacy or weakness. So I'm not suggesting you become a sissy, but I encourage you to delegate where needed. Having control of your life doesn't mean carrying the whole world on your shoulder. That need to constantly "run things" can become exhausting for yourself and others.

What to do: Invest a little time each day to have some quiet time where you can reflect, reset and regenerate. This quiet time will help you sort out your priorities and thoughts and help you feel more clear-headed and calm. Get in touch with nature by swimming in the ocean, hiking, biking, or walking in the local park.

ENNEAGRAM TYPE EIGHT UNDER STRESS

Enneagram Eights are typically stressed when they feel like they are being micro-managed, have to follow instead of lead, or can't see progress toward a goal. They also hate being around wishy-washy, lazy or manipulative people. As strong-willed as they are, feeling like they are not in control of things or dealing with failure can become highly stressful. But perhaps the thing that quickly causes a downward spiral to disintegration is a lack of challenge.

If you're an Eight and stress is mounting, don't wait for things to get out of hand. Instead, give yourself some distance from the thing stressing you and just allow yourself to decompress. Get clear-minded about the situation, and don't allow anger or feelings of injustice or rejection to crowd your thinking. Tune into your breathing and help your body calm down. If there's someone you trust, this would be a good time to let your guard down and share what's stressing you. Remember, letting someone in doesn't make you weak. It helps you gain perspective. And once you've got perspective and clarity, make your next move. You may not solve the entire issue instantly with a single move, but you should be fine as long as progress is made.

RELATIONSHIPS

Enneagram Eights are passionate, protective, daring, intense, purposeful, authentic, dynamic, and invested in their relationships.

In romantic relationships, Eights are interested in having a partner who can challenge them to become their best self. They seek loyal and independent partners who aren't afraid to go after what they want in life. To some, this might be too intense. In fact, some do perceive Eights as being overly competitive and a little intimidating. But if you're an Eight, then you also know there's a hidden softer layer that you only allow a chosen few to experience and those that do stick with you for a long time.

Relationship tips

Eights need to be the leader in the workplace, and they want to be responsible for the significant challenges and issues. They need a dynamic work environment with people who trust that their leader will get the results.

RELATIONSHIP TIPS WITH OTHER TYPES

Here are some ways to improve your relationships with other Enneagram Types.

Type 8 & Type 1: With a Type One, the relationship is based on truthfulness, fairness, and a lot of intentionalities. The One offers a systematic, detailed approach to life and your relationship. You and your partner are justice-oriented, responsible, and firm in your convictions. At the same time, you bring a sense of protection and deep loyalty that's comforting to your partner. Your relationship can be highly hospitable, family-oriented, and vibrant when operating at healthy levels. As a couple, you stay active, succeed in your careers, travel, and take any chance to change the world for the better.

A challenge that might create tension is how you prioritize your energies. You're more open and expressive of your anger. At the same time, the One is more self-controlled, carefully choosing their words and trying their best to repress anger. Your partner can easily get frustrated with your outbursts, and you might feel like you're being controlled. Grow together by reminding each other that you're on the same team.

Type 8 & Type 2: The relationship is passionate and energetic with a Type Two. You both see something needed in the other. You need that compassionate, gentle warmth that you want to protect, and your partner is drawn to your power and tenacity. The Two softens your edges, and you empower the Two to set healthy boundaries and learn to be more assertive. At healthy levels, you bring out the best in each other.

A challenge you might face is when you have a difference in opinion or a disagreement. You might also get into trouble for being too self-reliant and guarded, especially if still at average levels where opening up to intimacy is an issue. You might feel overwhelmed or smothered by the Two's need for constant affection. Meanwhile, your independent streaks could be interpreted as a loss of love by your partner, making them demanding. Grow together by continuing to develop to higher levels and embrace the safety and security you provide for one other.

Type 8 & Type 3: With a Three, you have a powerful dynamic relationship built on mutual respect, trust, and love. You are both intense, influential, and lively. That kind of passion and assertiveness enables you to go after anything you want in life. The relationship is highly satisfying because you finally find someone who can match your energy yet complements you in many ways. The Three finds a safe place to land because you aren't easily swayed and enjoy the high energy of your partner. They are never intimidated by your power, which is very comforting. You can finally let go of control a little because you know your partner is competent and responsible.

When your personalities clash, you might experience a challenge, especially when you fall to average and unhealthy levels. Just as you positively match each other's energy, the same is true when things go dark. You easily see the Three's outer mask, which can create doubt about your partner's authenticity. Your fear of betrayal can create tension, and unfortunately, when the Three reads this tension, they tend to withdraw. Grow together by learning to let go, trust each other more, and add more fun to the relationship. Things don't always need to be controlled and zipped up.

Type 8 & Type 4: With a Four, your relationship is filled with passion and intensity. It's authentic and deep. The Four offers sensitivity and emotional vulnerability, and you bring practicality, strength, and protection to the relationship. There's a magnetic pull between you as you constantly seek to understand and conquer the mystery of one another.

A challenge you'll encounter is during the conflict. Explosive tempers and disagreements can quickly get out of hand, given how emotionally reactive you are. Neither you nor your partner like to be controlled, and you're both highly expressive, meaning it's easy to say things you might regret later. Because you're both reactive and enjoy the excitement, it's easy to get into cycles of fighting and make-up. While that might keep things interesting for a while, it's not healthy for a lasting relationship. Grow together by increasing the level of compassion you express, especially during conflicts. Work on rising to higher levels of development to become less reactive and remind each other that what you want is to be fully heard and understood.

Type 8 & Type 5: With a Five, the relationship is deep, loyal, and autonomous. You both share that independent streak and find something needed in the other. The Five often feels as misunderstood in the world as you do and that bonds you together in a strange way. The Five offers you deep, thought-provoking conversations and makes you aware of higher knowledge and the impact your actions have in life. You help the Five become more practical and in tune with their power and intuition.

A challenge in this relationship comes from the fact that you both seek to isolate in different ways. You desire to be entirely self-reliant through attaining physical and material resources. The Five takes pride in needing nothing and wanting less physical or material attachments. When this goes too far, it can drive a wedge between you, especially when you refuse to admit your needs to each other. Grow together by learning to acknowledge that you have needs. It's okay to have needs, whether physical, emotional, intellectual, or spiritual. Recognize that you both crave a more profound connection that can only come from intimacy and embracing vulnerability together. It's scary but worthwhile if you do it together.

Type 8 & Type 6: Everything is an open book with a Six. The Six craves safety and security. Your partner feels they can trust and depend on you through your protective, decisive, and transparent nature. You like the loyalty and dependability of the Six. You're both direct in communication and get everything out on the table.

A challenge you might face in this relationship is mistrust and reactivity during conflicts. Things go wrong when you don't feel like you can trust each other. The Six might find your bullish approach off-putting and destabilizing. You might see the constant questioning and concern as a lack of trust. At this point, you might walk away, especially if you suspect rejection. Grow together by reassuring one another that you're looking out for each other and that your relationship is safe. Avoid always attempting to control the situation. Instead, work on creating safety and keeping communication open.

Type 8 & Type 7: With a Seven, the relationship is full of fun, adventure, optimism, and boundless energy. The combination of both your energies is explosive in a positive way. The Seven helps you lighten up and have fun; you help the Seven become more practical, attentive, and grounded in the present moment. You're both assertive, dynamic, and captivating. There's never a dull moment in your relationship.

A challenge in this relationship comes from your values and how you approach conflict. You might see the Seven's cheerful disposition as lacking maturity and authenticity. And when someone isn't authentic, you have a hard time letting your guard down. The Seven might find you too controlling, leading to a battle for autonomy. Grow together by slowing down long enough to notice your reactions. Ask yourself if overreacting is helpful or healthy for your relationship. Be more present and mindful. Encourage each other to work through unpleasant and uncomfortable emotions.

Type 8 & Type 8: The relationship is mirrored with a fellow Type Eight. You're both strong-willed, intense, powerful, and protective, and you just get each other. You know you can fully trust each other, and you love the respect you have in your relationship. You lead a dynamic lifestyle because you constantly challenge each other to grow and improve. There's never a dull season in your world.

A challenge that may arise here is how similar your temperaments are. Given your intensity and explosive nature, especially if anger hasn't been resolved, it's easy for things to get out of hand. If you feel like you're being controlled by the other, you may shut down and withdraw from the relationship. Grow together by maintaining an open dialogue. Work on rising to higher levels of development together and embrace vulnerability. Genuinely affirm one another. Do it frequently.

Type 8 & Type 9: With a Nine, the relationship is stable, calm, nurturing, and autonomous. The Nine helps you learn when to pull back and how to relax. They make you feel loved and accepted just as you are. It's safe to be yourself, and the relationship is earnest and respectful. You help the Nine find their voice, see their value and assert themselves more. You both enjoy the connection, companionship, and safety you offer one another.

A common challenge here is how you both deal with anger and conflict. Although you're both in the body triad, you deal with anger by expressing it, while a Nine deals with it by avoiding it at all costs. So when conflicts arise, a Nine will withdraw, become distant, and disengaged. That's probably going to frustrate you tremendously, and in your heated temper, the Nine becomes resentful of your behavior. They will never stand their ground and fight no matter how offended they feel, and it's easy for you to misread that. Grow together by allowing each other space to process negative emotions. Be open about this and communicate how you'll deal with disagreements. Create enough time to do some fun activities together regularly to keep that connection strong.

AFFIRMATIONS:

- I am in control of my own destiny.
- Life happens for me, not to me.
- I value collaboration over competition.
- I am learning to let my guard down and trust those I love.
- I aspire to lead and inspire others.
- What I judge in others is what I judge in myself.
- I am kind to myself and others.

Remember affirmations only work when what you say deeply resonates with how you feel. Make sure you pick affirmations that align with your emotions for best results.

DAILY TIPS FOR GROWTH AND HAPPINESS

Schedule reflective time

It's essential to have a little downtime where you can just "be." Allowing yourself time to clear your mind and refocus will give you more energy and open you to higher perspectives. It will also keep you calm. Speaking of calm, let's talk about some mindfulness practices.

Practice mindfulness daily

Find some mindfulness practices that can enable you to process emotions, stay calm, and ground yourself at any given moment. Some can become part of your morning or evening routine, while others can be little hacks to deploy whenever necessary. Consider journaling, meditation, yoga, nature walks, mindfulness baths/showers, and deep breathing. Find what works best for you. These mindfulness practices will keep you calm and in the present moment. The more present you are, the more powerful you become.

Embrace vulnerability and your softer side

This will be scary at first. You don't need to become vulnerable with everyone. Study some materials to learn more about what it means to be vulnerable, tune into your emotions, and pick a few people you can choose to let in. Brené Brown is an expert on vulnerability, so you might want to Google her and watch one of her many videos that describe what vulnerability is and its benefits. The most important thing is to shift that core belief around vulnerability so you can realize that it makes you stronger, not weaker. Take your time working on this, and trust that even a little bit of vulnerability will positively affect your relationships.

ENNEAGRAM TYPE 9

THE PEACEMAKER OR MEDIATOR

T he last two chapters of this book are dedicated to uncovering the details of the Enneagram Type Nine, commonly referred to as the peacemaker or mediator. As you may have guessed, this personality type values keeping peace above all else. Internal and external peace should be maintained at all costs, even if it means avoidance or conformity. Nines are absolutely loveable, and everyone loves to be around them because they are always accepting, assuring, loving, easygoing, and just nice to be around. They are very stable in their behavior and often too willing to just go with the flow even when it doesn't serve their highest good. Nines are part of the body triad along with Eights and Nines, which means they rely primarily on their gut to navigate life. Their core unresolved emotion is Anger, but unlike the Eights, who have no difficulty expressing their temper, the Nines do everything possible to suppress it. They don't redirect it inwardly as the Ones do but instead try to pretend it doesn't exist. There might be a leak often, and you may notice bouts of temper, which can be shocking for others around them since they come across as cool and calm. They are a brewing ocean of stored anger and resentment.

Nines always strive to achieve harmony and peace. Their primary focus is comfort. Driven to connect with the people around them and be part of a group or community, Nines have a tendency to go the extra mile to be part of the group, even if it means disregarding their own needs or feelings. So it's not uncommon for a Nine to feel like they've lost their identity or don't have a voice in a relationship or group, especially if the people involved are stronger in opinion and personality. When operating at high levels of development and at their best, Nines are optimistic, creative, all-embracing, and excellent at bringing people together and healing conflicts. Nines become stubborn, lethargic, and indecisive at average and unhealthy levels.

STRENGTHS OF A NINE

The Nine can see multiple people's perspectives at once. That's a unique quality that no one Enneagram Type possesses. It makes them great peacekeepers and mediators.

Another strength they possess is actively listening without judgment, offering a sense of acceptance and love. When you confide in a Nine, you feel "heard and seen," which makes people love being around them.

Key personality traits of a Nine

- Calm, collected demeanor
- Mellow and soothing
- Likeable
- Wide circle of acquaintances

Common hobbies for a Type Nine

- Meditating
- Exploring nature
- Napping

- Relaxing with friends
- Practicing spirituality

FEARS AND WEAKNESSES

Type Nines have a basic fear of loss and separation. They can't stand being separated from others and really fear a loss of any kind, unresolved conflict, and relational tension. Nines are known to avoid anything and everything that could jeopardize their sense of harmony because they never want to feel fragmented. Deep down, all a Nine really wants is to feel at peace all the time.

Another issue for Nines is the fear of being too needy and thus pushing people away. That's why Nines always strive to be the glue of a group or relationship. They do everything to maintain a harmonious state, even if it overrides their desires. Often this fear comes from the belief that their opinions and needs don't matter as much as those of others. This tends to become a weakness for Nines because as they avoid all disturbances and confrontations, they may become resentful. Average and unhealthy Nines also develop passive aggressive tendencies.

Somewhere along with their upbringing, they picked up the message that their opinions, needs, wants, and dreams don't matter. So you'll often find Nines struggling to express their own ideas or even saying "no" to something.

What's the Basic Fear driving this behavior? The fear of losing their connection and becoming fragmented.

How does this basic fear often manifest itself?

Of all Enneagram Types, Nines are the most self-forgetting. It's the most pronounced expression of their fear. They'll forget their thoughts, priorities in life, and goals. When faced with a conflict or confrontation, the Nine's natural reaction is to disengage from people and their emotions even when it would be in their best interest to participate.

Another expression of this fear is the brewing inner resentment and the outer passive aggressive behavior that's quite common for average and unhealthy Nines. At times their need to avoid anything that disrupts harmony can cause them to become numb to situations and negative emotions, leading to withdrawal.

DESIRES AND MOTIVATIONS

The basic desire for a Type Nine is to have inner stability, peace of mind, and to feel whole and connected. They are motivated to keep peace around them, which causes them to be very agreeable. Unfortunately, leaning too much into this motivation does lead to unhealthy behavior that creates inner turmoil for the Nine. That's why it's crucial for a Nine to be intentional and courageous enough to decide what kind of peace and harmony they want in life, and then practice speaking up when their peace is violated instead of withdrawing.

Nines desire to feel safe, accepted, and heard even though they may not articulate it. This desire feeds into the way they exist in the world, how they see themselves, and their relationships with others. Feeling seen, heard, and accepted energizes a Nine and further deepens their connection with others.

Core values

- Harmony
- Gentleness
- Compassion
- Balance

Type Nine celebrities and famous people you might know to include Former President Barack Obama, Former President Ronald Reagan, Former President Bill Clinton, Actor Morgan Freeman, Actress Audrey Hepburn, Actress Whoopie Goldberg, Former President Abraham Lincoln, Her Majesty Queen Elizabeth II, Actor Clint Eastwood, and the 14th Dalai Lama.

Wondering if you're a Type 9? Here are some personality indicators

1. Conflict of any kind is the worst thing in the world.
2. Coffee is the magic miracle working drink you can't live without.
3. It's easy for you to see all perspectives at any given time. One of your greatest strengths is that you can hold and understand multiple perspectives.
4. You struggle to believe that you matter and that your presence matters.
5. Routines rock, and you can't figure out how other people live without routines.
6. You easily procrastinate, especially when overwhelming kicks in.
7. Comfort matters to you a lot.
8. You're naturally very stubborn when you want to be.
9. Getting started on a new project is hard for you, but you see things through once you get started.
10. You're very easygoing and always going with the flow.
11. The outdoors is very calming and peaceful for you. You absolutely love the great outdoors.

YOUR WINGS

Wings are the numbers adjacent to your Enneagram Type. As a Nine, you have -

- The Enneagram Nine with an Eight Wing: "The Referee"
- The Enneagram Nine with One Wing: "The Dreamer"

While you may have tendencies that lean into both wings at various stages of your life, you'll likely be more dominant in one than the other. This will be your most influential and Dominant Wing.

Meaning of your Wing

If you're a 9w8 (Nine with Eight-Wing), you're more energetic and confident. The combination of being a personality that tries to avoid conflict at all costs yet is influenced by a wing that absolutely loves conflict is quite complex. It turns out, however, that this combination works in your favor because the Eight Wing gives you more access to your anger, so you're no longer afraid to express that emotion. However, because you're fundamentally a Nine, you never let it get out of hand, and you quickly restore peace once you've made your point. At unhealthy levels, the influence of this Wing can lead to a lot of contradicting behavior. You might be highly energetic in one area of your life while being neglectful and lazy in other parts. You can also become too stubborn, depressed, and resistant to any help, only to lash out in unexpected bursts of violence. However, when operating at healthy levels, the influence of the Eight Wing makes you assertive, strong, and still gracious. You're still gentle and easygoing, but you can slam down hard when the situation calls for it.

Common career types that best suit a 9w8 include:

- Judge
- Social worker
- Religious worker
- Veterinarian
- Salesperson
- Diplomat

- Editor

If you're a 9w1 (Nine with One-Wing), you're more idealistic and disciplined. The combination of a Nine and One (depending on how strong it is) can turn into a very principled, focused, and often more confident individual. The influence of the One-Wing gives you a stronger sense of right and wrong and a more idealistic view of the world. Your patient openness combined with the objectivity of a One makes you a wonderfully non-judgmental counselor with outstanding levels of integrity. On more unhealthy levels, the conflict avoidance typical of a Nine can mix with the smoldering resentment of a One to produce a particularly sarcastic and indirect form of anger. When things get pretty bad, this unhealthy Nine can feel morally superior towards others, and perfectionism can take over in certain parts of their life while they become totally neglectful in other areas.

But of course, there are also the healthier versions of a 9w1, and that's when you become really organized, rational in your thinking, and highly productive. You become more effective and willing to share your ideas with others. Your active listening skills and ability to see things from multiple perspectives are enhanced by the influence of the One Wing, making you a powerful counselor or mediator.

Common career types that best suit a 9w1 include:

- Museum curator
- Counselor
- Nurse
- Diplomat
- Environmental scientist
- Human Resources Director
- Pharmacist

Arrows and what they mean

Your Enneagram personality type is linked to two other "lines" or points that are worth noting. These lines are called arrows, and each indicates how you show up at your best and worst. One Arrow called the Arrow of Disintegration shows the lines of stress (your path of destruction), and for you, that path lies in number 6. As you disintegrate, you pick up the unhealthy habits of an Enneagram Six and become more anxious and worried. We'll talk more about stress and how to avoid falling into disintegration in the next chapter.

The other line connected to your Enneagram type is 3, which is the Arrow of integration. That means that moving on the path of growth and integration, you take on healthy traits from a Three that make you self-developing, productive and energetic like healthy Threes. To understand the relationship between these arrows and how we fall into unhealthy patterns or rise into healthy ones, let's discuss the nine levels of development. The goal here is to identify where you might be and move toward the highest level, i.e., healthy level 1.

THE 9 LEVELS OF DEVELOPMENT, FROM LOWEST TO HIGHEST

Levels of Development arise from Riso and Hudson's teachings and the founders of the Enneagram Institute, which is a great place to take your Enneagram Test. Their theory posits that all individuals fall into one of nine levels of functioning. The lowest level is nine, and the highest is level one. The levels are divided into a triad that subcategorizes these levels as healthy (1, 2, 3), average levels (4, 5, 6), and unhealthy levels (7, 8, 9).

Unhealthy

Level 9: This is the lowest and most destructive level for an adult Nine. We're all usually at this level during infancy, so there's nothing wrong with this level. Problems arise if we fail to grow, develop, and spiritually mature because then we get stuck expressing behaviors associated with this level, which leads to terrible consequences. For a Nine, this is where they become completely self abandoning, severely disoriented, and catatonic. Some even struggle with multiple personalities, feeling like shattered, empty shells.

Level 8: A this level, a Type Nine is numb, depersonalized, and unable to function as a productive member of society. In an attempt to block out anything that could affect them, they become completely disconnected from themselves and the world.

Level 7: The Nine at this level feel incapable of facing problems. Everything is simply too overwhelming making them highly repressed, undeveloped, and ineffectual. Some are so neglectful to the point of being a danger to others.

Average

Level 6: At this level, the Nine have grown enough to the point where they aren't completely disconnected and numb. However, they are still pretty bad at dealing with disturbances and conflict. Stubbornness is a key quality at this stage of their growth, and they tend to minimize problems. Some are fatalistic and resigned as if nothing could be done to change things, while others become frustrated and angry by their tendency to procrastinate and engage in conflict-avoidance.

Level 5: At this level, the Nine is active but inattentive and disengaged. They walk away from problems and prefer to sweep things under the rug to avoid discomfort. This Nine is emotionally indolent and totally indifferent to anything that threatens the harmony they crave.

Level 4: This Nine is the classic easygoing "yes" man or woman who will do anything to avoid conflict and maintain connections with others. They are highly neglectful of their own needs and tend to fall into conventional roles and expectations, losing their identity to accommodate others. This type of Nine often deflects and can be known to be quite philosophical as a coping mechanism to appease others.

Healthy

Level 3: At this level, the Nine have grown into the mature healthier levels of development. Here we witness an individual who is optimistic, supportive, reassuring, and great at communication. That facilitates connection and oneness in all their relations. They have a healing and calming influence that brings people together and facilitates great mediation.

Level 2: At this level, the Nine is emotionally stable, serene, self-accepting, and more in tune with their identity. They are at ease with life, themselves, and others. Their expression and behavior are simple and innocent. Everyone loves Nines at this level of development because they are genuinely nice, unpretentious, good-natured, and trusting of themselves and others.

Level 1: This is a Nine at their best and highest expression. The individual is autonomous, fulfilled, content, and intensely alive at this level. They have great equanimity and are fully present to themselves, making them even more powerful and present in their relationships. This Nine has found oneness with self and a deep connection to others simultaneously.

ENNEAGRAM NINE'S PASSION

Type Nine's Passion or deadly sin is sloth. It typically expresses itself as indifference. Nines like to spend energy keeping the outside world out and the inside world in instead of paying attention to the self. They seem to have psycho-spiritual laziness, which unfortunately causes them to lose touch with their core self.

What the Nine needs is the right action. This is the virtue that will bring much-needed aliveness, engagement, commitment, and a willingness to act on what they know is right. If you're reading this and recognize that you're a Nine, this is the work you must do. Bring yourself back into wholeness and reconnect with your core self. Come back into the present moment, right action.

CHILDHOOD AND EMOTIONAL PATTERNS FOR ENNEAGRAM NINE

One might wonder, how did the Nine develop this belief that their presence doesn't matter? Most of the time, it begins in childhood. As a child, a Nine might have been deeply connected to the parental figures but in some way felt overlooked. The Nine might have learned that it's easier to keep the peace by not being assertive at some point. They may have been a middle or younger child unable to get the attention they needed or a quiet voice whose opinion got lost in a sea of loud or forceful voices. Regardless of the details, the Nine got used to blending in and just going along to avoid getting upset or creating disturbances. Most Nines are easygoing children who accommodate the family's needs, cause no trouble, never ask for anything, and are great at keeping peace when conflicts arise.

Because Nines are so connected to the people they love, they have difficulty differentiating their own feelings from others. Connecting to their parents gives them a sense of identity. And so, they grow up out of tune with their own feelings and always in the background of other people's stories.

As adults, the same patterns show up as Nines assume it's best to reserve their involvement and numb themselves to pain. Because nothing is important to them, nothing can let them down. This is a perspective held by many wounded Nines. Their childhood wounds show up as procrastination, indecisiveness, sleeping for long periods, and indifference.

To heal the childhood wound, a Nine must reconnect with their Higher Self and realize that their ideas, opinions, and presence matter. They need to cultivate a new mindset concerning their value and worth. As a Nine, you need to remind yourself that you have a unique identity to you alone and that your true identity is whole, always peaceful, and confident.

SUBTYPES FOR TYPE NINE

The Enneagram profiling system allows for 3 subtypes in each type. These are Self-Preservation, Social, and One-to-One (Sexual) variants. Remember, all three instinctual variants exist in all of us, but the order in which they stack up determines their influence on our lives. One will be most dominant and the easiest for you to resonate with and observe as behavior and thought patterns in your life. The second will feel a little neutral and less influential, and the third will be the least significant. The third instinct becomes a blind spot for many because it's totally underdeveloped and out of their conscious recognition. Depending on which instinct is most dominant, it will shape your unique personality and how you approach life as a Nine.

Self Preservation Nine (SP)

SP Nines are most concerned with meeting their physical needs. They enjoy keeping a routine around their activities and creating comfort in their lives. Peace and time alone are vital to them, and they often become irritable and stubborn when others upset their balance. SP Nines prefer to collect things to fill that void to avoid dealing with their internal states.

Social Nine (SO)

SO Nines work hard to support their groups to find belonging and comfort. Their essential quality is participation because they like to feel like they are part of something. As the countertype of the subtype Nine, these individuals work really hard to keep the people in their life happy. Sometimes, that leads to overworking, pain, or stress, which they tend to hide by putting on a happy front to avoid burdening others.

One-to-One/Sexual Nine (SX)

SX Nines have the quality of fusion because they are most likely to merge with a significant other as a strategy to feed their sense of self and guarantee comfort. SX Nines tend to feel most secure when partnered with others and may find it challenging to be on their own. Boundaries? What boundaries? For an SX Nine, aligning their personal desires and attitudes with the other is what matters, even if it means sacrificing their Truth and personal identity.

WORK AND LIFESTYLE TIPS FOR TYPE 9S

As part of your discovery and transformation, it's essential to recognize your triggers, the areas that you struggle with most, and where your opportunities for growth lie.

STRUGGLES OF AN ENNEAGRAM NINE

Burying your voice under politeness

Placating others is detrimental to your happiness, yet many Nines are guilty of this. They say "It's fine" or "you decide" just because they want to avoid conflict. Unfortunately, opting to be polite and speaking up, especially when someone offends you, only leads to buried resentment, loneliness, and pent-up anger. It makes you feel invisible, unheard, and unloved even when the person didn't mean it to happen.

What to do: Talk about your interests with others and invite people to do things with you that you love. Refuse to say "whatever you want" for a week and notice how much better you'll feel. People who love you will not be offended when you have an opinion. They'll respect and love you even more for your presence.

Putting things off until the last minute

Procrastination is real for Nines. Putting things off until the last minute just seems to be second nature, but unfortunately, it's neither healthy nor productive.

What to do: Make a short list of what you want to accomplish each day. Break down large goals or projects into mini milestones and then set some deadlines for the mini goals. As you complete each mini goal, reward yourself with a small treat. When the big project or goal is achieved, do something wonderful to celebrate yourself.

Indecisiveness

This is a struggle all Nines experience. The gift of seeing and holding multiple perspectives when interacting with others also means that you may have difficulty choosing a side or having a clear opinion. You're not alone. Most Nines say it's tough to know what they really want or believe, especially when presented with equally good options. Average to unhealthy Nines struggle even more with this because, in addition, they are also out of tune with their own desires.

What to do: Stop trying to make everyone happy. It's impossible to lead a life where you make everyone happy all the time. In the end, you forget your own Truth. When you feel undecided or unsure about what you want, say, " I need some time to think it over." Practice a little assertiveness and watch the magic it will add to your relationships.

Denying your anger

All Nines desire inner and outer peace. They want to be authentic and understood. Being the calm, nurturing one is of great importance to them, and unfortunately, that tends to create conflict avoidance. It can also lead to denial because rather than acknowledge this emotion or the offense they've taken, they'll try to suppress it.

What to do: Become more aware of that anger and resentment brewing inside since childhood when you learned that your presence doesn't matter. Being cool on the outside but irritated on the inside doesn't do you any good. It certainly doesn't bring you closer to the lasting wholeness you seek. So it's time to let it go. Notice how often and quickly you get judgmental, irritable, or tense. What underlying issues are at play when you feel these emotions? Try to voice them sooner rather than later to avoid having outbursts that you'll regret.

ENNEAGRAM TYPE NINE UNDER STRESS

Enneagram Nines typically get stressed when dealing with peer pressure, when they are forced into a position they're not comfortable with or when there's conflict around them. They hate being with people who enjoy drama or divas who enjoy having the spotlight. It's also super stressful for a Nine to have too many demands on their time. But perhaps the most dangerous habit for a Nine is to suppress their anger for too long.

If you're a Nine, you already know you get stressed when you say "yes " to things you don't really want to do. You also know that relationships are essential to you, so you must find a way to be yourself and still maintain those healthy relationships. It comes down to developing enough courage to be yourself. Give yourself permission to own your voice and use it in your relationships. Start by finding healthy ways to "let out" all the anger, frustration, and resentment you've suppressed. Process this anger either on your own through journaling and mindfulness practices or with the help of a professional. Learn to tune into your body and emotions. What are your physical, emotional, and spiritual needs? What do you love? Recognize that you are a unique individual with unique strengths, talents, and dreams. Be courageous enough to pursue the things you love and allow others to support you on this journey. Trust that your loved ones will continue to love you even when you say no to their requests.

RELATIONSHIPS

Nines are supportive, patient, encouraging, pleasant to be with, and accepting in all their relationships. Because they value harmony and comfort, all their relationships are easygoing and offer soothing comfort and stability. Nines long to be loved and cared for in a way that supports their peace and creates genuine, deep, connected love.

Nines can merge so strongly with their partner that they lose their individuality and personal identity in romantic relationships. They are usually willing to go above and beyond to create a loving space for the relationship to thrive.

Creating an environment that fosters goodwill and togetherness is important to Nines. They are very good at keeping peace within a team setting. They are steady and balanced in their approach to projects and relationships at work. However, their main challenge is to stay focused on priorities and speak up when they need to stand their ground, especially when it's uncomfortable, or a potential conflict ensues.

RELATIONSHIP TIPS WITH OTHER TYPES

Here are some ways to improve your relationships as an Enneagram Nine.

Type 9 & Type 1: With a One, you're in a stable, comforting relationship. With a Type One also being part of the body triad, you both give of yourselves physically to others, often with minimal attention to yourselves. You take great satisfaction in loving others in the community and giving generously to each other. The One brings a sense of duty and is more task-oriented, which is very helpful to you because it enables you to create routines that facilitate the peace you desire. Your kind accepting nature is attractive to the Type One and causes them to be more self-forgiving and self-accepting. You also remind Type One to choose people over principle, and they help you speak your Truth more. You both value being ethical and considerate. It's a very purposeful and enriching relationship.

A challenge you might encounter here, especially if you're both operating at average or lower levels of development, is your unresolved anger. Both you and Type One tend to deal with anger in unhealthy ways. You're concerned with repressing anger to keep peace and avoid conflict. At the same time, Type One is concerned with suppressing it appropriately. That pent-up anger can leak out as explosive tempers or resentment/stubbornness/silence, all of which are unhealthy for a lasting relationship. Grow together by finding healthy ways to deal with anger and other negative emotions. Work on rising to higher levels of development as a couple and affirm one another and the relationship during tense situations.

Type 9 & Type 2: With a Two, you're in a warm, nurturing, loving, serene and comfortable relationship. It's a highly engaging and reciprocal relationship. You're not demanding and always accepting, which allows the Two freedom to tend to their own needs. You also offer the Two a sense of security and stability where they feel loved for who they really are. Your partner helps you get in tune with your own desires and offers a warm embrace for you to express them.

You might encounter a challenge if the Two's helpful energy feels overwhelming for you. Perhaps you find them too emotional, which might create an inner disturbance. Twos are also quite action-oriented while you're easier going and like to move through life in a relaxed way. When you become upset, you tend to become passive and distant, while Twos become resentful and indignant. To work through all these issues, grow together by learning to acknowledge and resolve conflict as it comes up. Take the time you need to process, but don't repress negative emotions. Remind each other that true peace is cultivated when conflict is addressed in healthy ways.

Type 9 & Type 3: With a Three, you're in a dynamic, purposeful, encouraging, and driven relationship. You give your partner the space to be themselves with total acceptance and love. The Three offers you encouragement to find your voice and follow your dreams. They see potential in you and become your biggest cheerleader. There's great balance and reciprocity in this relationship, and you enjoy the peace, respect, and trust that you both provide.

A challenge you might experience, especially when you're both at average or lower levels of development, is during the conflict. The Three might feel like you're holding them back from achieving their goals, and you might feel like they're just neglecting you and making no time for the relationship. Your easygoing nature can become a frustration for the Three, who see it as inaction. You might feel pushed and rushed to keep moving faster and chasing after targets. Instead of withdrawing, grow together by remembering that there's good in both of you. The speed you both operate is neither wrong nor right, so you just need to find a balance that works. Keep an open dialogue and encourage each other to grow to higher levels.

Type 9 & Type 4: With a Four, the relationship is deep, sensitive, empathetic, and non-judgmental. You both value independence and want to have a deep connection. The Four offers that acute emotional awareness that encourages you to go deeper and voice your emotional experiences. Your non-judgmental nature enables the Four to move toward self-love instead of drowning in self-doubt. As the pragmatic one in the relationship, you help keep things stable, which keeps the Four grounded. You also become a lot more energetic and outgoing under the influence of the Four.

A challenge you might face here comes from your opposing reactions to stress. When you get stressed or, a conflict arises, your natural response is to disengage to maintain peace. Meanwhile, the Four is emotionally reactive under stress and conflict. So when you withdraw, your partner sees that as a lack of presence and an unwillingness to work through things because they believe that it's important to express all feelings. While that becomes an overwhelming and unsettling experience for you, grow together by learning to give each other the chance to process stress in a manner that suits your personality. Consider finding healthy stress-releasing activities that you can use, e.g., journaling. When you do discuss the issue, do so with compassion and thoughtfulness.

Type 9 & Type 5: With a Five, you're in a thoughtful, calm, stable, accepting, and autonomous relationship. Because both of you can easily get overwhelmed by the demands of the world, you establish structures that enable you to maintain the peace you want. As the Five puts their attention on you with great curiosity, you're able to put to words your thoughts and ideas. That creates more self-awareness and a sense of connection. You help the Five feel more relaxed and at ease which is significant because often, Fives feel like they can't be comfortable in this world.

A challenge you might face in this relationship is, of course, when things get challenging. Your easygoing nature can turn passive-aggressive and quite stubborn during the conflict. On the other hand, Fives are rational and objective, so they'll have difficulty understanding your reaction. The other thing is that you both prefer to take time alone to process thoughts and feelings before verbalizing them, which can cause conflict to simmer for days before being fully addressed. Sometimes, you may cope with conflict in your own separate ways and never really come together to discuss and resolve it as a couple. Grow together by finding ways to stay grounded and present, especially when things get tough. Consider sitting down together to write down your feelings and discuss them until the issue is resolved.

Type 9 & Type 6: With a Six, you're in a stable, comforting, predictable, loving relationship. The Six offers loyalty, security, unity, affection, quick-mindedness, and action, which enables you to be a more active force in your life. Your calm demeanor stabilizes the Six, who tends to be more skeptical and alert to issues. Healthy interdependence is assured in a relationship like this, and you both enjoy it.

A challenge you might face with this relationship is again during moments of stress. The Six's questioning can feel accusatory to you, while your withdrawal can feel like abandonment to your partner. Another issue is that Sixes tend to be reactive during the conflict, primarily if operating at lower levels of development which, as you know, is very uncomfortable for your personality. Grow together by keeping an open dialogue and supporting each other in voicing your needs and wants. Be clear about what you really want in life and how you want your relationship to be.

Type 9 & Type 7: With a Seven, the relationship is full of energy, adventure, and optimism. The Seven brings fun, assertiveness, and self-confidence and helps you break out of your shell and try new things. You bring steadiness, calmness, and a personal touch that the Seven finds attractive. Both of you like looking to the bright side of life, and your differences complement each other.

A challenge you might face is the stubbornness you both have. When it rears its ugly head, things can go wrong, especially if you don't take the time to work through the issues as they come up. The Seven is more likely to surface conflict since they don't want to be trapped in unpleasantness. Unfortunately, this need to quickly move past negative issues can often leave you feeling trampled or overlooked because they don't give you enough time to fully process the issue. Another issue is that because you like to avoid conflict, sometimes your partner may not be aware that something is going wrong until it's almost too late. That can be very hurtful for the Seven. Negative issues and uncomfortable emotions are challenging for both of you, so after the tough talk, reward yourselves with something fun. Affirm each other regularly. Grow together by learning to work through conflict sooner rather than later.

Type 9 & Type 8: With an Eight, the relationship is dynamic, earnest, and autonomous. The Eight offers protection, and you admire how tenacious and powerful they are. You help the Eight learn how to relax, let their guard down and embrace their softer side, and they help you see your value and become more assertive. Given your strong values of fairness, justice, respect, and trust, the relationship feels safe. You enjoy the companionship and connection you share.

A challenge you might face in this relationship is rooted in the fact that you both belong to the body triad, yet you handle anger quite differently. When things get difficult, you tend to withdraw and become passive-aggressive and disengaged, which angers the Eight, who would prefer to confront the issue head-on. The Eight pushes harder when things get tough, and they want you to stand your ground and fight it out. This kind of intensity can feel overwhelming to you. Grow together by keeping an open dialogue and finding a middle ground when dealing with conflict. I also encourage you to plan something fun together and regularly affirm each other.

Type 9 & Type 9: With a Nine, you're in a mirrored relationship. This is harmonious, deeply serene, and comforting. The companion-ship is beautiful, and you offer each other constant acceptance and encouragement. Since you both like predictability, you've set a routine that works for you and built a safe, comforting space for each other. You're patient with one another and like to draw each other out without being too intrusive. While you make time to have fun and be silly, what you love most is the connection you've built and the life you have together, taking life's challenges in stride.

A challenge you may encounter, especially if operating at average or lower levels of development, is the struggle with knowing your identity, unique desires, and opinions. It takes a while for you to process things, and because you like to stay positive, conflict can be a scary thing. When things aren't going well, you both withdraw and disengage. Grow together by choosing not to ignore each other's withdrawing behavior. Instead of entertaining passive aggressive behavior, take the initiative. Remember that true peace often requires good communication. A little healthy conflict and addressing unpleasant emotions together are recommended. Just approach it with compassion and be patient with each other as you learn to work through conflict.

AFFIRMATIONS

- My feelings are valid and important
- I give and receive love generously
- I am not responsible for other people's happiness
- I am willing to express my Truth and desires
- Obstacles are opportunities for growth

Remember affirmations only work when what you say and feel are in synch. Choose only the affirmations that resonate deeply with you.

DAILY TIPS FOR GROWTH AND HAPPINESS

Practice being more assertive when interacting with others.

This will require practice and may feel very uncomfortable at first, so start with small action steps. For example, stand in front of a mirror and say something you've always wanted to say to someone in your life. Practice standing in a confident, assertive posture. Notice your body language and tone as you speak. Once you get comfortable with the mirror, test it on your mom, sibling, or someone you trust. Grow into being more assertive gradually.

Process your anger and negative emotions

Promise yourself to continually work through any and all negative emotions. This will help you get better at handling conflict without being confrontational. You can use journaling, talking it out with a friend, or any other healthy form of expression you prefer.

Be more active in life and explore new things

I know you like to stick to routines and stay in your comfort zone, but it will do you a world of good to add a little planned adventure every so often. Try going on hikes alone, go for dips in the lake or nearest sea. None of these activities are likely to lead to human conflict. If you like fishing, then do that often. Find something adventurous you enjoy doing alone.

Daily exercise

Put in some daily workout to move your body and break a sweat. It will give you an energy boost and enable your brain to avoid falling into procrastination. Do you enjoy jogging in the neighborhood? Weight lifting in the gym? Swimming? It doesn't matter what you do. Just do something you want and enjoy regularly.

CONCLUSION

We've taken a deep dive into all the Enneagram Types, their basic fears, and desires. You've learned about subtypes, struggles for your Enneagram type, childhood wound and emotional patterns that show up as an adult, and relationship tips. Now that you understand more about your Enneagram Type, it's time to draw parallels and manifest positive changes in your own life.

As you've learned, there is no Enneagram type that's better or worse than the other. We all have strengths and weaknesses, positive and negative traits that need improvement. At different phases in life, we might be operating at unhealthy, average, or healthy levels, and it's up to us to keep rising higher.

If you have successfully identified your Enneagram Type, you can use the suggestions given to improve your life. It begins by becoming self-aware. Go back to the chapters that cover your type and decipher the intricacies you may have missed to better understand yourself. Get to know your motivations, weaknesses, core values, and how you tend to react under stress. Read through the different levels of development and see if you can identify where you're currently placed so you can further work on cultivating habits that will lead you to your best self.

This book might be over, but your journey is just getting started. Awareness and commitment to this journey of self-discovery are mandatory if you wish to experience transformation. Take this knowledge and implement it. Find small changes you can make so you can see the benefits of the Enneagram firsthand. Remember, all the books in the world cannot bring you the healing, wholeness, and success you deserve. For that to happen, your participation and continuous integration are required. The Enneagram system will change your life if you work it. Take this next step and keep learning, implementing, and growing.

I wish you all the best.

RESOURCES

Traditional Enneagram (History). (n.d.). The Enneagram Institute. Retrieved May 20, 2022, from https://www.enneagraminstitute.com/the-traditional-enneagram

The Enneagram Personality Test. (n.d.). Truity. Retrieved May 22, 2022, from https://www.truity.com/test/enneagram-personality-test

User, G. (2021, May 13). *Enneagram: Arrows*. Cloverleaf. Retrieved May 20, 2022, from https://cloverleaf.me/blog/enneagram-arrows

Cloete, D. (n.d.). *Wings, Arrow Lines, Integration and Self-Mastery*. Integrative9. Retrieved May 20, 2022, from https://www.integrative9.com/enneagram/wings-lines-integration/

A. (2021, January 14). *Arrows: Each Type at their Best & Worst*. Full & Free Enneagram Co. Retrieved May 20, 2022, from https://kristirowles.com/best-worst/

Learn More About All 9 Enneagram Types | Your Enneagram Coach. (n.d.). Enneagram Coach. Retrieved May 20, 2022, from https://www.yourenneagramcoach.com/types

The Nine Enneagram Types. (n.d.). THE ENNEAGRAM AT WORK. Retrieved May 20, 2022, from https://theenneagramatwork.com/nine-enneagram-types

THE ENNEAGRAM GUIDE TO SELF-DISCOVERY, RELATIONSHIP FULFILMENT & AWAKENING:

USING THE ENNEAGRAM FOR FINDING YOUR TRUE SELF, DEEPENING YOUR RELATIONSHIPS & PSYCHOLOGICAL GROWTH

INTRODUCTION

It just feels to me like my life has been spiraling out of control ever since my dad died, and I've fallen into this rabbit hole of despair. Nothing I try works, and at first, I thought I could just fake it until things got better, but now it's starting to affect my marriage. These were the words of my client, Sally, who had just begun our coaching program, hoping that it would save her relationships.

The words she spoke echoed loudly in my mind as I recalled a distant past where I, too, faced similar frustration over my life. Despite my knowledge and training in human behavior and personal development, the experience of loss had thrown me off my game, and I didn't know how to get myself back on track. Do you know what that's like?

I don't know you or what made you pick up this book, but I do know this. We all want to feel more in control of our emotions, future, and lives.

Happiness, health, loving relationships, a fulfilling career are things we all care about, and we seek out solutions that will enable us to achieve these things in different ways. Most people look for external solutions, but you're not like most people, are you? That's why this book has piqued your interest.

How often do you find yourself thinking, "why did I do that?" or "what would cause that person to behave in such a way?" Social conditioning has led us to believe that we are stuck in a box, and there's nothing we can do to change things, but what if I told you there was a way for you to become wholly aware of this so-called "box" and not only that - to give you techniques that can enable you to perceive above and beyond it? Would that be of interest to you?

THE KEY YOU'VE BEEN SEARCHING FOR - A SECRET THAT IS FOUND

Our society encourages us to find answers to the important questions that ring in the back of our minds (e.g., how can I feel fulfilled, happy, and at peace with myself and others? How do I feel loved, and where can I find true love? Who am I really?) in the acquisition of material possessions. Sometimes it's implied that we can find it in another or by being with another human being, so we go out and look for that other who will complete us. Soon enough, we realize that no amount of material possessions and no other human being will satisfy us. If we want to feel whole and experience real happiness, we need to look for answers elsewhere. Don't get me wrong, having your material desires manifest is fantastic and a necessary part of enjoying life. Being with someone who brings you great joy and makes you feel loved is also critical to enjoying the whole human experience. But these aren't the foundation of a fulfilled life; they add to it. The foundation of a full, healthy, happy, satisfying life begins with a clear, deep understanding of yourself.

INTRODUCTION

So how much of yourself do you really understand?

Do you know the proper diet, lifestyle, career, romantic partnership, and friendships for you? How aligned do you feel with your purpose?

Let me share why this is important. Think about the most basic and trendy topic in the marketplace today, weight loss. It's a trillion-dollar industry with new fads and diets coming out every day. Many people want to lose weight so let's assume for argument's sake that you'd like to drop a few pounds before next summer. Which diet or workout program do you go for? A quick search online, and you'll realize the options are overwhelming. Each one claims that it will give you that magic solution to finally get you that six-pack you've always secretly desired. Regardless of which product you pick, there's likely a ton of testimonials from happy customers who successfully shed their belly fat in record time. That doesn't guarantee that you'd get the same results. As a matter of fact, you might purchase a particular product with high hopes only to end up feeling frustrated and disappointed by the lack of results at the end of the thirty days. You might have liked the guru that convinced you to buy the product in the first place, and he sure looked ripped and healthy, but if by the end you don't look anything like him, does that make the man a scammer?

Most people would argue yes. But this is where I want to share the first nugget of wisdom that one can only learn through this Enneagram quest.

Weight loss, like everything else, is dependent on far more than a particular diet or workout routine. Unless and until the root issues resulting in the weight gain are addressed, you will find no lasting solution. It really doesn't matter how much effort one puts in or how great the program is. When gurus offer prescriptions and solutions for personal development, health, or business success, the advice is often predicated on practices that have worked well for those individuals. And that same advice will likely work just as well for

305

someone with similar psychological makeup. In other words, there has to be a "match" of some sort. To better understand what makes a good match, we need to dive into the topic of personality. We are all unique as human beings with varying personalities. Recent reports in infant development and brain research have suggested that fundamental variations in temperament among various types of people possess a biological basis. As such, sound advice for one person may prove disastrous for another. Now, I know that it might seem like understanding other people is impossible, but this is where things get interesting. If we only make assumptions of others based on their surface-level personality traits, it would be hard to understand or even get along with those who aren't like you, and trust me when I say this; no one is exactly like you. But if we could focus on the layers beneath the surface, we can find a lot more substance that connects and groups us in ways that foster more harmonious interactions. So, in other words, instead of looking for any weight loss solution or picking one because the guru is famous, you'd look for a solution that aligns with your psychological makeup.

The filter through which we experience life

The primary filter we use to discover ourselves and the world around us—the thing that dictates how we show up, react, and even love—is our psychology. Our desires and yearnings might sound similar, e.g., freedom, health, happiness, and love but the way they are conveyed and expressed will be diverse and far more specific depending on the filter through which we look at all of life. Modern experts prefer to use the term personality type, and so it is this filter that we are most concerned about in this book. Because after a lot of digging, I've learned that an essential factor for great relationships and understanding oneself and others is this one thing - which type are you? It's not about race, religion, sexual orientation, or cultural traditions. All these are just add-ons that magnify that underlying psychological type. When I understand your filter, we have a much better chance of getting along regardless of external differences. That's what the Enneagram was designed to do. It's a tool that helps us spot out filters more clearly. We learn about our core internal issues and our interpersonal strengths and deficiencies. The Enneagram is not focused on your date of birth or any external attributes but rather on your psychological makeup and behavior. It won't just point out your personality type but also the core of who you are and who you can become.

If you've been looking for a way to uncover, discover and tap into your fullest potential so you can unlock the greatness you can feel lies within you, then you've landed on the right material. And if you're here simply because, just like my client, something feels off, and you want to tack an action step that could get you back on track, then this is also the right place to be. In your hands, you now hold the only book you'll ever need to learn about and understand the Enneagram and how you can use this tool to transform every area of your life. That's what it did for me, that's what it's done for countless others, and if you let it, you'll reap the same benefits. Buckle up because this is going to be a fantastic ride!

PART ONE
THE ENNEAGRAM
TOOL

CHAPTER 1

INTRODUCING THE ENNEAGRAM TOOL

As far back as the 4th century, we find ideas relating to the Enneagram tool, although some might argue against this. Perhaps it wasn't referred to by the same term, and it definitely didn't resemble the device we know and use today, but it's safe to assume the Enneagram model has been around for a long time. And that's one of the reasons it's a trusted model. Being both an old and modern tool, the wisdom and holistic approach involved in this self-exploration make it possible for you to finally learn the right way to observe and let go of worrisome practices and reactions. It gives you a spiritual wake-up call if you're ready to dive deeper into that exploration, but even if you're not, you still get as much as you need to continue improving yourself as a whole being.

WHAT EXACTLY IS THE ENNEAGRAM TOOL?

According to Wikipedia, Enneagram (pronounced Any-a-gram) is a model of the human psyche, principally understood and taught as a typology of nine interconnected personality types. The Enneagram is represented in the form of a geometric model symbolizing a map, which makes sense when one learns that in the Greek language, ennéa means nine and grámma means something written or drawn.

The enneagram figure is typically composed of three parts, as you shall see in chapter three, where we'll dive into the details of this ennea diagram.

To fully grasp the power of the Enneagram, you'll need to open your mind to new ideas and suspend all unbelief and limited thoughts regarding life and who you really are. You will also need to turn up the volume of curiosity so you can start asking questions like, what is my personality? Is there more to me than just my personality? How do I figure out what my real nature is, and how do I improve the areas of my character that I don't enjoy?

If you've already been asking these questions, that's excellent because the Enneagram is a perfect personality typing and personal development tool to help answer these questions and so much more.

How many other models are there?

If you're not aware, the Enneagram model isn't the only one in the market. Other personality typing models like the Myers-Briggs Type Indicator (MBTI), DISC, and Social Styles are also used. Similar to how MBTI, DISC, and Social Styles describe typical behavior meaning, the Enneagram teaches how different personality types behave and how to recognize these behaviors in ourselves and others. But here's where the Enneagram differs, in my opinion. It doesn't just leave things at that psychological surface level and instead integrates the spiritual aspect of our nature as well. By the very basis that it's derived from ancient teaching that views development as progressive integration and upward movement within one's type, it does far more than just talking about the inductive clusters of characteristics that we would find in the results of a research investigation. In other words, the Enneagram identifies why we do what we do, i.e., the motivation for our behavior. It looks at basic fears and desires as key drivers for behavior. Since these fears and desires are often subconscious or even unconscious, this process of discovering your true self using the Enneagram tool becomes more of a quest instead of a standardized report. And when we bond to the Enneagram, we get a simple idea planted inside that we are far more than just personality types. We are, in fact, spiritual beings incarnated through the material world.

Is it religious?

Absolutely not. This isn't about religion because the Enneagram sets itself apart from all doctrinal differences. People from every religion, creed, and walk of life have benefited from using this tool. It doesn't matter whether you identify as a devout catholic, Christian, Muslim, atheist, Mormon, Jew, man, woman, LGBTQ, rich, poor, black, white, or brown this tool can work for you. As you dive into the structure and workings of this tool, you'll realize that all Enneagram type Sixes are pretty much the same everywhere in the world. So, a devout Catholic who is a type Six is a great deal more like the Sixes who are Muslim than they could imagine. And that goes for every other type. In the end, it changes our perspective, and we realize how similar we are all at that deeper, more human level, creating a lot more compassion and empathy across the world. Just imagine how different our world could be and how many misunderstandings, wrongdoings, and pain we could obliterate if more of us realized just how similar we are from those we tend to discriminate against.

CHAPTER 2
THE ORIGINS

The mystery surrounding the Enneagram and its origins continue to gather much speculation and dispute for practitioners. While it is good to question the authenticity of this tool, and I'll do my best to offer some insights, don't allow that curiosity to turn into doubt. History around the Enneagram is clouded somewhat (like many ancient tools), but the model's effectiveness as a framework and a map for self-discovery stands solid.

So what's the actual origin of the Enneagram, and can we say with absolute certainty where it came from?

Well, here's what we do know. It is connected to different spiritual and oral traditions and certain philosophical and mathematical traditions. Some others believe that variations of the Enneagram symbol can be traced to the sacred geometry of Pythagorean mathematicians and mystical mathematics. Plotinus, in the Enneads, speaks of the nine divine qualities that manifest in human nature. We also see variations of the Enneagram symbol appear in the Sufi tradition, with specific reference to the Naqshbandi Order. It may have also entered into esoteric Judaism through the philosopher

Philo, later becoming embedded into the branches of the Tree of Life in the Kabbalah. There's a possible relationship with Christianity through medieval references to Evagrius' catalog of various forms of temptation (Logismoi), which much later, in medieval times, was translated into the seven deadly sins. The Franciscan mystic Ramon Llull taught philosophy and theology of nine principles in an attempt to integrate different faith traditions, and in a 17th-century text, we find an Enneagram-like drawing made by Jesuit mathematician Athanasius Kircher (Adopted from Wagner, 2010).

THE MODERN INTEGRATIVE VERSION OF THE ENNEAGRAM

The evolution of the Enneagram as we know it today took place recently in the 21st century. A Russian mystic and teacher named George Gurdjieff reintroduced this antiquated symbol in form and shape that we identify as the Enneagram diagram (to be discussed in detail in chapter 3). Only Gurdjieff did not draw it out but instead taught it primarily through a series of sacred dances or movements. He believed it was better when people directly sensed the meaning of the symbol and the processes it represents. Although Gurdjieff's teaching did not include a system of personality types associated with the symbol (that came later through another contributor, as you'll see shortly), he did reveal to advanced students that we all have what he termed "chief feature." This chief feature is the lynchpin of a person's ego structure and is the fundamental characteristic that defines that individual. When asked where he learned about the Enneagram, he said he was introduced to it during a visit to a monastery in Afghanistan in the 1920s, but nothing more is disclosed regarding the origin of this symbol. What we do know is that since then, Oscar Ichazo took the helm of the Enneagram studies and coined the term "Enneagram of Personality." Ichazo is credited as the person who originally put the system together in the way we use it today. This Bolivian-born teacher and healer, who also spent a significant portion of his early years in Peru, first moved to Buenos Aires in Argentina to learn from a school of inner work. Thereafter he journeyed to Asia to gather more knowledge before returning to South America, where he began putting together a systematic approach to all he'd learned. After many years of study, research, and practice, Ichazo created the Arica School (founded in 1968) as a means of sharing the knowledge he'd received over the years. In the 1970s, while living in Chile, Ichazo received a group of noted psychologists and writers from America who wanted to study and experience first hand the methods of attaining self-realization at Arica. Among these individuals were Claudio Naranjo and John Lilly (The Enneagram Institute).

The end result of weeks spent at the Arica School studying with Ichazo was the introduction of this tool into America and the rest of the world where modern psychology was in practice. Individuals such as Ochs, Almaas, and Maitri studied with Claudio Naranjo. Ochs introduced the Enneagram to the Christian communities in the United States, which got authors like Jerry Wagner, Don Riso, and Russ Hudson excited to further spread the teachings of the Enneagram (Integrative9 History of the Enneagram). Thanks to these contemporary theorists, our knowledge and development of the Enneagram tools continue to grow far beyond what anyone, including Ichazo (who passed away in 2020), could have foreseen.

IS IT SCIENTIFIC OR MYSTICAL?

There's no binary answer to this question. Given how popular and highly recommended this tool has become in personal development and professional settings, we cannot label it purely scientific or mystical. I like to think it's a little bit of both. While the Enneagram system as we know it dates back to the '60s when Ichazo started teaching it, the philosophy behind this tool contains components from all traditions that stretch back thousands of years. That's why we can confidently employ it to help us unlock our hidden potential, uncover our blind spots and enable us to grow in every area of life. Use the following chapters as clues that allow you to discover who you really are so you can feel more in charge of your destiny and your life story. The best part is that the more you know yourself, the easier it becomes to understand and predict other people's behavior.

The American Version of the Enneagram versus the original system taught by Ichazo:

Ichazo taught a system of 108 Enneagrams, but the American movement spearheaded by Claudio Naranjo, who still teaches the Enneagram to date, was based on the first four of the Enneagrams. These are called the Enneagrams of the Passions, the Enneagrams of the Virtues, the Enneagram of the Fixations, and the Enneagram of the Holy Ideas. Why were they categorized like this? In an interview with Ichazo, he said, "We have to distinguish between a man as he is in essence and as he is in ego or personality. In essence, every person is perfect, fearless, and in loving unity with the entire cosmos; there is no conflict within the person between head, heart, and stomach or between the person and others. Then something happens; the ego begins to develop, karma accumulates, there is a transition from objectivity to subjectivity; man falls from essence to personality." (Interviews with Ichazo, page 9)

WHAT ARE VIRTUES, PASSIONS, HOLY IDEAS, AND FIXATIONS ABOUT?

Later in the book, we'll name the virtues for each Enneagram type so you can see what your higher self is calling you toward in this lifetime.

According to Ichazo's theory, holy ideas and virtues are our higher spiritual qualities, and when these become distorted by the ego, they become fixations (head) and passions (heart), respectively. This relationship between the higher self and the ego is the real work we must undertake. That's what our self-discovery quest is all about.

Approaching this book and the Enneagram with the desire to label yourself a particular personality just because it feels good is wasted effort and a missed understanding of what this tool was intended for. Your purpose in self-discovery should be to bring about that balance between your ego and higher self that's been missing. The more you feel like you've lost your center and become distorted in your thinking, feeling, and behavior, the more you need to work on that relationship with self. Use your increasing self-awareness to recognize the patterns of distortion obscuring your connection and creating disharmony in your life. Get to know your type so you can direct your inner work and facilitate the transformation that's waiting to happen within you.

If you realize that your virtues are off, don't force yourself to become a virtuous person. It doesn't work like that. To become virtuous, we need to relax, reconnect with our higher self and become more awake so we can see through the fears and desires of our ego. Only then will virtuous qualities naturally manifest. And when it comes to reconciling our thoughts about passion, realize that having desires isn't bad. Passions merely point us to an underlying reality that something is missing; we've lost something, and we need to get it back. The thing we need to work on getting back in order to heal, make whole, and satiate that passion isn't what we usually chase after. Our ego might distort our thinking and cause us to work ourselves to death, sacrificing everything in our path just to become powerful, successful, or to be loved by another, thinking that will make us complete. Yet, once we're there, the emptiness still exits. This is one of the cornerstones Ichazo wanted his students to grasp. The misguided coping strategies that our ego uses under the disguise of passion are but a distortion of inherent essential virtue. What we're in search of is restoring contact with our Essential nature and our true identity as Spirit.

The other big idea here is that an individual's ego fixation is rooted in losing one's holy idea. We lose the ability to recognize the unity of being. We become stuck in duality and segregation, and our mind is constantly storming. Similar to what we've learned about virtue and passions when we become disconnected from our higher self, that sense of freedom that we innately know we should have turned into an ego-fixation.

However, all of these can be restored as we use the Enneagram knowledge to work on ourselves. How deep you want to go in this journey is up to you, but I can assure you, the deeper you go, the richer, more fulfilling, and enjoyable this human experience will become.

CHAPTER 3

THE ENNEAGRAM DIAGRAM

To use the Enneagram tool effectively, one must learn to read it accurately. This chapter will give you an overview of all the nine Enneagram Types, offer a visual illustration of the Enneagram diagram and its parts, and then teach you how to read the diagram. Only then will you be ready to dive into the details of each Enneagram type.

There are nine personality types that are placed around the Enneagram diagram, namely, The Reformer, The Helper, The Achiever, The Individualist, The Investigator, The Loyalist, The Enthusiast, The Challenger, and The Peacemaker.

Each of the enneatypes represents an archetype and worldview that the particular type identifies with. It's their home base and the framework through which they think, feel, act and relate to their environment, other people, and themselves. But this is far more than just personality profiling. In fact, if you only use the Enneagram to spot personalities, you might be disappointed when you discover that different enneatypes may display similar behavior. That's because the Enneagram model works under the premise that

321

behavior alone isn't enough to tell you who a person really is. As a matter of fact, it teaches that outward behavior can be deceiving when trying to figure out people or even the effectiveness of this tool for self-discovery. You should therefore identify yourself and others by exploring motivation. Become more curious about "why" you or another chooses to act in a certain way. That's the real value of using this model and the best way to discover why we do what we do in life.

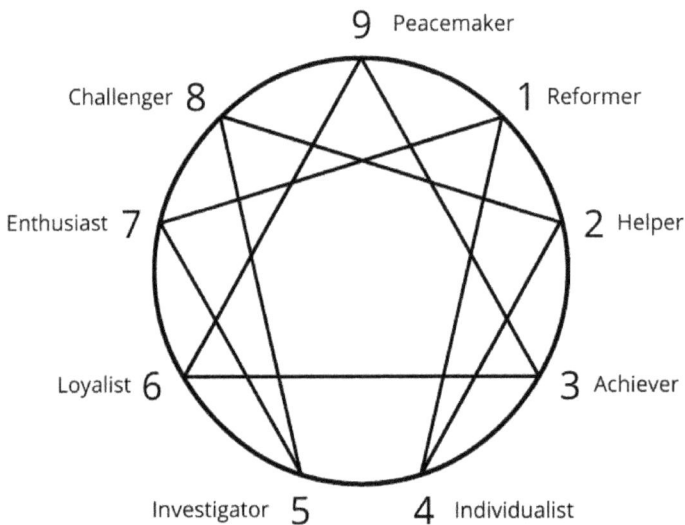

CHAPTER 4

UNDERSTANDING THE ENNEAGRAM SYMBOL

The modern-day Enneagram symbol is drawn as a geometrical shape with nine points. There's an outer circle on which the nine points that represent the nine personality types are numbered clockwise. The Enneagram uses a horizontal system to designate a number to each type, so no one number is better than another.

Inside the circle, there's a triangle between points 9, 3, and 6 and an irregular hexagon that connects all other points. If you're wondering what the circle represents, teachers of the Enneagram have said it represents the wholeness and unity of human life, i.e., the essence of life. The inner shapes represent the divisions, yet even with that, we can still see points of connections. This is important to remember as you go through your self-discovery. While you might be different from all the other types, you are still connected and form part of the whole.

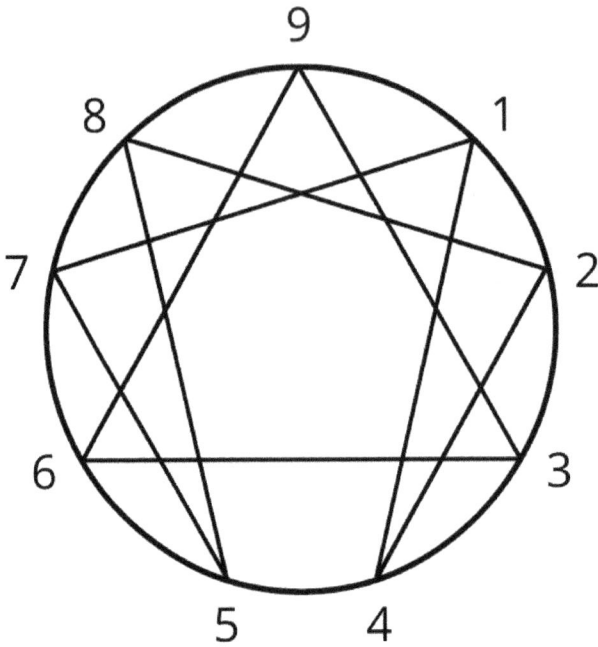

You'll find what we call wings on either side of each point (personality). Enneagram teachings tell us that wings represent related personality styles that lie dormant within us. We can choose to transition into a quality or mute a character trait that belongs to either of the wings our type is connected to and, in so doing, develop new facets of ourselves. For example, an Enneagram type One has the Nine and Two wing on either side. Type One can pull qualities from either the Enneagram Nine (The Peacemaker) or the Enneagram Two (The Giver). We'll be identifying each Enneagram type's wing in an upcoming chapter as well as how they may impact a person's behavior and personality.

HOW THE MODERN ENNEAGRAM WORKS

If you're a beginner on this journey of self-discovery, you'll find this section of the book especially helpful because it breaks down the fundamentals you need to focus on to get the most out of the Enneagram tool. Although the Enneagram can be quite complex, this is what you need to know at the beginning of your studies. Further knowledge and understanding will unravel as you get deeper into your quest and through the daily use of this tool.

The first thing you need to learn is your basic personality type. Each of us will identify strongly with one of the nine Enneagram personality types, depending on the motives and fears that drive us. One's primary type is influenced by biological and environmental factors, including but not limited to the family dynamic, parental relationships, childhood trauma, and any other significant occurrences during those formative years.

You'll likely find that you naturally relate more to one type than any other. The consensus is that people do not change from one Enneagram personality type to another. Instead, they resonate with different traits depending on their overall level of development and psychological and spiritual health.

The second thing you need to learn about is your wings. You'll see there are two wings associated with your personality type, as well as different levels of development for your specific type. You'll also get guidance on the directions your type can take, which could either lead to integration and growth or disintegration and stress.

The other super important thing you need to learn about are the three Centers of intelligence and the three instincts that drive all types. Becoming aware of the key motivations and fears that mainly guide your actions and decisions will give you increased self-awareness and the chance to make shifts in your personality.

Only then can you correctly type yourself and others. Remember, you must refrain from making assumptions about yourself and others purely through behavior and enneatype. Go deeper and uncover the instincts and levels of development first before determining which type you or anyone else is. Before we dive into each personality type, let's look a little more closely at the three centers and instincts.

THE CENTERS OF INTELLIGENCE

The Enneagram model is a 3 X 3 arrangement of nine personality types in the three Centers (Enneagram Institute). These centers are broken down into intellect, instinct, and intuition. This triad is based on how we habitually process and respond to each other and life in general. Let's get into a little scientific talk before you label the notion too *woo woo* for you. Neurobiologists have discovered that the human body has three "centers" where many nerve cells bundle together to serve the nervous system and pass information more efficiently. These centers are found in the head, chest, and gut or lower abdomen. Enneagram teachers worked with these three centers long before scientists formally proved them, and they termed them "centers of intelligence." In the context of the Enneagram, this triad enables us to understand the basic emotions that motivate various Enneatypes, all grouped within that 3X3 model.

Some teachers prefer to label them the thinking center (head), instinctive center (gut), and feeling center (heart). We tend to discuss this particular triad, even though there are many more because this one's easy for beginners to grasp. Although we have all three centers of intelligence, one is usually more dominant. Knowing whether you're in the thinking, feeling, or instinctive center can help you accurately determine your personality type. That can be especially useful when you're torn between a few types.

The Enneagram personality types are divided into three groups, as shown in the diagram below. The Instinctive center has enneatypes 1,8,9; the Feeling Center has 2,3,4, and the Thinking Center has 5,6,7.

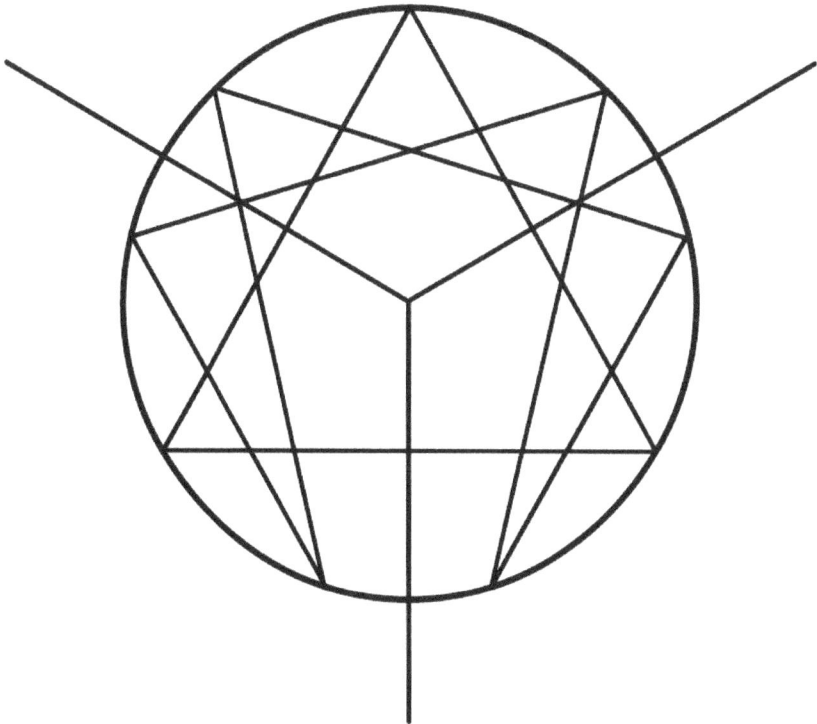

How did the original teachers of this system come up with these particular groupings? They believed that each type results from a specific relationship with a cluster of issues that characterize that center. Simply put, when you lose contact with your higher self, unconscious emotional responses arise from within, and until you can resolve these issues, these emotions become the default reaction.

So, in the Thinking Center (head), the unresolved emotion is fear. For the Feeling Center (heart), the emotion is shame, and for the Instinctive/body Center (gut), the emotion is anger or sometimes rage. That's not to say one only experiences the emotion associated with their center of intelligence because, as you know, we all feel shame, anger, and fear. Instead, the lesson here is that one of these emotions affects us most. It is a common theme that seems to follow us everywhere.

An illustration might help solidify this idea

I have a friend who grew up in the worst of conditions. Today she's a well-known Instagram influencer specializing in DIY fashion and vintage knitwear. She's been featured in magazines and speaks across the United States, motivating and inspiring young girls, especially those growing up in poor neighborhoods. Although her life seems almost like a fairytale, her early childhood and young adulthood were nothing but a nightmare. She was born into a single-parent household where there was barely enough money for food. Her uncles sexually abused her, and when her mom remarried, the new husband also abused her. She ran away by the age of sixteen, lived on the streets of California for a while before meeting someone, getting pregnant, and finding herself repeating that same cycle of abuse. It took a really long time for her to finally land a healthy, non-abusive relationship. However, through this Enneagram tool and extensive self-discovery work, she was able to start making permanent changes. When my friend tried to identify her personality type, she was torn between three types, but after learning about the centers of intelligence and realizing that her theme was predominantly shame and that this theme has been following her like a dark shadow recreating the same nightmares she had as a child, that's when it a lightbulb went on. Things have never been the same since.

Hence when it comes to your center of intelligence, the idea is to observe your life and determine which emotional theme is most dominant and recurring. Let's explore each center with a little more detail:

The Thinking/Head Center:

The Thinking Center aligns with types 5, 6, and 7. The Enneagram numbers might seem different, and, indeed, their outer behavior and personality traits differ from one number to the next. However, these three types all share the same "thinking," in the sense that their most dominant approach to life is thinking with their head rather than listening to intuition or gut feelings. These are the people who tend to be "too much in their head" when processing information or reacting to conditions.

All type 5s, 6s, and 7s are very concerned with strategies and seek out security and safety above all else. Their biggest underlying issue and a theme that recurs throughout their human experience until resolved is fear. Although they all deal with fear and anxiety, how they deal with it is very different due to their diverse personality traits. You'll find that Fives will be anxious and apprehensive about the outside world and thus prefer to isolate themselves. The Sixes handle their anxiety by suppressing it, which manifests as internal stress, wild imagination, and a lot of pessimistic "worst-case scenario" thinking. They are the most fearful in the group and some-times struggle to trust their own thoughts. That causes them to constantly seek external approval and validation. The Sevens deal with fear and anxiety by denial and avoidance. They already have the sense that there's too much pain, loss, deprivation, and fear within them, but they don't want to deal with it, so, instead, they do every-thing possible to stimulate their minds with things that excite them. This is manifested by constant busyness and physical distractions so their minds and bodies won't deal with the inner restlessness and fear they're suppressing.

The Feeling/Heart Center:

The Feeling Center aligns with Enneagram types 2, 3, and 4. As mentioned before, the thing that connects these seemingly different types is a layer deeper than personality traits or outer behavior. Instead, it's the fact that they process life predominantly through emotions. If you've been around someone who likes to say, "It just doesn't feel right to me, so I can't do," or, "I didn't hire her because something about her didn't feel right," then you've interacted with a heart-centered individual. Maybe you're that person, in which case you'll finally understand why a particular emotion lingers no matter what you do. Enneagram type Twos, Threes, and Fours are mainly concerned with how others perceive them, and they really love getting attention. The underlying issue that has to be resolved is a feeling of shame.

How does each type handle its recurring issue?

Twos tend to focus on doing things that appear to make them feel better, but that really just mask or mute out their inner shame. They want to convince themselves that they are good, loving people by focusing on positive feelings for others while repressing their unwanted feelings. In relationships, this creates a very fragile connection; as long as the Two gets positive emotional responses from the other person, they will feel wanted and somehow manage to tame that feeling of shame, but it is very conditional.

Threes are more resistant to their inner feeling of shame, and they try to deny this emotion as much as possible. In this group, Threes are the most out of touch with their feelings of shame and inadequacy. They use coping mechanisms and find objective ways to stave off their shame. Fours are more introspective. They are aware of their dark side, so they try to control it by burying it as deep as they can and turning their focus to how unique and special they are. As a general rule of thumb, you'll find Fours to be highly creative, and they use this ability to deal with shameful feelings. Unfortunately, they are also the most likely to succumb to feelings of inadequacy and take drastic measures to escape that unwanted reality.

THE INSTINCTIVE/BODY/GUT CENTER:

The gut center aligns with types 8, 9, and 1. These Enneagram types couldn't be more different in personality, but one thing they have in common is they really do listen to their gut instinct. That's how they make decisions, process information, and deal with difficulties in life. Eight's Nines and Ones are very concerned with justice, they love having autonomy, and one of the main underlying issues which can sometimes be hard to spot is anger. When you hear someone say, "I only use my gut to make any decision in life," you can be sure that person falls into this triad. And even if their logic or thinking tells them something different, they'll still go with what the gut tells them to do.

How do these different personality types deal with their unresolved anger?

Well, the Eights seem to be the easiest ones to spot because they don't hide their anger. They'd love to control it, and in fact, some do a pretty good job, but with a type Eight, you'll outwardly see displays of anger quite regularly. They tend to be quite "temperamental" or hot-tempered. Nines are in denial over their anger issues, so they try to suppress it because they don't want to come across as temperamental and upset anyone. In their desire to be good, they'd rather avoid owning that they have this negative emotion. Among the three types, Nines are the most out of touch with their anger and often feel threatened by it. Ones are pretty intriguing because they care so much about achieving perfection (and, of course, view anger as imperfection) and control that they cope by doing their best to repress this emotion.

In section II of this book, you'll discover some suggestions for resolving whatever dominant emotion you might be noticing in your life.

THE WINGS AND LEVELS OF DEVELOPMENT

As you start learning the various classifications, you'll notice there are certain qualities not on your dominant type that you resonate with. The wings are the two adjacent types located next to your primary personality type. The wings typically complement and support or at times contradict your basic type, giving you that overall personality that you identify with. You can think of this as the "second side" of your personality, and it also influences who you are. That's why it's good to know your wings and how they impact your behavior and life experience. How many wings can one have? Some schools of thought claim one, and others claim we have two wings.

Given that there are two adjacent types for each number, I reckon two wings make sense. However, one wing might resonate stronger when you assess the qualities, and that's okay. Experts on the matter say most people have a dominant wing, causing the other to be less visible. You'll get to see the different wings and what they represent for each type when we break down the types and subtypes over the following three chapters.

One last thing we need to mention here is the levels of development. A continuum of behaviors, motivations, and attitudes exists within each personality type that all come together to express a complete personality. A type Nine can be at different levels of development at various stages of their life. The same is true for all the other types. What's even more intriguing is that you and your friend could both identify as the same type but realize you're at differing levels of development. In 1977, Don Riso originally discovered and worked out all the traits that comprise each type, and further developed them, in collaboration with Hudson, in the 1990s. They are the only Enneagram teachers to include this critical factor in their treatment of the Enneagram (Enneagram Institute).

The levels are divided into healthy, average, and unhealthy traits. Think of this as a skeletal structure that enables you to dive deeper into any particular type to understand where they are in their journey and how far they need to go to unlock their highest potential. Each level helps us understand how any particular type is aligned with Presence, so the more aligned a person is, the better they will function and the higher they will be in their development. You may assume that the healthy levels of development indicate that the individual has achieved spiritual liberation and is no longer bound by the ego. Therefore, the lowest and unhealthiest level indicates that a person has lost their contact and connection to their higher self and feels the most constricted, bound vigorously by the ego. Such a person would be caught up in the fixations of their particular type and ruled by their basic fears and desires.

As you get to know your type, pay close attention to the level of development you most identify with. Be candid with yourself. Only then can you recognize the inner work that needs to take place.

CHAPTER 5

ENNEAGRAM PERSONALITY TYPING SYSTEM PART 1

TYPE 1: THE PERFECTIONIST OR THE REFORMER

Overview of type One:

Type Ones are called perfectionists because they live based on an ideology of perfection, order, and constant improvement both of themselves and those around them. Ones love rules and have a powerful sense of right and wrong. They need to feel like they have everything under control at all times. They will be very professional and objective at work and pay lots of attention to details and quality standards. Different types of Ones will view the world based on their level of development, but as a general rule of thumb, while healthy Ones see an abundance of situations that aren't quite right based on their ideals, they accept things just as they are. Despite their strong sense of justice and fairness, they are serene enough to tolerate and understand diversity in humanity. Average Ones are more rigid and less accepting. They compartmentalize as a coping mechanism and might suppress emotions to follow their strict ideals. Unhealthy ones have so disconnected from their higher self that their qualities become negative. Their rigidity and inability to accept those that don't match up to their ideals creates a lot of condemnation, anger, and disdain for humanity and the world in general.

Within the Centers of Intelligence triad, type Ones fall into the "gut" center where anger is the core emotion to resolve.

A healthy type One will come across as responsible, ethical, idealistic, earnest, self-disciplined, orderly, and conscientious. These are actually pretty distinct qualities that one would easily observe in type Ones.

You'll also recognize that they typically have very high standards, which is great until it's not. When things don't go as planned or if people don't meet their high expectations, Ones can become resentful, impatient, and highly critical.

At their best, though, Ones are pretty noble and wise. Some might even say they possess the ability to be morally heroic in their attitudes and behavior.

Core Desire: Type One's desire to be good, perfect, and live with integrity.

Core Fear: Their greatest fear is to become dishonorable or corrupted by evil. They are so afraid of being flawed or "bad."

What motivates type Ones? A type One wants the world and everyone around them to be the best and do so correctly. The strong urge is to be good and honorable and to live by their ideals beyond criticism so that no one can find fault.

Wings:

Type One has the Nine-Wing, which is "The Idealist," and the Two-Wing, which is "The Advocate."

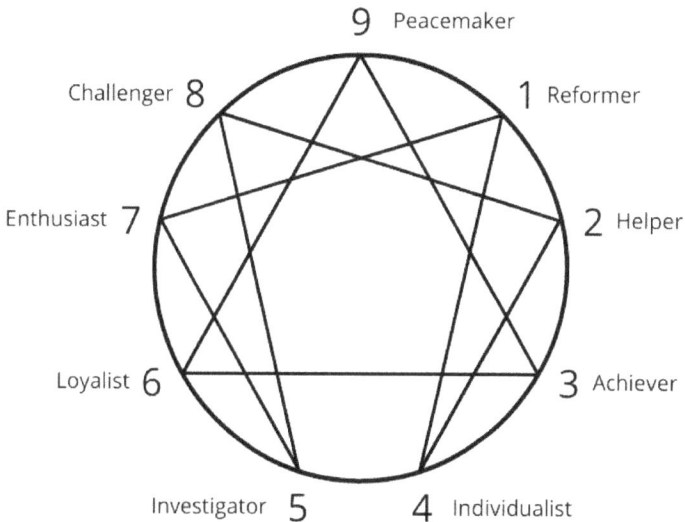

The type has two arrows, namely 4 and 7. When moving in the direction of disintegration and stress (four), Ones become moody, irrational, and too judgemental. However, the arrow pointing to growth and integration (seven) shows an angry, critical One transforming into a more spontaneous and joyful individual like a healthy Seven.

Examples of famous people:

Some well-known people sharing the Enneagram type One include Kate Middleton, Michelle Obama, Hillary Clinton, Nelson Mandela, Prince Charles, Martha Stewart, Osama bin Laden, Celine Dion, Jerry Seinfeld, Jane Fonda, Meryl Steep, and George Harrison.

Type one levels of development:

There are different expressions of type Ones that you'll need to learn. At various stages of development, a type One will exhibit certain behavior and attitudes depending on how disconnected they are from their higher Self. Let's look at each level.

Healthy levels

Level 1 is when the type One is at their best. At this point, the individual is extraordinarily wise and discerning, self-accepting, and serene. They are realistic, mission-driven, and they know the best action to take in each moment. Their interaction with others is inspiring, humane, and empathetic. This type One is highly hopeful and believes the truth always wins.

Level 2 is where type One is conscientious with strong personal convictions. The sense of right and wrong is extremely high, and this individual likes to work in a structured and systematic way adhering to all personal religious and moral values. A type One this stage of development is rational, reasonable, self-disciplined, mature, and moderate in all things.

Level 3 is still healthy, and a type One at this stage will be principles in their actions, objective, ethical and fair in all they do. This individual is very concerned with truth and justice. They have a strong sense of responsibility, personal integrity, often reaching for ways to express and share with others a higher sense of purpose, e.g., by teaching or leading a movement.

Average levels

Level 4 is the phase a type One becomes a high-minded idealist. They've become dissatisfied with reality, and they feel it's up to them to improve everything. You'll find most critics, advocates, and crusaders or Ones that are into "causes" fall under this level of development.

Level 5 is where type One becomes super rigid. Everything has to be "perfect," and they can't afford to make any mistakes. This individual is very organized and attentive but also puritanical and emotionally constricted. You'll hear words like "anal-compulsive" associated with such a person.

Level 6 type One is highly critical, judgemental, and suffers from perfectionism. Based on their perspective, they are highly opinionated about everything and the kind that will badger, interrupt and correct you in the middle of a sentence or an action just because they want you to "do the right thing." Impatience is more pronounced at this level, and you might even get a scolding look or an abrasive talk when you don't do things exactly as they desire.

Unhealthy levels

Level 7 type One is extremely self-righteous and dogmatic. They are intolerant of others and think everyone who doesn't think and act like them is wrong. At this level, the individual deals in absolutes and feel like they alone know "The Truth."

Level 8 type One is obsessed with the imperfections they see in themselves and others. The individual at this level wants everyone to fix their wrongdoings, and unfortunately, they might say one thing and do the opposite making them quite contradictory.

Level 9 is the most unhealthy and lowest level of development in type One. At this stage of development, the individual is condemnatory and cruel to themselves and others because they cannot stand the imperfections they see. The failure to live up to the ideal they deem perfect is too much to bear, and we often find such a person deeply depressed, suffering from nervous breakdowns, and even contemplating or attempting suicide.

Addictions:

To cope with and suppress some of the emotional and psychological unrest that this type faces, especially at the unhealthy levels of development, Ones may resort to Alcohol. Some, however, attempt to force their self-control by undereating, leading to bulimia or extreme diets and vitamins.

HOW TO RECOGNIZE IF YOU'RE AN ENNEAGRAM ONE

Let's look at some easy-to-spot traits for an Enneagram type One, and make sure you take note of how many you identify with. Bear in mind that some of these traits will be more pronounced in healthy Ones while others will be more present in unhealthy Ones.

- You hold yourself to extremely high standards in everything you do.
- Most people, including yourself, tend to use the term "perfectionist" or "strict" when describing you.
- You're incredibly organized, diligent, systematic, and you thrive in systems and structure.
- Rules? You love rules and believe that's the best way to get things done/
- Your communication style is direct, honest, and thoughtful.
- You like to take charge of your duties, and everyone knows you're super responsible.
- Patience isn't one of your strengths, especially when things aren't going your way.
- You work hard to control and civilize your natural impulses. Spontaneity and risk-taking sound silly and unnecessary.
- There's a super loud inner critic that you have to deal with every day, whether it's the voice of a parent or someone else, constantly criticizing you when you fail.

- Being grounded and fair is essential to you, so you do your best to detach emotions from a problem. That's especially true when the problem involves making a significant decision that impacts others.

STRUGGLES THAT TYPE ONES MIGHT HAVE

Unrealistic expectations

All Ones are driven by the need to make the world around them better and lead ethical, honest, honorable, and responsible lives. If a type One says he'll do something, then you can bet everything they will do it.

Many people respect and greatly depend on Ones because they're totally reliable, ethical, and carry themselves with great integrity. They set super high standards that only they can live up to, and it's pretty inspiring in some cases. But sometimes, these high standards can turn into a curse. The more unhealthy a type One is, the bigger this curse will be because they'll often project their own inadequacies to those around them. A type One is often their own worst critic, and even minor failures can become unbearable, causing them to take drastic measures, including self-punishment.

Taking everything too seriously

Average and unhealthy type Ones can come across as rigid, no-nonsense individuals who have little taste for fun. They just don't know how to relax and loosen up or enjoy life with a bit of spontaneity. Leisure activities seem like unnecessary and even immoral indulgences. Their self-control is somewhat forced because they don't want to deal with their emotions making it difficult for the person to express feelings naturally.

Not good enough

Average and unhealthy Ones tend to struggle with this most. They view their failures and defects as unacceptable, no matter how small. Self-judgment and criticism are high at these levels of development, causing the individual to feel defeated by life and not good enough for whatever they desire to have.

Overfilling your plate

By this, I mean taking on too much responsibility and pushing yourself to the limit. Many type Ones believe they need to carry the weight of the world on their shoulder. While that sounds really selfless, it's often not a smart idea as it creates a lot of anxiety, overwhelms, frustration, and undue stress. The need to do everything to perfection only exacerbates the matter creating feelings of guilt, especially when their high standards aren't met or if they fail at something.

GROWTH TIPS FOR ONES

#1: Give yourself permission to "play" and unlock some of your inner childhood, especially the easy-going aspects.

Allow yourself to be silly, fun, and free-spirited. Consciously choose to block out time for an activity that's fun, whether that's playing your favorite board games, dancing, painting, pottery, or simply going to the park with a friend and playing frisbee.

#2: Ask for help

It's normal for a type One to want to carry the weight of the world on their shoulder, but everyone knows we do our best work when it's a team effort. Don't burn yourself out trying to be perfect at everything. Instead, look at your current workload and the things you've been struggling with and just ask others to help. And when others come in to help, remind yourself that it's okay for them not to be perfect or do it exactly like you. They are unique and will do their best work when you give them space to do their thing.

#3: Quiet that inner critic

Your inner dialogue has to be kept in check immediately. Belittling yourself, fault finding, and dwelling too much on your weaknesses, failures, and shortcomings only destroy your self-esteem. It's time to silence that voice. It won't happen at the snap of a finger, but things will get better with practice and deliberate action to switch the conversation. Consider creating a silly avatar for that inner critic and change the tone of voice to match a cartoon character that you find hilarious. You can also practice more compassion and self-love, which we'll discuss next.

#4: Practice self-love and self-acceptance

The best way to enhance the positive qualities of your type and heal the aspects that don't serve you is to increase your self-love and acceptance. Learn to love yourself unconditionally, even the parts you don't particularly like about yourself. When that inner critic says something, respond with "thank you for bringing that to my attention. I still think I did a pretty good job."

#5: Acknowledge, embrace, process and heal your unresolved emotion

Anger doesn't serve you, so pretending it's not there only disconnects you from your higher self. Instead of repressing or suppressing anger, find healthy ways to process and heal yourself. For example, when someone hurts your feelings, don't fall into passive-aggressive behavior, let them know they've hurt you, or find another way to address it, such as writing a letter and then burning it. Or, when you feel anger brewing, find a private place where you can scream at the top of your lungs or punch your pillow until all the emotion is released.

TYPE 2: THE GIVER/HELPER

Overview of type Two:

Type Twos are called helpers because they are genuinely invested in helping others, especially at healthy levels of development. And even if they're underdeveloped, they are still highly invested in seeing themselves as helpful. Relationships matter a lot to type Twos. A sense of belonging and feeling loved is essential for a helper, which causes them to seek relationships where they can nurture, care for, and help others. They are eager to involve themselves in other people's lives and struggle with the word "No." In fact, sometimes they can agree to help someone even at their own expense because they feel the need to prove that they are dependable. Type Twos are warm, gentle, excellent team players, and radiate kindness to everyone. At work, they will be focused on building relationships, offering support, and doing their best to create a more peaceful, loving environment.

Different types of Twos will view the world based on their level of development, but as a general rule of thumb, healthy Twos are selfless and find their fulfillment through various acts of giving unconditional love. Not only do they understand the meaning of empathy, but they also embody it in their daily lives. Average Twos like to take on a martyr role in their relationships. They need constant validation and suffer significantly from people-pleasing. Unhealthy Twos are overly possessive, enjoy pity parties, and often use sympathy to get attention from people. Some become clingy and overbearing. The nurturing, generous aspect becomes poisoned and manipulative, making their intentions insincere.

Within the Centers of Intelligence triad, type Twos fall into the "heart" center where shame is the core emotion to resolve.

A healthy type Two will come across as kind, caring, compassionate, empathetic, gentle, patient, supportive, and loving. These are actually pretty distinct qualities that one would easily observe in type Twos. You might also notice they tend to be huge people-pleasers, especially at the lower levels of development.

At their best, Twos are considerate, generous, loving, and people-centered. They know their self-worth and strike a healthy balance between selfless service and tending to their own growth and needs.

Core Desire: Type Twos want to be appreciated, valued, and wanted. They have a strong need to belong and to be loved.

Core Fear: Type Twos fear rejection, losing love, or being unlovable.

What motivates type Twos? The need to belong and be desired by others. Twos want to feel needed, and they often look to others to express agreement and vindicate their claims about their goodness.

Wings:

Type Two has the One-Wing, which is "The Servant," and the Three-Wing, which is "The Host/Hostess."

Arrows and their meaning:

The type has two arrows, namely 8 and 4. When moving in the direction of disintegration and stress (eight), Twos are needy, possessive, highly aggressive, and dominating in their relationships. They have unhealthy levels of pride. However, the arrow pointing to growth and integration (four) shows us that a prideful, self-deceptive Two can transform into a more self-nurturing and emotionally aware individual like a healthy Four.

Examples of famous people:

Some well-known people sharing the Enneagram type Two include Mother Theresa, Maya Angelou, Eleanor Roosevelt, Monica Lewinsky, Luciano Pavarotti, Lionel Richie, Elizabeth Taylor, Bishop Desmond Tutu, Paula Abdul, Priscilla Presley, Dolly Parton, and Paramahansa Yogananda.

Type Two levels of development:

There are different expressions of type Twos that you'll need to learn. At various stages of development, type Two will exhibit certain behavior and attitudes depending on how disconnected they are from their higher Self. Let's look at each level.

Healthy levels

Level 1 is a type Two and their best. An individual operating at this level is altruistic, deeply unselfish, and humble. This person genuinely loves unconditionally and finds a healthy balance between loving and giving themselves to others and self-care. This type Two freely gives without expectation and feels it's a privilege to be in the lives of others and to have the power to nurture such powerful relationships. The connection with the higher self is optimum, and this type Two knows that feels that in giving to others, they are in fact giving to the whole.

Level 2 is where type Two naturally radiates empathy, thoughtfulness, forgiveness, and compassion for others. They are very concerned with the needs of others and are sincere in their attempts to care for and love others.

Level 3 is where type Two focuses more on serving others, praising, appreciating, and finding good in others. They are generous and absolutely reliable, yet they still know how to strike that balance between taking care of others and tending to their own needs.

Average levels

Level 4 is where type Two falls into the trap of people-pleasing in an attempt to be seen as helpful and reasonable. They become overly friendly, emotionally demonstrative, and want to prove that they are reliable.

Level 5 is where type Two's helpfulness starts to become intrusive. At this point, the Two starts sending mixed signals because their generosity comes with expectations. They need to be needed, which causes them to meddle and "control" in the name of love.

Level 6 is where a type thinks too highly of their giving nature and seems to wear an air of self-importance and self-righteousness. They are also quite needy, presumptuous, and condescending. As we start to see the decline of that healthy giving nature, this type two is more of a martyr than anything else, and they demand that others praise and acknowledge everything they do.

Unhealthy levels

Level 7 sees a turn to the dark side of type two, where that nurturing and relationship-building ability is used as a tool for manipulation and deception. This person isn't shy of using guilt and shaming tactics to get what they want. They start belittling those around them and using disparaging words. They've also lost touch with their emotions. Instead of tending to their needs, this type Two turns to food and medication as coping mechanisms. The sympathy they get for their problems is hugely pleasing, and it's where we find some keeping themselves permanently in this state as a way of getting attention and love from others.

Level 8 is a Two that's very domineering and coercive. All they want is to "get their way," They possess a strong sense of entitlement, feeling that people owe them something for being such givers.

Level 9 is the most undeveloped stage of development for type Two, and they thrive in victim mentality. They see themselves as taken advantage of, turning them into angry, resentful, bitter, and aggressive individuals. That usually leads to chronic health problems.

Addictions:

To cope with and suppress some of the emotional and psychological unrest that this type faces, especially at the unhealthy levels of development, Twos may resort to over-the-counter meds and binge eating. The overeating or "stress eating" comes from this need to fill the void or lack of love they are experiencing.

HOW TO RECOGNIZE IF YOU'RE AN ENNEAGRAM TWO

Let's look at some easy-to-spot traits for an Enneagram type Two, and make sure you take note of how many you identify with. Bear in mind that some of these traits will be more pronounced in healthy Twos while others will be more present in unhealthy Twos.

- You're strongly driven to create meaningful relationships with others, and you enjoy making people feel valued and important.
- Strangers tend to walk up to you and ask for directions or help. All your friends and family find it easy to ask you for advice or discuss personal matters because you feel warm and understanding.
- You're highly attuned to the needs of others and can quickly tell how someone feels even if they don't tell you.
- Your communication style is warm, loving, compassionate, and empathetic.
- You invest a lot of time staying in touch with the people in your world. Relationships are what you value most.
- When it comes to your romantic relationships, you enjoy playing a more supportive role, and you tend to be the more affectionate and affirming one in the relationship.
- You're attentive, engaged, and present when interacting with others which can sometimes become overwhelming, especially when they are being dramatic.
- You don't like criticism or competition.
- At your best, you feel creative, comfortable in your skin, and accepting of who you are.
- Sometimes, you worry that having needs and expressing them to another is wrong. Your fear of being selfish is

prevalent, and that can sometimes cause you to neglect your own needs or even say "no" to things you don't enjoy.

STRUGGLES THAT TYPE TWOS MIGHT HAVE

Saying "No."

Selfishness is a big deal to a type Two, and the last thing she wants to do is come across as such, so she never says no. It's hard for a generous giving type Two to say no even when she knows it's the right thing to do. Most of the time, a Two just over-extends herself because she doesn't want to appear unreliable or unhelpful. Because the self-worth and personal value of a type Two are centered on being good and giving generously, she often has a terrible time balancing the demands of others and tending to her own needs, which leads me to my next point.

Taking care of your needs

Type Twos are notoriously good at self-neglect, all in the name of serving others. Their self-sacrificing nature can often create many internal issues because they never have time to tend to their own emotional, spiritual, or physical needs. This is especially true for average and unhealthy Twos who are constantly battling between wanting to help themselves and helping others so they can continue to receive love.

Feeling unloved

Average and unhealthy Twos fear that they're unlovable, and so they do everything possible to serve others in return for that love they crave. It's not uncommon for a type Two to feel empty, unseen, misunderstood, or even underappreciated, but that's usually because they "overdo" things purely expecting to receive the same generosity back.

GROWTH TIPS FOR TWOS

#1: Set healthy boundaries

Saying No is hard, I know, but unless you start creating healthy boundaries for yourself, you'll end up resenting the very people you're trying to help. Remind yourself that it's okay to say "No, I can't do that right now" or No, [fill in the blank]. Start with small things that feel less selfish and work your way up. And whenever you feel like someone is just trying to take advantage of you, have the courage to speak up and let them know you won't do it because they don't feel genuine. Don't be afraid to use your words and express your feelings. Trust me, those that truly love you don't want you to be a doormat.

#2: Prioritize self-care

What are some things you can do to make yourself feel special? Take a special and long bath each week, sign up for a painting class just for the fun of it or treat yourself to weekly massages at the spa. Anything you can do to take care of yourself, including getting proper sleep, eating healthy, making time for exercise, and more, are all ways to practice self-care. This is not selfish; it's how you fill yourself fully so you can have the energy to generously give and take care of others.

#3: Practice self-love, self-acceptance, and compassion

Self-love and compassion are essential for all enneagram types, but it's paramount for you because your type tends to completely forget that you have needs, too. Average and unhealthy levels of development will require a lot more work because anger is strong at these lower levels, but you can learn to love, accept and heal yourself. There are many spiritual teachers who are great teaching strategies for self-love, including Louise Hay and Deepak Chopra. Find a spiritual teacher that resonates and implement the self-love practices they offer. Be patient with yourself as you go through these practices, and no matter what, don't quit on yourself.

#4: Affirm yourself

Consider leaving yourself little notes all over the house with statements that make you feel good about yourself. For example, "I am loved," "I am loveable," "I love and approve of myself," or "I am beautiful, and everyone loves and accepts me for who I am."

#5: Carve out some "alone time" as often as possible.

I would encourage you to make this a daily practice even if you're alone for half an hour. It's better than nothing. While alone, do some "check-ins" to see how you're feeling, what you're thinking and which needs are unmet. Regularly taking time out to be with your thoughts and emotions will ensure you avoid the trap of thinking your source of joy or love comes from others.

TYPE 3: THE ACHIEVER/ PERFORMER

Overview of type Three:

Type Threes are called competitive achievers because they love being the best and having the best in life. Threes are hardworking, often image-conscious, goal-oriented, and have an inner drive that's almost unstoppable. Their charisma and impressive outer appearance make them very appealing, and that makes an excellent first impression. People tend to like Threes a lot because they possess a lot of remarkable accomplishments and social niceties. They are energetic doers and eager to produce things that cause them to feel and be perceived as significant.

At work, they will come across as principled, resourceful, driven, motivated, and encouraging to others, especially when everyone is moving toward a shared goal.

Different types of Threes will view the world based on their level of development, but as a general rule of thumb, healthy Threes are authentic, self-accepting, and make great role models. Average Threes are overly concerned with their image and what others think of them. They typically struggle with workaholism and "busyness." Unhealthy Threes are excessively competitive, dismissive, and hard to deal with. Their entire self-worth and self-identity are tied to their possessions and accomplishments.

Within the Centers of Intelligence triad, type Threes fall into the "heart" center where shame is the core emotion to resolve.

A healthy type Three will come across as ambitious, courageous, confident, charismatic, optimistic, hardworking, adaptable, inspiring, and success-oriented. These are actually pretty distinct qualities that one would easily observe in type Threes.

At their best, Threes are great role models, the best in their fields, and excellent at inspiring others to unlock their potential.

Core Desire: Threes most desire to feel worthwhile and valuable.

Core Fear: Threes struggle with the fear of being worthless and failing. The fear of being insignificant drives this type to find ways to be successful and influential.

What motivates a type Three? Attention and admiration are the biggest motivators for this personality type. Their need to be significant and impressive causes them to stretch and do more and go the extra mile.

Wings:

Type Three has the Two-Wing, which is "The Charmer," and the Four-Wing, which is "The Professional."

Arrows and their meaning:

The type has two arrows, namely 6 and 9. When moving in the direction of disintegration and stress (nine), Threes are vain, disengaged, and apathetic. However, the arrow pointing to growth and integration (six) shows us that deceitful, competitive Threes can transform into collaborative and service-oriented individuals like healthy Sixes.

Examples of famous people:

Some well-known people sharing the Enneagram type Two include Bill Clinton, Arnold Schwarzenegger, Muhammed Ali, Andy Warhol, Oprah Winfrey, Deepak Chopra, Tony Robbins, Madonna, Sting, Will Smith, Whitney Houston, Lady Gaga, Brooke Shields, Tiger Woods, Elvis Presley, Jamie Foxx, Richard Gere, Cat Deeley, Anne Hathaway, and Reese Whitherspoon.

Type Three levels of development:

There are different expressions of type Threes that you'll need to learn. At various stages of development, a type Three will exhibit certain behavior and attitudes depending on how disconnected they are from their higher Self. Let's look at each level.

Healthy levels

Level 1 is a type Three at their best. This individual is self-accepting, authentic, charitable, humble, gentle, benevolent, and excellent at unlocking greatness in themselves and others.

Level 2 is where a Three is energetic, competent, self-assured, and believes in their own value. Their charming and gracious desirable nature draws people to them.

Level 3 is where type Three is pretty grounded in certain admirable cultural qualities depending on what they were conditioned into. If the person grew up in a family that values success in the form of fame, they would work to become a famous actor, model, writer, or some kind of public figure. Those that are from a religious family might become some kind of religious figure or somebody noteworthy who is admired by their community. At this level, type Three is ambitious and eager to prove themselves as the best.

Average levels

Level 4 is where we start to see a somewhat negating shade forming. Type three is highly concerned with performance, doing their job well, and getting credit for their work. They have a strong need to achieve goals, and their self-worth is tied to their accomplishments. This type Three is terrified of failure, and they constantly compare themselves with others in search of status and success. Nothing matters more than climbing as high as they can in their career and society so others can see they are the best.

Level 5 is where average Threes get too consumed by their social status and public image. They work hard to have the right "package" according to the expectations of others. While they are still very efficient and pragmatic, they've started losing touch with their emotions and true identity. To save their public image, they can sometimes do some questionable things. Intimacy at this level of development is very poor as they struggle to have real connections. Everything is staged and phony.

Level 6 is where type Three feels superior to others while also struggling with inferiority when dealing with those they consider more successful. They are pretty narcissistic and have inflated notions about their talents and accomplishments. Some even embellish information about themselves so they can appear more impressive. When dealing with people they feel are less competent, they can be pretty dismissive and condescending. Jealousy and contempt for the more successful start to take root at this point.

Unhealthy levels

Level 7 sees a turn to the dark side for type Three as they become opportunistic, exploitative, and jealous. They are willing to do "whatever it takes" to preserve the illusion of their superiority and struggle deeply with the fear of failure.

Level 8 is where a type Three really turns devious, malicious, and untrustworthy. At this point, the individual will betray their friends, sabotage other people's success, and "elbow" their way to the top. They've become petty and overly competitive about everything. Anyone who is doing better than them is now perceived as a threat, and their jealousy is now taking a toll on their judgment.

Level 9 is where a type Three goes full-on evil, turning into a vindictive, ruthless, obsessive person destroying whatever stands in their way, especially when they perceive that thing or person as a threat. This type Three exhibits psychopathic behavior, and their energy is completely misdirected, making them quite dangerous to their own well-being and that of others. Most people who have narcissistic personality disorder fall into this category.

Addictions:

To cope with and suppress some of the emotional and psychological unrest that this type faces, especially at the unhealthy levels of development, Threes may resort to excessive intake of stimulants, cocaine, steroids or partake in radical surgery for cosmetic improvement. They might also work themselves to exhaustion trying to prove themselves to the world.

HOW TO RECOGNIZE IF YOU'RE AN ENNEAGRAM THREE

Let's look at some easy-to-spot traits for an Enneagram type Three and take note of how many you identify with. Bear in mind that some of these traits will be more pronounced in healthy Threes while others will be more identifiable with unhealthy Threes.

- Your internal drive and entire DNA is set on productivity. You seem to have this innate desire and sense of urgency to do more in life. Where Enneagrams pursue "work-life balance" and peace through rest of relationships, you're running in the opposite direction. Peace of mind for you is knowing that you're building something magnificent.
- You tend to be overly competitive even when it's unnecessary, especially at those lower levels of development.
- There's an inherent gift of being able to read a room and change your persona accordingly. Some call it shapeshifting and think of it as something evil; you disagree, of course.
- You're poised, charismatic, and intuitively know what to say in almost any situation. You can make friends and create allies out of just about anyone.
- Your image matters to you greatly, and you enjoy accentuating your best features.
- You consistently think about the future and how it could be better. Many would call that being a visionary, and you agree!
- You struggle with insecurities and feelings of emptiness, especially at those average and unhealthy levels of development. That often causes you to cover up and "mask" those weaknesses, so you can still appear impressive.

STRUGGLES THAT TYPE THREES MIGHT HAVE

Having to put up with inefficiency and incompetence

Threes are naturally hard-working individuals who believe in developing their talents and skills. Nothing is more insulting than incompetence, so when they have to work with lazy, disorganized, or inefficient people, it's simply unbearable. It's crazy to a type Three that people can be so unfocused and easily distracted by trivial things. Working with these "regular" people is quite a struggle.

Inferiority superiority complex

This is more pronounced at average and unhealthy levels of development when a Three is very prone to comparing themselves with others. When surrounded by people less successful, the Three feels very proud and superior. On the other hand, when surrounded by more successful people, the Three experiences an overwhelming sense of insecurity and inferiority. Overcoming this struggle takes a lot of deep personal development work and self-discovery so that a Three can finally become content with who they are and what they've accomplished.

Feeling unloved

Many Threes feel that others love them because of their accomplishments and outer success. Sometimes, they struggle to practice self-love because of this very thing. Without your public image, special status, and achievements, do you know who you are? Would you still feel worthy and loveable if it was all taken away? That underlying fear that your self-worth is tied to what you do and what you have is the main reason you get fixated on competing and winning at all costs. Somewhere along with your development, you were conditioned to believe that in order to survive, your focus should be on performance and action. And while there's nothing wrong with excellence and performance, it should never be the measure of your value.

Burnout

Type Threes are obsessively focused on success and achievement. That often tunes them out of their physiological and psychological needs. Over time, they struggle with fatigue, sleep deprivation, and other health issues, all in the name of chasing after that dream. If any or all of the above sounds familiar, it's time to take control of your health. Take care of your mind and body if you want to accomplish more in life. Use the technology at hand to set timers that enable you to pause during the day and hydrate or even power nap. Do you need to work long hours? That's okay. Just make sure you eat well, exercise, drink plenty of water, avoid too much caffeine and as soon as you can get a break, take some vacation time to reset. You can also learn some of the techniques and practices shared at the end of the book so you can integrate some healthy rituals into your hectic lifestyle. No one is asking you to stop being who you are. Living the Enneagram isn't about giving up your dreams but pursuing worthwhile desires in a holistic way that positively serves you and everyone else.

GROWTH TIPS FOR THREES

#1: Ground yourself worth and value in something more than accomplishments

Although you're very success-oriented and value accomplishments, realize that nothing you do adds or detracts from your true self-worth. That will be a hard concept to grasp at first, but the more you discover your true self, the easier it will be to shift your anchor from earthly, transient things to a higher, indestructible Source. That will bring you a newfound sense of security, joy, and confidence to keep developing and accomplishing in life but with less egotism.

#2: Prioritise rest and downtime

It's common for a Three to work themselves to the ground. That's neither healthy nor necessary. To accomplish greatness in your life and have the lasting influence and legacy you dream of, rest, relaxation, downtime, and you should also prioritize family time. Make an effort to slow down regularly and enjoy the present moment. It doesn't have to interfere with your work if you get creative about this. For example, you could choose to make Friday mornings a time for connecting with people, calling up friends, having breakfast with family, doing some yoga, pilates, or some other form of relaxing, enjoyable activity. Find what routine aligns with your lifestyle and schedule, and then stick to it.

#3: Cultivate empathy and compassion

It's easy to get sucked into "doing" mode and forget that people skills are an essential factor for long-term success. Emotional talk and empathy don't come naturally for many Threes, so you might need to work on this. Have enough self-awareness to recognize how good or bad you are at showing compassion when interacting with someone. Catch yourself when you respond to someone's pain or complaint without empathy. There are plenty of small things you can do to increase these qualities where lacking. A good starting point is to practice mindfulness. We'll talk more about this in the last section of the book.

#4: Choose to be your authentic self instead of what the world expects you to be

A common belief among Threes is that the world only cares about winners. The limitations of such thinking need to be addressed, especially if you lack enough self-awareness to maintain your authentic self even as you pursue success. It's important to refocus your energy on becoming the best version of yourself instead of competing to beat others or impress them in any way. Will Smith has a great statement that goes something like this: "We spend money that we do not have on things we do not need to impress people who do not care." There's no upside to that kind of approach, so it's best to focus on unleashing your best self rather than impressing a world that doesn't really care.

ENNEAGRAM PERSONALITY TYPING SYSTEM PART 2

TYPE 4: THE INDIVIDUALIST/ ROMANTIC

Overview of type Four:

Type Fours are commonly called individualists because they are very self-focused and view themselves as unique and "different" from everyone else. They are passionate (sometimes over-emotional) and often moody. Many of the best artists and performers identify with this enneagram type.

The people who identify as type Four tend to be highly self-aware, sensitive, and often very creative, or at least very unafraid to express their creativity. As non-conformist and repelled by social status, individualists like to stand out and show the world how different they are either through their fashion choices or their unconventional lifestyles and creative output. They spend a significant portion of their lives reflecting on the past and ever seeking to discover their true identity. As such, every experience and feeling is considered valuable as though it offers a clue to some deeper meaning about life and themselves. This self-reflection can sometimes become dangerous, especially if the individual over identifies as being more flawed in some way than others. More than any other group, type Fours have difficulty detaching from what they consider personal inadequacies and deficiencies. They swing between feelings of true "aristocracy" and deep feelings of shame and fears that they are somehow deeply flawed. Fours are emotionally complex, to say the least. At work, they tend to fluctuate, sometimes being warm, compassionate, and emotional, while other times, they can be totally dry and cold. There's often an underlying tone of sadness in their communication, even when they've done good work.

Different types of Fours will view the world based on their level of development. Still, as a general rule of thumb, healthy Fours are compassionate, self-aware. They've found a way to live with and integrate both joy and suffering. Unhealthy Fours are trapped in a torture chamber of their own making and suffer from self-victimization, envy, and hopelessness. That makes them highly destructive.

Within the Centers of Intelligence triad, type Fours fall into the "heart" center alongside type Twos and Threes. In greater degrees than types Two and Three, the type Fours are more likely to fully embrace feelings of grief and sadness. Feelings of shame are more pronounced and expressed in this type as well. They really do have a hard time believing that they can be loved for who they are. Although they are in tune with their emotions, it's a very complex relationship and not always healthy.

Some descriptive qualities you might recognize in type Four include self-awareness, melancholy, expressive, idealistic, creativity, and emotional sensitivity.

At their best, Fours are compassionate, creative, and open-hearted. They seek meaning and depth in everything they do and constantly strive for personal discovery and creative expression.

Core Desire: Fours long to feel significant, be unique, and find their true identity. They also long to experience the same happiness they sometimes see in others.

Core Fear: There's a profound and piercing sense of missing out on happiness and connection that eats away at Fours. It's further amplified by the fact that they feel different and unique, which means they don't think anyone can truly get them or see their genuine magnificence.

What motivates a type Four? All Fours, to varying degrees, want to express their creativity and individuality. They are driven by this need to create and surround themselves with beauty (however, one may define beauty depending on their level of development).

Wings:

Type Four has the Three-Wing, which is "The Aristocrat," and the Five-Wing, which is "The Bohemian."

Arrows and their meaning:

Type Four has two connecting arrows, namely 2 and 1. When moving in the direction of disintegration and stress (two), aloof Fours become over-involved and clingy like an unhealthy Two. However, the arrow pointing to growth and integration (one) shows an envious, emotionally turbulent Four transforming into a more conscientious and objective individual like a healthy One.

Examples of famous people:

Some well-known people sharing the Enneagram type Four include Pyotr I. Tchaikovsky, Virginia Woolf, Miles Davis, Bob Dylan, Paul Simon, Rumi, Frédéric Chopin, Alanis Morrisette, Jonny Depp, Nicolas Cage, Cher, and Gustav Mahler.

Type Four levels of development:

There are different expressions of type Four that you'll need to learn. At various stages of development, a type Four will exhibit certain behavior and attitudes depending on how disconnected they are from their higher Self. Let's look at each level.

Healthy levels

Level 1 is when a type Four is at their best. They are incredibly creative, expressing both the personal and universal connection. Most of the time, this will be in a work of art. This type Four is inspired. They've found that inner emotional balance and have adequately understood their identity. That makes them self renewing, regenerating, and almost whimsical as they are able to make every moment seem magical. Every experience is naturally transformed into something meaningful for them and those around them.

Level 2 is where type Four expresses their compassion and gentle nature. This Four is keenly aware of their inner impulses and become sensitive to his or her feelings and intuition. They are introspective, highly self-aware, and spend most of their time alone searching for self.

Level 3 is when we see a type Four really fighting for that sense of uniqueness and individuality. They are emotionally honest, self-revealing, humane, and unafraid to show their vulnerability. Their perspective on life and who they are is quite ironic, and they have an uncanny way of being serious and funny all at once.

Average levels

Level 4 is where a type Fours holds a romantic orientation to life, and their main focus is creating beautiful aesthetic environments that promote certain inner moods. They are very in touch with their imagination and possess a heightened reality founded on fantasy and passion.

Level 5 is where we see a more self-absorbed and introverted Four. At this point, the individual is very moody, hypersensitive, overly self-conscious, and often withdraws from the public eye to protect their self-image. This Four takes everything personally and can be really hard to deal with at work. The reason is that it's better to be isolated while they try to figure out their turbulent inner world.

Level 6 is where introspection starts to create shadows that haunt the individual. A Four at this level feels that they are different from everyone else and lack access to the joys everyone else seems to have. This individual becomes very melancholic and often falls back into a self-created fantasy world where they feel safer. They use a lot of self-pity and already start showing signs of envy. Not much gets done from this point on because it's hard to be productive when one is giving up on living.

Unhealthy levels

Level 7 is where type Four takes a downward spiral into the dark side of their personality. A Four at this level is chronically envious of others, ashamed, emotionally paralyzed, depressed, and angry at themselves because none of their dreams are materializing. This drains them of all their energy, making them super unproductive.

Level 8 is where the torment starts for a Four. Delusion, self-contempt, self-loathing, and blame take center stage. When they are not hating themselves, they are busy blaming others for their torture-filled existence.

Level 9 is where a Four hits rock bottom and is most disconnected from their higher self. At this point, the individual feels hopeless, powerless, and incapable of becoming anything more than what they are now. That makes them highly self-destructive and extreme. Some use alcohol and drugs to escape this life of torment, and others consider suicide. This is a hazardous level for type Four, and getting immediate help is advised.

Addictions:

To cope with the emotional and psychological turmoil this type faces, especially at those unhealthy levels of development, Fours may resort to alcohol, tobacco, prescription drugs, heroin, or even cosmetic surgery depending on their thought process and what they are attempting to erase from their lives.

HOW TO RECOGNIZE IF YOU'RE AN ENNEAGRAM FOUR

Let's look at some easy-to-spot traits for an Enneagram type Four and take note of how many you identify with. Bear in mind that some of these traits will be more pronounced in healthy Fours while others will be more identifiable with unhealthy Fours.

- You're highly attuned to your emotions and sensitive to other people and their feelings.
- It's easy for your to form deep connections with people.
- You're imaginative, creative, and a deep thinker.
- Authenticity and vulnerability are words that best describe you when interacting with the world.
- You like to express yourself through dance, writing, music, poetry, or other creative expressions.

STRUGGLES THAT TYPE FOURS MIGHT HAVE

Using pain as fuel for creativity

Fours are notorious for chasing after pain and sadness to fuel their creativity among the heart-centered types. If you're a Four, have you found yourself doing that at any point? Most Fours believe that art or originality is only achieved through intense emotion (usually negative emotion). Do you? If so, that will keep you stuck in a sea of negativity. Contrary to popular belief among the Fours, you don't have to be in pain to create something precious for the world.

Melancholy

In stressful situations, almost all Fours struggle with feelings of melancholy which quickly leads to self-pity and depression for the unhealthy type Fours.

Feeling misunderstood

Fours often feel misunderstood by other people. It might be that others are simply confused by the Four's ever-changing mood or that they just aren't used to dealing with a person who openly shares their most vulnerable and painful emotion. Whatever the case might be, if you're a Four and feel that people don't appreciate or understand you enough, instead of doing what unhealthy Fours would do, i.e., withdraw from the world, choose to figure out a way to connect with others in a way that develops both you and them.

Envy

Many Fours (especially those at average and unhealthy levels) struggle with deep feelings of envy because they see in others what they feel is missing in them, which stirs up jealousy. If you often compare yourself to others and feel less about your own life, this should be addressed in healthy ways.

GROWTH TIPS FOR FOURS

#1: Watch your self-talk

Inner dialogue can either be negative or positive. It tends to be negative for many of us, which can poison confidence and self-esteem. In the case of type Four, negative self-talk can be detrimental, even destructive.

Pay close attention to that inner critic and determine to retrain that inner voice into a more loving, kinder, and positively affirming voice. This will require effort and practice on your end, so start small.

Whenever you catch yourself thinking ill about yourself or another, pause, take a few breaths and tell yourself, "Here I go again. Throwing myself down the pit of despair. Well, not this time. I choose to think a different thought."

Proceed to find the next best thought that is more positive than your previous negative thought.

#2: Don't believe every thought and feeling you have

Many Fours become slaves to their minds and assume the role of victim when negative, overwhelming thoughts and emotions kick in. Here's the thing, no matter how tormenting a thought is, it's just a thought. You can choose to think a different thought. Just because the idea came to you doesn't mean it should take residence in your mental home. For example, if you feel envious and think evil thoughts, you can refuse to hold on to that emotion. You could cast it away from your mind and body immediately and command it to stay away from your mental home. With your imagination, open the door of your mental home, command that thought or emotion to get out, and lock the door! Try it next time an unpleasant feeling shows up.

#3: Practice self-discipline

Given the tendency to be passive and even procrastinate, I'm encouraging you to develop healthy routines that enable you to practice self-discipline.

Everything should have its time and place, e.g., a time to just wander with your imagination and a time to be objective, pragmatic and productive. The key here is to build a healthy routine you enjoy and then stick with it. By developing your own personalized routine, not only are you exercising your power of individuality, but you're also giving yourself rules of engagement that foster the best quality of life possible.

#4: Find common ground between you and others

The only way to eliminate that horrid feeling of being "different" from others is to train yourself to find common ground while socializing with people. The more things you can find in common, the easier it will be to create connections with others and find the people who love and accept you for who you are.

#5: Celebrate your wins no matter how small

One way to avoid the trap of shame and inadequacy is to notice the things you're doing well and the strengths you possess. Whenever you set a goal and achieve it, celebrate that, no matter how small. If you have a work or health goal, create mini-milestones that will keep you accountable and also help you know when to celebrate yourself.

TYPE 5: THE INVESTIGATOR

Overview of type Five:

Type Fives are also called observers or quiet specialists because they are driven by the desire to gain knowledge and understanding. They are sober-minded, disciplined, and highly intelligent. Fives are most comfortable in the realm of thought where they can think, investigate, discover and objectively solve complex problems. They care a lot about finding out why things are the way they are and how the world works, whether it's the local environment, the planet, or the cosmos. While many type Fives are scientifically oriented, some are drawn to humanities and arts. In fact, it's not uncommon for a Five to be artistically inclined even if they pursue a scientific discipline.

Fives spend a lot of time curiously observing and contemplating everything around them to gain new knowledge. They don't care much about what's already familiar and established in society. Instead, they want to be on the leading edge of that new idea or discovery. A Five's attention is usually attracted to the unusual, the overlooked, the bizarre, or the unknown territory. Gaining knowledge that others don't have is thrilling for a type Five. That's why many of them choose to specialize in areas where they can get enough expertise to be considered an authority in that subject. At work, Fives are private, prefer to work autonomously, and tend to analytically approach each project or subject. You may notice they don't like small talk and generally refrain from social interaction unless it's a topic they have an intense interest in.

Different types of Fives will view the world based on their level of development, but as a general rule of thumb, healthy Fives are self-reliant, confident, influential pioneers who are great at dealing with emergencies or crises because they know how to remain calm and objectively analyze the situation at hand. Unhealthy Fives are withdrawn from society, radical, and lacking emotional awareness. They struggle to understand their own emotions and quickly develop tunnel vision, making it hard to have healthy relationships.

Within the Centers of Intelligence triad, type Fives fall into the "head" center alongside type Sixes and Sevens. The underlying unresolved emotion for the thinkers is fear. Fives attempt to avoid the feeling of fear and anxiety by withdrawing and protecting their inner resources.

Some descriptive qualities you might recognize in type Five include curiosity, scholarly, perceptivity, autonomy, insightful and private.

At their best, Fives are curious visionary pioneers who tend to be ahead of their time. They have incredible foresight and a calm demeanor that brings great comfort to others.

Core Desire: To be self-sufficient, free, and knowledgeable. Fives want to understand why things work as they do, and most desire to be competent and feel secure in their knowledge and inner resources.

Core Fear: Type Fives fear being incapable or helpless.

What motivates a type Five? All type Fives to varying degrees and depending on how healthy their development is long to understand their environment. They are inspired by their curiosity and desire to know and understand as much as possible.

Wings:

Type Five has the Four-Wing, which is "The Iconoclast," and the Six-Wing, which is "The Problem Solver."

Arrows and their meaning:

Type Five has two connecting arrows, namely 7 and 8. When moving in the direction of disintegration and stress (seven), detached Fives become scattered, absent-minded and hyperactive like an unhealthy Seven. However, the arrow pointing to growth and integration (eight) shows a detached Five transforming into a more confident and decisive individual like a healthy Eight.

Examples of famous people:

Some well-known people sharing the enneagram type Five include Albert Einstein, Stephen Hawkin, Friedrich Nietzsche, Stephen King, Siddhartha Gautama Buddha, Eckhart Tolle, Emily Dickinson, Bill Gates, Mark Zuckerberg, Jane Goodall, Jodie Foster, and Angela Merkel.

Type Five levels of development:

There are different expressions of type Five that you'll need to learn. At various stages of development, a type Five will exhibit certain behavior and attitudes depending on how disconnected they are from their higher Self. Let's look at each level.

Healthy levels

Level 1 is a type Five at their best and highest development. At this level, the individual is open-minded, engaged, and sees the world as whole and abundant. This Five sees large complex issues with clarity and precision. That leads them to pioneer discoveries and find entirely new ways of doing and perceiving things. They have also learned to acknowledge, process, and even embrace their emotional side, making them well-rounded and powerful human beings.

Level 2 is where type Five is intensely focused on their object of attention. They are extraordinarily perceptive and curious about whatever they study, preferring to invest most of their time in observation mode.

Level 3 is where a Five invests all their time to become an expert in a specific field. They are innovative, highly independent, and produce precious works. Knowledge thrills and excites them.

Average levels

Level 4 is where a Five spends most of their time thinking things through and building mental models and visuals to figure things out. At this point of development, the individual is slow to take action on their ideas because they prefer to gather as many resources as possible, prepare and test out their ideas in their head first.

Most people tend to be fascinated by off-beat esoteric subjects, even those involving dark and disturbing elements. They are intense and high-strung and spend most of their time alone. Level 5 is the point at which a type Five typically starts showing significant signs of detachment.

Level 6 is where type Five takes an antagonistic stance toward anything that threatens their inner world or personal vision. They are cynical, argumentative, and hold incredibly radical views on life.

Unhealthy levels

Level 7 is where we see a downward spiral into the dark side of the personality. This type Five is isolated from reality, eccentric and nihilistic. Their fear is beginning to take center stage, causing them to be very unstable and detached from everything and everyone.

Level 8 is where a Five becomes obsessed and frightened by their own thoughts. Threatening ideas overwhelm them, and they turn into horrific delirious individuals suffering from phobias and reality distortions. At this point, many develop poor eating and sleeping habits and even neglect their hygiene.

Level 9 is the rock bottom for type Five, and they become highly susceptible to suicide. Some people have a psychotic breakdown, and others become deranged, self-destructive, and entirely out of touch with their emotions.

Addictions:

To cope with the emotional and psychological turmoil this type faces, especially at those unhealthy levels of development, Fives may resort to psychotropic drugs for mental stimulation and escape. Some may use narcotics to deal with their anxiety.

HOW TO RECOGNIZE IF YOU'RE AN ENNEAGRAM FIVE

Let's look at some easy-to-spot traits for an Enneagram type Five and take note of how many you identify with. Bear in mind that some of these traits will be more pronounced in healthy Fours while others will be more identifiable with unhealthy Fives.

- Others often say you come across as emotionally disconnected, aloof, over-analytical, and distant. Maybe your romantic partner complains about some of these traits?
- You're not big on small talk, but you enjoy deep conversations around your topics of interest.
- Privacy is critical to you and non-negotiable. It's one of the reasons you're not a fan of social media.
- Being self-sufficient, independent, and having complete autonomy over your life are also non-negotiable.

- You're a minimalist.
- It feels like the world is very intrusive and draining. Hence, you do your best to create firm boundaries to protect your energy and resources.
- You like to hoard knowledge, space, and even time alone.
- You're not into large crowds, big gatherings, or many friends. Your relationships are few but very strong.
- Curiosity is one of the key qualities you recognize about yourself. There's an unquenchable thirst for knowledge and figuring things out.

STRUGGLES THAT AN ENNEAGRAM FIVE MIGHT FACE

Getting stuck in your head

There's a common statement you might have heard several times in your lifetime, especially if you are a type Five. "Get out of your head ." Let's face it, Fives spend a lot of time lost in their heads. While it is nice to dissect everything and everyone around you or to create internal models of the world, over time, this will create a deep struggle as the gap between your inner mental world and this outer objective world widens. A healthy Five learns to integrate both worlds and spend healthy amounts of time swimming in their ocean of thoughts and mental constructs without neglecting the objective world.

Underlying insecurity

In the book "Personality Types: Using the Enneagram for Self Discovery, Don Riso and Russ Hudson state that type Fives "usually try to avoid getting deeply involved with others because people are unpredictable and potentially demanding. The average and unhealthy levels of development struggle the most with this thought because they believe there's always a catch. This is a form of insecurity often masked with a detached, carefree demeanor. You might think that you don't care about others, but the underlying issue is that you fear you won't be competent enough to handle any unpredictable challenges that arise from engaging with others. That's something that needs to be resolved.

Distractions

Whether you're a healthy, average, or unhealthy Five, you'll appreciate the mention of distractions because that's a universal struggle for all Fives. Everyone who identifies as a type Five hates being interrupted or forced to deal with the noisy outside world. Technology is fantastic for a knowledge thirsty Five. But it can also be a source of anguish, especially if you have family and friends who keep nagging you offline and online. When there's a lot of noise, obligations, and too frequent interactions, it feels as though people don't respect your privacy and personality. Instead of suffering in silence or, worse still, shutting yourself away from people, consider speaking up and letting others know that you need quiet, uninterrupted time. If apps tend to irritate you, create a structure that enables you to enjoy them when convenient and shut them out when you need peace and quiet. Find healthy ways to protect your personal space without isolating yourself.

Connecting with your emotions

The thinker in your struggles to reconcile the value of emotions thus ensues the constant rift between reason and feeling. It's easy to detach from your feelings, block them out and hope they will disappear. What you need to realize is that your emotions serve a higher purpose. They are just as important to your growth and fulfillment as your intellect. Your ideas and execution ability will exponentially grow when you harmoniously integrate both thought and emotion.

Not having enough alone time

It's good to find a healthy balance between being alone and connecting with others. If you're a Five, you know that you need more alone time than most people. That can create friction within relationships, especially if you have to deal with someone extroverted. Forcing yourself to be around people isn't healthy for your development. Still, neither is detaching too much from the world of people.

GROWTH TIPS FOR FIVES

#1: Let the world in

Okay, maybe not the whole world but know that it's okay to step out of your comfort zone and trust people. The universe is benevolent. It's okay to have relationships, trust others and even share your feelings. I know it will take practice, so start small. One good friend at a time is all you need to get started.

#2: Invest time daily to connect with your body and emotions

While it is lovely to spend most of your time in your mind, it's even more powerful to consciously create that mind-body connection. Consider experimenting with different exercises and activities that link your emotions, body, and mind. Find something you enjoy: painting, playing an instrument, creative writing, journaling, yoga, or whatever else you can regularly engage in.

#3: Practice being generous with yourself

The more you can do and give to yourself, the easier it will be to perceive abundance and, in turn, give generously, whether it's your knowledge, time, or resources. Make some room for abundance in your life so you can eliminate that scary feeling of scarcity that often causes Fives to hoard things.

#4: Create a support structure that promotes your wellbeing

People who build you up and challenge you to be a better human being. Considering how obsessive and intense you can be about something you care about, I encourage you to have a support structure. Pick one or two people with whom you can absolutely share anything and everything. This can be a single individual who has access to your most disturbing thoughts emotions so they can help keep you grounded. Suppose you lose your grip on reality or get too carried away by an idea. In that case, they'll be there to bring you back into a healthy perspective so you don't lose yourself in the pursuit of knowledge. You might think it's unnecessary, but it does a lot of emotional good for both you and the one that loves you to know that you've got each other's back.

#5: Increase your self-awareness

Daily self-awareness practices will enable you to go through life mindful and more aware of how you show up and when you're starting to spiral downward in your development. Become aware when you're starting to close yourself in or when you've shut someone down. Then you can consciously take action to move in a more constructive direction.

TYPE 6: THE LOYALIST/SKEPTIC

Overview of type Six:

Type Sixes are commonly called loyalists because they are very committed to their relationships and values. Sixes are considered the most loyal, faithful, and dependable of all Enneagram types. They are also referred to as skeptics because they are often alert and trying to think several steps ahead so they can feel ready to handle worst-case scenarios. Sixes are generally incredible at troubleshooting and problem solving, but lower levels of development have Sixes who get paralyzed by this natural tendency to anticipate things going wrong.

In fact, at average and unhealthy levels, a type Six is often over-whelmed by their constant worry about the future and things going wrong.

In general, Sixes are hard-working, competent, and take their time to do things the right way. While they are the most loyal, it takes time to develop that trust. But once a Six trusts you or commits them-selves to something, they stick to it. They also respect rules and authority, provided they trust that source of authority and their intention. Unlike type Five, who are also thinkers, Sixes enjoy collab-oration and teamwork. At work, they thrive in healthy team environ-ments and aren't afraid to take a stand on behalf of the team's greater good despite concerns and risks. They are great at honoring commitments to people and plans and tend to approach issues with both logic and emotion. For a type Six, being prepared, safe and secure is a top priority.

Different types of Sixes will view the world based on their level of development, but as a general rule of thumb, healthy Sixes are

caring, generous, and hard-working team players who enjoy moti-vating colleagues and friends. They take great pride in serving their organization, developing a secure attachment style, and trusting others easily.

On the other hand, Unhealthy Sixes are highly paranoid, suspicious of everything, and paralyzed when it comes to taking action because the illusion of constant danger is too overwhelming. Unfortunately, unhealthy Sixes like to project their insecurities onto others which can cause a lot of friction in relationships.

Within the Centers of Intelligence triad, type Sixes fall into the "head" center alongside type Fives and Sevens. Within this triad, type Sixes struggle the most with their unresolved fear, and they keep swinging from trust and mistrust of the people around them and the world. The fear and anxiety in a Six can manifest in various ways, making this type the most difficult to describe and type. It also makes a Six more susceptible to mistyping their real personality. Many assume they are a type Two or a Nine.

Some descriptive qualities you might recognize in type Six include responsibility, commitment, persistence, loyal, trustworthiness, dependability, courage, attention to people, and strategy in their thinking.

At their best, Sixes are internally stable, self-reliant, trustworthy, and great team players.

Core Desire: Sixes seek security and support.

Core Fear: Losing their ground, being unprepared, and unable to defend themselves from the dangers of this world.

What motivates a type Six? Type Sixes are driven by the need to create a feeling of safety and security around them.

Wings:

Type Six has the Five-Wing, which is "The Defender," and the Seven-Wing which is "The Buddy."

Arrows and their meaning:

Type Six has two connecting arrows, namely 3 and 9. When moving in the direction of disintegration and stress (three), dutiful Sixes are arrogant and competitive like unhealthy Nines. However, the arrow pointing to growth and integration (nine) shows a fearful, pessimistic Six transforming into a more relaxed and optimistic individual like a healthy Nine.

Examples of famous people:

Some well-known people sharing the Enneagram type Six include Mike Tyson, Diana Princess of Wales, Marylin Monroe, Mel Gibson, Jennifer Aniston, Sarah Jessica Parker, Mark Twain, Woody Allen, and Eminem.

Type Six levels of development:

There are different expressions of type Six that you'll need to learn. At various stages of development, a type Four will exhibit certain behavior and attitudes depending on how disconnected they are from their higher Self. Let's look at each level.

Healthy levels

Level 1 is a type Six at their best. Here the individual is calm, trusts themselves and others, courageous, optimistic in their thinking, and makes a great leader. Their ability to affirm themselves and champion others into their greatness makes them extremely valuable in the world. This type Six has found his or her security and safety and doesn't look to external sources to provide them. They find a balance between independent and interdependent when in relation to others.

Level 2 is a type Six who is lovable, affectionate, and capable of forming permanent alliances and healthy relationships with others. Trust is essential, and they can bond quickly with others.

Level 3 is a type Six who is highly devoted to the people and things they believe in. This individual is often a great community builder. They are trustworthy, hard-working, great at troubleshooting. They bring about that cooperative spirit that glues people together, whether offline or online.

Average levels

Level 4 is a type Six not yet grounded in their own stability and safety. That means they spend most of their energy and time trying to create structures and alliances that give them that feeling of continuity and security. This individual is always on the alert and anticipating problems.

Level 5 is a type Six who struggles with anxiety and internal confusion. They keep switching from feelings of trust to mistrust, safety, and danger. This individual becomes evasive, indecisive, overly cautious, and ambivalent. They might also become a little passive-aggressive in their relationships.

Level 6 is where a Six become increasingly insecure. They turn sarcastic and blame others for their problems. At this point, their tunnel vision causes them to be very black and white, creating divisions and labeling people either as friends or enemies. This type Six loves to be authoritarian yet is highly suspicious and even fearful of authority. They find comfort in instilling fears in others as a coping mechanism to silence their own fears.

Unhealthy levels

Level 7 is where a type Six spirals downward into their dark side. Fear is pronounced in this person, and they turn panicky, volatile, and challenging to be around. They feel defenseless and desperately seek out a stronger external authority or something that can help them resolve their problems.

Level 8 is typically where the Six feels like others are out to get them. Some might even turn a little violent as they lash out and act irrationally. Ironically, their actions cause them to produce the very thing they fear.

Level 9 is the most unhealthy level for a type Six. At this point, we are dealing with a self-destructive, hysterical, and maybe even suicidal person. Most of their behavior is passive-aggressive, and they are prone to self-sabotage even the little good that they do.

Addictions:

To cope with the emotional and psychological turmoil this type faces, especially at those unhealthy levels of development, Sixes might resort to alcoholism, drug abuse, or even working excessively, all in an attempt to eliminate the dangers they perceive and fortify their security.

HOW TO RECOGNIZE IF YOU'RE AN ENNEAGRAM SIX

Let's look at some easy-to-spot traits for an Enneagram type Six and take note of how many you identify with. Bear in mind that some of these traits will be more pronounced in healthy Sixes while others will be more identifiable with unhealthy Sixes.

- You're incredibly loyal to the people you care about.
- Stability, safety, security, consistency, and predictability really matter to you.
- In some ways, you're super confident, but sometimes you're also super insecure.
- You like being direct in your communication and prefer when people are direct with you.
- You're more interested in supporting the group than being the star or having the spotlight on you.
- You value loyalty and trust in relationships.
- The desire to always do things the "right way" causes you plenty of anxiety.
- You fear being abandoned or left alone by those you trust.
- When you believe in something, you'll stick to it and will rarely change your mind no matter what.

STRUGGLES THAT AN ENNEAGRAM SIX MIGHT FACE

Pessimism and suspicion

Painting worst-case scenarios is a huge obstacle for all Sixes. While it is good to consider all angles, allowing your brain to fall into the rabbit hole of pessimism and anxiety will only do your work and health harm. Consider bringing yourself more into the present moment whenever you find yourself falling too far into skepticism.

Thinking in circles

Most unhealthy and average Sixes will find themselves thinking in circles, getting nowhere. It's easy to get stuck in a loop that breeds anxiety and fear. That's why you need to catch yourself as early as possible when your thinking starts to spiral downward and stop that momentum. Instead of overthinking things, pause and ask yourself, "what if the worst happens?" Once you answer that follow up with "and then what?" Once you answer that, keep leaning in that direction until you find yourself identifying the resources you have to handle whatever your brain tells you will go wrong. Sometimes all you need to do is show your brain that anticipating "bad things" isn't very productive and that no matter how bad your brain thinks it is, there's always a solution to every problem. Show yourself that your thinking can be brilliant enough to create constructive ideas, not just anxiety-building ones.

Phobias or counter-phobic behavior

Some Sixes avoid facing their fears and become phobic over everything as a defense mechanism. Others go to the polar extreme and put up a show of tough exterior, often putting themselves in risky situations to prove that they are fearless. This is used as a way of masking their internal uncertainty. Either way, none of these expressions are healthy, so it's best to address and resolve them in healthy ways.

GROWTH TIPS FOR SIXES

#1: Take safe risks and try new things often

Consistency and predictability are great, but they'll make you too rigid. You need to stay flexible and adaptable, so do something that regularly takes you out of your comfort zone. Start with small things like ordering a different sandwich at your favorite cafe or changing up your workout routine. The more you can show yourself that some risks are reasonable, the easier it will be to embrace change, and you might just realize that the world isn't as bad as you imagine.

#2: Cultivate self-belief

This is one of the most important things you can do to develop and improve your life. How does one increase self-belief? It starts with small, consistent steps taken daily that increase your self-esteem. Consider listening to a podcast or reading a book daily that feeds your mind with nourishing thoughts about who you are and what you're capable of. You should also set big and small goals that you move toward. As you accomplish each one (especially the mini-goals), remind yourself that it's you doing this and give yourself permission to feel good about it. Find your Truth, and you will have a solid ground to build yourself.

#3: Create daily practices and habits that help you release anxiety

Instead of spending a lot of time on your head, refocus that energy on constructive things that enable you to stay in the present moment and release stress and tension. If unsure what activities can help you with present moment awareness, check out the last section. I've shared various techniques to help you grow into a healthier version of yourself.

#4: Work on your trust meter

Trust is a big issue for you as a Six, and that means you need to give it generously if you desire to have it. That tendency to be skeptical of everything and everyone might serve you some of the time. Still, you should have it on a tight leash because, for the most part, it's easier to build healthy, lasting relationships when you're not pessimistic and skeptical. Don't be afraid to give someone your trust if it feels right, and trust in your judgment. Sure, you will come across a few mistakes here and there. The trick is to get more attuned to your inner guidance and believe that you can choose the right people to be around you.

CHAPTER 7
ENNEAGRAM PERSONALITY TYPING SYSTEM PART 3

TYPE 7: THE ENTHUSIAST

Overview of type Seven:

Type Sevens are enthusiastic pleasure-seekers because they love adventure and possess boundless energy. They are ever pursuing the next big thing that will create feelings of pleasure and happiness in their lives. Sevens are often practical with multiple talents and high-level skill sets. They are quick thinkers, creative, and able to do several things simultaneously. Their positive energy makes them highly attractive, so people really enjoy being around them. The central theme for the optimistic Seven is to plan, prepare for and seek out the next new thing because they are generally convinced that something better is just around the corner. And although their energy and personality are great for networking, promoting themselves, and their interests in the workplace, this constant restlessness can create a lot of friction. Focus doesn't come easy for a Seven, and they like to keep all their options open, so they struggle with commitment a lot. They enjoy having creative freedom and having options and flexible schedules at work. They love being around people, but it cannot be under rigid rules and structures as that will kill the spontaneity and freedom that Sevens most enjoy about interactions. Sevens thrive in environments that utilize their creative thinking and imagination. They will be the ones to explore and offer up new possibilities and future ideas. Most Sevens are extroverted and enjoy experiencing the world mainly through their physical senses.

Different types of Sevens will view the world based on their level of development. Still, as a general rule of thumb, healthy Sevens are more serene, focused, and able to concentrate their energy wisely, producing results that benefit themselves and others. They possess contagious positive energy that naturally draws in all the right opportunities and people. They can easily find that perfect work-life balance that enables them to enjoy the best of both. Unhealthy Sevens are illogical, irritable, great procrastinators, and unproductive. They struggle with responsibility and accountability and can never finish what they start. Ever jumping from one thing to the next or relationship to relationship, unhealthy Sevens aren't grounded or in control of their compulsive need for pleasure. That makes them pretty moody and emotionally unstable.

Within the Centers of Intelligence triad, type Sevens fall into the "head" center alongside type Fives and Sixes. With fear being their underlying unresolved emotion, Sevens react differently to this disconnect. They choose to do everything possible to find and sustain pleasure through their senses as their way of locking out the negative states and fear they don't wish to deal with. They seek distractions in external environments to ensure constant stimulation, which is why they are more prone than most types to fall into all kinds of addictions.

Their fear and pain avoidance are also projected onto others. You'll notice a Seven will not want to confront anyone's dark emotions, not even their own. They'd rather downplay or deny pain rather than acknowledge it. Of course, the extent to which a Seven is manifesting this denial and avoidance depends entirely on their level of development.

Some descriptive qualities you might recognize in type Sevens include curiosity, optimism, spontaneity, versatility, adventurousness, adaptability, agility, and open-mindedness.

At their best, Sevens are focused and working on worthwhile goals. They've learned to be appreciative, joyous, and satisfied with themselves and life as a whole.

Core Desire: Type Seven's most basic desire is to feel happy, satisfied, and engaged. They want to soak in all the goodness that life offers and desire to live all their lives in that pleasure.

Core Fear: The most basic fear of a Seven is that the inherent fear and negative emotions that are unresolved within them will take over and cause inescapable pain. They also fear being deprived of freedom and excitement in life, so they hate rigid rules and strict deadlines.

What motivates a type Seven? Their biggest motivation is to avoid pain, discomfort, and negativity at all costs.

Wings:

Type Seven has the Six-Wing, which is "The Entertainer," and the Eight-Wing, which is "The Realist."

Arrows and their meaning:

Type Seven has two connecting arrows, namely 1 and 5. When moving in the direction of disintegration and stress (one), scattered Sevens become critical and perfectionistic like unhealthy Ones. However, the arrow pointing to growth and integration (five) shows a scattered Seven transforming into a more focused individual like a healthy Five.

Examples of famous people:

Some well-known people sharing the enneagram Seven include Amelia Earhart, Ram Dass, John F. Kennedy, Richard Branson, Katy Perry, Elton John, The 14th Dalai Lama, Bette Midler, George Clooney, Brad Pitt, Robin Williams, Jim Carrey, Robert Downey, Jr., and Leonardo DiCaprio.

Type Seven levels of development:

There are different expressions of type Sevens that you'll need to learn. At various stages of development, a type Sevens will exhibit certain behavior and attitudes depending on how disconnected they are from their higher Self. Let's look at each level.

Healthy levels

Level 1 is a type Seven at their best. This individual lives in awe and wonder over the goodness that life offers. They assimilate experiences in-depth and experience deep appreciation and gratitude for where they are and what they have. They have accessed the joyful ecstasy of finding that much-needed spiritual alignment that provides the pleasure they were seeking externally.

Level 2 is where a Seven is most extroverted. They are cheerful, resilient, spontaneous, curious, excitable, and want to experience life to its fullest. This individual finds everything invigorating.

Level 3 is where a Seven is more of a generalist and still very invested in their multifaceted interests but in a focused way, making them highly productive. This individual accomplishes more than most and is usually great at everything they put their attention on.

Average levels

Level 4 is where a Seven starts becoming restless. They want to have more options and choices tied directly to their sense of freedom. Their sense of adventure and pleasure-seeking is more worldly as they seek external experiences and new things. This Seven is a massive consumer of the latest trends.

Level 5 is where a Seven becomes hyperactive and unable to control their compulsive need for stimulation. They are swamped and distracted doing whatever comes to mind. At this point, the fear of being bored and missing out starts to kick into high gear. They are still optimistic, witty, wisecracking, and love things that entertain them. Creative ideas continue to flow, and as they are still trying to pursue all their different interests but without a clear focus, not much is getting accomplished. They might start something or develop a great idea, but there won't be any follow-through.

Level 6 is where a Seven turn excessive in their consumption. They just can't say "no" to themselves. That causes them to become self-centered, too materialistic, and even greedy as they seek to have more and more. Nothing is ever enough for them. In terms of behavior, this Seven becomes pushy, jaded, and really demanding.

Unhealthy levels

Level 7 is where we see a downward spiral to the dark side of a Seven. At this point, the person is desperate to quell their increasing anxiety and excessive behavior. Unfortunately, they don't know how to create discipline because they've never created any structure or healthy habits, so they fall into addictions and abusive behavior. In an attempt to escape negative states of mind, they fall deeper into the dark pit of addiction.

Level 8 is where a type Seven attempts to run away from their own horrid self. Their optimism has faded, and now all that's left is never-ending anxiety and erratic mood swings.

Level 9 is the lowest level of development and definitely rock bottom for the enthusiast. At this point, the Seven has depleted all their energy and often give up on life and themselves. They quickly fall into depression and despair. Some develop dangerous and self-destructive behavior and are prone to overdosing or attempting suicide.

Addictions:

To cope with the emotional and psychological turmoil this type faces, especially at those unhealthy levels of development, Sevens might resort to all kinds of stimulants ranging from caffeine to more dangerous stuff like Cocaine. They are more likely to indulge in ecstasy pills, psychotropics, narcotics, and alcohol. Those that are into physical appearance might also take up excessive cosmetic surgery.

HOW TO RECOGNIZE IF YOU'RE AN ENNEAGRAM SEVEN

Let's look at some easy-to-spot traits for an Enneagram type Seven and take note of how many you identify with. Bear in mind that some of these traits will be more pronounced in healthy Sevens. In contrast, others will be more identifiable with unhealthy Sevens.

- You're passionately obsessed with the future and all its possibilities. In fact, you prefer focusing on the future and find the present pretty dull.
- You enjoy having lots and lots of options when it comes to just about everything. That includes your social and professional life.
- FOMO is real, and you can't stand it.
- You don't get people who say "find what you love" because you love lots of things and are pretty much multi-talented.
- "Zen" is the last word you would ever use to describe yourself.

- You have childlike enthusiasm and curiosity despite how old you are.
- People find you magnetic and say your positive energy is contagious.
- You love planning a lot. In fact, you can easily map out the next fifteen years... but two weeks from now, you'll probably have another new detailed plan.

STRUGGLES THAT AN ENNEAGRAM SEVEN MIGHT HAVE

Lack of focus

Being able to focus and concentrate is a skill that all Sevens will need to master if they want to be productive and accomplished. It's harder for average and unhealthy Sevens to concentrate and focus on a single thing long enough to see it through. If that mental fog and "out of control" feeling is getting to you, work on creating healthy routines that enable you to develop more self-discipline and focus.

Feeling constricted and trapped by routine and schedules

Since freedom is one of your core values, it's easy to feel like commitments, schedules, and other people's expectations cage you. You might desire loyal lasting relationships like marriage or long-term work contracts. Still, at the same time, these things bring you a sense of anxiety and restlessness. The key here is to reframe some of these critical commitments in your life and come to the full realization that freedom and responsibilities are not mutually exclusive.

Jack of all trades and a master of none

Most average and unhealthy Sevens will struggle to stick with something long enough to gain mastery. That can be in their professional and personal interests. Their curiosity at these lower levels of development causes them to bounce from one thing to the next. They can easily pick up new skills and abilities but quickly drop them for the next new thing. If this has been one of your struggles, the solution is to develop yourself so you can get to the point where you can pursue what you love long enough to gain real expertise.

Pain and negative emotions are your enemies

As a classic type Seven, acknowledging and processing anything that threatens that upbeat vibe is obviously going to be hard. And that's okay. Sevens are known to rationalize and justify everything that threatens their happiness because they don't want to deal with these uncomfortable emotions. If you realize this to be true of you, start catching yourself in those moments when things are bad, and you're attempting to "gloss" over or "closet" them for later. Instead, get out of your head and into your body. Become aware of those emotions and take time to explore them. Give yourself permission to experience both pleasure and pain because it enables you to become well-rounded and resilient.

GROWTH TIPS FOR SEVENS

#1: Learn to see the value of all your emotions, including the dark ones

I know this is hard if you're a Seven because you avoid all negativity and pain, including other people's. I would encourage you to keep an open mind and educate yourself a little more about the purpose these emotions serve. It will be hard to feel whole if you go through life denying certain aspects of yourself. And while dwelling in pain and negativity is not healthy, acknowledging it when it happens is ideal.

#2: Allow yourself to go deep and process all your emotions

Give yourself permission to feel all your emotions, not just the pleasant ones. The next time a negative emotion comes over you, don't run. Sit with it and take time to process it. Ask yourself, "what am I feeling, and where are you feeling it in your body?" If you can identify exactly what this negative emotion is, that will empower you to label and tame that emotion. Done well, and with much practice, this can be a liberating process.

#3: Integrate a little more discipline into your life

You might associate schedules and structure with boredom and constriction. Still, a little more discipline and self-control will actually enhance your life and aid your development. The more discipline you bring to your work and life, the more focus you'll have and the bigger the reward as you finally start seeing the results of your hard work.

#4: Slow down and be more present

I know it's fun to stay focused on the future and limitless possibilities but remember your power lies in the present moment. It's essential for you to invest more time cultivating your power in the here and now. That's the real key to further growth and progress. Check out the last chapter on practices that can enable you to become powerfully present regardless of your current level of development.

TYPE 8: THE CHALLENGER/PROTECTOR

Overview of type Eight:

Type Eights are known as challengers because they rebel against the status quo and have no problem challenging something that doesn't align with their values or take advantage of others.

Eights are powerful and strong-willed with the natural charisma and persuasive abilities that cause others to follow them into all kinds of endeavors. They are known to enjoy taking up new challenges, creating initiatives that propel change, and being in charge of everything around them. Sometimes they are also referred to as protectors because inasmuch as they like to challenge others to step out of their comfort zone, they are also very protective of the people under their care. Although Eights can come across as intimidating, aggressive, and at times argumentative, their intentions are usually in the right place because nothing is more important to them than standing up for what they believe and protecting those under their care. All Eights tend to be quite domineering, even the healthy ones. The difference is with a healthy Eight, that tendency is kept in check.

Most Eights are hard-working, self competent, pragmatic, and goal-oriented. They are often the trailblazers in our society, taking great pride in their independence and sharpness of mind. Their perception is that the world is made up of "strong" and "weak" people; they being in the "strong" category, have the responsibility of protecting the weak. One of the great passions for an Eight is to bring about justice, end oppression for and protect the vulnerable.

At work, Eights are better when they have some kind of leadership role. Most people refer to them as "bossy" because they're assertive, authoritative, and can get pretty angry when things don't go their way. They can be pretty impatient with rules and regulations and have difficulty following other people's instructions. However, they bring great energy and enthusiasm to the team. As long as things are getting done their way, everyone enjoys working with them.

Different types of Eights will view the world based on their level of development. Still, as a general rule of thumb, healthy Eights are

brave, charismatic, generous, powerful protectors who are resourceful and committed to their team or mission. They are also intensely loving and protective of their close friends and family members. Unhealthy Eights, on the other hand, are tyrannical. They are power-hungry and will destroy anything that gets in their way. Anger is a big issue for this type, and they aren't afraid to unleash it to the world, especially when they don't get what they want. In the lower levels of development, Eights can become quite vengeful and emotionally numb.

Within the Centers of Intelligence triad, type Eights fall into the "Gut" center alongside type Nines and Ones. The core unresolved emotion for this triad is anger, and Eights isn't afraid to show it. Unlike the Nines and Ones who try to repress or ignore their anger, Eights aren't shy of confrontation, issuing threats and throwing temper tantrums at a moment's notice.

Some descriptive qualities you might recognize in type Eights include brave, enthusiastic, energetic, charismatic, determined, confident, fierce, independent, self-sufficient, assertive, and protective.

At their best, Eights are inspiring, generous, and capable of achieving great things. Their self-mastery and commitment to justice and creating a good life for themselves and others strengthens and propels them into success. They are natural-born leaders, and people love following them.

Core Desire: Eights desire to have a good life and control their own destiny. They want to be the hero in their world.

Core Fear: Eights fear being controlled or harmed by others.

What motivates a type Eight? Their biggest motivation is the need to be in control, powerful, and invulnerable to external forces. They want to have enough power, energy, and resources to protect themselves and others (especially the underdogs). Eights are also driven by the need to impact and stand for something meaningful.

Wings:

Type Eight has the Seven-Wing, which is "The Maverick," and the Nine-Wing which is "The Bear."

Arrows and their meaning:

Type Eight has two connecting arrows, namely 2 and 5. When moving in the direction of disintegration and stress (five), self-confident Eights suddenly become evasive and fearful like unhealthy Fives. However, the arrow pointing to growth and integration (two) shows a lustful, controlling Eight transforming into a more caring and warm-hearted individual like a healthy Two.

Examples of famous people:

Some well-known people sharing the enneagram Seven include Winston Churchill, Martin Luther King, Jr., Saddam Hussein, Aretha Franklin, Pablo Picasso, Frank Sinatra, Mae West, Barbara Walters, Clint Eastwood, Jack Nicholson, Serena Williams, Donald Trump, Alec Baldwin, Franklin D. Roosevelt, and Ernest Hemingway.

Type Eight levels of development:

There are different expressions of type Eights that you'll need to learn. At various stages of development, a type Eight will exhibit certain behavior and attitudes depending on how disconnected they are from their higher Self. Let's look at each level.

Healthy levels

Level 1 is a type Eight at their highest and best. Here the individual possesses excellent levels of self-control and feels very connected to their higher self. This Eight has cultivated and developed their gentle caring side, and they have a deep sense of gratitude and joy. They are magnanimous, merciful, courageous, and generous. They are willing to put themselves in serious jeopardy to achieve their vision and have a lasting influence.

Level 2 is where type Eight is strong, powerful, self-confident, and assertive. They have a strong inner drive to accomplish their goals and meet their needs and wants. They know how to stand up for what they envision and have an unbeatable "can do" attitude. And they do all this from a place of emotional stability and self-restraint.

Level 3 is where an Eight is pretty decisive, authoritative, and commandeering, always wanting to be the person others look up to.

This individual takes the initiative and knows how to make things happen. Consider them a champion of the people, a provider, and protector. They carry themselves with honor and integrity, and they enjoy championing others as well.

Average levels

Level 4 is where the Eight begins to deny their own emotional needs. Self-mastery, especially of their emotions, isn't yet attained. They are, however, very hard-working, resourceful, and self-sufficient. At this point, the Eight is more concerned with financial independence and having enough resources to live life on their own terms. This individual is typically quite rugged, enterprising, and pragmatic.

Level 5 is where we see the oppressive aspects of an Eight taking over. This individual wants to control their environment and the people around them. There might be quite a bit of boastfulness, pride, and egotism in their demeanor as they attempt to impose their will and vision on others. At this point, the Eight doesn't see that equality anymore, and the internal disconnect and emotional conflict are more significant, so they will have difficulty respecting others.

Level 6 is the level of development where an Eight is aggressive, intimidating, and confrontational. This individual will have plenty of adversaries. They won't be afraid to issue threats and reprisals to get obedience from others. They might even go as far as instilling insecurity and fear in others to tame them, which creates plenty of resentment and hostility. Competition is the name of the game, and they believe everything is a battlefield and emotions are for the weak.

Unhealthy levels

Level 7 is where a type Eight spirals downward into the dark side of their personality. This Eight is hard-hearted, immoral, and in some cases, pretty violent. In an attempt to control everything and everyone, they usually turn into ruthless dictators in their own right.

Level 8 is when the Eight becomes too reckless and over-extends themselves. In an attempt to feed their power-hungry addiction, they take actions that scare and even hurt those around them. They might develop delusional ideas about their power, feeling omnipotent and unstoppable, which often causes them to make grievous mistakes.

Level 9 is rock bottom for a type Eight. This Eight has the emotional range of a teaspoon, making them stone-cold, antagonists who are highly antisocial. At this point, the individual is vengeful, almost barbaric in their thoughts and actions, and will destroy anything and everything that doesn't conform to their will.

Addictions:

To cope with the emotional and psychological turmoil this type faces, especially at those unhealthy levels of development, Eights might resort to alcoholism, tobacco, and other narcotic substances for relief. They also tend to ignore their physical and emotional needs even if they feel an issue.

HOW TO RECOGNIZE IF YOU'RE AN ENNEAGRAM EIGHT

Let's look at some easy-to-spot traits for an Enneagram type Eight, and make sure you take note of how many you identify with. Bear in mind that some of these traits will be more pronounced in healthy Eights while others will be more present in unhealthy Eights.

- You vehemently despise being controlled or manipulated in any way.
- Vulnerability is something you seriously struggle with, even when it's someone with whom you're intimately involved.

- Your attitude can sometimes come off as intimidating and abrasive even when you don't mean to. But that doesn't bother you much because you feel the world absolutely needs people like you.
- Though you don't usually express it openly, nothing gives you as much joy as seeing the people you've taken under your wing thrive and prosper in life.
- You refuse to enable self-sabotage or self-pity in the people you love. That's why you're not afraid of giving a little tough love from time to time, especially to those you care about.
- When backed up against the wall, your first instinct is to tackle it head-on single-handedly.
- You hate asking for help or relying on others.
- Leading others and taking the initiative come naturally to you. And something about your personality just seems to compel others to follow your lead.
- You have a great deal of respect for those who show resilience, courage, and perseverance in the face of adversity.
- If you had a mantra, it would probably be "you create your own luck through hard work, a strong character, and relentless pursuit."
- You believe respect should be earned through competency and reason, not status or age.

STRUGGLES AN ENNEAGRAM EIGHT MIGHT HAVE

Impatience

You have a keen sense that time is limited, and you want to make the most of your time on earth accomplishing as much as you can. That's a great driver, and it enables you to make things happen. But it can also create a lot of impatience, especially with people who seem slow. Procrastinators and time-wasters tend to get on your last nerve, and they might not enjoy the reaction they get from you. While it is great to be so motivated, becoming too impatient with yourself, others or conditions beyond your control can be detrimental. Learn to trust in the process.

Dominating or even intimidating others without meaning to

As stated earlier, the need to be in charge, in control, and to lead the way comes naturally for an Eight. Even at the most healthy levels of development, you'll still need to keep this trait in check so that others don't feel too controlled by you. This aspect is pretty pronounced and tends to suffocate others when it comes to the more average and unhealthy Eights. I know you don't like sugarcoating anything or coddling people, but you'll need to be mindful of how straight and direct you are if you don't want to come off as offensive. The struggle is real because sometimes you'll feel like you're being forced to choose between being your authentic, bold self and playing diplomat (which you can't stand). Still, I encourage you to be mindful of your reactions. Take time to consider the effects of your reactions, especially when dealing with relationships you deeply value.

Putting too much pressure on yourself

With so much strength, power, boldness, ideas, and the belief that you can make the impossible a reality, it's easy to go too hard on yourself. Eights are notorious for physical and emotional self-neglect, especially at average and unhealthy levels. You might feel like you don't need help from anyone or that you can't afford to slow down and take a break because the mission is too critical. Here's the thing, to build a lasting legacy, you'll need all the help and rest you can get. Rest and relaxation are equally as important as going hard. And even though you struggle to delegate, feel vulnerable, or do anything in a less than perfect way, understand that these are not signs of weakness. I encourage you to give yourself permission to stop running all the time and just enjoy healthy downtimes regularly.

Struggling with emotions and the V-word

If there's one word that gets you all conflicted, it's got to be - vulnerability. You might have associated vulnerability and emotions with weakness for a long time. Having heart-to-heart conversations is probably one of the hardest things you can do, even with the people you care about the most. Your strength and independence seem to be at odds with compassion, gentleness, and vulnerability. Many Eights often worry that others might take advantage of them or try to control them if they openly share their feelings. Start slow if you realize it's hard to let someone in (as is often the case with many Eights). Open your mind enough to start developing that level of intimacy and tenderness with just a few people who earn your trust over time. Don't feel forced into it but do put some effort so that it can actually happen. Being vulnerable with another, even if it's just one person, will ultimately make you stronger and more grounded. It can be scary, but it's always worthwhile.

GROWTH TIPS FOR EIGHTS

#1: Prioritize self-care

This is one of the most significant shifts I encourage you to make immediately. Make time each day to do something that grounds you and brings you into the awareness of the self. Neglecting your body, mind, emotions, and higher self only weakens your power and creates unnecessary hurdles on your path of greatness. Think about this, you have big plans and require boundless energy to make those dreams a reality. How do you source this energy? Where will it come from in unlimited ways? Average Eights assume they can rely on external stimulants to keep them going. That is not only very detrimental, it's also quite temporary and unreliable. There is a better way, and that is through self-care rituals and time spent connecting with your higher self. You will need to create a routine that incorporates practices that serve all three domains of yourself, i.e., body, mind, and spirit. Find things you enjoy doing like sports, swimming, massages, etc., to take care of your body; feed yourself nourishing mental food to take care of your mind, and take up practices like yoga, Tai Chi, and meditation to nurture all three domains. The more these three are working harmoniously, the more unstoppable you become.

#2: Connect with your thoughts and emotions

As a body or gut-based type, you tend to act out of instincts which is excellent but not holistic. You might notice a big shift in your temperament just making this one move - reconnect with your thoughts and feelings before taking action. When you combine all three, i.e., gut, thoughts, and feelings, your decisions and actions will be more accurate and powerful.

#3: Open yourself up to unconditional love

The tendency is to view people as strong or weak, with you or against you. This way of thinking can make you intensely loving to your close friends and family members but numb you out when it comes to so-called strangers. Unfortunately, that can make it difficult to establish solid relationships built on trust and mutual respect. To do big things, you'll need a lot of people working with you, and the best way to lead these people and gain their loyalty is through love rather than intimidation and force. Practicing unconditional love and recognizing that you can give and receive love more freely will liberate and empower you. It will strengthen your professional and personal connections. I know you like everything to be on a merit-based system but make love the exception to this rule.

#4: Prioritize rest and downtime

Work hard and remember to rest enough too. Schedule downtime and sleep time just as you do work time. All great decisions, ideas, and actions occur when a mind is refreshed, sharp, and alert. Listen to your body and give it ample resting time not based on what others say but solely based on what your mind and body tell you is right for you. Some people like Kevin Hart can operate sharply on four hours of sleep, while others like Gary Vee need seven hours. There's no right or wrong here. Just make sure you do what's suitable for your body.

TYPE 9: THE PEACEMAKER

Overview of type Nine:

Type Nines are commonly referred to as peacekeepers or even mediators because they value peace and harmony above all else. These individuals are unselfish, easy-going, and very amicable. All Nines prefer to avoid conflict, making them somewhat withdrawn from life in varying degrees. Some Nines are introverted, so it's easier for them to isolate and avoid anything that threatens their peace of mind. Others lead more active and social lives, but even then, you'll always see a degree of disengagement and lack of involvement as if they are trying to insulate themselves from threats.

For the most part, Nines will be optimistic, supportive of others, and adopt a "go with the flow" attitude at all times. They enjoy being outdoors and trying their best to live in serene environments. Although Nines appear conservative, they can still be highly resilient in the face of change and uncertainty. As a matter of fact, most Nines are more resilient and open to change than they think. One unique struggle this type experiences far more than any other in the Enneagram typing system is their tendency to lose themselves in personal relationships. Often they will take on the characteristics of their partner and completely mute out their own unique qualities and voice. That makes it easy for a Nine to mistype themselves. Mothers can also give themselves up to the family entirely and lose their unique identity causing them to mistype as a Two. And while that dissolving of one's self is driven by the need for harmony, it often breeds resentment and anger, which periodically explodes. Even though it's not easy to spot, Nines don't like outer control, just like type Eights. The only difference is, they don't show it upfront. Instead, they show their resistance passively, resulting in passive-aggressive behavior.

At work, type Nines will get along with everyone and genuinely see each person's perspective, making it easy for others to feel understood. They will, however, do everything possible to avoid or end conflicts around them.

Different types of Nines will view the world based on their level of development, but as a general rule of thumb, healthy Nines are: calm, honest, supportive, and use their natural conflict diffusing superpowers to maintain harmony and social fluidity in every setting.

Unhealthy Nines are lethargic and struggle significantly with procrastination. They may become overly passive and highly self-critical.

Within the Centers of Intelligence triad, type Nines fall into the "Gut" center alongside type Eights and Ones. The core unresolved emotion for this triad is anger. Although Eights are excellent at expressing their anger and Ones resist it, Nines prefer to avoid it altogether. Their only focus is to find inner peace.

A healthy type Nine will come across as agreeable, gentle, kind, calm, stable, honest, accepting, optimistic, creative, and trusting. These are actually pretty distinct qualities that one would easily observe in type Nines. This type has the natural superpower of healing conflicts around them without much effort. They are also great persuaders, and others easily listen and follow their advice.

At their best, Nines are sturdy unifying individuals who bring people together and heal disputes.

Core Desire: To have complete inner stability and peace of mind.

Core Fear: Nines fear separation and loss

What motivates a type Nine? The need to find inner and outer peace and harmony. Nines want to avoid conflict at all costs.

Wings:

Type Nine has the Eight-Wing, which is "The Referee," and the One-Wing, which is "The Dreamer."

Arrows and their meaning:

The type has two arrows, namely 3 and 6. When moving in the direction of disintegration and stress (six), Nines becomes anxious, stressed, and worried like unhealthy Sixes. However, the arrow pointing to growth and integration (three) shows a self-neglecting and lethargic Nine transforming into a more energetic, purpose-driven individual like a healthy Three.

Examples of famous people:

Some well-known people sharing the Enneagram type Nine include Walt Disney, Audrey Hepburn, Sophia Loren, Kevin Costner, Queen Elizabeth II, Abraham Lincoln, Carl Jung, Janet Jackson, George Lucas, Lisa Kudrow, Tobey McGuire, John F. Kennedy Jr., George W. Bush and Ronald Reagan.

Type Nine levels of development:

There are different expressions of type Nines that you'll need to learn. At various stages of development, a type Nine will exhibit certain behavior and attitudes depending on how disconnected they are from their higher Self. Let's look at each level.

Healthy levels

Level 1 is type Nine at their best. This individual is self-possessed, fulfilled, and at one with all. They have great autonomy, equanimity and enjoy a deep sense of contentment with who they are and life as a whole. Having found that inner peace and authentic self, they are able to form deeper connections with others and facilitate great healing all around them. People naturally trust in and follow their sage advice. This Nine is alive and deeply connected to themselves and others.

Level 2 is where the Nine is emotionally stable and serene. Their level of trust is high, and they approach life, relationships, and challenges with ease and an unshakable calmness. This type Nine is receptive, accepting of themselves and others, totally unpretentious, patient, and genuinely lovely with people.

Level 3 is an optimistic type Nine who is still aware of their persuasive and healing superpower and uses it positively to harmonize groups and bring people together. This individual is reassuring, supportive, a strong communicator, and excellent at mediations.

Average levels

Level 4 is where a type Nine starts idealizing others and going along with whatever people say whether or not they agree. They tend to deflect things and have trouble speaking their truth, especially when they aren't sure whether it will be well received.

Level 5 is still an active but somewhat disengaged Nine. This individual is unreflective and a little absent-minded. Those that are social and outgoing will still be around people. Still, they won't be responsive to other people's problems choosing instead to walk away. For the most part, this type Nine is "tuned out" and oblivious because they would rather be indifferent than exert themselves or focus on problems that will only heighten their inner issues.

Level 6 is where type Nine prefers to minimize problems and seek peace at any price. That means they will agree with things just to maintain peace and even resign themselves in matters where they feel nothing can be done to create change. We also start to witness a lot of procrastination in the individual as they prefer to put off anything in the real world that adds to their inner disturbance and instead turn to wishful thinking and magical solutions.

Unhealthy levels

Level 7 is where a Nine takes a downturn to the dark side of their personality. The person is stubborn, obstinate, and feels powerless. They isolate and disassociate themselves from all conflicts to the point where they can walk away and leave someone else in danger just to avoid getting caught up in the conflict.

Level 8 is where the type Nice seeks ways of blocking out anything that causes conflict in their world. They are numb, neglectful, and depersonalized in all their interactions wanting nothing to do with an inharmonious world or environment.

Level 9 is where the type Nine can barely focus on any task as lethargy, powerlessness, and self-criticism kick into high gear. They suffer from passive-aggressive behavior in whatever existing relationship they have, and most become severely disoriented and catatonic.

Addictions:

To cope with and suppress some of the emotional and psychological unrest that this type faces, especially at the unhealthy levels of development, Nines may resort to alcohol, marijuana, overeating, depressants, and psychotropics. They might also avoid any physical activity.

HOW TO RECOGNIZE IF YOU'RE AN ENNEAGRAM NINE

Let's look at some easy-to-spot traits for an Enneagram type Nine, and make sure you take note of how many you identify with. Bear in mind that some of these traits will be more pronounced in healthy Nines while others will be more present in unhealthy Nines.

- Your biggest desire is to have a world without violence, disease, or anything negative.
- You can't stand seeing sadness in another person.
- Everyone sees you as that genuine friend who is always laid back and easy to be around.
- You have a hard time picking sides in a fight.
- People naturally trust and open up to you.
- You've always been the mediator and peacekeeper in family gatherings.
- You realize your personality tends to shift when you're around certain people. It's almost like you gell and become more like them.
- You're in the habit of dealing with problems by not dealing with them, hoping that by not acknowledging them, they'll somehow just disappear.
- Going through the Enneagram model and identifying your type feels impossible because you see yourself in all of them and can't decide which is the real you.

STRUGGLES AN ENNEAGRAM EIGHT MIGHT HAVE

Indecisiveness

Almost all Nines struggle with decision making especially when several parties are involved. Their natural inclination to maintain peace and harmony can stand in the way of making even the most uncomplicated choice like "do we go for Chinese or Italian?"

It's tough for a Nine to voice their opinion because they are so gentle and caring about others in their life. At average and unhealthy levels of development, this can lead to a loss of identity as the Nine merges themselves with the other (especially a romantic partner). Besides, most underdeveloped Nines have never taken the time to know what they really want. So they might go through life doing things others suggest because they don't know their own personality.

Putting things off because they stress you and take you away from your zen

Procrastination is a huge problem for the less developed Nines. The need to move at a slow, calm speed can sometimes cause them to procrastinate, especially on things that require high energy. Deadlines sound like death to a Nine, and it's easy for overwhelm and lethargy to get the best of them.

Feeling the pressure to give in

Do you ever feel like people are taking advantage of your goodness? Have you been screwed over by friends over and over again? Do you often wonder whether the people in your life love you for who you really are or if they just love you because they need something from you? These are common thoughts for Nines. As troubling and upsetting as it may feel, the main cause of this experience is that you're not feeling safe enough to be your authentic self. It is you who lets people push you over and take decisions on your behalf because you've never emphasized your voice. In the name of politeness, you've said yes even when it was a self-betrayal, and now people have become accustomed to that. But all is not lost. You can still change things for the better without creating disharmony in your life.

Calm and cool on the outside, burning on the inside

Nines are considered extremely calm, but we know their unresolved emotion is anger. So even though you might not see it externally,

Nines can harbor a lot of resentment and even rage. Since a typical Nine doesn't want to cause conflict, they'll often remain silent or even bury their opinion if it contradicts what others say. They are often terrified of losing their temper not just because of the external relationship but because they're trying really hard to find and keep that inner peace. If you're a Nine and you've noticed a wave of brewing anger, it's time to grow further along with your personal development and learn healthy ways of dealing with this emotion. Don't repress the anger or resentment. Use the Enneagram tool to heal and cultivate the confidence to speak your truth even if no one else agrees.

GROWTH TIPS FOR NINES

#1: Become aware of your anger

Notice when judgment, resentment, and anger start brewing. As soon as you become tense or irritable, get curious and ask yourself, "what underlying issues have just been triggered?" If you can label and tame the issue, it will get easier with time. But even if you can't get a clear answer, I encourage you to find healthy ways to voice that emotion instead of suppressing it.

#2: Ask for time to make your decisions

Indecision is a big struggle for you so, train yourself to become a better decision-maker. Start with small things like deciding before-hand where you want to go for dinner with friends this weekend. When they ask and throw around suggestions, give yours as well. If someone at work asks you to choose something at a moment's notice and you need time to think, rather than say "whatever you want," request some time to think it over. This will take practice, but the more you do it, the better it gets.

#3: Share your interests, values, and ideas with others

Make a vow to yourself right now that you'll stop placating others just to avoid conflict or that uncomfortable feeling in your stomach. And once you make that commitment to yourself, start taking an interest in the things you enjoy. Try different things and when you find something you genuinely like, let the people you care about know even if they don't like that activity. When you have a new idea or someone steps on your values, make it known. Have the courage to speak up with kindness and candor (yes, these two qualities can go well together). Given your calm demeanor, you'll have an easy time disagreeing with someone and voicing your truth without necessarily triggering their nerves. Trust that your peacemaking superpower can enable you to transform into a peaceful warrior. And if you're worried about losing friends and loved ones - don't be. The people who love you already know how good you are. Showing up as more of yourself will only increase their respect and love.

#4: Set mini targets daily

As you continue to work on your personal development, set mini-goals of things you'd like to accomplish. Write these down and select definite completion or due dates. Keep a small list of short to mid-term targets and an even smaller list of daily things you want to accomplish. As you complete an important project or hit a target, reward and celebrate yourself. This small change in how you approach your life can have a tremendous shift in your energy and overall growth.

PART TWO
YOU AND THE ENNEAGRAM

CHAPTER 8

DISCOVERING WHO YOU REALLY ARE

A fter going through the contents of section one, you likely have an idea of which personality type most represents you. If not, that's okay. Sometimes, finding yourself in the Enneagram system requires more thought and brutal self-analysis. As a matter of fact, I always encourage everyone to read all nine types comprehensively before taking the test to identify their own type. Realize that we all have a basic personality type but learning about all nine enables us to understand ourselves and others better. It's also essential to see the connections from one type to another because regardless of our number, there's a tiny facet of other types existing in us.

On this quest for self-discovery and uncovering more of your true Self, we're going to approach this on two levels. First, we help you figure out your core type - pretty straightforward and easy to do.

Second, we dive deeper to uncover - who you really are. Have you ever asked yourself, "who am I?" If so, that second level won't be as scary, and you'll likely pick up a few new insights to add to your current understanding. For those who've never pondered this simple yet profound question, get ready for an awakening that will set you on the right path of self-discovery. Let's not get ahead of ourselves here. First things first, how do you figure out your core type?

IDENTIFYING YOUR ENNEAGRAM

There are countless tests that you can take to determine your enna type. The most common one is the Riso-Hudson Enneagram Type Indicator (RHETI) and is considered by experts to be among the best with about 80% accuracy. You can also take the TAS questionnaire. I will include links in the resource sections for some of the recommended online tests, many of which are paid. If you don't yet want to pay for a test, you can ponder specific reflective questions to gain more clarity about your type.

- How do you react to stress, strangers, happy or unpleasant situations on a daily basis?
- What's a predominant underlying emotion that you just can't shake for as long as you can remember? Is it mostly fear, shame or anger?
- What are some defining qualities or character traits that you and others associate with you?
- What is your worldview and frame of mind? Could you spot some of your thought patterns in any of the enneagram types?

The key to identifying your type is 100% honesty.

You need to identify which driving emotions and basic fears guide most of your behavior. That way, you can avoid basing your type purely on outer traits. So let's briefly go through each of the nine fears as listed by Don Riso and Russ Hudson in their book "The Wisdom of The Enneagram":

- Type 1 fears being evil or corrupt.
- Type 2 fears being unloved or unwanted by others.
- Type 3 fears being unaccomplished and worthless.
- Type 4 fears losing or not finding their identity and expressing how unique and different they are.
- Type 5 fears being inadequate, incompetent, and helpless.
- Type 6 fears being without guidance and support.
- Type 7 fears pain and deprivation.
- Type 8 fears being controlled and harmed by others.
- Type 9 fears loss and separation.

Most of us will have more than one basic fear. Still, as I said earlier, through observation, you'll recognize the dominant basic fear and underlying emotional theme that's ever with you no matter where you go.

Once you've identified the triad with the primary unresolved emotion and the dominant basic fear, you'll easily find the corresponding number, and the rest should fall into place. Your basic fear will feel most intense, pervasive, and maybe even a little horrifying. You might start to recognize it showing up as different experiences in different domains of your life.

The Enneagram Test:

Getting an online test is always recommended. It gives you a comprehensive understanding of your personality, blind spots, thought patterns and validates your existing ideas about your right enneagram type. So, even after identifying your type, I want to encourage you to take an online test. If you go on Google to find an Enneagram test, you'll be flooded with countless options, some of which aren't very good. The best one is the "Riso-Hudson Enneagram Type Indicator" created by The Enneagram Institute. Please check the resources section for the links I recommend.

WHO ARE YOU REALLY?

The whole point of studying personality types and taking an ennea-gram test is to know who you really are. Most people lack the courage to begin this quest, and understandably so. It's scary and hard. Our society doesn't encourage us to figure out our true selves at a young age. Instead, we are encouraged to complete and be like others around us. The social norms around what constitutes a respectable, successful human being are pretty vain and shallow. Own a fancy car, get a high-paying job, mortgage a home, buy the latest shiny gadgets, and have an Instagram-perfect life - then we consider you a successful human being. Unfortunately, this is anything but a successful life.

Martin was successful by this shallow measure of society. By the age of twenty-nine, he'd mortgaged his first house, married a beautiful wife, and drove his dream car. Martin also had a corner office at his firm and frequently vacationed at the Hamptons. It took an illness, losing his job, and getting a divorce for Martin to realize that he really didn't know himself at all. When he finally hit rock bottom, he was fortunate enough to come across Deepak Chopra's books and online content, which forced him for the first time to ask the questions "who am I? What do I believe in? What is my purpose in life?" These questions served as a launchpad for his journey of self-discovery. It took a lot of work on his part and much therapy, meditation, study, and daily reflection, but Martin was finally able to transform his life and reconnect with his true Self.

What is the difference between the true Self and the ego-self?

Your ego self or everyday self is the you that gets mixed up with daily stuff. Within you lies a deeper, wiser, and more powerful self who is often a silent observer. If you pay attention, you'll realize that Self. How will you know it's your true Self? In the same way, you can identify the difference between salt and sugar. Each possesses certain qualities, and as you taste them even with a blindfold, you can pick them apart. The same is true for your ego-self and your true Self. When you experience the qualities of your true Self and learn to cultivate them as part of your well-being, you'll quickly tell when you're operating from the everyday self or the higher Self.

- *The true Self is stable and secure.* Ever had those moments where you just felt more solid than a rock and sound in your thinking? You had tapped into a quality of your higher Self. Your higher Self is ever reliable and secure, but your ego-self is constantly shifting.
- *The true Self is always at peace.* There's an inner knowing that all is well that's only possessed by your true Self. On the other hand, your ego is easily disturbed, doubtful, agitated, and tumultuous.
- *The true Self is clear and sure about things.* In every moment, no matter what you face, your higher Self knows what step to take next. Unfortunately, the opposite may be said for your ego, who is ever confused, easily distracted, and influenced by outer circumstances. Again, there's a fundamental knowing that's only possessed by your higher Self.
- *The true Self is love.* We can quickly identify this quality because most of the time, living from the ego's perspective, we seek love outside of us. We become dependent on outside sources and people to make us feel loved. That's a clear sign we're not living from the true Self. When you live from your true Self, there's no void to fill, no loneliness or loss, and you don't seek to find love. Instead, you long to give from your overflow.

Looking at these qualities, you can start figuring out what perspective you live from on a day-to-day basis. And that becomes a good indicator of how much development you need to unlock your highest and best Self. In the Enneagram types, we discussed the different levels of development so that you could know what to work on to rise to the highest level where you get to live primarily from your higher Self. That doesn't mean you destroy or deny the ego-self. It means you've transformed it into its healthiest version, where it serves your Soul and life's purpose.

Our society operates mainly at average and lower levels of development where that connection to the true Self is significantly severed. That's why negativity seems to win the day, and our actions are more selfish, ruthless, and divisive. But once we can each learn to recognize and encourage the qualities of the true Self to rise within us, positive change will take place. All it takes is one individual taking on that responsibility in their life to expand their awareness, make better choices, and know more about who they really are. By reading this book, you have made that choice for your life. As long as you keep asking the right questions and move forward in your path of self-discovery, you'll not only positively impact your life but also those around you.

10 QUESTIONS TO HELP YOU DISCOVER MORE ABOUT YOUR PERSONALITY

Although the quest of finding your true Self cannot be completed by a simple questionnaire, answering the following questions will offer a clear starting point, bring in some new perspective and guide you on the next steps. These questions were developed by Dr. Phil and curated by Lifehack (Chui). Fire up your word document or notes, and let's begin. You'll find the points for each question and what they indicate at the end of the questions.

Question 1: When do you feel at your best?
a) in the morning
b) during the afternoon or early evening

c) late at night

Question 2: You usually prefer to walk...
a) fairly fast, with long steps
b) fairly fast, with little steps
c) less fast head up, looking the world in the face
d) less fast, head down
e) very slowly

Question 3: When talking to people, you...
a) stand with your arms folded
b) have your hands clasped
c) have one or both your hands on your hips or in pockets
d) touch or push the person to whom you are talking
e) play with your ear, touch your chin or smooth your hair

Question 4: When relaxing, you sit with...
a) your knees bent with your legs neatly side by side
b) your legs crossed
c) your legs stretched out or straight
d) one leg curled under you

Question 5: When something really amuses you, You react with...
a) a big appreciative laugh
b) a laugh but not a loud one
c) a quiet chuckle
d) a sheepish smile

Question 6: When you go to a party or social gathering, you...
a) make a loud entrance, so everyone notices you
b) make a quiet entrance, looking around for someone you know
c) make the quietest entrance, trying to stay unnoticed

Question 7: When you're working or concentrating very hard, and you get interrupted you...
a) welcome the break
b) feel extremely irritated
c) vary between these two extremes

Question 8: Which of the following colors do you like most?
a) red or orange
b) black
c) yellow or light blue
d) green
e) dark blue or purple
f) white
g) brown or gray

Question 9: When you're in bed at night, in those last few moments before drifting, you lie...
a) stretched on your back
b) stretched out face down on your stomach
c) on your side, slightly curled
d) with your head on one arm
e) with your head under the covers

Question 10: You often dream that you are...
a) falling
b) fighting or struggling
c) searching for something or somebody
d) flying or floating
e) you usually have dreamless sleep
f) your dreams are always pleasant

Points for each question
1. (a) 2 (b) 4 (c) 6
2. (a) 6 (b) 4 (c) 7 (d) 2 (e) 1

3. (a) 4 (b) 2 (c) 5 (d) 7 (e) 6
4. (a) 4 (b) 6 (c) 2 (d) 1
5. (a) 6 (b) 4 (c) 3 (d) 5 (e) 2
6. (a) 6 (b) 4 (c) 2
7. (a) 6 (b) 2 (c) 4
8. (a) 6 (b) 7 (c) 5 (d)4 (e) 3 (f) 2 (g) 1
9. (a) 7 (b) 6 (c) 4 (d) 2 (e) 1
10. (a) 4 (b) 2 (c) 3 (d) 5 (e) 6 (f) 1

Now add up all the points to see your result:

OVER 60 POINTS

Others see you as someone they should "handle with care." You're seen as vain, self-centered, and one who is extremely domineering. Others may admire you, wishing they could be more like you, but don't always trust you, hesitating to become too deeply involved with you.

51 TO 60 POINTS

Others see you as an exciting, highly volatile, rather impulsive personality, a natural leader, one who's quick to make decisions, though not always the right ones. They see you as bold and adventuresome, someone who will try anything once, someone who takes chances and enjoys an adventure. They enjoy being in your company because of the excitement you radiate.

41 TO 50 POINTS

Others see you as fresh, lively, charming, amusing, practical, and always interesting; someone who's constantly in the center of attention but sufficiently well-balanced not to let it go to their head. They also see you as kind, considerate, and understanding, someone who'll always cheer them up and help them out.

31 TO 40 POINTS

Others see you as sensible, cautious, careful, and practical. They see you as clever, gifted, or talented, but modest. Not a person who makes friends too quickly or easily, but someone who's extremely loyal to friends you do make and who expects the same loyalty in return. Those who really get to know you realize it takes a lot to shake your trust in your friends, but equally that it takes you a long time to get over it if that trust is ever broken.

21 TO 30 POINTS

Your friends see you as painstaking and fussy. They see you as very cautious, extremely careful, a slow and steady plodder. It would really surprise them if you ever did something impulsively or on the spur of the moment, expecting you to examine everything carefully from every angle and then usually decide against it. They think this reaction is caused partly by your careful nature.

UNDER 21 POINTS

People think you are shy, nervous, and indecisive, someone who needs looking after, who always wants someone else to make the decisions, and who doesn't want to get involved with anyone or anything! They see you as a worrier who always sees problems that don't exist. Some people think you're boring. Only those who know you well know that you aren't.

How many points did you get?

A TIP FOR FINDING YOUR TRUE SELF

While personality tests and questionnaires are a great starting point, always remember that your true Self is far greater and that it takes a lot more than just identifying your personality. Use them as clues but never stop there. The deeper you go, the more you'll uncover the real you. One great approach that's been helpful in my quest has been the emphasis on finding what's meaningful to me. I learned this from reading Viktor E. Frankl's book "Man's search for meaning," which transformed how I approached my life. Frankl survived some of the most horrific circumstances during the Nazi war. He was held prisoner in the Nazi concentration camp and witnessed his entire family killed, including his wife and kids. The fact that he survived was mainly because he could maintain a sense of meaning. Frankl said, "Life is never made unbearable by circumstances, but only by lack of meaning and purpose."

How does that help us in our quest for self-discovery?

The more we seek our personal sense of purpose and live from a grounded place of personal values and the principles we hold true for ourselves (uncorrupted by society and parental influence), the closer we are to living from our true Self. But don't assume that will be an easy feat.

It's one thing to understand your personality and identify the traits and quirks that make you - you. But without a deeper cleanse of the influences that have shaped that personality and the ability to see who you are underneath that social cloth, you'll struggle to access that grander "Self" that we discussed earlier. Purpose and meaning seem to be the summoning energies that draw out that higher Self. Perhaps that's why people like Viktor Frankl, Nelson Mandela, and others were able to endure things our egos consider impossible. They were living from their true Self, not their personalities, which made all the difference in the world.

SUBTYPES PART 1

S omething strange will occur as you get familiar with the enneagram personality typing system and start using it to understand yourself and others. One of these days, you'll come across someone of the same ennea type, yet they'll act totally different. The first time that happened to me, I thought the system was broken, or the person had mistyped themselves. Turns out, neither of those was accurate. We shared the same Enneagram type but differed significantly in our expressions, mainly due to our subtypes. In subsequent chapters, we'll cover what subtypes are, why they matter, and the different subtypes for each Enneagram type.

WHAT ARE ENNEAGRAM SUBTYPES?

Subtypes are rich, nuanced ways of understanding more about yourself and the things that influence your behavior. They combine your Enneagram type and natural instincts, i.e., how you're wired for survival. They are commonly referred to as instinctual subtypes or instinctual variants and have everything to do with your basic survival instincts. Why would we care about survival instincts in today's modern society? We may not be hunters and gatherers or at the risk of being eaten by a lion on our way home from work, but that part of our brain is still active and operational. The drivers and motives that enabled us to navigate those dangerous times still influence our day-to-day experiences more than we know. Perhaps that's why we can see a highly educated, well-dressed politician behaving like a caveman. Instead of pretending that your instincts aren't there, it's better to become more aware of how they influence your reactions. The more awareness you have about your subtypes, the easier it will be to bring them into balance and create alignment with your higher Self.

THE THREE INSTINCTUAL SUBTYPES:

The three classifications are self-preservation (SP), social (SO), and sexual (aka intimate or One-to-One). We all possess each of the three instincts, but a dominant one combines with our specific Enneagram type to form a subtype. Let's look at the difference between these three subtypes. Think of it in the same way that you have two arms, but one is more preferred and is likely why you refer to yourself as either right-handed or left-handed (depending on which arm you rely on most). In the case of subtypes, you have three, but one is more influential, and you use it as your default setting. Most of us can quickly identify the dominant instinct. We might, however, feel indifferent or neutral about the second place instinct and barely recognize the third and least influential instinct.

Self-preservation (SP)

As the name suggests, self-preservation is about prioritizing physical needs such as food, shelter, health, family, and finances. In other words, safety and security is the top priority here. Most of the focus goes into preserving resources and energy as the strategy for basically getting through life and feeling safe and protected. If you have this instinct as your dominant one, you tend to prioritize family, physical, and mental well-being. You likely manage your energy levels and resources in ways that help you avoid becoming overwhelmed or too stressed.

Social (SO)

Social instinct prioritizes belonging and being accepted by the group or community. It's about working toward shared goals with others as the strategy for getting through life and feeling safe and protected. If you have this as your dominant instinct, you most enjoy being part of a group or working in a team with others who share a common goal. You value feeling that you belong and that you're wanted by those in your group. Your focus is often on how others respond to you, and you're quick to notice your standing in any particular group setting. Feeling connected to others and to the greater good matters to you.

Sexual (SX)

As the name suggests, sexual or intimate instincts prioritize connecting one-to-one with individuals. It's about creating a spark or "chemistry" with others. Please bear in mind that the connection doesn't have to be of a sexual nature; it can and often is purely platonic. If you have this as your dominant instinct, you value passion, excitement, and intimacy. You likely have boundless energy, love activities, and experiences that enable you to bond with another individual. Perhaps you tend to seek out friendships and relationships that complete you somehow and offer you that sense of security and safety as you go through life.

Which instinct stood out most for you? Think about how your subtypes are stacked into first, second, and third positions.

Instinctual stacking and counter types:

The subtypes are yet another way of deep diving into who you really are (derived from the model of Claudio Naranjo's system). We all have an instinct stacking whereby one is overused, another is underused, and another still is totally neutral. Shifts may occur at different phases in our lives to switch between the neutral and overused instinct (e.g., when you face challenging circumstances). But in general, we tend to stack them in a particular order which gives rise to the specific way we express our Enneagram type. Knowing which instincts drive your reactions can be an invaluable way of transforming your character and managing your energy. Why is this helpful? Because when your emotional patterns or "passions" and your dominant instinctual drive come together, they create a particular focus of attention that usually reflects a unique insatiable need that drives your behavior.

We study subtypes because they reflect the three different subsets of the patterns of the nine types creating even more nuance in our quest to describe and understand ourselves and others.

You also need to know that for each Enneagram type, there's a countertype. A countertype is a cool way of naming the subset that goes against the main energetic direction of the "passion" for any given enneagram type. This is especially important if you're having difficulty identifying your enneagram type. People who don't seem to fit into any stereotypical enneagram type often have the countertype subtype. That means their dominant instinct clashes with their Enneagram type's emotional pattern (passion), resulting in atypical behavior. Notice, however, that the individual's motivation would remain the same (e.g., if fear is a big thing for that type and their stereotypical behavior is to be phobic, the countertype might clash, causing the person to deal with that fear by taking bold risks). That might cause the individual to mistype themselves. Still, if they go back to the basic desire, fear, and unresolved emotion in their intelli-

432

gence center, they will find their real enneagram type even if they express it differently.

HOW TO FIND YOUR ENNEAGRAM SUBTYPE:

Now that you understand the basic concept behind subtypes, you're ready to engage in the practical work of identifying your subtype. The best way to do this is to first read through the 27 subtypes and notice what resonates. It's also a good idea to become more mindful as you go about your daily duties in the coming days. Where does your attention go, and what things matter to you? As you go to work or any social gathering, pay attention to what you're noticing and prioritizing. Do you place a lot of value in one-to-one connections or the entire group? When you walk into a room, are you often quick to notice the setup of the place, exit signs, temperature, fire extinguishers, etc.? These clues show you which instinct is dominant in your life. There's no wrong or correct answer here. The goal is self-awareness and self-discovery. If you're still feeling lost and confused, try asking people you trust for their objective opinion about you once you're done going through the subtypes.

THE ENNEAGRAM TYPE ONE SUBTYPES

Self-Preservation One: Worry

The Enneagram One's primary desire is to be good and live with integrity. Dissecting the subtle nuances of SP One, this subtype is often plagued with worry. Their basic fear is to be corrupt or evil. They have a pattern of anger.

Self-preserved Ones are the true perfectionists. They suppress their anger through hard work and rigid rules, all in an attempt to produce perfection. This subtype represses anger the most and has the uncanny ability to transform the heat of anger into warmth resulting in a friendly, benevolent character, especially when operating at those healthy levels of development.

Some characteristics of the Self-preservation One:

- Tendency to be a control freak over their own life.
- Often suppresses anger or resentment.
- Kind and gentle when at healthy to average levels of development.
- Focuses on predicting the future.
- Strives for perfection all the time.
- Tendency to be too hard on themselves.
- Strives to be forgiving, compassionate, and tolerant of others.

Social One: Non-adaptability

In an attempt to be good and manage the fear of becoming corrupt or evil, this subtype enjoys reforming and advocating for change. Social Ones believe themselves to be perfect.

They focus their energy on being the perfect role model they can be through doing things "the right way." Typically possessing a teacher mentality, there's an unconscious need for superiority. In expression, their personality type is more of a cool intellect with a strong need for control. These type Ones are pretty rigid, idealistic and tend to seek out leadership roles within a group so they can show "the rest" how to do things right. Social Ones can be extremists and highly judgemental at unhealthy levels with unrealistic standards for themselves and others. They are also pretty stubborn, argumentative, and stubborn.

However, a Social One is ethical, conscientious, discerning, and helpful at healthy levels.

Some key characteristics of the Social One:

- Tendency toward idealism.
- Strong opinions and convictions.
- Lives by example and enjoys being a role model for others.
- Skilled at reasoning.
- Tendency to take things personally.

Sexual One: Zeal

By now, you know all Ones desire to live in integrity and fear being evil or corrupt. But how is this impacted when we layer on the richness of the sexual subtype? As the countertype for the Enneagram One, Sexual Ones are idealistic and passionate, but their drive is purely focused on improving others (especially their partner/s) and the world at large. They tend to be more reformers than perfectionists and seek to find those who share their ideals and convictions.

Unlike the other two subtypes, this type One isn't afraid to show anger. In fact, they usually act out their anger through their intense desire to improve others. They possess a strong sense of entitlement and believe they have a right to change society and get what they want because they have a higher understanding of the truth. As the countertype for type One, this individual will express their character as more impulsive, pushy, irritated, outwardly angry, and typically goes against the "counter-instinctive" tendency of repressing anger and impulses stereotypically associated with type Ones. Unhealthy sexual Ones are controlling, jealous, pushy, and entitled. They can even go as far as punishing themselves in unhealthy ways to purge themselves of desires they view as immoral (remember, moral perfection is of great importance to this enneatype). Healthy Sexual Ones are more compassionate and pragmatic. They still have high morals but know how to temper their idealistic visions and ideals.

Some characteristics of the Sexual One:

- Idealistic and passionate.

- Determined and brave.
- Tendency to be impatient.
- Often orderly and responsible.
- Prone to jealousy.
- More focused on perfecting others rather than themselves.

CHAPTER 10
SUBTYPES PART 11

THE ENNEAGRAM TYPE TWO SUBTYPES

Self-preservation Two: Privilege

Enneagram Two's primary desire is to be loved for who they are. Their basic fear is being unwanted or unloved. They have a pattern of pride. In dissecting the subtle nuances of type Two, this subtype is perhaps one of the more challenging to identify because pride isn't apparent. It's the countertype of type Two, meaning they behave in atypical ways. As such, self-preserved Twos "seduce" like a child would in the presence of grown-ups. It's their way of inducing others to take care of them. A self-preserved Two adopts a youthful stance as a way of getting special treatment beyond childhood. This Two desire to be loved, prioritized and treated with privilege for being who they are, not because of what they give to others. In expression, their character will be playful, charming, irresponsible with very little pride.

Some characteristics of the Self-preservation Two:

- Playful, warm and childlike.
- Want to be taken care of but fear depending on others.
- Tendency to mistype or appear like type Sevens.
- Idealize people, especially at the beginning of relationships.
- Want to be loved just because they exist.
- Commonly drawn to pleasure and fun.
- More guarded than the other two subtypes in Enneagram Two.
- Fear of rejection caused this subtype to become withdrawn and hurt.
- Extremely tender and emotionally expressive.

Social Two: Ambition

In their endeavor to be loved and manage the fear of being unwanted, this subtype enjoys identifying and connecting with the influential people around them.

Social Twos are seducers who take pride in being perceived as influential leaders and attaining their audience's attention. Pride is an undeniable trait in this subtype Two. As the name suggests, this individual desires to be "on top," beloved, and receive advantages and benefits corresponding to their lofty position. They tend to be quite competitive and less sensitive to other people's emotions compared to the other subtypes within this Enneatype.

Similar to the Enneagram type Three, Social Twos want to stand out and be successful. They can go to great lengths to reach their goals and make an impact. But in keeping with the core desire of all Enneagram Twos, goals still revolve around being loved, wanted, and included in the group (unlike a typical Three whose goal is to be the ultimate achiever).

So, although Social Twos are giving and affectionate, that benevolence comes with expectations. In expression, you'll observe a lot of pride and less than altruistic generosity. Unhealthy Social Twos are manipulative, exploitative and enjoy gossip a little too much. Healthy Twos, however, are charming, empathetic, loving, and generous.

Some characteristics of the Social Two:

- Hardworking and competitive.
- Strives to stand out.
- Tendency to be more introverted than the sexual or self-preservation Two subtypes.
- Aims to be close to those in power.
- Less empathetic than the other subtypes in the group and highly aware of their public image.

Sexual Two: Seduction/Aggression

By now, you know that all Enneagram Twos desire to love and be loved for who they are and they're very afraid of being abandoned or unwanted. But how is this impacted when we layer on the sexual subtype?

Well, Sexual Twos tend to invest all their energy in key individuals intending to forge intimate, passionate connections. They enjoy giving lots of attention to people and aren't shy of employing classical seductive methods to attract those who will meet all their needs.

Sexual Twos are aggressive in their seduction. Unlike the self-preserved Two, they possess a more adult-like approach because they want their needs met and want to have some power.

Besides their need to gain affection and closeness, these individuals are also great listeners taking great pleasure in having intimate conversations about the struggles of a friend or partner. They genuinely believe love conquers all, but underneath that passionate exterior is deep-seated anxiety about their desirability. They depend on their charm to win others over, receive validation and love as a way of solidifying their self-worth.

In expression, this Two's character is energetic, irresistible, and inspires great passions and positive feelings, all for the sole purpose of getting their needs met in life. Unhealthy Sexual Twos are pushy, demanding, and really prone to possessiveness, jealousy, and obsessive behavior. Healthy Sexual Twos, however, are deeply romantic without any ulterior motives. They ooze unconditional love.

Some characteristics of a Sexual Two:

- Charming and highly seductive.
- Less ashamed of having needs than the Self-preservation or Social Two subtypes.
- Generous and supportive.
- Aims to form strong intimate bonds.
- Caring, nurturing, empathetic, and loving unconditionally.

THE ENNEAGRAM TYPE THREE SUBTYPES

Self-preservation Three: Security

Enneagram Three's primary desire is to be desirable and highly successful. What they fear most is failure or a feeling of worthlessness without achievement. As the countertype of Enneagram type Three, these individuals will work hard, strive for success and covertly seek admiration and recognition. Even though they sense their vanity, they try very hard to conceal and deny it.

SP Threes are more concerned about being good people, not just "looking good." That, however, doesn't mean they're not interested in being the "best" in whatever they do. If anything, their concept of being the best is tied to hard work and modesty. They possess a strong code of honor and a need to be self-reliant and hard working. A self-preserved Three will care about their image and cultivate virtues that model the qualities they believe shape a good human. They can also combine material success with hard work and even service to others.

Some characteristics of the Self-preservation Three:

- Wants to be the best at everything.
- Believes in earning admiration from others through hard work.
- Typically mistypes themselves as a Six or One.
- Avoids talking about their achievements or successes in life.
- Works hard to attain a certain level of security.

Social Three: Prestige

In their endeavor to be successful, desirable, and accomplished while managing the fear of failure or a sense of worthlessness, this subtype works hard to maintain a powerful public image. Social Threes only care about one thing - moving up in the world. They are the most competitive and aggressive of the Enneagram type Three. Social Threes are driven by the need to be the best, whether in school, a group setting, or at work. Vanity is present and evident in these Threes, and they very much enjoy the spotlight. With plenty of charm, great energy, focus, and desire to accomplish their goals, social Threes tend to do well for themselves and typically possess a sales or corporate mentality. At unhealthy levels, Social Threes are desperate for attention and validation from others. They will go to any lengths to receive recognition and live to impress others by any means necessary. That often leads to unhealthy and reckless choices. Conversely, a Social Three is pretty inspiring at healthy levels and more of a visionary that people love to follow. Their energy, competency, and charm quickly rally people behind their grand visions.

Some characteristics of the Social Four:

- Charming.
- Highly competitive.
- Skilled at networking and forming strategic relationships.
- Cares deeply about their public image and social status.
- Success and goal-oriented.
- High levels of confidence.

Sexual Three: Charisma

By now, you know all Threes desire to be successful and fear failure or being perceived as worthless. But how is this impacted when we layer on the richness of the sexual subtype? Unlike Social Threes, who are mainly focused on career success and being seen by their community as influential, Sexual Threes are more interested in personal attractiveness. They have a strong desire to be desirable, alluring, and wanted by others, especially their ideal mate.

Sexual Threes neither flaunt nor deny their vanity. Instead, all their energy goes into creating an attractive, irresistible outer image. Often seen as supporters of others, Sexual Threes like to use their charm to promote and please others, especially those they want to win over to their side. As a result, their innate skills and power are often less obvious to others, as are their true intentions. It's a more subtle form of influence because, in the end, they still get to accomplish their goals by putting others first and making them feel more important. Many people mistype this Sexual Three as a type Two because of how supportive, helpful, and people-pleasing they are. Still, closer observation will reveal this individual is more focused on being attractive to others, not necessarily meeting the emotional needs of others.

Unlike the SP Three or Social Three, this type Three isn't focused on money or prestige. Instead, that energy and desire for accomplishment will be redirected to personal appeal and magnetism. However, underneath all that attractive exterior is a deep sense of emptiness.

Sexual Threes have a hard time practicing self-love or acknowledging their own strengths. Sexual Threes are vain, narcissistic, jealous, and vindictive at unhealthy levels. They typically get addicted to the pursuit of sexual encounters to feel attractive. Conversely, healthy Sexual Threes are self-accepting, self-improving in mind and body, inspiring, and supportive. They can focus on their own desires and live authentically instead of hiding behind the guise of "supporting others."

Some characteristics of the Sexual Three:

- Enthusiastic.
- Longs to be desired and attractive to others.
- Tendency to people please to get what they want.
- May use their talents and strengths to support and uplift others.
- Long to be and find the perfect lover/partner.
- Often insecure about themselves but won't show it.

THE ENNEAGRAM TYPE FOUR SUBTYPES

Self-preservation Four: Tenacity

The Enneagram Type Four's primary desire is to be authentic in every way possible and to find their true identity. They fear most that they are flawed and lack a true identity. With self-preservation being the countertype of the Fours, they express their pattern of envy through atypical behavior. Rather than dwell in envy and feeling defeated, SP Fours focuses on going after their objects of desire.

Healthy and average SP Fours will be persistent, goal-oriented, creative, resilient, empathetic, and highly self-aware. They have a lot of endurance and are willing to take the initiative to actively seek out the authentic life and material security that's missing. Instead of accepting that void, these individuals will attempt to fix themselves.

From an emotional standpoint, this Four is likely more stoic in the face of pain and doesn't share their feelings as much. Instead of dwelling in jealousy, SP Fours will work hard to get what they lack, making them a bit more masochistic than melodramatic.

Some characteristics of the self-preservation Enneagram Type Four:

- Unlike the rest of the Fours, SP Four works hard to gain the things they desire.
- They dislike complaining.
- Empathetic and compassionate with themselves and others, especially those in healthy and average levels of development.
- Want to be loved because they demonstrate strength and steadfastness.
- Can be Self-absorbed and self-rejecting if they operate at unhealthy development levels.

Social Four: Shame

The social Four is the classic individualist who enjoys being involved and sociable. They enjoy forming close bonds but struggle with envy and jealousy, easily succumbing to these negative emotions. Driven by the basic desire to discover their true identity, live authentically, and the fear of lacking significance in this world, this subtype struggles with shame and rejection a lot.

Unlike the SP Four or the Sexual Four, this subtype is much more sensitive and dwells a lot on their perceived "ingrained flaws." They are melancholic and often lament about their inferiority and how different they are from others. In a group setting, the person constantly compares themselves to others and shows how much they are "lacking" in something. That said, they possess a certain charm that others find appealing which is why they get by in social settings. The deep sense of sadness for this subtype causes them to use pain and suffering as a way to attract attention and affection, hoping that it will bring in their savior to rescue them from their condemned existence. At unhealthy levels, pain and suffering are greatly amplified, and these social Fours tend to play the victim role all the time. However, at healthy levels, social Fours are creative, loving, curious, profound, and empathetic.

Some characteristics of the Social Four

- Tendency to compare themselves to others.
- Struggles to care for their own needs.
- Socially friendly and charming in their own way.
- Tendency to play the victim, especially at unhealthy levels.
- Experiences guilt over wanting things or wanting to fit in.
- Feels like a misfit wherever they are.
- Highly sensitive and keenly focused on their emotions.
- Wants recognition.

Sexual Four: Competition

By now, you know all Fours desire a sense of authentic identity and fear having no significance or identity in the world. But how is this impacted when we layer on the richness of the sexual subtype? Unlike the SP Four or the Social Four, who are often overwhelmed by sadness, the Sexual Four mostly battles anger. Because of this, they tend to mistype as Eights because of how intense and emotionally "hot" they come across.

Sexual Fours deny their suffering and try to suppress their shame. Their focus is mainly on making others feel worse than they do in an attempt to feel better. That's why these Fours come across as competitive and dramatic. They actually want to be the best and most elite in their chosen passion-based endeavor. This Four takes the power of others as a personal challenge, and their value is ever fluctuating depending on who they are comparing themselves to.

And just like other Sexual subtypes, the Sexual Four longs to be the object of desire to another. But they tend to have mixed emotions, including admiration, envy, and hatred. At unhealthy levels, this will be more pronounced and will, in fact, go to great lengths to be the only person that matters to the individual they're with. Unhealthy Sexual Fours can be pretty wild and have no problem sabotaging other people to get revenge or merely out of jealousy. They can be arrogant, elitist, superior, and hold grudges without good reason. Healthy Sexual Fours are more composed, Self-aware, forgiving, inspiring, and capable of finding harmony between their inner and outer world. They learn to embrace both their individuality and their emotions, even the darker ones, and find better ways of handling them rather than externalizing them in angry outbursts or taking offense.

Some characteristics of the Sexual Four:

- Envious and jealous of other people's success.
- Highly competitive.
- Deeply struggle with feelings of inferiority and crave feeling superior to others.
- Romantic and individualistic
- Highly creative and imaginative.
- More assertive than SP Fours and Social Fours.
- Tendency to externalize their suffering through anger.

THE ENNEAGRAM TYPE FIVE SUBTYPES

Self-preservation Five: Castle

The Enneagram Type Five's primary desire is to be competent and knowledgeable. They fear incompetency and lack of proper resources to maintain their independence. When this ennea type combines with the self-preservation instinct, it causes them to build thick boundaries and isolate themselves to protect their energy and resources. Hence the term "castle" because the behavior expressed is that of creating a little sanctuary of their own making.

SP Fives are the least expressive of the type Fives and do everything possible to live within the confines of their resources so they can remain completely self-reliant. This need to have enough supplies behind their castle walls can sometimes lead to hoarding and cause these individuals to be very stingy and aloof. Healthy Fives respect the space and needs of others and don't take from others without giving back in equal measure. Unhealthy SP Fives are stingy and unwilling to open up to others.

Some characteristics of the self-preservation Enneagram Five:

- Typically introverted.
- Tendency to view the world as hostile, intrusive, and overwhelming.
- Intensely private.
- Struggle with their emotions and understanding them.
- Tendency to place a lot of boundaries between themselves and the outside world.

Social Five: Totem

In their endeavor to be knowledgeable, competent, and manage their fear of becoming dependent on others or lacking resources, this subtype seeks to become a master in their field and be the go-to person on a particular topic. The Social Five finds their sense of belonging by being highly skilled and supporting those who need academic help. Most of their social interactions are with people who are drawn to their topics of interest which is usually scientific, philosophical, or educational in some other way.

Although the social Five relates to others in a group, it is always through common interests based on knowledge and shared values rather than emotional connection. They are passionate and hungry for knowledge and understanding the meaning of life. While these Fives are more social than the rest of the Enneagram type Five, they still hate small talk, gossip, or anything that wastes their precious mental or physical resources. Social Fives are condescending, antisocial, and out of touch with reality at unhealthy levels. Conversely, healthy Social Fives are observant, trustworthy, unbiased, logical, authentic, and highly informed.

Some characteristics of the Social Five:

- Want to become someone important.
- Prefer to interact with and engage with people they admire intellectually.
- Socialize with people who share the same ideals.
- Very idealistic.
- Driven to discover the ultimate meaning of life.

Sexual Five: Confidence

By now, you know all Fives desire knowledge and independence and fear being incompetent. But how is this impacted when we layer on the richness of the sexual subtype? Sexual Fives are passionate, intensely imaginative, and might even possess a romantic streak as the countertype for the Enneagram Five. They love creating mental utopias and visions of the ideal partnerships. Sexual Fives long for a mystical union (a merging with someone that results in unconditional love). When they find that connection, they are like an open book. To the outside world, however, the Sexual Five will still remain a mystery, but to their chosen partner, they are transparent, caring, and share all their secrets.

Sexual Fives are the most emotionally sensitive of the Fives. Although they might appear reserved and analytical like the others, deep down, the Sexual Fives are emotionally intense and romantic. Are they a little strange? Sure. But for those who can accept their eccentric ways, these individuals are fantastic. If, however, the Sexual Five feels misunderstood or unappreciated, they quickly recoil and disappear. At unhealthy levels, they are isolated, impossible to please, and prone to dangerous sexual experimentations. Conversely, healthy Sexual Fives are loving, authentic, visionary, wise, and are constantly learning and growing.

Some characteristics of Sexual Fives:

- Deeply imaginative.
- Romantic and sensitive side that isn't quite present in the other subtype Fives.
- Innovative and perceptive.
- Tendency to indulge in lush fantasies.
- Values one-to-one connections.
- Wants to find the ideal relationship.

CHAPTER 11
SUBTYPES PART 111

THE ENNEAGRAM TYPE SIX SUBTYPES

Self-preservation Six: Warmth

The Enneagram Type Six's primary desire is to have security and guidance. They fear being unprepared to face a situation or lacking proper support. The self-preserved Six is the most "phobic" of all the other Sixes. They express their fear by seeking protection through friendly and protective alliances. This Six strives to be warm, friendly, and trustworthy but underneath that demeanor is deep anxiety. Their focus is on relationships as a means of securing the sense of safety and security that they need in the world, but they constantly worry about losing that alliance, being rejected, and being alone. A self-preserved Six will often get stuck in analysis-paralysis because they doubt themselves and others too much, especially at unhealthy levels of development. Healthy SP Sixes, however, tend to trust themselves more and feel connected to the world around them. The radiate serenity and security that comes from within.

Some characteristics of the self-preserved Six:

- Skeptical and doubtful (increases exponentially at unhealthy levels of development).
- Warm and friendly, especially at healthy and average levels of development.
- Tends to mistype themselves as Enneagram Type Two.
- Oriented toward relationships and personal connections as a survival mechanism.
- Fears letting people down.
- Feels a lot of responsibility and guilt when things go wrong.

Social Six: Duty

In an attempt to feel safe and secure while managing their fear of being unsupported and unprepared, this subtype cares a lot about finding a community or group that they can fit into and feel safe and protected.

Social Sixes are loyal, dutiful, and care a lot about their commitments within the group. They enjoy following rules and guidelines that offer a form of protective authority. Social Sixes want to feel that they are part of something bigger than themselves and are willing to make sacrifices for that experience. They have a tendency to think more about how others will react to their choices and decisions in life, which often promotes analysis-paralysis in their decision-making.

Social Sixes are most comfortable when surrounded by like-minded individuals in a community where everyone helps each other out and wants what's best for the whole. They express their fear as anxiety and cannot stand uncertainty, so they seek to deal with these emotions through abstract reasoning and ideologies. A social Six focuses on precision and efficiency in all their endeavors. Social Sixes are controlling, impatient, judgemental, and self-critical at unhealthy levels. They struggle with passive-aggressive behavior and often question their own beliefs. However, a healthy Social Six is courageous, more confident in their own thoughts, ideas, and beliefs. They are loyal, dedicated, and filled with integrity.

Some characteristics of the Social Six:

- Tendency to seek out rules and structures to guide them.
- Punctual and precise.
- Prefer to rely on authority for protection and guidance.
- Seek to understand and fulfill their role within a group structure.
- Tendency to become a fanatic for their belief system, especially at the lower unhealthy levels of development.

Sexual Six: Beauty/Strength

By now, you know all Sixes desire security, protection, guidance, and fear lacking support or guidance from authority. But how is this impacted when we layer on the richness of the sexual subtype? As the country for the Enneagram Six, this subtype deals with underlying fears by becoming aggressive risk-takers. Sexual Sixes adopt the mindset "me against the world." They do everything possible to fight their fears and hardly ever let their guard down. Sexual Sixes believe that the best defense is a good offense, and they attempt to live by that frame of mind. Because of their constant suspicion and fear of being duped, they can seem like they're always about to explode.

This Six believes in preparation and skill development as a way of staving off both anxiety and their enemies, so they work hard to look good and feel powerful. They do this by building up their strength, both emotional and physical. They often subject themselves to extreme sports that build their endurance. At unhealthy levels, they are erratic, combative, dominating, depressive, and may violently lash out at others. They are often obsessed with watching their perceived enemies for any attack signs. Healthy Sexual Sixes are more chilled, courageous, protective, reliable, and self-reliant.

Some characteristics of the Sexual Six:

- Tendency to be impulsive.
- Often contrarian.
- Extremely loyal and reliable, especially at healthy levels of development.
- Strives to be physically strong and attractive.
- Tendency to run towards fear to fight it off.
- Often mistypes as an Enneagram type Eight.

THE ENNEAGRAM TYPE SEVEN SUBTYPES

Self preserved Seven: Keepers of the castle

The Enneagram Type Seven's primary desire is freedom and happiness. They fear pain, negativity, suffering, or missing out on life. They're also terrified of feeling trapped in situations, relationships, etc., that might cause them to lose their sense of freedom and adventure. The added nuance as a self-preserved Seven is that they'll seek safety and security in material things and networking opportunities.

SP Sevens are great at establishing alliances that are advantageous to their well-being. Pleasure is something they absolutely love and seem to be great at getting their way when dealing with people, perhaps due to their cheerful, charismatic nature. A healthy self-preserved Seven is pragmatic and content with what they have, but the unhealthy SP Sevens tend to be demanding, greedy, and even manipulative.

Some characteristics of the self-preservation Enneagram Seven

- Practical and realistic.

- Highly opportunistic.
- Charming and talkative.
- Skilled at networking.
- Great sense of humor.
- Enjoy having the best and newest material things.

Social Seven: Sacrifice

In an attempt to pursue their desire for freedom and happiness while suppressing their fear of pain or being caged, this subtype is the most idealistic of the Sevens. They are also the countertype in the group, which means they exhibit the opposite behavior of what a Seven would typically express. Hence, while all the other Sevens succumb to gluttony, a social Seven is often altruistic and focused on helping others.

They are keenly aware of their tendency to exploit others and strive to purify themselves of this paradigm by sacrificing their own needs to support others. Their passion is to be perceived as good as they make personal sacrifices. A social Seven will express enthusiasm and idealism as a way of making themselves feel valued and active in the world, demonstrating that they can get by with very little. Often visionary, they see many new opportunities and enjoy finding friends and advisors who share their interests and enthusiasm. Most Social Sevens will position themselves in roles that enable them to work with others to pursue a cause that excites them. That doesn't eliminate their urge to pursue various things and gain further knowledge. At times, their speed can be a bit too unrealistic for others in the group. This can cause a strain as the Social Seven turns impatient and might even consider "moving on" to do things on their own.

At unhealthy levels, impatience and restlessness are high. They become irresponsible, never quite finishing any project they start and scattering their energy all over the place as they jump from one thing to the next. However, at healthy levels, Social Sevens are bold, visionary, adventurous, resilient, and dedicated to their chosen goal. They've learned to tame that inner child and know how to find freedom in commitments.

Some characteristics of the Social Seven:

- Idealistic.
- Enthusiastic.
- Helpful and generous.
- Visionary.
- Fears being excessive or indulgent.
- Craves admiration.
- Capable of taking on great responsibilities.

Sexual Seven: Suggestibility

By now, you know all Sevens desire freedom and happiness and fear missing out or feeling trapped. But how is this impacted when we layer on the richness of the sexual subtype? Sexual Sevens aren't shy of expressing gluttony and do so by imagining better than their current reality. They are romantic dreamers with a passion for living in their imagined states. Some refer to them as overly naive and suggestible because they tend to look at the world through rose-colored glasses. Ever optimistic and light-hearted, everything is possible to a sexual Seven. Their primary focus is experiencing as many pleasurable fantasies as possible. They quickly feel trapped and overwhelmed by the mundane routines of life, so they attempt to create more thrill around them. That often makes them restless and impulsive, embellishing everyday life just so it can seem more intoxicating. Sexual Sevens are fickle, fearful of commitment, and prone to falling for crazy schemes at unhealthy levels. Healthy Sexual Sevens, on the other hand, are joyful, enthusiastic, imaginative, hopeful, and productive. They've learned to be content with everyday life.

Some characteristics of the Sexual Seven:

- Spends more time fantasizing than in reality.
- Trusting and hopeful.
- Tendency to jump from one activity to another.
- Constant search for the next new, exciting and extraordinary thing to bring more pleasure and magic in their life.
- Idealistic and highly imaginative.

THE ENNEAGRAM TYPE EIGHT SUBTYPES

Self-preserved Eight: Satisfaction

The Enneagram Type Eight's desire is to be in control and have autonomy. What they fear is being controlled by others. When it comes to the nuances of a self-preserved Eight, they are practical and willing to do whatever it takes to ensure their needs are met. That makes them pretty aggressive in some cases. They're also not big on small talk or "chit-chat." these Eights like to cut past formalities and niceties and get straight to the point.

Self-preserved Eights express their lust by focusing on their needs and the needs of those they care for. They need to satisfy their material needs instantly and don't handle frustration or disappointment very well. SP Eights are the least expressive of the group and often look for symbols of power and impact such as fancy cars, nice houses, etc. Unhealthy SP Eights can quickly turn into selfish, impatient bullies who stop at nothing to get what they want. On the other hand, healthy SP Eights are strong, protective of others, and enjoy motivating others to reach their dreams.

Some characteristics of the self-preservation Enneagram Eight:

- Practical and realistic.

- Direct in their communication.
- Hardworking and highly productive.
- Exudes a quiet strength.
- Always goes for what they want.

Social Eight: Solidarity

In an attempt to pursue their desire for autonomy and have complete control while managing their deep-seated fear of being vulnerable and losing control, this subtype is the most intellectual among the Enneagram Type Eight. As the countertype of the Eights, these individuals come across as warm and more mellow than the other two subtypes. They deeply value harmonious relationships and friendships. Once loyalty is established, they go above and beyond for their friends, caring for and protecting them against any and all threats. They like to tend to their own needs leading a life of intense action, various activities, and minimal downtime for self-care. Unlike your typical Eight, a Social Eight is often less aggressive and genuinely more helpful. At unhealthy levels, Social Eights are anti-social. They turn self-destructive, reckless, and blind to the damage they cause others. Conversely, healthy Social Eights are charismatic, goal-driven, fearless, self-reliant, and passionate about caring for and protecting those they care about.

Some characteristics of a Social Eight:

- Friendly and charismatic.
- Enjoy debating with others.
- Pursues adventure and thrill.
- Keep busy with different types of projects.
- Stands up for others.

Sexual Eight: Possession

By now, you know all Eights desire control and autonomy, and they fear being vulnerable or controlled by others. But how is this impacted when we layer on the richness of the sexual subtype? Sexual Eights are the most rebellious of the Eights and naturally hate rules. These Eights are intense, charming and they love having control and influence. Rather than seeking material security like an SP Eight, a sexual Eight prefers to get "power" over things and people. Their focus is on becoming powerful and dominating their whole environment. While they can be loving and devoted, they tend to struggle with intimacy, seeing it as a risk that could give control and power to others. Sexual Eights like a challenge and aren't shy of being direct even if it leads to conflict and confrontation. Sexual Eights are possessive, jealous, dominating, and controlling at unhealthy levels. Healthy Sexual Eights are the opposite. They are self-reliant, forgiving, and protective of others, almost to the point of being heroic.

Some characteristics of Sexual Eights:

- More emotional than the SP Eight and Social Eight.
- Pragmatic and enterprising.
- Rebellious and anti-authoritarian.
- Often perceives intimacy as a struggle for control.
- Demands loyalty from loved ones.
- Strives to attain pleasure.
- Action-oriented more than reflective.

THE ENNEAGRAM TYPE NINE SUBTYPES

Self-preserved Nine: Appetite

The Enneagram Type Nine's primary desire is inner peace and stability. What they fear most is conflict and fragmentation, especially internally. All type Nines express the passion for laziness. Self-preserved Nines are more concerned with seeking security and comfort in the material world. They are practical and routine-oriented, preferring to focus on everyday things in the present moment rather than idealism or distractions. Books, television shows, good food, rest and relaxation are very attractive to this Nine, so they invest their energy in these activities. Some are pretty talented, but their focus on immediate minor rewards typically hinders them from pursuing something grand. At unhealthy levels, SP Nines are apathetic and emotionally shut down. They get hooked on their creator comforts and turn a blind eye to everything else in their environment. However, at healthy levels, they are peaceful unselfish, level-headed, and patient.

Some characteristics of the Self-preservation Nine:

- Enjoys predictable routines.
- Prefers and seeks out physical comforts.
- Fun-loving and accepting of themselves and others.
- At times, food and drink are used as anxiety suppressants.
- Prefers to focus on the real concrete world.

Social Nine: Participation

In the pursuit of inner peace and stability, while managing the fear of conflict, disconnection from Self, and fragmentation, this subtype is known for being influential, caring, and giving themselves to others without reservation. Nothing means more to a Social Nine than just being part of a meaningful group. As the countertype of the Nines, the Social Nines are cheerful with a warm exterior. They enjoy participating and prioritizing other people's needs ahead of their own. That's because underneath all that giving is a fear of abandonment and exclusion.

Social Nines most enjoy fusing with groups and work hard to be the fun-loving, friendly, peace-keeping character in the various groups they join. There exists an underlying sense of insecurity regarding their self-worth, which often causes them to "people-please" in an attempt to fit in. At unhealthy levels, Social Nines are needy, inse-cure, emotionally out of touch with themselves, and tend to fall into depression. Conversely, healthy Social Nines are energetic, thought-ful, non-judgmental, and extremely kind.

Some characteristics of the Social Nine:

- Generously and unconditionally gives.
- Longs to fit in.
- Tendency to overwork or overextend themselves in the group.
- Cheerful and friendly.
- Prioritizes the group needs ahead of their own.

Sexual Nine: Fusion

You know all Nines desire inner peace and fear internal instability or conflict by now. But how is this impacted when we layer on the rich-ness of the sexual subtype? Sexual Nines express their pattern of lazi-ness by merging with the important people in their lives. Unknowingly, this Nine will take on the attitudes, opinions, and feel-ings of others. While they are kind, gentle characters who typically lack assertiveness, this inability to stand on their own identity tends to backfire in the long run. They often live out their dreams and fantasies through others and spend most of their time imagining their future with other people but nothing else beyond that. Their anger is easily sparked if their relationship with that significant other is threatened, which surprisingly turns them into the sassy, passive-aggressive type. While the relationship they merge with is often intimate, such as with a spouse, it can also be with a best friend or God. Sexual Nines are so tied to another individual that they become self-neglecting, repressed, codependent, and prone to resentment at unhealthy levels. Healthy Sexual Nines, however, are empathetic, comforting, peaceful, and loving from a place of their own true connection and personal identity. They've done the hard work of eradicating the tendency to merge with another's identity and live from their true personality.

Some characteristics of the Sexual Nine:

- Tendency to lack a sense of Self, especially at those unhealthy levels of development.
- Empathetic and emotionally aware.
- Tendency to merge inside relationships and lose their sense of Self.
- Kind, peaceful, and genuinely loves.
- Always prioritizes the needs of others.
- Calm, poised, and possess a powerful presence that can offer a sense of comfort and healing to those nearby.

The Enneagram system is indeed a wealth of information that can at times feel overwhelming. It can feel a little overwhelming when you first encounter these concepts, from standard Enneagram types to triads, wings, and now subtypes. Understand, however, that all these different aspects are nuances that are meant to add richness to your understanding of yourself. By going through the subtypes in this section, I hope you've developed more awareness and understanding of why you navigate life as you do and why someone else in your same Enneatype will appear so radically different. The more you understand yourself, the easier it will be to understand others. Speaking of which, it's time to start applying your knowledge of the Enneagram in practical ways, starting with existing relationships.

PART THREE
DEEPENING RELATIONSHIPS

CULTIVATING HEALTHY RELATIONSHIPS

R elationships are an integral part of our mental, emotional and physical well-being. Research now shows that having healthy, strong relationships can contribute to a long, healthy, and happy life. In contrast, there is compelling evidence that being isolated or alone in life is comparable to the risks associated with obesity, blood pressure, and cigarette smoking. A significant percentage of people who first look to the Enneagram for help are usually driven by the need to improve their personal or professional relationships. So in this chapter, we'll focus on how you can improve your personal relationships. In the next chapter, we'll focus on work relations.

WHY HEALTHY RELATIONSHIPS MATTER

A review of 148 studies found that people with strong social relationships are 50% less likely to die prematurely (Kreitzer, RN, Ph.D.). And that's not all. Being in a healthy committed relationship is linked to less production of cortisol (a stress hormone) and faster healing. Studies show that recovering from an illness or procedure happens faster for long-term partners than for single patients. Of course, it's not just about surviving hard times. It's also about cultivating great habits together, and again, having a healthy relationship is linked with a healthy lifestyle. Think about it; if you're in a relationship with a lover or best friend who takes up all your free time and they are into eating healthy, exercising, and developing their mind, you're more likely to pick up those habits as well. It's much easier to take on new healthy habits when the people around you do the same. So there's no denying that relationships influence our lifestyles, and the quality of that relationship affects our well-being. Author Brené Brown explains, "A deep sense of love and belonging is an irreducible need of all men, women, and children. We are biologically, cognitively, physically, and spiritually wired to love, to be loved, and to belong."

Can the Enneagram really help?

Kaley Warner openly shares how the Enneagram helped save her marriage. Let's hear it from her own words.

"I was a newlywed. I had moved to New Jersey and was struggling. My husband was in a Ph.D. program, and I felt isolated. I had left all my friends and found the prospect of making new ones daunting. My husband and I had a bike crash, and the physical and mental toll from those tangled handlebars hung heavy over us. His energy was gone. I was escaping my pain through working harder and traveling. The more critical and demanding I become of him, the more he checked out. We were reaching an impasse. I remember telling a friend that he wasn't the man I fell in love with and married. I'm sure I wasn't the woman he wanted to share his life with either. That winter, while home for the holidays, my mom suggested that we attend the same Enneagram training she and my dad had attended a few years earlier. I don't remember the details of how she did it, but Nate and I both thought it was our idea to go, and so we registered. In a small room in Atlanta, as Russ Hudson described each of the Enneagram Types and the intricacy

of the system, I felt like I was being reminded of something I already knew. Everyone, he said, just made sense. The Enneagram described patterns of people's behavior that I'd seen in my life better than anything else I'd learned. When he got to Type 1, my husband laughed with recognition. And I cried. Russ put words to the invisible experience of my life. He explained my inner critic and striving for perfection in a way that didn't make me feel judged but understood. All of my attempts to improve our marriage that had instead been driving us apart came to light. I had been trying so hard but creating the opposite result. As I learned about my personality, there was grace for myself that I hadn't experienced before. When Russ got to Nate's type, the same thing happened, only in reverse. I laughed; understanding the behaviors that had just the day before made me angry. And Nate cried, having his inner experience articulated in such a way that we now shared a vocabulary to discuss what had been happening. We spent the rest of the training in deep conversation about our types, how we had been triggering each other and how we could appreciate the other person instead of getting lost in the conflict."

— KALEY WARNER KLEMP

HOW THE ENNEAGRAM WILL HELP YOU DEEPEN AND HEAL YOUR RELATIONSHIPS

As with the story above, the Enneagram works because it's a perfect tool for communication with another. As you understand yourself and the other person, you can use a common language to address existing conflict, pinpoint the triggers and unhealthy habits, and genuinely learn to see the world through the lens of the other. So if you've struggled with relationships in the past or if you don't even know what kind of relationship would be right for you, it's time to understand how your strengths and weaknesses affect your personal relationships. Take responsibility for the energy you bring to any relationship, and things will change for the better. Used properly, the insights you're learning throughout this book will naturally aid you in cultivating healthy relationships.

ENNEAGRAM TYPE 1 - THE PERFECTIONIST IN RELATIONSHIPS

Type Ones are sticklers for rules and doing things the right way. Achieving perfection is a huge driving factor, and these individuals know what they want every time. In relationships, Ones are loyal, dedicated and want the relationship to move in a specific direction.

If you're a type One, perhaps you'll notice friction arises when dealing with types who are more ambiguous and less interested in structure. You're incredibly organized, tend to see the world in shades of black and white, and you're uncompromising in your strong moral code.

Your strengths include being faithful, conscientious, and focused on personal growth.

Your weaknesses in relationships include being too critical, controlling, and uncompromising. You might be placing too high expectations on your partner. In an attempt to make everything perfect, you could drive a wedge between you.

How to improve:

To bring out the best in you and others, embrace a little bit of spontaneity, playfulness, and creativity. Tell your partner or friend what you need instead of expecting them to read your mind. Find ways of relaxing and hit the snooze button on your rules from time to time, especially on things that you know will bring joy to your partner, friend, child, etc. For example, let your kid have ice cream before dinner if he's been such a good boy all summer, and allow your partner to surprise you with an unplanned weekend getaway. It's okay if you get lost and miss a reservation at your favorite restaurant.

What you need:

As a One, you need a partner that can encourage you to become a bit more playful and relaxed. Someone who can add a bit of spontaneity into your life in ways you enjoy. Someone who understands and respects your need for perfection and rules but still facilitates fun in your relationship.

ENNEAGRAM TYPE 2 - THE GIVER IN RELATIONSHIPS

Type Twos are nurturers, helpers, and love supporting others. In relationships, they'll put others first, even if it comes at the expense of their own needs.

If you're a type Two, perhaps you've realized that it's easier for you to give love and attention to another, but it's not so easy to provide the same to yourself. I want to remind you that one can never pour from an empty cup. The more you fill yourself up first, the more you'll naturally have to give to those you care about.

Your strengths include knowing how to make people feel loved and appreciated.

Your weaknesses in relationships include becoming possessive and too dependent on your partner. It might also be that you struggle with self-care.

How to improve:

To bring out the best in you and others, resist the urge to fix every-one's problems. Sometimes you just have to sit back and allow others to solve their issues. And make sure you prioritize self-care and, when needed, put yourself first, even if that means saying no to another's request. Those who love you will appreciate and respect your decision to first tend to your own needs.

What you need:

As a Two, you need a partner who will respect, appreciate and show you how much they love you just as you are. Your romantic partner should encourage you to create healthy boundaries and tend to your own emotional well-being.

ENNEAGRAM TYPE 3 - THE ACHIEVER IN RELATIONSHIPS

As a type Three, I can tell you we put a lot of time and energy into career, achievement, success, and building legacy. In relationships, Threes want to be appreciated for their hard work and accomplishments. Sometimes this can be too extreme to the point of emotional neglect, which leads to unhealthy behavior patterns.

I want to remind you that you can have thriving relationships and a successful career. If you're a Three, perhaps you're now becoming aware of how obsessive you can get with your work and accomplishments. You just need to realize that your value isn't tied to your achievements. The people in your life who love you will love you for who you are if you can just carve out a little time to be present with them.

Your strengths include high energy, charisma, creativity, and an eagerness to live up to others' expectations.

Your weakness in relationships includes being impatient, too self-absorbed, absent-minded, and too focused on your career at the expense of your personal relationships.

How to improve:

Find a way to be there for the people who love you that you want to nurture in your life. It is possible to strive for success, meet your emotional needs, and spend time with your loved ones. Customize a plan that works for your particular situation and, as much as possible, have some downtime where you can switch off from work stress and just have fun with those who love you.

What you need:

As a Three, you need a person who can encourage and support you in taking care of your emotional needs. A romantic partner that can help you unwind and gives you compelling reasons to put work on mute for a little while and just connect with each other.

ENNEAGRAM TYPE 4 - THE INDIVIDUALIST IN RELATIONSHIPS

Type Fours are the sensitive, creative types who care more about living authentically than fitting into society. In relationships, they want to be understood and appreciated for their uniqueness and individuality.

If you're a type Four, it's time to let go of this tension that causes you to feel alone, misunderstood, and inherently flawed. That doesn't mean that everyone will "get you." It means some will, and it's essential to remain open and positive enough to recognize when you come across the few that will accept, embrace, appreciate and love you in all your uniqueness.

Your strengths include being empathetic, intuitive, romantic, playful, and open to new experiences. You have a natural gift of understanding how your partner really feels, and you probably want to find a partner who can reciprocate that.

Your weaknesses in relationships include a tendency to be quite moody and dramatic. Some Fours are also needed, super sensitive to criticism, and are prone to recurring cycles of depression.

How to improve:

Learn to balance that common emotion of sadness and melancholy with gratitude and hopefulness so you can bring positive energy into the group.

What you need:

As a Four, you need a romantic partner who is open, understanding, Self-aware, and expressive in their appreciation of you and all that you are. The more emotionally stable and in-tune your partner is, the richer your connection will be.

ENNEAGRAM TYPE 5 - THE INVESTIGATOR IN RELATIONSHIPS

Type Fives are thinkers. They prefer to observe in the safety of their own privacy, preferably where very few can access. Generally introverted, most Fives prefer isolation and appear secretive and mysterious, but once they find their partner, they become an open book, often sharing everything with their chosen one. If you dig deep, some Fives might even have a romantic streak in relationships. They do, however, require enough time alone to process, think and reset even from their loved ones.

If you're a Five, perhaps you've noticed how hard it is to relate to others. You might be thinking that being isolated and detached is the best solution. I want to remind you that a truly fulfilling life comes from enjoying all that life offers. That includes healthy relationships as well. The meaning and understanding of life that you seek cannot be found if you neglect your emotions or deny yourself the possibility of having a few thriving relationships.

Your strengths include being a curious lifelong learner, kind and perceptive. Your keen interest in activities that foster growth and satisfy your thirst for knowledge can be highly appealing to someone with shared interests.

Your weaknesses in relationships include being aloof and withdrawn from the world. You might also have a tendency to become cynical and irritated with a partner, especially when they interfere with your space or drag you out of your comfort zone.

How to improve:

To bring out the best in yourself and others, open up some more to your chosen partner and allow yourself to sometimes tread outside your comfort zone (thoughtfully, of course).

What you need:

As a Five, you need a partner who is comfortable giving you as much time as possible to yourself. Someone with similar passions in life who isn't afraid to talk about "deep stuff."

ENNEAGRAM TYPE 6 - THE LOYALIST IN RELATIONSHIPS

Type Sixes are known for their loyalty, integrity, dedication, and honesty. They like to know that they're in a steady, secure relationship.

If you're a Six, it's time to start trusting yourself first and foremost. It's easy to go through life being skeptical and mistrusting of everyone, and there's value in having that alert mind. But don't let it ruin your entire existence. Slow down and breathe before responding to others. That will help you get out of your head and make grounded decisions. Make this your truth: The world isn't all bad. In fact, many good, honest people desire to connect with me."

Your strengths include being trustworthy, dependable, supportive, warm, committed, and interested in long-term relationships, even if they're purely platonic.

Your weaknesses in a relationship include defensiveness, being too self-conscious, and struggling to trust others quickly. Some Sixes can turn anxious, fearful, insecure, and controlling.

How to improve:

Work on building your self-confidence and self-esteem. The more you feel good about who you are and come to learn your true worth, the less insecure you'll feel around your partner. Enneagram experts also suggest increasing your capacity to be vulnerable. Brené Brown's book "Daring Greatly" might be a great starting point if you want to strengthen yourself while embracing vulnerability simultaneously.

What you need:

As a Six, you need a trustworthy partner who will be loyal to you. Someone who recognizes how valuable you are and isn't afraid to be vulnerable with you and play the long game in your romantic relationship.

ENNEAGRAM TYPE 7 - THE ENTUSIAST IN RELATIONSHIPS

Enneagram type Sevens are energetic, passionate, full of ideas, and almost always happy. These are the people who have this electrifying energy that you just want to be around. In relationships, they bring that special spark and know how to have a good time.

If you're a Seven, being optimistic and open-minded comes naturally. Perhaps you've noticed, though, that in your quest for novelty and freedom, you're struggling to build anything substantial. Being future-oriented is excellent, and I know you love only the best in life. I want to encourage you to find strength, freedom, and power in the present moment as well. Learn to be more mindful and patient with yourself. When hardships come, (and they will) allow you the grace to explore rather than escape those feelings. If you genuinely want to live life fully, you must learn to experience it all (the please and the pain).

Your strengths include spontaneity, enthusiasm, great positive vibes, and adventure.

Your weaknesses in relationships include a tendency to be narcissistic, distracted, and unable to stay committed in any relationship.

Perhaps you have difficulty finishing any project you start, and your partner often complains you have a short attention span.

How to improve:

Work in finding that balance between adventure and stability. There is a way for you to have both. Freedom and commitment do go hand in hand if you just change perspective. Suppose you can resist the urge to run away or abandon ship, whether things get tough. In that case, you'll finally start experiencing the joys of a committed relationship.

What you need:

As a Seven, your best romantic partner is someone stable, confident, patient, and someone willing to guide you as you slow down in life. Trust your partner enough to let them be serious and weigh in once in a while, especially on important matters.

ENNEAGRAM TYPE 8 - THE CHALLENGER IN RELATIONSHIPS

Enneagram Eights are confident, naturally rebellious, and contrarian, but they are pretty outgoing. In relationships, they can be very protective of their own to the point of arrogance.

If you're an Eight, perhaps you've noticed how hard it is for you to put down your guard and become vulnerable with another. Even intimacy scares you a little, doesn't it? Your ability to see dynamic power plays in every relationship is a gift, but don't let it become a curse. I want to encourage you to let someone in. Remember, not everyone is out to take advantage of you or control you in any way.

Your strengths include being honest and direct in your communication which is great for any kind of relationship. You also tend to be generous, supportive, and extra protective of the people you care about.

Your weaknesses in relationships include being too demanding, uncompromising, too intense, and wanting to control everyone and everything. That can really choke your romantic partner and create a disconnect between you.

How to improve:

Being vulnerable doesn't make you weak. It strengthens your relationship. Work on allowing your softer side to show, at least to your romantic partner. You should also improve your active listening skills and allow your partner to weigh in on matters that concern you both.

What you need:

As an Eight, you need a romantic partner who loves your intense energy and shares your passions and vision in life. Someone who loves how fierce you are and cheers you on.

ENNEAGRAM TYPE 9 - THE PEACEMAKER IN RELATIONSHIPS

The Enneagram Nines are peaceful, kind, gentle, and excellent mediators. In relationships, they often play the supportive, gentle, non-judgmental role.

If you're a Nine, you've got an extraordinary gift, and it's time to use it. Your ability to see all sides in any conversation make your presence powerful and an antidote for many conflicts. However, that doesn't mean that all conflicts are destructive. Instead of turning a blind eye or avoiding them at all costs, cultivate more of your confidence and increase your self-mastery so that you can serve others without losing yourself. Find your voice, live your truth and become the inspiration you were born to be.

Your strengths include being easy-going, calm, loyal, stable, and emotionally sensitive to your partner's feelings.

Your weaknesses in relationships include being passive-aggressive, stubborn, defensive, and at times resentful. Perhaps you've noticed that you've lost your identity in this relationship. That's a common occurrence for a Nine that turns them into people pleasers just to avoid conflict.

How to improve:

Not all conflicts have to end in an argument. There's always a way to maintain peace, even during a disagreement. Work on having healthy conflicts and learn to see the value in expressing your ideas even if they aren't pleasant.

What you need:

As a Nine, you need a romantic partner who will support you and encourage you to speak up and find your voice.

WHICH ENNEAGRAM TYPES PAIR WELL TOGETHER?

Although I don't believe in a "perfect match" because relationship success is based on two individuals and the work they put in, Enneagram experts do have suggestions. The idea behind this Enneagram compatibility isn't to restrict one type to only engage with someone from a specific type but rather to make them aware of the common trends and patterns they've observed. Given how granular the Enneagram system can get and the fact that it focuses more on underlying motives rather than outer behavior, I believe any two types can get together and produce a happy, healthy, thriving relationship. In the book "The Enneagram in Love & Work, researcher Helen Palmer notes that her study uncovered combinations that are more common than others. However, it's important to mention that the research did not consider the combination's satisfaction or compatibility. And what are these common combinations?

Type Ones naturally pair well with Twos and Sevens.

As the detail, oriented, conscientious perfectionists, Ones are drawn to those who can help them lighten up and find beauty in the imperfect moments of life.

In a One-Two romantic partnership, the nurturing, attentive Two can bring a certain warmth to a rigid and task-oriented One. Type Two can help encourage a type One to be more soft and relaxed even as they courageously pursue their perfect ideals in the world. Likewise, type One can bring a sense of structure, security, and consistency to the Two. That can be super appealing for the Two as they often struggle with abandonment issues. These Enneagram types also happen to share wings, so they'll notice some overlap in their traits.

In a One-Seven romantic partnership, the two types connect through their Enneagram Line. Ones might be attracted to the adventurous, joyful spirit of the Seven. This is especially great in helping the hard-working, self-restrained One to let loose and just have fun. Likewise, Sevens might find One's sense of purpose and direction quite attractive. It helps the Seven feel grounded.

Type Twos naturally also pair well with Threes and Eights.

One of the key areas we identified for improvement in type Two is prioritizing and even vocalizing their own needs. Having a romantic partner who can reciprocate intimacy, encourage self-care and not take advantage of the Two's generosity is vital.

There's a high energy match in a Two-Three romantic partnership because these two share similar charisma and interests. The charming Threes often galvanize the Twos to reach their potential instead of focusing on others. Likewise, Twos support the Three with unconditional love and approval, which helps them feel more confident in just being themselves rather than struggling to prove themselves to others through work or status.

In a Two-Eight romantic partnership, these two share an Enneagram line and create a natural attraction. The Twos like the strength, passion, intensity, and conviction that the Eight brings to the relationship. It encourages them to step up and embrace their own power. Likewise, the Eights find this kind of connection appealing because being around a Two enables the Eight to let down their walls and embrace that gentle, loving, and softer side they tend to hide. Twos are excellent at facilitating this vulnerable kind of affection which is super essential for a healthy Eight to have.

Type Threes naturally also pair well with Nines.

Type Threes have a strong image-oriented personality, hindering their vulnerability and authenticity. In a Three-Nine romantic partnership, a calm, poised and stable Nine can enable the Three to accept themselves for who they are, not what they can do. This shift from outer success to inner self-worth reconnects the Three to their emotions. Likewise, Threes help the easy-going Nine move toward the spotlight and find respect and value in their self-identity.

Type Fours naturally pair well with Fives and Nines.

Fours are artistically inclined, highly self-aware, emotionally sensitive, and reflective. They love authentic people who are living their unique truth.

In a Four-Five romantic partnership, the emotionally expressive Fours find comfort in the naturally occurring "straight-talking" no b.s nature of type Five. The "logic first" frame of mind that a Five possesses is very appealing and grounding for a type Four. Why? They admire how authentic and unafraid Fives are in exploring deep things in life, whether science, emotions or art.

In a Four-Nine romantic partnership, the Fours ignite passion back into the mellow Nines, creating an intensity that can be pretty thrilling for the Nine. Likewise, the Nine is appealing to a Four because of their gentle, non-judgmental nature. This kind of self-acceptance is very appealing to a Four who struggles with emotions and finding their identity.

Type Fives naturally pair well with Ones and Twos.

Besides the compatibility with a type Four, these objective, intellectual Fives also commonly pair well with Ones and Twos.

In a Five-One romantic partnership, the Fives are very attracted to the Ones' curiosity, independence, and integrity. When they find a mutual interest, there can be an instant connection. Likewise, the One's appreciate the Five's lack of judgment and commitment to lifelong learning and improvement. Their partnership can build a strong foundation of trust and dependability.

We're witnessing a true "opposites attract" scenario in a Five-Two romantic partnership. The emotionally attuned and loving Two wouldn't be considered viable for an objective, intellectual Five. Yet it happens more often than you might think. The Two's are very attracted to the Five's firm boundaries, independent and objective nature. Also, knowing how much alone time Fives need, the Twos are better able to self-care and tend to their own needs. Fives also benefit from this connection because having a Two around creates a cozy, domesticated atmosphere that colors the Five.

Type Sixes naturally pair well with Nines.

The loyal, trustworthy, security, and stability-oriented Sixes benefit most from a stable and drama-free relationship. In a Six-Nine relationship, they can have all that and more. The gentle, accomodating, and peaceful presence of a Nine is very soothing for a Six. Likewise, this kind of partnership creates that predictable routine-like connection that Nines find most appealing.

Type Sevens naturally pair well with Nines.

It seems many of the Enneatypes fine Nines naturally irresistible, including the enthusiastic, playful, and adventure-seeking Sevens. In a Seven-Nine romantic partnership, an upbeat and positive atmosphere is created when the agreeable, always peaceful Nine hooks up with the free-spirited Seven. Nines are great at helping Sevens slow down and enjoy the present moment more, which is critical for a healthy Seven. Likewise, the energetic Seven ignites a fire in the often passive and too chilled Nine.

Type Eights naturally pair well with Nines.

In an Eight-Nine romantic partnership, the attraction factor is pretty high on both sides because a Nine is often drawn to strong personalities. The powerful, authoritative Eight, some-times aggressive and forceful, likes to pair with a Nine. The Nine sees the high energy and competence radiated by an Eight as very appealing. They admire the Eight's ability to take on chal-lenges. For an Eight, the appeal is more on the calmness of the Nine and how soothing their peaceful energy is to their rela-tionship.

Type Nines naturally pair well with Ones and Twos.

As the peacemakers, their reassuring, harmonizing nature obviously draws in most Enneagram types.

In a Nine-One romantic partnership, the easy-going, peaceful nature of the Nine is very comforting and appealing to the type One. That inner critic and self-judgment are met with self-acceptance and gentleness from the Nine, which soothes anxiety and reduces the need to be right all the time. Likewise, the Nines benefit greatly in the structure, a sense of purpose, and clarity that a type One brings to their relationship.

In a Nine-Two romantic partnership, the loving and self-accepting Nine values and shows affection to the Two without taking advan-tage of them. They value the Two for who they are and not what they give. That's very comforting for a type Two who longs for that. Like-wise, the Two's nurturing and attentive nature can help motivate the

Nine into action. That takes him from that passive lethargic tendency into a more active and productive lifestyle.

None of these pairing types are set in stone. Often you might find success in same-type parings or even an Enneagram type that wasn't mentioned above. How much self-awareness you and your partner bring to the relationship matters. It's the determining factor of how fulfilling and healthy any relationship can be.

Now that you know your Enneagram number, wings and subtypes, start noticing how your instincts and motivations influence your reactions and behavior. Your temperament, early childhood, and unique experiences are ever-present when you begin a new relationship. Love is more than just that initial attraction. It's what happens after that initial "honeymoon" phase sizzles out. The more growth work you partake in together and individually, the better your chances of having a healthy and thriving relationship.

CHAPTER 13
HOW TO USE THE ENNEAGRAM AT WORK

As the business environment shifts and marketplace volatility increases, many organizations in the United States and abroad find it necessary to adjust their leadership and people management approaches. Technology, customer expectations, and many other factors add extra strain to employees of any business type and size. Smart business owners and employees are looking for different solutions that can enable them to improve productivity, teamwork, and emotional intelligence. The Enneagram has become one of those go-to tools for professionals who seek enlightenment, efficiency, and a better bottom line at their organization.

Why would businesses care about a tool that's rooted in ancient mysticism and spiritual teachings?

Understanding what drives people and discovering their strengths and weaknesses can influence company performance. In fact, it does impact performance way more than you think. If you are a leader or working within a team structure that seems to have plenty of gaps and incongruencies, this is one of the best ways to bring about positive change in the workplace. The Enneagram isn't about promoting a particular religious or psychological belief. Instead, it's about celebrating human diversity and prioritizing self-awareness and personal development as pre-requisite skills for professional growth.

BENEFITS OF USING THE ENNEAGRAM AT WORK

Healthy conflict resolution

Conflicts are part of a healthy team, and it's time we learn how to disagree respectfully. The Enneagram helps people come to a better understanding of their triggers, fears, motivations, and how to best communicate with others.

Greater meaning and productivity

As employees feel more cared for, valued, and understood at work, their commitment levels increase. In a 2017 Gallup study led by Dr. Amy Edmondson, they found that environments that improved their psychological safety experienced a 12% increase in productivity and less employee turnover. But fostering an environment where everyone feels safe and valued is hard if you don't have a tool like the Enneagram. What one employee perceives as a sign of care might threaten another depending on their Enneagram type. By deploying this tool across your organization, you will have clarity on the strategic moves to make that will ensure everyone experiences their version of "psychological safety."

Diversity and maximizing potential

After experimenting with the Enneagram tool, one of the core benefits different businesses have had is the ease by which the senior leadership can tap into each individual's uniqueness and highest potential. Accurately identifying where each person can be best positioned in a given project and allowing various types to tackle the same problem from different angles can maximize team contribution and performance.

EACH ENNEAGRAM TYPE AT WORK

We've already gone through the details of each Enneagram at a personal level. Now let's look at how you can relate to the various Enneagram Types in the workplace for better communication and team building.

Enneagram 1 - The Perfectionist

If you want to establish rapport with a type One, learn to respect their integrity and seriousness. Be a little more serious when interacting with them and know that they value the details that many of us tend to overlook.

To promote a healthy professional connection, engage in discussions of how things can be improved.

Avoid taking shortcuts or neglecting proper procedures when around Ones. It also doesn't hurt to keep good manners as they care a lot about doing things correctly. When making promises or arrangements, only agree to what you know you can see through to completion.

During conflicts, request them to be direct with their anger, so they don't harbor resentment. Genuinely acknowledge your mistake if you're in the wrong. Remember, Ones speaking style is precise and detail-oriented. When addressing them, do so with personal conviction and authority. If you know there's more than one right way, challenge them to see that too, but do it with kindness. When communicating with a One, always be clear about your expectations. Keep in mind they're trying to answer this unspoken question. "How can I fulfill my responsibility with integrity and in the perfect way?"

Whatever you can do to support answering that question will go a long way in ensuring success.

Want to support their growth? If you're leading a type One, the best thing you can do is to encourage them to be less critical of themselves and more accepting of their mistakes and other people's seeming imperfections. You can also encourage them to share responsibilities with fellow team members and once in a while to just chill and have fun even while working on serious projects.

Enneagram 2 - The Helper

If you want to establish rapport with type Two, take the initiative and make that first contact. Regularly show your appreciation and approval.

To promote a healthy professional connection, encourage them to build partnerships and friendships that are warm and fulfilling for them.

Avoid being too critical, taking advantage of their generosity, or ignoring them as that deeply hurts their feelings. Twos are highly emotional, and it's essential for them that they are liked and accepted by others.

During conflicts, insist that they take responsibility for getting what they want instead of passing on the blame or evoking guilt. They tend to become resentful, so make sure to address that with as much empathy as you can. A Two's speaking style is sympathetic and nice. They love giving advice and being around a lot of people. Remember to regularly communicate your appreciation and say simple things like, "I really appreciate what you did there."

Want to support their growth? Encourage them to develop healthy boundaries and pay attention to their own needs and feelings.

Enneagram 3 - The Achiever

If you want to establish rapport with a type Three, acknowledge the hard work they put in. Be fast and efficient in your communication, so they don't feel like you're just wasting time.

To promote a healthy professional connection, become more proactive in the projects you work on together and focus on getting results.

Avoid getting in the way of their forward momentum. Threes have a lot of energy, and they can't stand failure or anyone hindering their success.

During conflicts, you have to be okay with getting a bit more aggressive in your exchanges, especially when things aren't going right. But don't let that deter you from staying on track with the overall goals. Threes are very enthusiastic, and they enjoy motivating themselves and others for success. Use that to your advantage in your communication. If you want them to get things done, offer incentives, including monetary rewards and public recognition. Threes can sometimes forget the value of people in the pursuit of success, so be assertive in reminding them that people have an essential role to play in success. Challenge their rhetoric while allowing them to save face when the situation calls for it.

Want to support their growth? Value them for who they are, not what they do, and make sure they know this. Encourage them to slow down once in a while and pay attention to their health. Create an atmosphere at work where failure is considered a good learning opportunity so they can stop demonizing it.

Enneagram 4 - The Individualist

If you want to establish rapport with a type Four, learn to vocalize your appreciation of their creativity and emotional sensitivity. Often these people are brilliant in their output and even if you may not agree with their art or sense of style, just acknowledge it.

To promote a healthy professional connection, value their individualism and effort into being unique and different.

Avoid making everything conform to logic and rationale if you want to win them over. They also don't enjoy doing status quo things, so try not to force them into conformity.

During conflicts, challenge the person to avoid withdrawing from the unresolved conversation and, at the same time, don't entertain their dramatic outbursts. The best you can do during disagreements is find a middle ground and refrain from taking everything they say to heart. Most of the time, type Fours say things they don't mean as their emotions run wild. Always remember that. A type Four's speaking style is sometimes warm and full of positive feelings, and sometimes it's dry and flat. To make your communication effective, I encourage you to validate and acknowledge their unique insights frequently. And try not to take their fluctuating moods personally.

Want to support their growth? Encourage healthy, respectful disagreements in your environment and let them know they are safe to express their emotions as long as they do so mindfully. Get them to watch what they say and consider the implications of their words and actions on others in the team. Promote mindfulness practices and self-awareness techniques that can enable them to create more emotional balance within and silence the inner critic.

Enneagram 5 - The Investigator

If you want to establish rapport with a type Five, be thoughtful in your approach and make sure you give them plenty of room to think and process information.

To promote a healthy professional connection, get together to discuss interests and deep and meaningful ideas. No small talk, please.

Avoid pressuring them into making immediate decisions or taking fast actions without proper thinking time.

During conflicts, you can agree to disagree with a Five. They are rational, technical, and can't stand chit-chat, which means they'll directly tell you what's going on if you ask the right way. Be mindful of signs of withdrawal, especially during a disagreement. When communicating, keep things professional and focused on their area of expertise. Give the person plenty of information and data, then allow them time to process. Don't pry into their personal life and if your business is flexible, consider allowing some flexibility in their work environment, e.g., remote work.

Want to support their growth? Encourage them to be warmer, generous and to forge strong relationships with a few key people in the team or organization. Make it safe for them to share as much or as little of their emotions as they feel comfortable doing. Remind the person that they need to let other team members know that they care but need plenty of alone time and space to work in solitude.

Enneagram 6 - The Loyalist

If you want to establish rapport with a type Six, make an effort to appreciate the natural tendency to worry and focus on problems. Let them know that you understand their need to guard and create a sense of safety. Agree on rules and procedures that aid in meeting that objective.

To promote a healthy professional connection, embrace their insights and acknowledge that you see value in dissecting all the worst-case scenarios before moving ahead with a given project.

Avoid changing rules too abruptly or withholding information from Sixes. As natural skeptics, lack of transparency or omission of critical details breeds doubts, leading to conflict.

During conflicts, don't be ambiguous. Speak clearly without discounting the person's concerns. At the same time, they refuse to take on their projections and insist that the individual takes responsibility for the situation at hand instead of creating external excuses. Sixes are naturally full of questions, so in your communication, let them know you are open to answering even the most tedious question as long as it helps put their mind at ease.

Want to support their growth? Sixes need a lot of psychological safety at work before mentally relaxing and stopping scanning for threats in every conversation. If you can create a "safe zone" where they can relax more, speak openly about their fears, and get reality checks without feeling judged, you're more likely to get the best out of this loyal individual.

The Enneagram 7 - The Enthusiast

If you want to establish rapport with a type Seven, learn to embrace their vibrant energy and enthusiasm for life. Learn to appreciate their endless stories and ideas.

To promote a healthy professional connection, encourage discussions that are fun, future-oriented, and filled with possibility.

Avoid being too negative or "reasonable" in your goal setting or ideas around Sevens. I also encourage you to always seek out various options for solving problems - challenge the Seven to help you find them.

During conflicts, challenge the person to take responsibility for their actions and insist on listening to other people's side of the story instead of talking over them. You might need to repeat this often. It's also important to be clear about what's expected and what the person should deliver because Sevens can easily get sidetracked. In your communication, switch it up a little when addressing a Seven and be more optimistic and excited about the project. But don't fake it.

Want to support their growth? The biggest support you can offer a Seven is to help them become a little more grounded and balanced between their constant desire for new and their ability to see things through before moving on to the next. Stress the importance of feedback and active listening, especially with fellow team members. Considering how much they hate pain, consider how you dish out negative feedback.

Enneagram 8 - The Challenger

If you want to establish rapport with a type Eight, make direct contact, be assertive, and don't back down in the face of their strength.

To promote a healthy professional connection, become proactive in helping them build momentum toward the desired result.

Avoid coming across as controlling or disrespectful. Given how energetic and domineering they are, I would avoid giving them assignments that cause them to sit still for too long.

During conflicts, you need to be bold enough to have healthy confrontations. Be authentic to yourself but deal with them directly and get ready to embrace the angry energy that's bound to come your way. Allow them to express their anger, but don't let it get out of hand. If they start to demonstrate destructive or violent behavior, do not stand for it at all. Since Eights are assertive speakers, they are more receptive to the same direct and bold communication style. Set clear goals, deadlines, and expectations in your communication, then leave them be. If you're savvy enough, figure out ways to plant ideas in their mind so they can "feel" more in control about taking the desired action. The more persuasive you are, the further you'll get with an Eight.

Want to support their growth? The best way to support type Eights is to figure out healthy ways for them to express their energy and emotions.

Enneagram 9 - Peacemaker

If you want to establish rapport with a type Nine, take time to listen, and I mean really listen to them. Encourage them to share what they care about so you can find common ground.

To promote a healthy professional connection, maintain peace. Nines cannot stand internal or external conflict, so if you can find ways to sustain a peaceful relationship at work, you'll win them over. It's that simple.

Avoid putting pressure on the person or making them feel bad for not moving as fast as the others. Of all the Enneagram types, Nines have the least energy, so their pace in execution is likely to be the slowest. Getting impatient or being too pushy will be counterproductive to your business goals.

During conflicts, do your best to demonstrate fairness in all matters. Find ways to disagree in healthy, non-threatening ways. When dealing with a Nine, it pays to slow down and dig deeper, asking them to share what's really going on inside them. Sometimes a Nine will have an angry outburst or become passive-aggressive in their behavior. Let them know neither of these behaviors will be tolerated, and encourage them to work with you in resolving the issue. Nines speak with a lot of kindness and inclusivity. Try to use the right tone in your communication, so they don't interpret you as harsh and dismissive, leading to withdrawal. You should also establish clear priorities and give the person enough time to contemplate and process the task/assignment.

Want to support their growth? One of the best things you can do to support a Nine is to work with them to create structure and schedules around their work to keep them on track. Find small ways to constantly push them out of their comfort zone in ever so subtle ways so they can keep growing and contributing more to the organization.

PART FOUR
USING THE ENNEAGRAM FOR GROWTH IN ALL AREAS

ACCELERATING YOUR PERSONAL GROWTH PART 1

N ow that you've learned quite a bit about the Enneagram system and hopefully identified your personality type, what happens if you wish to change it? What if you're not happy with what you've discovered? What next? This is actually a pretty common experience, so don't worry if you're looking for answers on how to change your personality. Before I can give the long and short version answer, we should probably agree on a definition of personality.

Personality originates from the Latin word "persona," which refers to a theatrical mask that performers wear to project different roles during a play. Entertainers also used it to disguise their true identity during the performance. Your true identity is far grander, more real, and lasting than the persona that you're accustomed to wearing on a day-to-day basis. Based on that, let's agree that personality has nothing to do with who you really are.

And while at the most fundamental level, personality is about the thought patterns, feelings, and behaviors that make you unique, they are indeed not who you are. According to experts who study human personality, the consensus is that personality arises from within the individual and remains fairly constant throughout one's life. Enneagram experts seem to believe the same, which is why they say that an individual's Enneagram type cannot really change. To attempt to change your personality or your Enneagram type is a losing battle that I wouldn't encourage anyone to partake in. But all is not lost if you desire to grow and transform into a better version of yourself.

WHY PERSONALITY IS ALMOST IMPOSSIBLE TO CHANGE

Our personalities arise and are shaped based on many interacting factors that we can sum up into two broad categories - genetics and environment. Author and psychologists Carol Dweck asserts that, for the most part, our personalities are out of our control because even if we change the environment, genetics still influences us significantly. So if you're predisposed to being short-tempered and uptight but end up spending a long time in an environment that was zen-like and friendly, you'd likely see some shifts in your temperament to match that setting. Dweck often shares a story about twins to make this point. Two boys born identical twins were separated at birth. Raised in entirely different environments, one might expect no similar personality traits. As adults, however, the two men married women with the same first names, shared identical hobbies, and had similar levels of specific characteristics that experts could measure on personality assessments. Dweck proves the bias for the notion that we don't have control over our personality, but I do like that she continues to explore the solution that exists for those of us who desire change.

The secret to change and growth:

If you'd like to improve your current personality and the quality of your life, don't focus on what you cannot control, e.g., your Enneatype or genetics, and instead focus on what we know is within your control. And that is your behavior. Dweck believes that by changing habits, behavior patterns, and beliefs under the surface of your broad personality type, you can experience lasting personal transformation. That's where the Enneagram becomes super helpful because it gives you access to the aspects of you that lie beneath the surface of your overall personality. It also teaches you to move from a lower, underdeveloped version of your character to a higher and more "aligned" version of your personality. What do I mean by aligned? The alignment and connection between your personality and your higher self. After all, your real identity lies with your higher self rather than your persona. You have the ability to change your belief system, habits, coping strategies and close the gap that's responsible for all your anguish and restlessness.

HOW TO LEVERAGE THE ENNEAGRAM TOOL FOR POSITIVE CHANGE AND PERSONAL GROWTH

Embrace and accept your number

It's common to feel resistance about your Enneagram type once you've taken the test. If you're feeling uncomfortable and exposed, if perhaps you broke down in tears after reading some of the negative emotions and tendencies associated with your number, that's okay. I know it can feel intrusive, but the point of this quest is to bring awareness into your life and finally get to know who you are. Your personality type isn't better or worse than mine. Each Enneagram type is perfect as is and the best we can do is recognize, accept and make peace with where we are. What we discover and uncover about ourselves shouldn't drown us in self-defeat or pity. It should empower us to consciously and purposely plot out how we'll approach the rest of our lives. All Enneagram types possess great strengths, unique offerings, and plenty of untapped potentials that can bring so much good into the world. Focus on unlocking more of that potential within yourself.

Identify the areas you'd like to improve

Now that you've accepted and embraced your Enneagram type, it's time to take an honest look at your life. Look at the state of your health, finances, career, mental and emotional well-being, relationships, and any other domain that matters to you. Where do you need to grow in the next 12 months? Is there a negative pattern you've identified that has to change? Are you looking to reconnect with your spiritual nature? Do you feel it's time to find your purpose or perhaps become more in-tune with your emotions? Whatever led you to pick up this book and study the Enneagram tool is the first thing you should improve. As you improve on one area and hone your skills, add more and more goals that bring you joy.

Put this knowledge into practice

It's one thing to read a book or attend a weekend seminar and an entirely different thing to put what you learn into practice. Many people who read this book will finish it proudly and pat themselves on the back. But unfortunately, they'll go back to doing exactly what they did before reading it and claim the book was a waste of time. The Enneagram and all the contents in this book work if you're willing to put in the effort and apply the lessons to your daily life.

The Enneagram tool shouldn't be used as a weapon to attack or manipulate others. It's meant to be used as a self-discovery tool so that as you understand yourself, you can meet others with more compassion. Instead of being at the mercy of your core fears and weaknesses, you can learn to tame them and still show up as the best version of yourself, even in the most challenging situations. When you catch yourself falling off track or reverting to old habits that no longer serve you, gently bring yourself back to focus without self-judgment or dwelling on past mistakes. This is the real purpose for the Enneagram teaching, and you can only reap the benefits when you apply the knowledge in your own life and track the progress you're making.

If you don't know what to focus on for your specific Enneagram type to see progress, let's break down some of the essential qualities you can cultivate, plus how to expedite your strengths.

ENNEAGRAM TYPE ONE - THE PERFECTIONIST – PATH TO GROWTH

Your essential qualities are integrity, goodness, and sacredness.

As you grow and awaken, the virtue you're moving toward realizing is serenity.

When it comes to accelerating your personal growth as a One, it's time to get deeply acquainted with your inner critic. That is, that little voice in your head that never shuts up. Ever measuring yourself up against certain ideals that are often unrealistic, it's easy to assume that becoming perfect is the way to self-actualization. Unfortunately, this couldn't be further from the truth. The way to use the Enneagram to accelerate growth and self-actualize is by focusing less on perfecting yourself—instead, practicing self-acceptance. Make an effort to relinquish the constant need for harsh judgment on yourself and others. It will transform you into a more compassionate, empathetic, and graceful person.

To bring you into a more serene and self-accepting state, here are some calming statements that can enable you to practice present moment awareness.

- *May I be at ease with myself.*
- *May I let go of judgments and forgive me and others knowing that this doesn't mean I agree with any particular behavior.*
- *May I be at ease with the things I consider imperfect realizing that serenity comes from knowing that the present moment is perfect just as it is.*

Once you've stabilized this way of thinking and feeling, here are some positive affirmations to add to your daily rituals.

- *I am at ease with life.*
- *I embrace myself completely.*
- *I am gentle with others.*
- *Everyone is doing the best they can at their current level of awareness, and I am accepting of this.*
- *I choose to be compassionate, understanding, and accepting of others.*
- *I forgive myself.*
- *Life is perfect as it is.*
- *I choose to be flexible, adaptable and embrace change.*

ENNEAGRAM TYPE TWO - THE HELPER – PATH TO GROWTH

Your essential qualities are love, affection, and nurture. The virtue you're moving toward as you grow and awaken is humility.

When it comes to accelerating your personal growth, it's time to stop people-pleasing and start tending to your own needs and living by example. The way to use the Enneagram to self-actualize is to invest time daily to get grounded within and to reconnect with your emotions first before jumping in to help others. Notice when feelings of pride push you to do things for others. And when the fear of being unloved tempts you to betray yourself and refuse to act from that perspective. Ask yourself regularly, "Am I tending to my own needs?" and "Is my giving authentic or set on expectations to get something in return?" Become emotionally present with yourself. Cultivate your confidence so you can start making the shift toward self-care and humility.

To begin walking the path of humility and unconditional love, here are some calming statements that can enable you to practice present moment awareness.

- *May I learn to love myself genuinely and see my own worth regardless of others' thoughts.*
- *May I give as much love to myself as I give to others.*
- *May I learn to give generously and authentically from a place of abundance.*
- *May I relinquish my send of pride and walk the path of humility.*

Once you've stabilized this way of thinking and feeling, here are some positive affirmations to add to your daily rituals.

- *I am loved for who I am.*
- *I am confident in myself.*
- *I have healthy emotional needs.*
- *I give sincerely from my heart.*
- *I establish healthy boundaries between myself and others.*
- *I feel accepted for who I am.*
- *I am able to express and ask for what I want.*

ENNEAGRAM TYPE THREE - THE ACHIEVER – PATH TO GROWTH

Your essential qualities are value, glory, and preciousness. The virtue you're moving toward as you grow and awaken is authenticity.

When it comes to accelerating your personal growth, focus less on status and the mask you wear in public and more on your true self. Creating an illusion of what you think will make others perceive you as successful is counterproductive in the long run and will lead to the very things you fear. Instead, lean into your truth, strength, and ability to do more than others. But do so from a holistic place where your emotional needs aren't sacrificed. Embrace your natural leadership qualities and, at the same time, cultivate rich relationships. Regularly check in with your feelings and give yourself downtime to reset when needed.

To begin walking the path of practicing present moment awareness, here are some calming statements.

- *May I cultivate stillness and reconnect with my true feelings.*
- *May I allow greater patience into my day.*
- *May I have compassion in the face of suffering for myself and others.*

Once you've stabilized this way of thinking and feeling, here are some positive affirmations to add to your daily rituals.

- *I am open to acknowledging my feelings.*
- *I am enough.*
- *I inspire leadership in others.*
- *I am loved by others who appreciate me as I am.*
- *I am aligned with my true self.*
- *I am ready to acknowledge the efforts of my team.*
- *I celebrate the accomplishments of others.*

ACCELERATING YOUR PERSONAL GROWTH PART 11

ENNEAGRAM TYPE FOUR - THE INDIVIDUALIST – PATH TO GROWTH

Your essential qualities are beauty, intimacy, depth, and mystery. The virtue you're moving toward as you grow and awaken is equanimity.

When it comes to accelerating your personal growth, it's time to stop clinging to the brokenness you see in the world and start becoming the solution. Embody what you see is lacking or missing in the world. Perhaps as a child, you craved compassion and just leadership. Now that you're an adult, it's time to cultivate those qualities so you can become the change you wish to see in the world. Use the Enneagram tool to practice self-love and reconnect with your true identity. Finding your true self and feeling deeply loved matter to you, and rightly so, the knowledge of the Enneagram can enable you to finally realize that you're not broken, and finding yourself can only be accomplished by going within. Take time to notice and catch yourself when you start dwelling on what's missing or lacking. Bring yourself to the present moment. Cultivate high self-esteem and practice a little more enthusiasm. It will do you a world of good to allow your feelings to spin over to the good side of life.

To begin walking the path of equanimity and gratitude, here are some calming statements that can enable you to practice present moment awareness.

- *May I delight in the happiness of others.*
- *May I learn to appreciate what is rather than dwell on what isn't.*
- *May I appreciate and rejoice in myself as I increase my awareness about how life really works.*
- *May I learn to treat all beings with equal and positive regard.*

Once you've stabilized this way of thinking and feeling, here are some positive affirmations to add to your daily rituals.

- *I am centered in my true essence.*
- *I draw on my gifts to inspire the world.*
- *I am more than my emotions and my human experience.*
- *I choose to live in the present moment.*
- *I choose to release the past and find grace.*
- *I am happy to be me.*

ENNEAGRAM TYPE FIVE - THE INVESTIGATOR – PATH TO GROWTH

Your essential qualities are clarity, illumination, insight, and solitude. The virtue you're moving toward as you grow and awaken in nonattachment.

When it comes to accelerating your growth, it's time to take action and use your vastly deep knowledge and understanding to pinpoint which changes need to be made in the world. Allow your competence to serve your mission rather than making your research and knowledge the mission. You have the ability to do great things and positively impact the world, and it's time to lean more into this ability. Use the Enneagram tool to enable you to embrace the physical world so you can channel more insight. Freely offer your knowledge without fear. Learn to make the distinction between knowledge, wisdom, and insight.

To begin walking the path of openness, nonattachment, and being in the flow of the universe, here are some calming statements that can enable you to practice present moment awareness.

- *May I realize that the universe is abundant.*
- *May I feel secure within myself and trust that I will receive what I need.*
- *May I be at peace with not knowing, all the while realizing I already have ample knowledge.*
- *May I open my heart to engage fully in life's energy.*

Once you've stabilized this way of thinking and feeling, here are some positive affirmations to add to your daily rituals.

- *I am grounded in my being.*
- *I am calm, serene, and at peace even amidst life uncertainties.*
- *I thrive well in this world.*
- *I choose to connect with others.*
- *I experience life fully.*
- *I develop healthy relationships with the people around me.*
- *I appreciate the awe of being in my body.*
- *I have general trust in the people around me.*
- *I love myself.*
- *I feel abundant.*

ENNEAGRAM TYPE SIX - THE LOYALIST – PATH TO GROWTH

Your essential qualities are truth, guidance, and intuition. The virtue you're moving toward as you grow and awaken is courage.

When it comes to accelerating your growth, it's time to realize that your constant search for trustworthiness and security is actually concealing your insecurities. In the long run, it becomes counterproductive because the fear only grows. Use the Enneagram tools to finally address the internal insecurities. Understand that your imagination tends to dramatize situations, so catch yourself and notice this is a blind spot whenever you get trapped in a worst-case scenario. Then act accordingly, leaning more into the situation with curiosity rather than fearfully running away from the situation or person because most of the time, nothing is as bad as you see it in your imagination. As you get better at using the Enneagram tool and teaching, you will trust more in your inner guidance and let go of fear patterns.

To begin walking the path of courage, here are some calming statements that can enable you to practice present moment awareness.

- *May I turn fear into a friend instead of becoming victimized and imprisoned by its story.*
- *May I cultivate courage instead of constantly changing after security and certainty.*
- *May I have faith in myself and in life itself.*
- *May I learn to live more in the present moment and notice my tendency to magnify situations.*

Once you've stabilized this way of thinking and feeling, here are some positive affirmations to add to your daily rituals.

- *I am calm and centered.*

- *I choose to trust myself and my inner guidance.*
- *I am well supported by my team members and friends.*
- *My inner counsel is wise.*
- *I love myself.*
- *The world is a safe place, and the universe supports me.*
- *I make independent and clear decisions for myself.*

ENNEAGRAM TYPE SEVEN - THE ENTHUSIAST – PATH TO GROWTH

Your essential qualities are joy, hope, and freedom. The virtue you're moving toward as you grow and awaken is sobriety.

When it comes to accelerating your personal growth, the best you can do is increase your curiosity about what it truly means to be free. The tendency is to seek out growth and freedom by pursuing a new challenge, adventure, or opportunity. Unfortunately, this rarely leads to the change you truly crave. Use the Enneagram tool to go within and increase your understanding of yourself. Dive deep into the nature of being and find your lasting freedom there. Learn to process both positive and negative emotions.

To begin walking the path of sobriety and emotional mastery, here are some calming statements that can enable you to practice present moment awareness.

- *May I allow myself to feel all my emotions, including sadness, suffering, and sorrow, and reflect without being judgmental or harsh on myself.*
- *May I have compassion for myself and all other beings.*
- *May I learn to find freedom from within, which will allow me to have freedom in everything I do, even when it's mundane or repetitive.*
- *May I learn to find joy in the present moment ordinary activities.*

Once you've stabilized this way of thinking and feeling, here are some positive affirmations to add to your daily rituals.

- *I am abundant.*
- *I am content, fulfilled, and joyful.*
- *I am free to express who I am.*
- *I am grounded in my being and engaged in all I do.*
- *I am in touch with my emotions and inner guidance.*
- *I find joy in the present moment.*
- *I choose to focus my energy and attention.*

ENNEAGRAM TYPE EIGHT - THE CHALLENGER – PATH TO GROWTH

Your essential qualities are strength, aliveness, and power. The virtue you're moving toward as you grow and awaken is innocence.

When it comes to accelerating your growth, it's not about giving up your desired challenges and taking massive action. It's about getting into alignment first. The need to control everything and impose your will over others tends to be more counterproductive than helpful for your development. You also struggle with the belief that vulnerability means weakness, but the truth is, allowing yourself to be vulnerable, especially to your closest relationships, will only make you stronger. To be truly courageous and strong, one must also tune with their emotions.

As a natural leader, your powerful, authoritative and decisive instincts will be amplified as you use the Enneagram tool to get in tune with your emotional side. It will also enable you to be more open to receiving counsel from the person you most love who is also looking out for your well-being. Instead of being dismissive, pause for a moment and become more receptive. Listen with both your head and heart before rejecting input from a loved one.

To begin walking the path of innocence, here are some calming statements that can enable you to practice present moment awareness.

- *May I learn to embody gentleness and compassion.*
- *May I be receptive to the truth in all beings.*
- *May I cultivate more of a growth mindset and the innocence of a beginner's mind so I can enter each new situation with a fresh perspective.*

Once you've stabilized this way of thinking and feeling, here are some positive affirmations to add to your daily rituals.

- *I am peaceful and calm.*
- *I am in touch with my emotional needs.*
- *I respect the decision of others.*
- *I am sensitive to the needs of others.*
- *I can be gentle and firm at the same time.*
- *I practice patience.*
- *I embrace every part of me, including what I perceive as weakness.*

ENNEAGRAM TYPE NINE - THE PEACEMAKER – PATH TO GROWTH

Your essential qualities are harmony, wholeness, and interconnectedness. The virtue you're moving toward as you grow and awaken is engagement.

The best gift you can give to the world is using your natural ability to create peace and wholeness in your relationships. But to do that, you'll need to activate more of your innate powers and embody the solutions that others are struggling to see. When it comes to accelerating your personal growth, it's time to stop going along with things or blending in when you know it's not of the highest good just to avoid conflict. Do your best to notice when the resistance kicks in, and you withdraw simply because you want to avoid creating conflict by stating your truth. Cultivate the courage to speak up and find healthy ways to deal with disagreements. Use the Enneagram tool to help you notice your unproductive habits and tendency to revert to passive-aggressive behavior instead of boldly speaking up and actively working out solutions to problems. Allow the knowledge gained from the study of the Enneagram to aid you in exploring the underlying message that causes you to withdraw and ignore your own voice.

To begin walking the path of wholeness and right action, here are some calming statements that can enable you to practice present moment awareness.

- *May I discover my purpose and live more intentionally.*
- *May I become more aware of my inertia toward myself, knowing that the right action comes from valuing myself the same as I value others.*
- *May I focus on what's important, especially in the face of discomfort and conflict.*
- *May I remember my priorities and values.*

Once you've stabilized this way of thinking and feeling, here are some positive affirmations to add to your daily rituals.

- *I am peaceful and whole.*
- *I can honor my voice and speak my truth even when it's not comfortable.*
- *I can bring a healing presence to others without neglecting myself.*

- *I am loved just as I am.*
- *I am grateful, and I actively participate in the joys of daily living.*
- *I acknowledge and value my own identity.*

.

UNLOCKING YOUR POTENTIAL AND A FULFILED LIFE

Will you choose to live the Enneagram? Too many people get stuck in the theory and study of this wonderful system. That's quite unfortunate because, without daily practice and integration, the teachings of the Enneagram can never translate into results. A significant weakness in personality tests and personal development is the lack of emphasis on practicing what one learns.

I see the Enneagram as one of the best tools for shifting perspectives about life, our past, present, and future. The Enneagram tool enables us to discover more of who we really are. It's all about growth and development, helping us embody what makes us distinctly who we are. Our personal and professional lives benefit greatly when we begin to show up more as our true selves. Use the Enneagram model as a map that points you in the direction of your highest and best self. Take note of your strengths and weaknesses, so you can make better choices as you continue to navigate life.

HOW DO YOU WANT THE NEXT 12 MONTHS TO PLAY OUT?

Regardless of external factors or what the news tells you, the next year can be whatever you choose it to be. That's because you have control over your mind and, in turn, how you'll navigate experiences and circumstances. Think about this: No matter what's going on with the government or economy, some people will struggle tremendously, and some will succeed tremendously. Even during a crisis, some people continue to thrive. Wouldn't it be nice if you could be among those that thrive in all seasons?

The key to ensuring the next twelve months are significantly different from the last lies within you. You can use the Enneagram to help you unlock all the dormant power and potential that remains unutilized so that you can finally take charge of your life. This doesn't mean striving for more, hustling more, or forcing things into place. The more self-aware you become of both your conditioned limitations and untapped opportunities, the easier it will be to make the right choices for your life.

So far, we've gone through personal growth recommendations for each Enneagram type. Go back and re-read as much as you can about your Enneagram type and the simple action steps you can take to move your life forward. Besides understanding what your specific Enneagram type needs and wants to continue developing in healthy ways, there are some universal practices that will work for all of us regardless of our type. Some are ancient practices passed on by spiritual teachers and sages, while others are scientifically researched and discovered. Pick a handful of practices from this list, make them a daily habit and commit to living the Enneagram, not just studying it.

PRACTICES AND TECHNIQUES YOU SHOULD KNOW ABOUT

Cultivate Self-love

We've mentioned self-love several times throughout this book. But most people tend to misunderstand what it means. It's not just about feeling good or taking time to rest and self-care. Self-love is much deeper and more fundamental than that. It's a state of total awe and appreciation for oneself that grows from the actions that support your physical, psychological and spiritual growth. Self-love is one of the most important practices you can incorporate into your daily life if you live the Enneagram. It enables you to accept both strengths and weaknesses, meet your failures with compassion, and find personal meaning and fulfillment in life. When viewed through the lens of self-love, your life and the world takes on a different tone, one that's more in harmony with universal laws. How you see the world and interpret others doesn't come from outside, it comes from inside. The lower your self-love levels, the darker your vision, and conversely, the higher your self-love, the brighter your vision.

HOW DOES ONE BEGIN TO CULTIVATE SELF-LOVE?

As with all good things in life, it's a matter of forming a habit. Take small steps daily to reconnect with your whole self, nurturing and tending to your physical, psychological, and spiritual needs. Over time, those small actions will add up into habits that become your new norm. You must also notice how you communicate with yourself. Is your inner dialogue constantly negative? Are you often doubting, berating, and betting against yourself? The more time you spend compassionately checking in with yourself, the easier it will be to catch and prune all the unruly thoughts and emotions.

Forgiveness as a practice

One of the best tools you can use in this journey of self-discovery is the practice of daily forgiveness. Realize that forgiveness doesn't mean abdicating responsibility or even justifying a wrong. It simply means giving yourself (or another) compassion and shifting your perspective from how things are to how you'd like it to be. Why would you need to do this? Because your point of power will always be in the present moment. But each time you're holding on to any blame or resentment, you're stuck in the past. It robs you of your power and takes you off the path of living the Enneagram.

Here's the thing, you'll make many mistakes on this journey, and you'll also realize how much your ignorance has hurt you and others. Once we realize how short we've fallen from our true potential, we tend to self-loathe and self-punish. That is the worst move for us to make. The right thing to do is to exercise forgiveness. Learn to practice self-compassion when you fall short of whom you want to be. The same is true for those you feel have ill-treated you. As Louise Hay says, " No matter how justified you feel you are, no matter what "they" did, if you insist on holding on to the past, then you'll never be free."

A few statements to practice forgiveness:

- *I forgive myself for not being perfect. I know I am doing my best and living the very best way I know-how.*
- *I forgive everyone in my past and present for all perceived wrongs. I release all people with love.*
- *I love and approve of myself.*

Gratitude

Equally as important as practicing forgiveness daily regardless of your Enneagram type is the habit of feeling grateful. Humans have a negative bias (I can't tell you why, but we tend to remember bad things more than the good in our lives). That means that you're likely to dwell on your inadequacies or problems or things that are going wrong far longer than dwelling on everything that's going well. The antidote to this bias is gratitude.

Gratitude transforms our everyday experiences (personal and professional) into more positive and enjoyable experiences. There's compelling evidence showing that the daily practice of gratitude makes everyone feel better and positively impacts their health, creativity, relationships, and productivity. Use gratitude to neutralize your brain's negativity bias and as a tool to enable you to live the Enneagram model. Start by picking a time of day (first thing in the morning or last thing before sleep time) to write down three to five things that you feel grateful for on that particular day.

Make an effort to find unique things to praise and appreciate, no matter how small. Some mornings the thing I am most grateful for is the sound of a bird singing outside my window as I wake up. Other days I'm just so thankful for the air that I breathe. Find magic in the things you often take for granted, and it will enable you to understand what life is all about in more profound ways.

Mindfulness practices

Many people hear the word "mindfulness" and immediately assume it means sitting in silent meditation with a blank mind. That's a very limited view of what mindfulness means. Whether you enjoy meditating or not, adding mindfulness practices to your daily routines at home and work will be instrumental to your growth. Unless you can figure out ways of bringing that mindfulness factor into your activities, you won't experience the full benefits of being mindful. But how can one become mindful in the context of a busy workday or a demanding lifestyle?

Choose to be more present in your life. Take it moment by moment, hour-by-hour at first, until it turns into a habit. Mindfulness is not about blanking out your mind. It's about being intentional as you move through your life. It's about becoming more aware of your mind, environment, and inner world.

When you're absent-minded at work or during a meeting (or a date), you're lacking mindfulness, and that's when pre-programmed impulses usually step in and wreak havoc. Functioning on autopilot isn't always a good thing, especially if you're looking to create new changes in your life. So here's an idea that can help you stop being mindless in professional and personal settings. Choose to train yourself into present-moment awareness. Each morning before you start interacting with the world, decide with the intention that you're going to be as present as you can in all your activities. Pause for a few minutes before switching from one activity to another and remind yourself of this decision. For example, when you enter your car to drive to work, decide that you will only focus on that activity. Keep yourself grounded in that present moment by listening to the sound of your car's engine as you accelerate. Notice how your hands feel against the leather and how tight or relaxed your grip is. Pay attention to what's in front of you and around your as you drive. Try to notice things you wouldn't usually look too keenly at, such as how long it takes the traffic lights to switch or how fast the lady crossing the pedestrian walk in front of you is moving. Avoid thinking about Helen and her new promotion or John's tendency to procrastinate on projects.

When you get to work, before getting into your boss's office, intentionally pause and remind yourself to be as present as possible with them. If you take this intention with you into every activity, sooner or later, you will start to see some changes.

What if I struggle to remember to practice mindfulness?

Use the tools at your disposal to keep you accountable. Set the alarm on your phone so that at least three times a day, you pause for 30 seconds to "check-in" and see how well you're doing. If you're at work, make sure the alarm only vibrates, so it doesn't constantly nag others. Each time the alarm goes off, excuse yourself and find a moment of silence at the balcony, bathroom, or your office. Take a deep mindful breath. Notice how you're feeling. Reflect on how the day is going so far. Were you acting from your highest level of aware-ness? Are you noticing patterns of thought or impulsive, emotional reactions that perhaps need to be addressed during your free time? The more self-aware you can be, the easier it will be to reclaim the self-control and self-mastery you seek.

CONCLUSION

Finally, you come to the end of this first step in what will be a lifelong quest of self-discovery. By now, it should be evident that living the Enneagram is your surest path to the freedom, sense of unity, and the sense of wholeness you've been seeking all your life. You have learned your Enneagram type and the richness of the wings, subtypes, and triad that the model teaches. And you've also learned about your virtue and the inner calling from your spirit. Should you choose to pursue that path of spiritual awakening, you'll need to continue developing yourself and bravely dive deeper and deeper into the study of the Enneagram model.

Understanding yourself better should also equip you with the ability to understand others better and show more empathy and compassion. Remember, everyone is fighting a hard battle as they strive to find that unity of being and heal their ego fixations and passions. The filter through which others view the world determines why you notice their reactions and behaviors to be as they are. Suppose you desire to establish and strengthen rich nourishing relationships. In that case, it's essential to keep in mind that their level of development and current level of awareness limits them to act as they do. Your responsibility is to forgive, embrace and practice acceptance. Since you know how to be and do better, thanks to your investment in the teachings of the Enneagram, step up and be that shining example in the relationship.

Growing into your best self is ultimately what living the Enneagram is all about. And while you cannot change from one type to another, there's so much room for you to grow and more than enough potential for you to unlock. Once you discover all the magnificence you possess, you'll never want to be any other type. Even more remarkable is how the Enneagram tool enables us to transform professional and personal relationships. With your newfound understanding of yourself and others, you'll have a better grasp of why one person behaves as they do and others don't. But that doesn't mean you'll have all the answers to why your boss is so aggressive in meetings or why your new girlfriend wants you hitting the clubs every weekend. What you'll have is a better understanding of the motivations behind these behaviors.

Another critical thing to remember is that you can't assume anyone's Enneagram type - that's for them to figure out. If you're in a leadership position at work and can advocate for everyone to take the test, then great. Only after the person confirms their actual Enneagram type can you approach them in the manner directed in this book. Don't pressure anyone to take the test, especially not your romantic partner. It has to be something the person wants to do.

Once you surround yourself with people who know their Enneagram type and are willing to improve themselves just as you are, what's next? Well, keep growing, learning, and experimenting with developing even further. There's no end to living the enneagram knowledge. But there are two last nuggets I will leave for you.

First, be easy on yourself. Embrace both the positive and negative things you discovered going through this book. You started reading it for a reason. You wanted to know yourself better, and now you're well on the way to self-mastery. Take deep breaths, one day at a time, and cultivate one new habit at a time as you soak in this information. The human journey is full of speed bumps and unforeseen obstacles, but as long as you give yourself the grace to get back up when you fall, the journey will be fulfilling. If you're an Enneagram One, this might be hard to hear because you want everything perfect all the time. Keep working on that inner critic so you can go a little easy on yourself. I know you can do it. For Enneagram Two, being easy on yourself would mean investing time in self-care, not just tending to the needs of others. Enneagram Three, as hard as this might be for you, it's time to recognize that success isn't just about accomplishing stuff. Don't be too hard on yourself. Enneagram Four constantly remind yourself that there are those who get you and love you in all your uniqueness, and they wouldn't change a thing about you. Be easy on yourself as you find those people to connect with and learn to see the good in you.

Enneagram Five, this world sorely needs your knowledge and ingenuity, but please be more open and gentle with yourself. Be easy with your emotions and find the value in having a rich relationship with another. Enneagram Six, your anxiety, worry, and mistrust does get the best of you all too often, but no matter how many times you catch yourself falling, dust yourself up and keep moving forward. Identify your triggers, and with time you'll counteract them. Enneagram Seven, I know negativity, pain, and suffering feel unbearable. Still, I promise you, if you practice sitting with that emotions and processing them (allowing them to flow just as a river would), you'll eventually crack that aspect of you as well. Enneagram Eight, be patient with yourself toward the road of embracing vulnerability. It's not easy, but I know you are strong enough to do it. Enneagram Nine, I know conflict is challenging for you but find the courage to face uncomfortable conversations and speak your truth. Be easy during this process and start slowly.

The second and final word of wisdom that I encourage you to do regardless of your Enneagram type is to be easy on others. Compassion and empathy are sorely lacking in our population, and it's time we take steps to cultivate them personally. Now that you know how different types interact in relationships, their driving motivations, and behaviors, is it too much to ask for a little more patience and empathy? I am not suggesting you excuse or even accept bad behavior. But I insist that we increase our tolerance and understanding for each other. Forgiveness becomes the magic ingredient here. As you learn to forgive yourself and others, you will find better, more humane ways to communicate and get along with others. That is the kind of growth we should all aim for because it fosters the kind of future that promotes a healthy population. May the Enneagram tool guide you on this journey of becoming your best version.

Enjoy the journey of awakening to your true Self.

Dan Davis.

RESOURCES

Enneagram Tests Online:

Enneagram. (n.d.). The Enneagram Institute. Retrieved January 17, 2022, from https://tests.enneagraminstitute.com/

The Enneagram Personality Test. (2021, October 25). Truity. Retrieved January 17, 2022, from https://www.truity.com/test/enneagram-personality-test

Other useful resources:

Traditional Enneagram (History). (n.d.). The Enneagram Institute. Retrieved January 17, 2022, from https://www.enneagraminstitute.com/the-traditional-enneagram/

Christian, K. (2021, October 20). *How To Cultivate Healthier Relationships Based On Your Enneagram Type.* The Good Trade. Retrieved January 17, 2022, from https://www.thegoodtrade.com/features/enneagram-in-relationships

Yuan, L. (2021, August 23). *Breaking Down the Enneagram: A Guide for Total Beginners*. Truity. Retrieved January 17, 2022, from https://www. truity.com/blog/breaking-down-enneagram-guide-total-beginners

SAGE Journals: Your gateway to world-class research journals. (n.d.). SAGE Journals. Retrieved January 17, 2022, from https://journals. sagepub.com/action/cookieAbsent

www.ingramcontent.com/pod-product-compliance
Lightning Source LLC
Chambersburg PA
CBHW032056040426
42335CB00036B/215